The Arms of the Future

New Perspectives on Defence and Security
Published in collaboration with the Royal United Services Institute

Published in association with the Royal United Services Institute (RUSI), this cutting-edge series interrogates issues on the frontline of security and defence. With a global reach and perspective, books in the series explore emerging geopolitical conflict, competition and cooperation in strategically important areas. The series draws on the latest research, fieldwork and theoretical insights into what this means for UK defence and security.

The **Royal United Services Institute** (RUSI) is the world's oldest and the UK's leading defence and security think tank. A unique institution, founded in 1831 by the Duke of Wellington, RUSI embodies nearly two centuries of forward thinking, free discussion and careful reflection on defence and security matters. It incorporates the world-leading expertise of a community of staff, trustees and fellows, including research specialists and those with operational experience. RUSI's mission is to inform, influence and enhance public debate to help build a safer and more stable world.

The Arms of the Future

Technology and Close Combat in the Twenty-First Century

Jack Watling

BLOOMSBURY ACADEMIC
LONDON · NEW YORK · OXFORD · NEW DELHI · SYDNEY

BLOOMSBURY ACADEMIC
Bloomsbury Publishing Plc
50 Bedford Square, London, WC1B 3DP, UK
1385 Broadway, New York, NY 10018, USA
29 Earlsfort Terrace, Dublin 2, Ireland

BLOOMSBURY, BLOOMSBURY ACADEMIC and the Diana logo are
trademarks of Bloomsbury Publishing Plc

First published in Great Britain 2024

Series design by Toby Way

A catalogue record for this book is available from the British Library.

Library of Congress Cataloging-in-Publication Data
Names: Watling, Jack, author.
Title: The arms of the future : technology and close combat in
the 21st century / Jack Watling.
Description: London ; New York : Bloomsbury Academic, 2023. |
Series: New perspectives on security and defence ; Vol 1 |
Includes bibliographical references and index.
Identifiers: LCCN 2023001411 (print) | LCCN 2023001412 (ebook) | ISBN 9781350352964
(hardback) | ISBN 9781350352957 (paperback) | ISBN 9781350352971 (epub) |
ISBN 9781350352988 (pdf) | ISBN 9781350352995
Subjects: LCSH: Tactics. | Strategy. | Military art and science–Technological innovations.
Classification: LCC U165 .W38 2023 (print) | LCC U165 (ebook) |
DDC 355.4/2–dc23/eng/20230531
LC record available at https://lccn.loc.gov/2023001411
LC ebook record available at https://lccn.loc.gov/2023001412

ISBN: HB: 978-1-3503-5296-4
         PB: 978-1-3503-5295-7
       ePDF: 978-1-3503-5298-8
      eBook: 978-1-3503-5297-1

Series: New Perspectives on Defence and Security

Typeset by Integra Software Services Pvt. Ltd.

To find out more about our authors and books visit www.bloomsbury.com
and sign up for our newsletters.

Contents

Figures

Introduction

Opinions are sharply divided concerning the employment and operations of tanks. This should occasion no surprise, since all armies are burdened by a strong, if not limitless, power of inertia. The lessons of the world war point without exception to the importance of concentrating large masses of tanks on the decisive spot ... To many observers, however, the experiences of the war fail to offer convincing guidelines.[1]

General der Panzertruppen Oswald Lutz

Writing in 1979 the historian John Keegan lamented how descriptions of battle often succumbed to the stylized 'battle piece', characterized by 'extreme uniformity of human behaviour ... very abrupt, indeed quite discontinuous movement ... ruthlessly stratified characterization ... [and] a highly simplified depiction of human behaviour on the battlefield'.[2] The tendency to generalize the performance of whole units – the sudden transition from a defender holding their position only to rout – may conjure up strong images in the mind of the reader. But those images are unlikely to be consistent between readers, for the style leaves much to the imagination, and the imagination is apt to fill in the blanks from experience, which differs from person to person. In this way many of the descriptions of battle from historical texts have created popular mythologies that are difficult to reconcile with the practicalities of fighting.

The distortionary effects of narrative are not confined to writing about historical events. Consider, for example, a hypothetical attack described by retired US Marine Corps General John Allen, set on 2 January 2018:

> Our captain and his crew had not anticipated the incoming swarm because neither he nor his ship recognised that their systems were under cyber attack. The undetected cyber activity not only compromised the sensors, but "locked out" defensive systems, leaving the ship almost entirely helpless. The kinetic strikes came in waves as a complex swarm of drones tore into the ship. It was attacked by

---

[1] General der Panzertruppen Oswald Lutz, 'Preface', Heinz Guderian, *Achtung Panzer!: The Development of Tank Warfare*, Christopher Duffy (trans.) (London: Weidenfeld & Nicolson, 1999), p. 19.

[2] John Keegan, *The Face of Battle: A Study of Agincourt, Waterloo, and the Somme* (London: Pimlico, 1976), pp. 39–40.

a cloud of autonomous systems moving together with purpose, yet also reacting dynamically to one another and to the ship. More than anything the speed of the attack stunned and overwhelmed the sailors. Though the IT specialists on board the ship were able to release some defensive systems from the clutches of the cyber intrusion, the rest of the crew simply didn't have enough decision-making time to react – mere seconds. In these few seconds, some of the sailors ascertained, with their limited situational awareness, that the enemy's autonomous cyber and kinetic systems were collaborating. But in a matter of minutes, the entire attack was over.[3]

This passage may be considered arch typical of visions of future war replete with a full house of cliches: from swarming drones and cyber-attacks to artificial intelligence and a frenetic pace of activity. The scene as described seems a dizzying and terrifying warning of what is to come. And yet, such descriptions rarely survive scrutiny. For example, given the complex manoeuvring described, and the use of the word 'drones', we may assume that the ship is struck by relatively slow-flying munitions. If we assume that the ship is in blue water, then it must be some distance from land and the munitions would have easily taken over ten minutes to reach the ship, during which time their radar cross sections would have been visible. The 'cyber-attack' could have affected the defensive systems earlier, but if this were the case then the crew had rather longer than 'seconds' to deal with the problem. Perhaps more curiously however we might ask how the cyber-attack was delivered against an air-gapped naval system. If the systems was corrupted while the ship was in port, how did the attacker make it begin to lock out the defensive systems just as the drones approached, and how did they know the time and place to set up the strike when the cyber-attack was implanted? More fundamentally, given that small drones have less kinetic energy than missiles, are slower and carry smaller payloads, why did the attacker not just fire a cruise missile at the ship, especially since its defences were apparently dysfunctional. A cruise missile would give less time to react and have a high probability of destroying its target. Swarming behaviour is hardly necessary if the defensive systems are not working. Did the adversary use 'swarming drones' because they made military sense, or because to write 'cruise missile' would turn the whole vignette from coming across as a dire warning of future war to an incident that would sound broadly familiar to naval officers who served in the Falklands conflict of 1982?[4]

It would be unfair to single General Allen out; he is cited above because the problems with the vignette typify the genre. Peter Singer and August Cole's *Ghost Fleet* was explicitly written as an exploration of how technological developments are transforming warfare. The book was recommended for reading across the US military. Admiral James Stavridis described it as 'a startling blueprint for the wars of the future'.[5]

[3] John R. Allen and Amir Hussain, 'On Hyperwar', *Proceedings Magazine* (Vol. 143, No. 7, 2017), p. 1373.
[4] Max Hastings and Simon Jenkins, *The Battle for the Falklands* (London: Pan Books, 1997), pp. 180–205.
[5] James Stravridis, 'Review', Ghost Fleet Book: https://www.ghostfleetbook.com/reviews/, accessed 20 July 2022.

Blueprints should provide a detailed technical drawing of how something works. Yet consider the following description from *Ghost Fleet* of a modern Pearl Harbour in which Chinese forces conduct a surprise attack on a US Marine Corps base during the invasion of Hawaii:

> He saw one of the tiny Chinese quadcopters firing, its autocannon peppering a parked Osprey tiltrotor aircraft. First, the starboard wing buckled, and then the MV-22's massive engine dropped to the ground, tipping over the ungainly aircraft ... As [a marine on the ground] drew the magazine from a pouch on her flight suit, the quadcopter dropped to within a few inches of the ground and circled back around her position. She spun around too; Worm saw her chambering the next round as she raised her weapon. He willed his jet's cannonarming protocol to speed up. She fired and then darted to the other side of the wreckage, racing to keep it between her and the quadcopter, like a lethal game of musical chairs. Then she slipped in a pool of oil seeping out of the gutted Osprey, twisted her left leg, and fell down in a heap. The pistol skittered a few feet away ... Worm found the Z-10 strafing a smoking hangar 100 yards away from her. One of the quadcopters saw her and raced toward her position, then hovered to beckon the helicopter over. Worm dipped the nose of the jet and eased the throttle forward. With a gentle adjustment, he rolled out and centered the helmet-mounted pipper on the Z-10. He relaxed his g slightly to stay on the target and then squeezed the trigger ... As the F-35 accelerated away, the robotic quadcopter turned and loosed an air-to-air missile. It then blithely went back to its original task of raking the row of Ospreys on the runway ... With the missile homing in on him, he pulled the F-35 hard right toward the Ulupau Crater at the end of the base ... Worm dove toward the palms of the Ulupau Crater in a bid to mask his plane from the missile's radar.[6]

There are some basic technical problems with the scene. The F-35 is at times in the hover, at times flying – the pilot able to watch a scene play out in slow time, and then decide to try and escape an anti-aircraft missile travelling at mach-2 that was launched from close range. The quadcopters meanwhile are simultaneously described as 'tiny', flying around bits of damaged vehicles while armed with autocannon and anti-aircraft missiles. With each missile weighing upwards of 24 kg and autocannon having fierce recoil, no drone thus armed could be described as small. But there are more fundamental problems arising from the narrative than the authors' blasé approach to physics. Like General Allen's vignette, along with all the other opening clashes described in *Ghost Fleet*, the effectiveness of the adversary is ultimately achieved through surprise. The sense of helplessness is a result of the narrative being told from the perspective of isolated defenders who do not know how their adversary is able to defeat them. It is the unknown that causes dread. This makes for a strong narrative. But it also allows the authors to avoid having to think through the limitations and consequences

---

[6] Peter Singer and August Cole, *Ghost Fleet: A Novel of the Next World War* (New York: Houghton Mifflin Harcourt, 2015), pp. 75–8.

of how the systems they are describing work. For instance, the Chinese quadcopter is described as beckoning a helicopter. How did it do this? Did the helicopter have a command link to the quadcopter? The quadcopter seems to not prioritize engaging the F35 before the destruction of the helicopter, but then reprioritizes its targets after the helicopter is destroyed? Why did it not see the F35 as a higher threat before? Was this because it was executing priorities assigned by the helicopter? If so, once the helicopter was destroyed, who could issue orders to the quadcopter? Who launched the quadcopter? Who recovers it? These questions are answerable. But the answers would suddenly constrain what the adversary could do because it would fix the force to a particular structure. It would also expose some vulnerabilities. For example, why was the helicopter and quadcopter able to communicate but the F35s electronic systems were completely disabled, when the F35 has a powerful electronic attack capability through its active electronically scanned array radar? By positioning the narrative with a surprised defender none of the implications of how the adversary is actually operating are exposed. Instead, we are simply told that American technology doesn't work and that Chinese technology works perfectly. Far from providing a blueprint *Ghost Fleet* at best offers an impressionist sketch. But such a sketch does not provide a realistic demonstration of how forces might be organized or how they may need to fight. It does not effectively convey the design choices that militaries increasingly face as they try and build complex systems. Despite the volume and uniformity of much writing about the future of war, it remains wholly inadequate.

To argue that current visions of the future of conflict provide an inadequate basis for military forces to modernize does not mean that the status quo is sustainable. Exercise Warfighter, run by the US Army with participation from its allies, is a major war simulation with a high fidelity of modelling.[7] For several iterations reading the fallout has been harrowing, with frontline combat brigades routinely emerging from the serials at 20 per cent combat effectiveness.[8] While NATO often takes its objectives, it does so at a staggering rate of attrition in both personnel and equipment that could not be readily replaced. The weight of enemy artillery fire often devastates manoeuvre elements long before they reach the direct fire zone. There are many problems with Exercise Warfighter, and it should not be taken as an exact representation of how fighting would unfold. However, the vulnerability of large, armoured manoeuvre elements on the modern battlefield is born out in a wide range of tactical and operational exercises, as well as being hinted at in recent conflicts like Nagorno-Karabakh.[9] It is also entirely consistent with the fate of Russian armoured columns attempting to envelop Kyiv in March 2022.[10] It should also be noted that NATO's

[7] John Mead, 'Winning the Firefight on the Road to Warfighter', *British Army Review* (Vol. 175, Summer 2019), pp. 64–73.

[8] Author interviews with participating brigade command staffs, UK, Germany and US, June–July 2020.

[9] Oryx, 'The Fight for Nagorno-Karabakh: Documenting Losses on the Sides of Armenia and Azerbaijan': https://www.oryxspioenkop.com/2020/09/the-fight-for-nagorno-karabakh.html, accessed 20 July 2022.

[10] Jack Watling and Nick Reynolds, *Operation Z: Death Throes of an Imperial Delusion* (London: RUSI, 2022), pp. 2–7: https://static.rusi.org/special-report-202204-operation-z-web.pdf, accessed 20 July 2022.

command post exercises often actually ease armoured manoeuvre rather than making it more difficult, by for example erasing water obstacles on the simulated map.[11] This is not to assert the tired cliché that the 'tank is dead',[12] but rather that concentrated forces – whether armoured or not – are increasingly vulnerable as the fidelity of sensors, range and lethality of munitions increases. The futurists may be imprecise, but they are right that armies must adapt.

Despite abundant evidence of the need to change how armies fight, militaries are struggling to modernize. Here the inadequacy of the future visions of war is crippling because the lack of precision means that they do not provide militaries with a realizable path or even a clearly defined goal as to what they need to become. Armies have good reason to be cautious of leaping headfirst into transformative changes to their force structure, equipment and doctrine. The complimentary system of combined arms manoeuvre represented by tanks, armoured infantry and self-propelled artillery is difficult to match. It is also premised upon a great deal of expensive hardware, doctrine, training, infrastructure and culture that would be difficult to regenerate once lost. So long as armies lack a clear alternative, this model will persist, even as its effectiveness progressively erodes. Institutional inertia is unfortunately bolstered by the understandable emphasis in much military education upon continuities in war. In reaction to the evangelism of military futurists there is a community of historians and strategists who have strenuously argued that warfare will remain fundamentally unchanged: centred around violence in pursuit of political ends, visceral, terrifying and filled with uncertainties.[13] This is undoubtedly correct. But the tenor of such arguments has arguably reinforced the reluctance within the military to shift from the tried and tested structures with which armies are familiar to a force optimized to fight on the future battlefield. Until armies can identify what the future combination of systems comprises, they are unlikely to change.

Instead of transforming their combined arms elements armies today are largely seeking to retain tried and tested structures while adding new capabilities onto their platforms. In some respects the academy has encouraged this tendency, because some of the best work on emerging capabilities has pinpointed specific technologies and focused on how they may shift warfare, rather than looking at a range of technologies and considering how they interact. Excellent examples of the genre include Paul Scharre's *Army of None*[14] and Kenneth Payne's *I, Warbot*.[15] Both authors give highly provocative insight into what is technically possible and the level of potential strategic disruption this could entail. Neither, however, is precise as to the effects on concepts of

---

[11] Kevin Copsey, RUSI Waterways Conference: Obstacles and Opportunities, London, 27 April 2022.

[12] David Johnson, 'The Tank Is Dead: Long Live the Javelin, the Switchblade, the …?', *War on the Rocks*, 18 April 2022: https://warontherocks.com/2022/04/the-tank-is-dead-long-live-the-javelin-the-switchblade-the/, accessed 20 July 2022.

[13] Hew Strachan, *From Waterloo to Balaclava: Tactics, Technology, and the British Army, 1815–1854* (Cambridge: Cambridge University Press, 1985); John Spencer, 'The City Is Not Neutral: Why Urban Warfare Is So Hard', *Modern War Institute*, 4 March 2020; Ben Barry, *Blood, Metal and Dust: How Victory Turned into Defeat in Afghanistan and Iraq* (Oxford: Osprey, 2020).

[14] Paul Scharre, *Army of None: Autonomous Weapons and the Future of War* (New York: W. W. Norton, 2018).

[15] Kenneth Payne, *I, Warbot: The Dawn of Artificially Intelligent Conflict* (London: Hurst, 2021).

operation or combined arms integration. What is missing from these works is the detail as to how these capabilities are fielded and sustained over the course of an operation, or the operational implications of a force structured to employ such systems. The leap, from the technical to the strategic which characterizes works focusing on individual technologies, often creates a cognitive dissonance between the continuities of warfare and the possibility for radical transformation.

The anguish of officers struggling with these contradictory imperatives – caught between continuity and transformation – is perhaps encapsulated in the ritual incantation by every senior officer from the United States to India when discussing modernization that 'though the character of war changes, its nature is immutable', as if to reassure the audience that 'we shall adapt, but not too much'. This is typified by the US Army's Modernisation Strategy. On one level the United States has been conceptually bold. *The US Army in Multi-Domain Operations*[16] articulated a clearly identified threat and has since been mapped down echelon from Field Army to Corps and is now branching out across NATO.[17] However, acquisition for Army modernization began long before the concept was complete. Its modernization priorities – future vertical lift, long-range precision fires, the army network, soldier lethality and the next generation combat vehicle – intentionally mimic the Army's modernization process from the 1980s.[18] The intent is to take existing platforms and to refine and optimize them. Artillery will be longer ranged, helicopters will fly further and faster, the network will be more robust and have more bandwidth, rifles will be more lethal at greater ranges, and so on. This will mean a significant increase in complexity and cost of all these systems. Yet the 1980s introduction of AirLand Battle was a refinement of mechanized warfare rather than a transformation to a new system of fighting. It may therefore serve as a poor model for what must be done today. The future vertical lift platform may give the US Army greater reach, but it is unclear whether forces are any more survivable so far into the enemy deep. If survivability against proliferating threats cannot be reduced then one must ask whether aviation assault remains viable, and if it does not then the significance of such assets as a modernization priority diminishes. In short, if fundamental elements of the character of war are changing – and senior military leaders regularly contend that this is the case – then armies must transform rather than optimize.[19] In codifying its modernization priorities before writing its tactical concepts the US Army has in many respects pre-empted itself. What emerges from the US Army's cross-functional teams will undoubtedly be technologically impressive and with experimentation the force may be structured in novel and effective formations.

---

[16] US Army, 'The US Army in Multi-Domain Operations 2028', TRADOC Pamphlet 525-3-1, 6 December 2018.
[17] 1 German Netherlands Corps, *Corps Operating Concept*, Muenster, January 2022.
[18] Eric J Wesley, 'AUSA Global Force Symposium: Day 3 – Opening Remarks and Keynote Speaker', 28 March 2019: https://www.dvidshub.net/video/668339/ausa-global-force-symposium-day-3-opening-remarks-and-keynote-speaker, accessed 20 July 2022.
[19] Mick Ryan, *War Transformed: The Future of Twenty-First Century Great Power Competition and Conflict* (Annapolis: Naval Institute Press, 2022), chapter 1.

But it appears to be going about this in a manifestly inefficient manner. Moreover, the model whereby new capabilities are bolted onto old platforms ensures that they are harder and more expensive to maintain, deploy and require greater enablement, increasing the cost to project power.

In peacetime the United States has the largess to tolerate inefficiency. In wartime it could not afford to do so. For the United States' allies – lacking a comparable degree of resource – inefficiency in modernization is simply not viable. We thus see quite a stark divide between those who are trying to transform and those that are doubling down on existing systems. The US Marine Corps is fundamentally altering how it is equipped, structured and fights to seek to be competitive on the future battlefield, though in doing so is specializing for a very specific set of missions to the exclusion of others.[20] The British Army is divesting from many legacy capabilities and is experimenting to try and understand where to place its bets.[21] By contrast, Germany – unwilling to test many emerging capabilities for political reasons – is doubling down on an order of battle optimized for the 1980s.[22]

This book aspires to set out the choices that armies face in building a combined arms formation that will remain competitive over the coming decades. By evaluating emerging technologies, assessing how they interact, identifying where they are complimentary and where they are impractical, the book will endeavour to reach conclusions as to what a competitive combined arms formation will need to comprise, and where decisions must be made about trade-offs to seek advantage. In short, the book sets out to identify the arms of the future.

This is a bold aspiration, and it is therefore necessary to explain in some detail how the book sets about this problem. Firstly, where military concepts have tended to start from the top and work down – Multi-Domain Operations begin with identifying the strategic threat – this assessment begins with the technical level of war and works up to the strategic. Working from the strategic downwards makes sense if one is identifying campaign objectives, which thereby allows for the prioritization of resources at the operational level, and therefore determines how a force's tools are to be applied. The aim of this project by contrast is to understand what new tools are available, what it takes to employ them in a coherent manner, and therefore what pieces are available to be assigned by operational planners. It is all very well to say that drones will hunt tanks, but how many drones are needed, how many vehicles to carry them, and personnel to launch, oversee and recover them, to make this capability effective against an opposing manoeuvre element. How, moreover, is such a capability to be protected? Is the juice worth the squeeze? Since the emphasis is on how technical components work in combination, the focus of the research is on tactical echelons and specifically at

[20] David Berger, Commandant's Planning Guidance: 38th Commandant of the Marine Corps (2019): https://www.hqmc.marines.mil/Portals/142/Docs/%2038th%20Commandant%27s%20Planning%20Guidance_2019.pdf?ver=2019-07-16-200152-700, accessed 20 July 2022.

[21] Lucy Fisher, 'Soldiers and Machines Join an Army of 'Boots and Bots', *The Times*, 30 September 2020: https://www.thetimes.co.uk/article/soldiers-and-machines-join-an-army-of-boots-and-bots-mkwz9l2dt, accessed 20 July 2022.

[22] Alfons Mais, RUSI Land Warfare Conference, London, 2 June 2021.

those of a sufficient size to function as combined arms teams. The analysis is therefore centred on defining what a force looks like among company groups, battlegroups and brigades, and how these are integrated at the divisional echelon. The book essentially considers the components necessary to be able to execute an operation in a high-intensity warfighting context.

The timeframe for analysis is between today and 2050. The book examines emerging technologies currently being experimented with but which are largely unfielded and explores how their use poses challenges for existing formations, and the implications of employing them on the battlefield. Historically military acquisitions take between seven and fifteen years in the land domain.[23] If we consider that some of the technologies are not yet sufficiently mature to be tied into acquisition, then we may reasonably assume that the capabilities to be discussed will only be entering service at scale between 2030 and 2040. They will likely remain in service beyond 2050, but by then there will be additional technologies that cannot be part of the analysis in this book because they have not yet been discovered that will start to enter service and alter the balance. This book therefore expects to be most relevant for the period between 2030 and 2050, but the conclusions will need to inform decisions made by armies before 2025.

At a time when the emphasis in defence is on multi-domain activity, it might reasonably be asked why this study is focused on the land domain. The answer is that while operational art and higher tactical planning are increasingly aimed at achieving the convergence of military tools across warfighting domains, at a technical and tactical level the ability to field coherent force packets remains domain specific. The support, training and capabilities necessary to put a naval squadron to sea are specific to the maritime domain and the ability to force generate the capability is a prerequisite for any particular multi-domain activity. The same may be said of a brigade. It must link with aircraft and ships and may depend upon space-based supporting infrastructure and be supported by cyber capabilities, but these other activities are irrelevant if the brigade cannot function as a land formation.

It remains to explain how the relevant technologies have been identified and their likely effects and requirements analysed. The technologies considered comprise a range of technical capabilities observed by the author in development or being used in experimentation and in some cases on operations. They may be grouped into a range of categories: active and passive sensor arrays, novel transmission, complex weapons, novel power generation, autonomous systems, artificial intelligence, electronic warfare and active protection and multispectral concealment. For any technology being examined the approach has been to map out its functional logic and therefore dependencies when applied practically. For example, a radar must have a power source. Although the exact performance of a given radar is highly sensitive, reasonable estimations of the level of power required to produce a radar picture over a given distance allow for realistic projection as to the size of vehicle, its signature, weight and fuel necessary to actually field that system. By mapping the enablement required it becomes possible

---

[23] Jeremy Quinn, RUSI Land Warfare Conference, London, 2 June 2021.

to build a rough demarcation of capability and the density with which systems can be fielded. With this information this book adopts the approach taken by Paul Kennedy in *Engineers of Victory*[24] – a study of operational problem solving in the Second World War – and applies it to tactical problems in the future.

The first part of the book, *From Mechanized to Informatized Warfare*, examines how the battlefield application of combinations of emerging technologies creates fundamental problems for how ground forces have historically operated. This is important because unless the problems can be defined, there is neither an imperative to change nor an ability to measure whether a solution has been found. The first chapter, *Navigating the Transparent Battlefield*, outlines the transformative effectiveness of sensors that will provide high fidelity and timely detection of movement across large areas. The challenge for land forces is that this prevents manoeuvre elements, as presently constituted, achieving one of the key tenets of warfare: surprise. Chapter 2 – *Contesting the Spectrum* – explores how the desire to minimize traffic in the electromagnetic spectrum has been replaced by an imperative to maximize access. Yet that access is precarious. Consequently, existing military concepts for information management will become increasingly impossible to maintain on the future battlefield. *When Protection Is an Illusion* examines the impact of the logarithmic trajectory in advances in protection, capped by size and weight limits on platforms, versus the exponential increase in lethality, driven by higher power, more precise and longer-range munitions. This dynamic is threatening one of the core tenets of mechanized warfare: the need to concentrate forces at the decisive point. Between the increased fidelity of sensors, the range of munitions and the risks of concentration, Chapter 4 – *When the Tail Needs Teeth* – examines how armies will need to restructure logistics and enablement to sustain their capacity to operate. In Chapter 5, *Blood in the Streets*, there is an examination of how armies must reconcile the measures necessary to survive described in the previous chapters, with the enduring requirement for concentrated mass in the inevitable conduct of urban operations.

Having defined the problems that are confronting today's mechanized forces because of emerging capabilities, it becomes possible to consider how combinations of technologies and appropriate tactics can overcome these challenges. This is the aim of the second part of the book, *The Arms of the Future*. This section intends to outline what future-combined arms elements will need to comprise, and where armies may seek advantage through trade-off decisions as to the composition of units. Part two comprises five chapters. The first, *The Geometry of the Future Battlefield*, breaks down the problems identified in the first part of the book into operational tasks that must be carried out. The chapter also outlines how a commander might understand the future battlefield and measure their progress across it. When the components of a fighting force change, so too does the capacity of the force to move, fight and control different kinds of terrain. The force's centre of gravity also shifts. The result is that an enemy must recalibrate their priorities for targeting. Thus, the objectives are altered by both

---

[24] Paul Kennedy, *Engineers of Victory: The Problem Solvers Who Turned the Tide in the Second World War* (London: Allen Lane, 2013).

the bounds of the possible and desirable to both sides. The chapter concludes that there are four critical systems that make up a force suited to winning on this battlefield: the manoeuvre system, fires system, assault system and support system. The subsequent four chapters examine each of these systems in turn. The approach is to begin from their fundamental task and outline the tools they can employ to complete them along with the structures required to field them. This is to some extent descriptive – highlighting all of the components required to overcome the problem – but not prescriptive. There are, necessarily, alternative methods of solving the operational problems described. But by highlighting the interdependencies the chapters seek to demonstrate the interrelations between future capabilities and their limitations. Chapters 7–9 end with a vignette, showcasing how a force organized and equipped in the manner described could overcome forces armed and structured in the conventional fashion.

Land forces do not operate in a vacuum, nor can a force spring fully formed from concept to fielded capability. The third part of this book, *The Continuation of Policy*, seeks to place the force described in the second part of this book in a joint, institutional and policy context. The eleventh chapter, *Divergent Domains*, outlines the trajectories for development among space, maritime, air and cyber forces, to identify where land forces will increasingly interact with their counterparts and where there are mutual dependencies. The twelfth chapter, *Priorities in Transformation*, examines what modern militaries should prioritize if they are to transform the legacy force they currently field into a force capable of functioning on the battlefield described in this book. The chapter also seeks to highlight those areas where this book may have identified optimized platforms for the task, but current platforms are not rendered obsolete, even if they are not ideally suited to their future tasks. The final chapter, *An Instrument of Power*, considers the consequences of how land power is likely to be employed in the future, and how the operational options that the system of fighting described in this book entails may impinge upon how states decide to commit the military instrument. The book therefore works upwards, from the technical, through the operational and ending with the strategic.

A note on prediction. As Lawrence Freedman observed in *The Future of War*, 'prediction is difficult and likely to be wrong'.[25] His survey of the many attempts to predict how war would develop bears this out. Nevertheless, prediction is not futile. J. F. C. Fuller was more right than wrong in his predictions about armoured warfare.[26] Billy Mitchell accurately predicted the method and target for Japan's eventual assault on the United States. Robert Leonard was decades ahead of his time in his assessment of the impact of information on war.[27] Perhaps the most perceptive writing on the future of the character of war – strongly affirmed by the research conducted for this book – emerges from the writings of Guy Hubin.[28] What is curious is that very few transformations of warfare have been accurately predicted by the relevant responsible

[25] Lawrence Freedman, *The Future of War: A History* (London: Penguin, 2018).
[26] J. F. C. Fuller, *On Future Warfare* (London: Sifton, Praed & Company, 1928).
[27] Robert Leonhard, *The Principles of War for the Information Age* (New York: Ballantine, 1998).
[28] Guy Hubin, *Perspectives Tactiques* (Paris: Economica, 2009).

military institutions. Military force development aimed at refining capability is often highly effective; personnel are committed to getting better equipment. In transformation by contrast there will be winners and losers, and institutionally the losers are powerful. Given that military personnel tend to move jobs every two years – sometimes three – and that their promotion and advancement is dependent upon the approval of seniors from across the force, a soldier tasked with examining a fundamental problem who concludes that things must change risks having the conclusions dismissed by those higher in the chain of command who have not done the research, but do not like the answer. If the soldier persists in trying to drive the change in spite of discouragement from above, their short posting means that they will usually fail to get the change implemented before having to hand over to someone else. This does not mean that soldiers are not able to critically analyse the future of war. This book owes a debt of gratitude to many more serving personnel than can be named who have contributed their expertise, experience and advice. But few of their ideas will survive their institutions and be codified while they are in uniform. It is for this purpose that the Royal United Services Institute where I am privileged to work was established. Initially, RUSI enabled former service personnel to examine the future of their profession unencumbered by institutional inertia. I do not expect that the predictions made in this book will be entirely correct, but I am confident that they are more right than wrong.

Finally, it is important to discuss sources. I have worked as the Research Fellow for Land Warfare at RUSI for four years. In that time, I have worked extensively with the British Army on force modernization and liaised broadly with the Australian, Dutch, French, Finnish, German, Indian, Iraqi, Irish, Israeli, Italian, Korean, Lebanese, Norwegian, Polish, Qatari, Swedish, Ukrainian and US militaries. I have participated in hands-on, practical experimentation, in several countries. I have observed drones flying from inside both Russian-made and Western air defence systems. I have accompanied platoons in horizontal sleet conducting attacks using remote autonomous weapons. I have been inside and used a range of as-yet unfielded and legacy-armoured vehicles and have participated and observed exercises and operations from company, battlegroup and brigade headquarters. I have also observed new capabilities employed on operations by and against the Russian military in Ukraine.

Most soldiers work in two-year postings during which time they are given a very bounded area of responsibility about which they will become expert. As they become more senior they will also gather a wider perspective, but rank also limits their ability to engage. I am not and have never been a soldier. Having no rank, I have been tolerated by a group of soldiers emplacing an observation post in a woodblock one day, and found myself in a meeting with two-star general officers discussing force development the following week. In short, what I lack in expertise I hope to remedy by perspective, and the capacity to draw upon a very wide base of data. Much of what is described in this book is based upon hands-on experience of using and testing novel technologies. The exact ranges and capabilities of specific items of equipment are of course sensitive, and readers should consider all distances used in this book as nominal, but the principles underpinning the technology should provide a sufficient basis to outline their effects on military concepts. Of course, the gap between how equipment works in a lab as compared with how it functions in the field must always be borne in mind. Although I have never served in the military, I have spent time with military units in Iraq, Mali, Ukraine and elsewhere. Watching Iraqi forces attempting to deploy and maintain equipment vitally important for staving off attack from VBIEDs gives a strong sense of both the challenges and frictions produced in war. Observing Ukrainian troops seek to find targets using UAVs against dense Russian electronic warfare and air defence systems underscores the complexity in planning and the risks in execution of utilizing UAVs on the battlefield. From such experiences I feel that I can make an educated appraisal as to how difficult some capabilities are to use in practice. Where my naivety got the better of my analysis, I have benefitted from the advice and feedback from a significant number of current and former serving personnel of all ranks, whose patience will hopefully spare the reader from being afflicted by my errors. It must be acknowledged that when I embarked upon writing this book I did not know that I would spend a significant proportion of the time allocated to drafting it in Ukraine. This has provided invaluable insights into the practicalities of employing new capabilities in a high-intensity conflict. It also separated me from access to much of the academic literature that I would otherwise have cited extensively. I must apologize to colleagues for this limited engagement with wider scholarship. This book does not claim to be the final word on the future of war, but it does hope to drive a more grounded discussion about the trajectory of modern conflict.

Part One

From mechanized to informatized warfare

1

Navigating the transparent battlefield

Every war is rich in unique episodes. Each is an uncharted sea full of reefs. The commander may suspect the reefs' existence without ever having seen them; now he has to steer past them in the dark.[1]

Carl Von Clausewitz

'Got something', the first operator called out, making some adjustments to his console to reduce the clutter on his screen. Behind him the second operator brought the target acquisition radar to bear and started to try and determine range and altitude to achieve a lock. Sitting at the teleconsole station of the 1S91 radar of a 2K12 Kub surface to air missile battery, I slewed the camera to the bearing of the target and zoomed in. Eventually I caught a small shape moving low above the tree line. Then it turned about and disappeared from view. As the UAV banked its radar cross section spiked and the second operator achieved his lock. It had taken nine seconds. 'Got it', he announced to the officer standing outside the vehicle. Although no longer visible with the electro-optical sensor the lock remained steady. The officer nodded and spoke into his radio. Over the subsequent minutes he would lean in and ask what the UAV was doing and whether we could see it. The operators reported that it was flying an array of patterns, but that the lock was holding. The officer walked off and spoke some more into the radio. Returning he asked what they could see. I couldn't see anything with the camera but the lock was still good. 'The trouble is', said the officer, 'we've just landed the thing so we're trying to work out what exactly you've fixed on'.[2]

As it turned out someone else had put another UAV in the air a couple of kilometres further out and held it in the hover in almost perfect alignment with the target. In consequence, as the first UAV dropped out of sight the Kub locked on to the second, but because the Kub's three constituent sensors fed into separate consoles, overseen by separate operators, who did not know about and therefore did not expect the second UAV, they missed the transition. Other than the teleconsole operator the crew were experienced with the Kub. Against familiar air targets they could quickly sort through the returns from their sensors. But humans are easily distracted, vulnerable

---

[1] Carl Von Clausewitz, *On War*, Michael Howard and Peter Paret (trans.) (Princeton, NJ: Princeton University Press, 1989), p. 120.
[2] Author observations, joint military exercise, April 2021.

to assumptions, and without a fused sensor picture gaps between what operators are focusing on can be exploited. The Kub is an old system, entering Soviet service in 1967. Modern systems have a clearer interface and can therefore present a greater number of targets. However, the fundamental weakness of such systems highlighted above largely remains.[3] The next generation of such systems is unlikely to suffer from these shortcomings due to two increasingly common components, fused multi-sensor arrays and machine learning.

The finest tooth comb

Two months before the incident with the Kub described above, an NFL match took place near Tampa, Florida. As part of the security wrap there was an experimental mast mounting acoustic panels, a spectrometer, an electro-optical camera and laser unit, all feeding into three computer processors, each the size of a car battery. The system was designed to monitor UAVs. The acoustic panels would detect and isolate the rhythmic rotor sound from the background noise while the spectrometer would catch control frequencies. These – in isolation or combination – would then align the camera and laser range finder. This data would be passed to the computer which would measure the UAV based on the image and confirmed distance to target and then compare its silhouette and the acoustic signature from its rotors against a database and thereby identify the UAV.[4] The operator would be presented with a continuous list of detections being tracked, stacked in order of threat, with a range of options. Sensor fusion like this is not in and of itself remarkable. But what was transformative was that against the background noise of an NFL match the system had no difficulty filtering out the clutter and returning a 100 per cent accurate set of identifications with no false positives. Indeed, even when presented with a UAV that it had not seen before in its training data, the system correctly categorized its properties. Furthermore, where the Kub's hardware was focused on tracking fast jets and helicopters, with the radar picture presented to the operator in a way that best highlighted these objects, the experimental sensor array tested near Tampa was not only able to track UAVs. The same system could be employed to isolate individuals speaking in a large room,[5] or the origin and fall of shot, identifying the position, type and status of shooters.[6] In other environments minor adjustments to the software made precisely these detections possible in parallel with detections of UAVs. This is because machine-learning algorithms seek to establish unique signatures for prioritized objects and then match them. Thus, the size of signature needed to separate it from surrounding clutter, irrespective of the type of sensor being employed, is orders of magnitude smaller than that which is required

3   Jack Watling, Justin Bronk and Sidharth Kaushal, 'A UK Joint Methodology for Assuring Theatre Access', *Whitehall Report*, no. 4 (RUSI, London, 2022), pp. 30–44.
4   Briefing provided by system design team, US, March 2021; author inspection of the system, US, October 2022.
5   Briefing on alternative applications, manufacturers, Oslo, March 2021.
6   Ibid.

by a human trying to interpret the sensor data. The result is not just that sensors are becoming more sensitive in what they can detect, but that because of machine learning the quality of return to get a positive identification is rapidly diminishing.

Another important implication of machine learning is the breadth of the battlespace that can be simultaneously monitored by a single sensor array. During the 1982 liberation of South Georgia the Argentinians deployed a Guppy class submarine in an attempt to disrupt the British amphibious assault. Searching for this boat a Royal Navy Wessex 3 antisubmarine warfare helicopter momentarily turned on its radar to try and detect the conning tower. Because the radar operator – Chris Parry – had previously surveyed the environment and had marked off all known returns, he was able to detect the conning tower as an anomaly.[7] For decades humans have been able to focus on and pick out individual or isolated groups of objects from sensor returns. Doing so, however, often comes at the expense of a broad focus. For this reason, the current Royal Navy Seaspray radar, mounted on the Wildcat helicopter, places a cap on the number of objects it will track at 100.[8] Although the radar can detect and track many more than this, the human operator would struggle to do so. But a digitized monitoring system will not lose track of additional returns, while a machine-learning algorithm can rapidly sift signal from noise, so that the human operator can focus upon objects of interest rather than spend their time trying to avoid false positives. The transformative effect of machine learning is not just the centralized fusing of information at higher echelon – which will be considered later – but also the drastic increase in the effectiveness of distributed sensor arrays, whether passive or active, across the force.

The integration of multi-sensor arrays and the application of machine learning is not viable on most of the current generation of military platforms because they lack an open digital architecture. An AH-64D Apache Longbow for example, developed and delivered in the 1990s, has an impressively effective radar. But the processor that allows the radar's readings to be displayed to the crew is a mechanical structure. Not only does it offer less processing power than a smartphone while being the size of a person, but its ability to function is intimately tied to its mechanical functioning and therefore inseparable from the hardware.[9] New generations of military equipment by contrast have both more processing power and open architecture operating systems that allow software to be updated even while hardware remains fixed. The result is that as the next generation of military equipment enters service, the capabilities of sensors will begin to be adaptable at the speed of software updates, producing a six-month update cycle rather than a seven- to fifteen-year procurement cycle for upgrades.[10] Furthermore, sensors can be changed, with the supporting software updates enabling their immediate employment. Sensors therefore are going to become less tied to specific families of platforms and instead begin to appear across wider fleets. Machine learning too will soon be something that can be utilized across the force. Thus, we are

---

[7]   Cedric Delves, *Across an Angry Sea: The SAS in the Falklands War* (London: Hurst, 2018), pp. 69–80.
[8]   Capability demonstration, Yeovilton Air Station, August 2020.
[9]   Author inspection of an AH-64D and its systems, Wattisham, August 2020.
[10] Author interview, Gil Sukhbinder, London, June 2021.

on the cusp of a step change in which capabilities that are currently highly novel will increasingly proliferate across more modular platforms. To appreciate the magnitude of the change it is important to grasp the extent to which sensors have become ruggedized, miniaturized and significantly more sensitive. What follows therefore is an overview of the key classes of sensor that are likely to become pervasive among tactical echelons on the future battlefield, namely AESA radar, EW spectrometers, acoustic arrays, vibrometers, electro-optical sensors and tracking of civilian devices.

Surveying the senses

One of the most far-reaching developments in sensor technology is the proliferation of active electronically scanned array (AESA) radar. First-generation radar pushed out a narrow band of frequencies through its antenna from a single transmitter and had a single receiver. Thus, the radar had a fixed field of view unless it turned.[11] The invention of passive electronically scanned arrays saw multiple antenna elements attached to a single transmitter and receiver, so that by adjusting the timing of when energy was released from each element it became possible to focus the radar dynamically without moving the radar.[12] The system could still only survey a limited band of frequencies at a time, however. AESA radar comprises arrays of multiple antenna elements where each element has a dedicated transmitter and receiver. The system can therefore emit and detect multiple frequencies in multiple directions simultaneously.[13] The elements can also detect incidental radar reflections from other sources, thus remaining passive. An AESA radar can maintain wider situational awareness using a wider band frequency and then assign a proportion of its emitters to direct a narrower band frequency at an object of interest, increasing resolution, without losing sight of the wider context. Whereas earlier generations of radar required multiple radar to collaborate to retain situational awareness while generating useful returns, AESA radar can combine these functions on a single platform. Thus, an airborne AESA radar will reliably detect moving objects on the ground, adversary radar, artillery fires and other aircraft over considerable distances. Whether it records and classifies these detections is a function of the software directing and supporting it, rather than the hardware's capability. Furthermore, if the radar moves, then an AESA radar can create a synthetic aperture to generate an image of an area of interest at considerable resolution. Thus, if a radar is tracking a suspicious object that goes static and therefore disappears from the radar screen, it can then be captured through SAR and thereby identified.[14] The limitations

[11] L. Brown, *Technical and Military Imperatives: A Radar History of World War 2* (London: Taylor and Francis, 1999).

[12] Wulf-Dieter Wirth, *Radar Techniques Using Array Antennas* (London: Institution of Engineering and Technology, 2001).

[13] Arik Brown, *Active Electronically Scanned Arrays: Fundamentals and Applications* (Hoboken: John Wiley and Sons, 2022).

[14] John Curlander and Robert McDonough, *Synthetic Aperture Radar: Systems and Signal Processing* (New York: Wiley, 1991).

of AESA radar – ever since their introduction into military service in 1995 – have been imposed by power and cooling. This will continue to constrain the range at which smaller AESA radars can detect activity. Nevertheless, helicopter or UAV-mounted AESA radar can be expected to survey an area out to 150 km from 5,000 feet. AESA radar mounted on masts with a dedicated generator can often detect dismounts moving at a walking pace in dense country in the brigade deep.[15] Even small AESA radar drawing on the energy from vehicle engines and mounted at ground level has sufficient power to reliably detect movement at walking pace over a company's depth.[16] Passive radar, while able to make detections over comparable ranges, is often less reliable, but has the advantage of not emitting.

Discerning the significance of sources of emissions is the job of electronic warfare direction finding using spectrometers. This is not a new capability, having been extensively utilized throughout the Second World War.[17] However, direction finding has historically relied upon human operators getting a bearing from two or ideally three points on a transmission and thereby triangulating the coordinates of its source. It has also been possible to use frequency hopping and burst transmission to evade detection. This is increasingly difficult because sensors are more precise and because machine-learning-supported systems will pick out anomalies from the background environment irrespective of frequency. The dispersion of receivers to achieve an effective triangulation has also narrowed, making it easier to achieve multiple lines of bearing. Direction finding like this is not only effective in locating points of interest but often in determining the relationship between emitters. For example, if there are three points of emission and the third always illuminates shortly after the first or second has finished illuminating, then there is a high likelihood that the third is the command post acknowledging receipt of the messages from the first two points. The range of EW detection varies depending on the frequency being monitored, the climactic conditions, geographical context and masking tactics employed. Nevertheless, dedicated EW collection platforms like Russia's Torn-MDM can survey signals out to 30–70 km depending on type, giving an indication of the area that can be covered.[18]

Acoustic signatures are another form of battlefield sensor that unlike EW suites have only recently matured in the land domain. Shot indicators were a feature of the war in Afghanistan, setting off an alarm to warn of incoming fire.[19] They had a high false positive rate, often mistaking the popping of sealed waste bags under the Afghan sun as small arms fire, for example.[20] Next-generation acoustic panels are drastically more effective. Tracking a conversation between two people across a crowded 100 m space is eminently feasible. Organic noises however can prove difficult to distinguish.

---

[15] Author observation, capability demonstration, UK, August 2020.
[16] Author observation, Exercise Autonomous Warrior, Salisbury Plain, November 2018.
[17] Alfred Price, *Instruments of Darkness: The History of Electronic Warfare, 1939–1945* (London: William Kimber and Company, 1967).
[18] Technical assessment of captured Torn-MDM SIGINT station, Ukraine, June 2022.
[19] John Matsumura et al., *Rapid Force Protection Technologies: Assessing the Performance of Advanced Ground Sensors* (Santa Monica, CA: RAND, 2005).
[20] Author interview, Veterans of Herrick Operations, London, May 2019.

Mechanical sounds, because of the regularity of their signature, can be detected over much greater distances. Small UAVs for example can be reliably detected at between 300 and 1,200 m depending upon type. Deeper sounds from armoured vehicle engines or helicopters travel further, often being detectible out to 10 km with sufficient fidelity to be classified. That a microphone can be this sensitive is not remarkable, but that such a microphone can achieve this effect over a wide area while being robust, small and light enough to be carried by a dismounted soldier is impressive. Of course, a battery-powered system has limited endurance, and such capabilities are more effective when vehicle mounted, but they do not require dedicated platforms to deploy. They are also entirely passive.

Whereas an acoustic sensor detects sound waves that travel to the sensor, a vibrometer directs a laser to an object and measures vibration of a surface to calculate noise, or to assess other characteristics of the target surface.[21] While the former may have a practical conic field of regard of 120 degrees with the ability to pick up noise through some vegetation and over or around certain obstacles, a vibrometer has around a 3-cm field of regard and requires line of sight unobstructed by cloud, let alone solid objects. Nevertheless, a vibrometer is substantially more sensitive, being able to listen – for example – to a pigeon's heartbeat at 30 km.[22] The challenge is to get the laser pointed at the pigeon. Although vibrometers have existed for a long time, they have had limited military application and been mainly utilized by intelligence agencies to conduct covert surveillance. Once paired with sensors with a wider field of regard however the military application becomes more viable. Imagine, for example, a UAV with an passive radar that could detect movement of vehicles out to 30 km. Although it might confirm movement, it would struggle to identify the target at that range. If, however, the UAV also had a vibrometer, the laser could then be aligned to the bearing of the detected movement from the paired sensor and thereby directed onto the target object. All of a sudden the exact vibration and noise pattern of the vehicle can be precisely measured and since armoured vehicles have very unique vibration characteristics, this would be able to determine the engine and type of vehicle using a machine-learning algorithm. Because the sensors of such a system can be fused, the radar can then classify the return from a particular vehicle and move the vibrometer onto the next return, thereby building up a real-time picture of positively identified objects.

Similar effects can be achieved using electro-optical sensors ranging from image-intensifying, infrared and thermal imaging systems. On a fixed platform with effective gyro stabilization the range achievable with modern optics is considerable. Satellites, for instance, can achieve sub-centimetric resolution from orbit. Lenses that can be practically carried by humans are often more constrained by unobstructed lines of sight rather than distance, though 30 km is a reasonable planning assumption for modern

[21] Enrico Primo Tomasini and Paollo Castellini (Eds.), *Laser Doppler Vibrometry: A Multimedia Guide to Its Features and Usage* (Berlin: Springer, 2020).
[22] Capability briefing and demonstration, Qinetiq, UK, May 2021; Brian Perrett, 'Guiding Light: How Lasers Can Inform Military Operations', *Qinetiq*, 19 November 2020: https://www.qinetiq.com/en/blogs/how-lasers-can-inform-military-operations, accessed 20 July 2022.

man-packable optics. Image-intensifying capabilities meanwhile, which amplify the signature of available light, mean that clear images with limited degradation in resolution and colour fade can be retained throughout the night. Infrared systems can continue to function with a much crisper image, though the limited colour spectrum can make detection of certain objects harder. Thermal imaging is available at comparable resolution and increases the contrast for distinguishing objects from the surrounding environment. These capabilities will become widely available on practically any military vehicle and to dismounted infantry. They are effective within relevant combat ranges. Although these methods are to some extent more limited than radar and longer-range sensors, they also provide returns that provide immediately comprehensible data for humans, enabling rapid positive identification.

Although this book is concerned with the tools available to tactical echelons, and is not therefore concerned with wider intelligence collection, tactical monitoring of civilian activity within an environment can provide detailed intelligence about enemy movement, especially when combined with the inexhaustive list of sensors mentioned above. The pervasive availability of cellular phones in the battlespace has transformed the interaction between military personnel and civilians on the battlefield. Historically civilians have been largely passive observers or victims of fighting. Today, the information they share with one another increasingly makes them participants,[23] able to organize as groups and intentionally or unintentionally provide significant quantities of information to military forces.[24] For higher echelons collection from social media can be a valuable source of tracking adversary movement. For lower echelons however live metadata on phone locations can provide a great deal of information about adversary dispositions. SS7 tracking of phones in urban areas for instance can rapidly show groupings of people.[25] If an adversary manoeuvre element is tracked entering a town, and phone numbers associated with local officials congregate at a civic building, the meeting of adversary officers with civic leaders is likely trackable in real time. Displacement is also a powerful measure for troop movement.

For much of the last century the employment of sophisticated sensors has been constrained by the ease with which they can be detected and targeted. Air defence radar for example has tended to remain off to avoid being destroyed by radiation homing munitions. However, the miniaturization, proliferation and use of multisensory arrays have made the sensor picture much more robust. As already mentioned, modern sensors can often work against a range of targets, meaning that dedicated sensors for specific targets are less necessary. The integration of passive and active sensors on single platforms ensures that active emissions can often be brief and yet focus accurately on

[23] Anna Reading, 'Mobile Witnessing: Ethics and the Camera Phone in the "War on Terror"', *Globalizations* (Vol. 6, No. 1, 2009), pp. 61–76; Matthew Ford and Andrew Hoskins, *Radical War: Data, Attention and Control in the 21st Century* (London: Hurst, 2022).

[24] Lukasz Olejnik, 'Smartphones Blur the Line between Civilian and Combatant', *Wired*, 6 June 2022: https://www.wired.com/story/smartphones-ukraine-civilian-combatant/, accessed 20 July 2022.

[25] Samuel Gibbs, 'Your Phone Number Is All a Hacker Needs to Read Texts, Listen to Calls and Track You', *The Guardian*, 18 April 2016: https://www.theguardian.com/technology/2016/apr/18/phone-number-hacker-read-texts-listen-calls-track-you, accessed 20 July 2022.

points of relevance. Moreover, the sheer number of sensors on the battlefield means that there is a lot less given away by any given sensor turning on. Proliferation also ensures that degrading the sensor picture requires many more targets being struck and consequently reduces the risk of a particular sensor being exposed. In consequence, where historically armies have been able to gather snapshots of isolated data about the battlefield, today sensor coverage is broader, denser and more persistent.

From surprise to uncertainty

When Alexander the Great of Macedon led his armies into Asia Minor, he was opposed by local Hellenes allied with Persia who took up position on the banks of the Granicus River.[26] Always preferring the offence, Alexander ordered his army to ford the river and fight from the water to secure the bank. His force succeeded, but they did so with considerable difficulty. Alexander appears to have learned from the challenge, for when he faced King Porus across the Hydaspes River he resorted to guile. Alexander had his camp followers maintain a din while the Army marched up stream at night, crossing the river and thereby gaining the far bank unopposed.[27] Achieving surprise has long been an imperative in war. The grand envelopment achieved by the 'left hook' during the first Gulf War, whereby large, armoured formations conducted a rearward passage of lines, cut off much of the Iraqi Army in the Kuwait desert.[28] Among Soviet forces fighting the Mujahideen in Afghanistan, whether they could achieve surprise would often decide whether their operations were successful or ended in failure.[29] When surprise cannot be achieved the consequences are often sub-optimal. In many respects the grinding attritional struggle on the Western Front during the First World War may in no small measure be ascribed to the inability to generate surprise. Infantry, it was found, could not advance against prepared positions without the systematic preparation of the battlefield by artillery. The volume and duration of fire required however gave the adversary a clear warning as to the sector that was being threatened and the axis of advance, while the range of the artillery would amount to the limit of exploitation of a given assault. Thus, the defender could prepare additional defence lines behind the limit of exploitation and ready reserves to counterattack, ensuring that the attacker lost much of the ground taken in the initial assault. Heinz Guderian, in his analysis of armoured warfare during and after the First World War, noted that 'surprise is the third precondition for a thoroughgoing success on the offensive'.[30] Because the limit

[26] Lucius Flavius Arrianus, *The Campaigns of Alexander*, Aubrey de Selincourt (trans.) (London: Penguin, 1971), pp. 69–75.

[27] Ibid., pp. 259–74.

[28] Peter de la Billière, 'The Gulf Conflict: Planning and Execution', *RUSI Journal* (Vol. 136, No. 4, 1991), pp. 7–12.

[29] Lester Grau and David Glantz, *The Bear Went Over the Mountain: Soviet Combat Tactics in Afghanistan* (Washington, DC: National Defence University Press, 1996).

[30] Guderian, *Achtung Panzer!*, p. 75.

of exploitation of armour was so much greater, and its protection obviated the need for prolonged artillery preparation, it enabled breakthrough. But it also required that armour be massed behind the frontline without enemy observation or breaches of operational security.

Against the array of modern sensors that will permeate the future battlefield, it must be seriously doubted whether operational surprise is achievable by the current force. A modern combined arms brigade comprises somewhere in the region of 80–120 main battle tanks, 30–70 artillery pieces, around 800–1,400 infantry, and their supporting engineers, logisticians, maintenance and medical personnel. If it is to fight as a formation, it must concentrate to some extent and in doing so it generates a great deal of dust, noise and disruption of civilian traffic. For an adversary radar operator, 50 km behind their own air defences, the signature of such columns using ground moving target indication radar is unmissable. Moreover, days before the brigade reaches its assembly area behind the lines, civilians will have photographed its vehicles en route, uploaded them to social media, and civilians will have purchased satellite images of their support area as it is established.[31]

There is a certain type of old soldier – some still in service – who will opine that what is needed is a return to the discipline of the 1980s, with units manoeuvring in radio silence, without lights, always at night and the meticulous camouflaging of positions. These are all sensible TTPs. But while such prescriptions are deeply reassuring because they imply that resolving the challenge posed by sensor proliferation can be achieved by every soldier doing their part, it obscures the need for wider changes. It is certainly true that many such techniques do increase survivability. However, such propositions fail to appreciate the scale of the challenge. For example, during the Cold War satellite coverage of much of the world was severely limited. It was therefore possible to time movements to avoid the areas of regard of adversary satellites, or to coincide with gaps in coverage. Today, by contrast, any detailed assessment of the trajectories of hostile and neutral satellites – to which adversaries can often purchase access – will reveal exceedingly short gaps in coverage, and that coverage is often hyperspectral and can achieve very high resolution images. In fact, using commercial satellites it is possible today to gain synthetic aperture radar images of any location on earth within twenty minutes.[32] Given that the marks on the ground left by tracks can be traced, camouflage must extend beyond the positions, and this takes time. The result is that movement becomes highly constrained, and when it does occur is likely to be immediately detected by radar. The range of sensors meanwhile means that countermeasures would need to be taken at considerable distances from the front, and this would therefore slow progress to a point where the desire not to be seen would extend the length of time for enemy reconnaissance assets to find the brigade. The

[31] Emily Sakzewski, 'These Satellite Images Show Russia Has Ukraine Surrounded', *ABC News*, 23 February 2022: https://www.abc.net.au/news/2022-02-23/satellite-images-russian-troops-surround-ukraine/100827810, accessed 20 July 2022.
[32] Florence Cross, RUSI Waterways Conference: Obstacles and Opportunities, London, 27 April 2022; capability demonstration, UK, February 2022.

uncomfortable truth is that such large manoeuvre formations will be seen. If armies are to avoid being highly predictable and are to prevent being drawn into highly attritional assaults on prepared and forewarned positions, then they will need to operate differently. Moreover, manoeuvre elements will need to be equipped and structured to operate effectively on an increasingly transparent battlefield.

Transparency may be interpreted in two ways. The first is to suggest that everything is visible. The second is that something is see-through, and therefore cannot be seen. Asked to look through a series of glass panes one might well be able to identify an object on the other side. It would however be harder to accurately determine how many panes of glass were between the object and the viewer. If we accept that achieving surprise is critical to a force's likelihood of succeeding, then we must ask how – in an environment where all movement has a high probability of being detected – are armies to be unpredictable. Here, it is important to begin with some principles that armies can exploit, since these will create required characteristics and capabilities that any future force structure must have. The key principles to be explored are the difference between stand-off and stand-in sensors; the value of ambiguity; the virtue of being self-conscious; and the difference between system speed and component speed.

Sensors may be described as standing off or standing in. Stand-off sensors are those that can be operated from a distance sufficient to be unthreatened by the adversary echelon against which they are being tasked. In general, these sensors tend to survey a wide area, and offer persistent observation. Perhaps the most important characteristic of stand-off sensors however is that they usually rely upon the adversary doing something to be detected. GMTI radar requires the adversary to move. EW requires that they radiate or transmit. Acoustic arrays depend upon the enemy making noise. Space-based observation and synthetic aperture radar may fall into a special case because they can provide high-fidelity imagery at a stand-off distance and therefore achieve proactive detection. However, these assets can only do this against a specific target and one must ask how they know where to look without first having a wider indication of activity. Furthermore, these activities are constrained in the angles at which they can achieve an effect and so the risk of incidental detection via these means can in part be mitigated. Stand-in sensors may be defined as those that require the user to be situated within a distance that can be threatened by an adversary and tend to have a high fidelity but narrow field of regard. In contrast to stand-off sensors that depend upon the adversary to achieve a detection, these sensors must be proactively used to find the enemy. Because getting them into a position where they can achieve a detection requires manoeuvre, and because of the greater fidelity of the sensor picture, these sensors tend to be harder to mitigate against once they achieve a solution on a given position. The angle is harder to predict, and the level of detail discernible is greater.

In order to positively identify a target it is usually necessary to locate it using a stand-in sensor. This means exposing the sensor to threat. Planning the insertion of stand-in sensors is made easier by the situational awareness available from stand-off sensors, which also provides the targets for stand-in sensors to confirm. However, if stand-in sensors cannot establish a positive identification of the target, then there is a much greater risk of falling victim to deception or being shaped by false positives.

If we accept that surprise is a necessary condition for successful offensive action, then it follows that forces must both have a distributed array of stand-in sensors with which to confirm their targets and simultaneously have means of countering adversary stand-in sensors. Sensors, while they are proliferating across the battlefield, are nevertheless expensive, valuable and difficult to replace. Imposing a high rate of attrition on sensors tasked with confirming specific targets therefore will progressively give one side a better understanding of the operating environment while posing dilemmas on the other through the creation of ambiguity. Those resisting change may wish to argue that this process of rolling back stand-in sensors is merely an evolution of the recce battle. In many respects, this is correct, but when one considers the number of avenues of threat, the range of sensors and therefore the depth of the recce battle, and the magnitude of the advantage to be gained in winning this fight, it must be recognized that existing reconnaissance structures and their narrow capabilities are not equal to the task.

Screening areas of the battlefield from stand-in sensor coverage does not prevent the enemy-tracking movement with stand-off sensors. If forces wish to survive and achieve surprise, they must embrace the advantages of ambiguity. Imagine a situation in which an adversary is tracking movement in an area via GMTI. Group 1 comprising recce vehicles moves to a woodblock. Group 2 comprising logistics vehicles also moves to the woodblock. Both are tracked but disappear from the screens as they go static. A short time later the two groups move out of the woodblock, but in pairs driving close together. Initially the adversary notes one group of vehicles and therefore concludes that one group is moving and another remained in the woodblock, but does not know which. Without stand-in sensors the adversary consults its EW equipment and finds the radio signature from the logistics group. They therefore mark the reconnaissance group as having remained in the woodblock and track the logistics group as moving. Suppose now that in a fold in the ground the logistics vehicles decelerate to below walking pace and turn off the road into some trees. The reconnaissance vehicles continue at their previous speed. Upon emerging from the fold in the ground the enemy is now tracking a reconnaissance group as a logistics group and believes that the reconnaissance group is somewhere that they are not, while having lost the actual logistics group's location. In this way, layering ambiguity as to what a stand-off sensor is capturing can lead to errors that, if codified, begin to layer up to provide a false and misleading sense of where on the battlefield there are threats and where there are targets or opportunities. Suppose the enemy moves its own reconnaissance element around the empty woodblock and tries to intercept what they think is the logistics group. Not only have they failed to move through unoccupied ground – treating it as denied – but they are also susceptible to being surprised upon running into the reconnaissance group. To achieve this kind of ambiguity it is necessary to have enough small units of action to be able to create the 'noise'. If the units of action are too large, then one unit will not disappear behind another. It also helps if units are equipped – using multispectral concealment – to be able to minimize or maximize their signature against certain sensors so as to make their signatures as comparable to one another as possible. Finally, the pursuit of ambiguity requires that units are self-aware.

Units seeking to cover off all of the vectors by which they can be detected by modern sensors are liable to waste an inordinate amount of time-taking countermeasures against sensors that are not being directed at them. Conversely, units that do not understand what is being pointed at them are likely to have their efforts rendered pointless by the fidelity of modern sensors. Being able to make effective judgements as to what concealment efforts should be prioritized within the limited time available, and what the minimum standard is to drive up the material commitment required to achieve detection, will be vital. To do this units must understand the sensors fielded by their adversaries and how they are doctrinally employed. They will also need to understand their own signature and how it is shaped by their activity. Historically units have striven to minimize their signature. This has become a more and more onerous burden and if pursued to a level whereby it is effective would cripple the tempo of operations. Instead, therefore units need to be self-aware and understand what picture they are painting to their adversary. Sun Tzu's most famous dictum to – 'know your enemy and know yourself' – remains sound. Furthermore, they need the flexibility to proactively shape that picture. This is helped by building a force that is designed to have a more ambiguous signature. More importantly however it requires the generation of adversary sensors in training to be realistic so that troops understand what can and cannot be detected and can experiment with how to alter that picture. Without such training, there will be much wasted activity.

There is also a need to understand how terrain interacts with sensors. Woodblocks clearly provide good cover – as they have always done – but urban clutter is another source of ambiguity and concealment from adversary detection. There has been a great deal of literature on the challenges of urban combat over the past decade. The perspective in much of this literature is that militaries will have to fight in cities because they are economically important and expanding.[33] There is much less attention given to the advantages of urban terrain that will draw in militaries, however.[34] Historically, while ports and other infrastructure have provided important avenues for theatre sustainment, the density of a civilian population has driven military logisticians to separate themselves from urban environments. Given the large signature of logistics and support elements however, and the ambiguity created by dense urban terrain for stand-off sensors, there is likely an increasing incentive to base sustainment efforts in urban areas and project from them. There are therefore push and pull factors that draw forces into the urban environment. The complexity of urban terrain necessarily forces the commitment of greater numbers of stand-in assets for seeking targets, and this slows down the acquisition and accumulation of information by the adversary. Using dense terrain therefore has a comparable effect to the pursuit of ambiguity but by passive rather than active means.

Although the speed at which manoeuvre is detected and its components identified has accelerated, this does not mean that the speed at which the adversary can react is consistent or commensurate. The final principle that combined arms forces will need to appreciate if they are to survive on a transparent battlefield and achieve surprise is

---

[33] David Kilcullen, *Out of the Mountains: The Coming Age of the Urban Guerrilla* (London: Hurst, 2013).

[34] A point that has recently been made convincingly by Anthony King, *Urban Warfare in the Twenty-First Century* (London: Polity, 2021).

the difference between system and component speed. System speed may be understood as being analogous to John Boyd's OODA Loop. It is the time necessary for a process to be completed from start to finish. For example, let us suppose that a GMTI radar is tracking a moving object, which goes static. The operator therefore uses SAR to get an image of the object for positive identification. Let us say that this nominally takes four minutes. The operator then interrogates the image to ensure that it is in fact an object of interest. If it is, then they may wish to pass the raw data to a higher echelon, or simply to notify a headquarters as to what they have found. In either case they must transmit the data. Then the headquarters must assess the information and decide how it shapes their plans. New plans must be drawn up taking it and other additional information into account, made coherent and then distributed to subordinate units. For fires this may be a relatively short process lasting minutes, with additional time for the fires assets to align and for the time in flight of the munitions. For a response involving manoeuvre the time taken will be tied to a wider planning cycle. The system speed therefore may nominally be six minutes for a fires response and progress on four-hour cycles for a manoeuvre response. But these system speeds are made up of components. Component speed comprises the time taken to conduct each discrete action. Let us say the time in flight for a munition to reach the target is two minutes, for example. In an engagement cycle 30 per cent of the system speed may therefore be taken up by the component speed of the time in flight.

The importance of the difference between component and system speed is that certain components can be targeted to slow down the system speed or to have other effects. For instance in the above example jamming the frequencies used by enemy communications may prevent the enemy sensor sharing the location of the target for a time. It could cause them to send the information as text, rather than the raw data, stripping the context for the headquarters. Alternatively, if the adversary system speed for calling in fires is understood to be six minutes, then the force could move every five, causing rounds to be fired, but for the target to have moved before impact. Creating opportunities for adversary guns to unmask could create opportunities to conduct counterbattery fire, or cause the enemy to expose their guns further by seeking to reduce the system speed by moving the guns closer to the front, thereby reducing the component speed of the time in flight of the round. The difference between component and system speed can be even more problematic for enemy planning. If we assume that planning requires judgement and that those judgements must be communicated to subordinate units, then it must function in a cycle. If the enemy is conducting activity near the beginning of the cycle, then information about their activity can inform the judgements that produce the orders. However, if the adversary knows the rough timings of their opponent's planning cycle, then they can increase the tempo of movement as the cycle is supposed to conclude. Changing facts on the ground as a plan is about to be implemented can have several effects; it can lead to a loss of initiative as the headquarters tries to update plans to reflect the changing information, or it can lead to plans being distributed that disconcert recipients because they do not match the picture available on their sensors. If we assume that sensor coverage is continuous but that planning cycles are necessarily delivered at intervals, then it becomes possible to use ambiguity between stand-in and stand-off sensors to disrupt the enemy planning process and indeed to lead them to follow rather than task their sensors, becoming fixated on changes they can observe. The point is that even if the enemy can see activity, they cannot necessarily respond to it. Being able to surge activity therefore becomes a useful disruptive capability within the force.

This chapter has sought to argue that the drastic increase in the number and fidelity of sensors on the modern battlefield, combined with the ability to fuse and process returns from multi-sensor arrays, has brought about an increasingly transparent battlefield. If forces move, they will be detected. It has also argued that this poses fundamental challenges to forces as they are currently structured because they depend upon surprise to succeed with acceptable losses. To regain the capacity to achieve surprise ground forces will need to be able to seek and destroy stand-in sensors to create ambiguity. Ambiguity can be used to deceive but this requires self-awareness as to what a force's signature actually is to the enemy. Understanding the enemy's planning and engagement cycle meanwhile can allow manoeuvre to be calibrated so as to make the available sensor data as disruptive as possible. Ideally this can produce paralysis or cause the adversary to cede the initiative. To exert this kind of shaping effect it is necessary to coordinate dispersed forces and therefore communicate across multiple units, and to do that one must have access to the electromagnetic spectrum. How to secure that access is the subject of the next chapter.

2

Contesting the spectrum

*Whoever can limit the capacity for precision for the adversary through electronic
warfare will win this war.*[1]

Colonel Ivan Pavlenko, Commander,
Ukrainian CEMA Command

All military activity is dependent upon communication. Insofar as armies seek
to carry out the organized application of violence, they are dependent upon
communication to coordinate their efforts. Revolutions in communications
technology have always revolutionized warfare. The telegraph enabled the
synchronized coordination of theatres of war. Prior to the telegraph it was
possible – as at the Battle of New Orleans in 1815 – for major combat operations
to be undertaken after the signing of peace treaties.[2] The wireless enabled the
synchronization of tactical activity beyond line of sight. Satellite communication
meanwhile has eliminated the need for a fixed hierarchy of communications, with
it now possible for sub-tactical units to speak directly to strategic decision makers
in real time. This progression of technology has first and foremost increased the
speed and flexibility of communication.

Today we are in the midst of another fundamental shift in communications.
Up until the last decade there have been more people seeking information than
producing it. The capacity to process information has been greater than the volume
of information requiring processing. While certain communications architectures
have created bottlenecks and inefficiencies, the historical burden of effort has been the
production of information worth communicating and its transmission to the multitude
of persons for whom it is relevant. Today, by contrast there is a vast proliferation of
information producers. Almost every civilian carries devices that are passively producing
information, while they themselves will actively communicate, produce and post
content. Infrastructure, from street lights to door bells, contains sensors, transmitters
and receivers, and is constantly producing and sharing data. As described in the
previous chapter, military vehicles are bristling with battlefield sensors, producing data
at a volume that far exceeds the bandwidth available in any conceivable data network.[3]

---

[1] Author Interview, Colonel Ivan Pavlenko, Commander, Ukrainian Cyber and Electro-Magnetic
   Activities Command, Ukraine, August 2022.
[2] Daniel Walker Howe, *What Hath God Wrought: The Transformation of America, 1815–1848* (Oxford:
   Oxford University Press, 2007), p. 16.
[3] Leonhard, The Principles of War for the Information Age, p. 17.

At the same time the electromagnetic spectrum, through which most communication is routed, is now flooded, with few frequencies uninhibited by routine traffic.

The fact that there is more information available than is relevant changes how armies must prioritize and manage information. It is this abundance of data that drives some of the most transformational visions of warfare articulated by officers and academics. The idea of a perfectly coordinated system encompassing a whole force, whether that be along the lines of a joint firepower campaign as envisaged by the People's Liberation Army[4] or Joint All-Domain Command and Control (JAD-C2),[5] pursued by the United States, is perhaps where emerging military technologies come closest to the vision brought to life in science fiction like *Ender's Game*, in which military power can be orchestrated centrally under the supervision of a singular, situationally aware intelligence.[6]

The ubiquity of connectivity however, like the assurance of the data being transmitted, is far from guaranteed. A pure military network is likely targetable by its unique signature and vulnerable to suppression. Networks that leverage non-military infrastructure are often harder to detect but also expose the military to risk of penetration and compromise. The future information environment will likely deviate from the visions that tantalize military bureaucracies because connectivity is increasingly contested, while assuring it is becoming an active struggle in which commanders at all levels must balance risk and reward. This chapter seeks to outline the challenges imposed on tactical echelons by the transformation of information on the battlefield. It seeks to outline what is – under the best conditions – possible, the challenges for traditional information architectures in a contested electromagnetic spectrum and the requirements to be competitive in maximizing one's own communications and denying access to the adversary.

The promised panopticon

On a sweltering summer morning in Vauxhall, I sat across a table from a retired soldier in an air-conditioned office, watching a wall-mounted monitor and drinking from cans of flavoured water. In the southern United States an aircraft was taking off, en route to a military testing area. As it approached it was detected by a number of military aircraft, fixed installations and mobile defences. This information was relayed in real time to the office in Vauxhall. Reviewing the detected aircraft type, its response to challenge and its flight profile, the man sitting opposite me flagged the detection red, meaning hostile. A drop-down menu appeared with effects to choose from. My interlocutor selected one, opening a new set of options highlighting the available means of destroying

---

[4] Sugiura Yasuyuki, 'The PLA's Pursuit of Enhanced Joint Operations Capabilities', NIDS China Security Report 2022: http://www.nids.mod.go.jp/publication/chinareport/pdf/china_report_EN_web_2022_A01.pdf, accessed 20 July 2022.

[5] Congressional Research Service, 'Joint All-Domain Command and Control (JADC2)', 21 January 2022: https://sgp.fas.org/crs/natsec/IF11493.pdf, accessed 20 July 2022.

[6] Orson Scott Card, *Ender's Game* (New York: Tor Books, 1985).

the target, weighted according to speed, assurance and risk. There was the option to launch a surface to air missile from a battery on the base, or task one of two defensive counter-air patrols to intercept the incoming aircraft. Clicking the option would send the order via the relevant network. Another notification appeared on the screen; this time indicating that the system was 98 per cent confident that it had detected a person walking along the boundary of the testing site. The system was less confident that it had identified the person from the relatively grainy footage from the security camera. Again there were a list of options as to what to do.[7] This system was being tested as part of the attempt to build the Advanced Battlespace Management System (ABMS),[8] for the US Air Force. The USAF has since been tasked as the leading service in the development of Joint All Domain Command and Control (JAD-C2),[9] so the system was also being examined as a contributor to battlespace management across the US military.

There are numerous advantages to the centralization of battlespace management. Firstly, when fires are managed across multiple networks and coordinated at different levels, there is a risk that multiple assets respond to the same threat, or that threats are not engaged because controllers at different levels assume that another system is already covering it. Furthermore, when a fire control headquarters does not have an up-to-date picture of the location of blue forces, response times are slowed by the need to confirm that a target is hostile and that it is not immediately adjacent to friendly forces. This can become particularly cumbersome in joint fires where, for example, the parabolic trajectory of mortars may cross through the airspace occupied by aviation assets, requiring deconfliction between assets owned by different branches or services.

A second efficiency offered by the centralization of battlespace management is that so long as the higher headquarters has appropriate situational awareness, they are likely to have a broad field of regard and can therefore make informed trade-off decisions as to who is best placed to manage a given task. Placing fires in the hands of tactical units usually leads to their prioritizing the threat that is most acute to them. This leads to highly capable munitions being employed against operationally insignificant targets.[10] Alternatively, if the centre lacks sufficient data but wishes to prioritize resources, then the response to a threat is slowed down while the fire control headquarters tries to understand what is threatening a given sector and compares this to other challenges. Accumulating data and control of fires at a higher echelon therefore ensures the efficient employment of resources. Armies almost always have insufficient munitions available to strike all identified targets.

A third advantage to the aggregation of data and centralization of battlespace management is that it removes those making the decisions from immediate threats that shape judgement among those directly engaged in fighting. Personnel in a combat

---

[7] Capability demonstration, Vauxhall, July 2021.
[8] John R. Hoehn, *Advanced Battle Management System (ABMS)*, Congressional Research Service. February 2022.
[9] Congressional Research Service, 'Joint All-Domain Command and Control (JADC2)', 1 July 2021: https://fas.org/sgp/crs/natsec/IF11493.pdf, accessed 26 February 2021.
[10] A tendency chronic to Russian forces operating in Ukraine, where Tochka-U was readily employed for counterbattery fires missions, author interviews, Ukraine, June 2022.

zone must necessarily be limited in number to reduce their signature. They are likely to be lacking sleep, physically drained, having irregular meals and be uncomfortable owing to climactic conditions whether hot, cold or wet.[11] By contrast a battlespace management system that can be operated at a secure distance from operations can have enough personnel working in it to ensure a reliable rotation, having facilities to feed and hydrate personnel appropriately, can have climate control, and the personnel will not be suffering from the fear and stress of being hunted. These individuals should make better decisions, and have access to the expertise and processing power to assist them in coming to evidence-based judgements as to the best course of action.

Although centralized battlespace management has been a prominent feature of science fiction for the best part of a century – fuelled in part by the narrative ease of having one group of collocated characters directing events – it is only recently that militaries have bought into the belief that such a system may be feasible. Chinese concepts emphasize placing all relevant tools under a unitary commander, able to orchestrate their effects in pursuit of a clear directive or mission.[12] This is shaping not only command and control but also the requirements for munitions. The C803 Anti-Ship Cruise Missile for example has been integrated onto land-based launchers, ship-board launchers and strike aircraft so that a single logistics chain can supply munitions deliverable across three domains. The United States has a range of programmes, from Project Convergence, run by the US Army, to Naval Integrated Fire Control-Counter Air (NIFC-CA) run by the US Navy and the aforementioned ABMS all contributing to JAD-C2, with a similar standardization of munitions like the SM-6 and protocols.[13] In the UK the concept is being explored through Multi-Domain Integration.[14] The reason for this shift in what militaries believe to be possible is largely driven by digitization. So long as hardware can support a common open architecture for an operating system, software can be written to integrate and make compatible the various platforms across a military formation. Once compatibility has been achieved, there is the hurdle of connectivity. Here militaries are aided by the fact that wireless communications have become so prevalent in civilian life that they are not the sole contributor to the development of supporting infrastructure, whether terrestrial or orbital. Thus, many parts of the world have multiple avenues for moving data which the military can use to patch and support the limitations of the networks it can deploy and sustain. Despite the faith that centralized battlespace management is on the verge of realization, there are a great many hurdles towards making it a reality, and in practice militaries are likely better off pursuing systems that anticipate and function in a degraded state.

---

[11] Daniel Kahneman and Amos Tversky, 'Prospect Theory: An Analysis of Decision under Risk', *Econometrica* (Vol. 47, No. 2, 1979), pp. 263–92.

[12] Li Yousheng, *Lianhe zhanyi xuejiaocheng [Lectures on the Science of Joint Campaigns]* (Beijing: Military Science Press, 2012), p. 72.

[13] Raytheon Missiles and Defence, 'SM-6 Missile': https://www.raytheonmissilesanddefense.com/what-we-do/missile-defense/interceptors/sm-6-missile, accessed 20 July 2022.

[14] Defence Concepts and Doctrine Centre, Joint Concept Note 1/20: Multi-Domain Integration (Shrivenham: Ministry of Defence, 2020): https://assets.publishing.service.gov.uk/government/uploads/system/uploads/attachment_data/file/950789/20201112-JCN_1_20_MDI.PDF, accessed 23 November 2022.

Fighting to be heard

Three months after the meeting in Vauxhall I was sat over an expanse of desert in a Mi-35 helicopter. The Mi-35, bristling with anti-tank missiles, rocket pods and a chin-mounted chain gun, was providing close air support to a unit in a large-scale military exercise. The gunner could see the enemy in a series of camouflaged positions along the floor of a valley some miles to the Southwest. On the other side of a ridgeline was a friendly unit whose forward air controller (FAC) was having difficulties. To keep eyes on the enemy position the helicopter had to cross a ridge and the terrain feature would sever communications between the FAC and pilot. When they could speak, the pilot could not confirm the enemy's current position but could provide a grid and description for where it had been. The friendly units on the ground meanwhile were being subjected to jamming and were having difficulty reporting their positions. The FAC therefore lacked confirmation that the target being reported was not a friendly unit. The Mi-35 circled over the ridgeline. It did so for twenty minutes. By the time the FAC had managed to establish where his own forces were the enemy, who had initially been unaware of the threat circling to their north, were alerted to its presence and getting ready to shoot down the helicopter.[15]

For anyone who has spent time with signallers in the field – rather than in the demonstration areas where industry partners swarm backstage to keep everything working – the predicament faced by the Mi-35 pilot likely sounds tame. In another recent exercise, despite the radios being set up the night before, it took five hours for units to gain basic connectivity at company level within line of sight.[16] In another several communications systems never worked for the entire duration of the exercise.[17] The impact of climactic conditions, component failure, terrain, enemy interference and a failure to coordinate frequencies, encryption or timing can disrupt communications. For most of the era of mechanized warfare, armies have resolved this problem by retaining a fixed communications architecture that is consistent with the structure of the force. For the most part this has comprised a company net enabling line of sight communication between the company headquarters, platoon commanders and more recently section leaders, with soldiers able to listen but not speak, and a battlegroup net from command posts enabling information to be passed between echelons. Individual augmentees performing specialist functions like artillery spotters, forward air controllers or air defence units have often carried their own radios linked directly to the battery or aircraft they are supporting. Communication on any given network has been minimized for several reasons. Firstly, each net has comprised a defined frequency scheme, and anyone speaking on that net therefore takes up that frequency for the area within which they are transmitting. One person can speak at a time, and so if one net is supporting a company, keeping that net decluttered is critical, so that it can be accessed when it

---

15 Author observations, MWX22, Twentynine Palms, October 2021.
16 Author observations, air defence exercise, UK, July 2021.
17 Author observations, multinational exercise, Sweden, September 2021.

is needed.[18] The second reason is that any transmission will produce a spike in the electromagnetic spectrum that can be subjected to direction finding by the enemy and thereby located. If a company employs the net continuously, they will also continuously provide the enemy with information about their location and over time enable the enemy to identify where key assets of the company are, including its command post. Historically many units have stayed off the net until in combat where coordination is most important and in which the enemy knows the location of the unit anyway.[19]

The architecture described above is both inflexible and vulnerable. If an augmentation joins a unit, they may or may not be able to join the company net, and because the company net must remain uncluttered, there are limits to how many subordinate units can be connected to it. Furthermore, in order to prevent the enemy listening to the net it must be encrypted, but this means that any new attachment must be able to set their radios to use the same encryption key so that they can access the information being passed. The requirement to maintain line of sight to communicate means that a company is constrained in how far it can spread out. It is constrained in how effectively it can coordinate if straddling elevated or dense terrain, a problem that is exacerbated in urban areas where buildings block communications, preventing units in adjacent streets or buildings talking. It also limits the extent to which sections and fireteams can break up to overcome specific tactical problems, since each new node risks clogging the net. At the same time the whole system is vulnerable to jamming. Its frequency can be identified and if the enemy pushes white noise into that frequency, then they can sever communications across the area in which the company is operating. This is achieved by saturating the receivers on the radios which have an automatic cut-off to protect their electronics when too much energy is being pushed into them. Systems can be made resistant to jamming. Frequency hopping is the most common method, where a radio network regularly changes frequency. This must be by a pre-arranged sequence however, for if radios within a network end up tuned to different frequencies, then they will not receive the transmissions, irrespective of what the enemy is doing. This – in addition to encryption – adds another setting that must be enabled for any attachment joining a unit.

The factors outlined above should make it clear why there is a gulf separating communications architectures for mechanized forces, and those needed in an information enabled force that can move data from any sensor to any shooter in real time. The panopticon described at the beginning of this chapter depends upon the location of all friendly units being shared across the force. It also requires that images and other data sets – many of which are megabytes in size – are transmitted from point to point. This would not only saturate any traditional network but would also lead to a high proportion of nodes to be transmitting all of the time, thereby exposing the position of the relevant units to the enemy continuously and in a manner that tactical operators could not control.

[18] Neville A. Stanton et al., *Digitising Command and Control: A Human Factors and Ergonomics Analysis of Mission Planning and Battlespace Management* (Farnham: Ashgate, 2009).
[19] David Adamy, *EW 101: A First Course in Electronic Warfare* (Norwood, MA: Artech House, 2001).

To manage routing, bandwidth limitations and emissions control militaries shifted from the straightforward net described above to one that was managed by a router. The invention of computing and its miniaturization meant that it was possible to write algorithms that could break up data into packets and coordinate their distribution across a network of transmitters and receivers in such a way as to avoid network saturation. The decoupling of routing protocols from the physical infrastructure of transmitters and receivers also meant that the encryption and authentication of devices could be separated from the physical platform of the transmitter and receiver. This meant that the network could increasingly comprise multiple kinds of transmitter and receiver, connecting dismounts to vehicles, forward observers to batteries and other links within the same network. Rather than an attachment to a unit having to set their hardware to send and receive with the network, the router could authenticate whether a piece of hardware should interact with the network. The result is a hub and spoke architecture managed by centralized routers. This is not dissimilar to the home wireless router.

There are problems with the hub and spoke model. One significant problem is that it is centralized and therefore has a single point of failure. The central hub must emit and, while regular movement and the separation of the router from its transmitter can reduce risk of its being targeted, if it is hit the impact on the network can be the decapitation of the communications architecture. Putting aside the risk of kinetic strikes against the hub, directional jamming against its receiver can have a disproportionate effect against the network. Another problem is that if there is a technical fault and a component is struggling to connect, all of the troubleshooting capability lies at the hub, but the end of the spoke is not able to speak to that hub unless the communications system is working. Units can therefore drop off the network and it is entirely ambiguous as to whether this is because they have been destroyed, are choosing not to emit or have encountered a technical problem. This can lead to whole units being forgotten by formations.[20]

In order to get around the hierarchical structure of hub and spoke communications militaries are increasingly working with mobile ad hoc networks (MANETs), often known as mesh networks.[21] MANETs comprise bearer agnostic networks of devices that collaboratively route information between themselves. Thus, if Point A does not have line of sight to Point B but both Points A and B have line of sight to Point C, information will be routed from A through C to B and vice versa without the need for a centralized router to manage the data traffic. Similarly, if one bearer is denied, data can be routed through an alternative available bearer.[22] MANETs can also increase the volume of data that can move across the network by breaking up

---

[20] As occurred to a reconnaissance unit during an exercise in Oman in 2019.

[21] Jeroen Hoebeke et al., 'An Overview of Mobile Ad Hoc Networks: Applications and Challenges', *Journal-Communications Network* (Vol. 3, No. 3, 2004), pp. 60–6.

[22] In this MANET offer a tactical variant of Mosaic Warfare, in which combat groupings can be organically constructed based upon mission or circumstance; see Bryan Clark, Whitney McNamara and Timothy Walton, *Winning the Invisible War: Gaining an Enduring U.S. Advantage in the Electromagnetic Spectrum* (Washington, DC: CSBA, 2019).

a large data package into packets and sending these concurrently through different routes across the nodes in the network. The network therefore has greater bandwidth as the number of interconnected points increases. There is therefore an advantage to having additional attachments join a net. Each device, being its own router, also has a unique identifier so that data can be sent from A to B without preventing C and D communicating concurrently. A software-enabled MANET can further strengthen its resilience by working across multiple transmitters, exploiting radio frequencies, and civilian infrastructure like 4G and 5G masts,[23] also allowing beyond line-of-sight communication links to feed data into the network.[24] A further advantage of MANETs is that although communication is constant and emissions are no longer controlled by the individual – since information may be routed through a transmitter held by one individual without their knowledge or consent – it reduces the susceptibility of the force to direction finding. Mesh networks tend to look like a mist or blur across the electromagnetic spectrum, with very limited indication of the exact position of transmitters and receivers.[25] The fact that information is continuously passed around the network also means that it is very difficult to determine the point of origin and receipt, thereby hiding the structure of the formation that is communicating and evading attempts to locate headquarters and other specific nodes through their pattern of behaviour.

There are downsides to MANET systems. First, by switching the burden of responsibility for joining and leaving the network to the device holder, rather than a central router, it shifts the burden of problem solving to each device holder. In a combat situation this pushes the obligation to trouble shoot down echelon to individuals who should be focused on fighting the close battle. Secondly, a system that allows external components to be authenticated and join the network, and in doing so gain administrative privileges to route information, is far more susceptible to cyber-attack than one that is centrally managed and uses propitiatory military equipment. This vulnerability is expanded further if military systems are also drawing upon civilian infrastructure to expand their bandwidth.[26] Thirdly, it becomes much harder in a MANET for an operator to understand their own signature. While a MANET may appear in the EMS as a mist rather than a set of clear points, if someone is at the edge of the mesh, their movement will be confirmable as a node because it will cause the edge of the mist to shift position. There are therefore vulnerabilities that are contextually derived and hard for individuals to monitor as routing decisions and transmission windows are determined by the stress on the network. If different units are on different MANETs, the mists can also clearly demarcate unit boundaries for the enemy.

---

[23] Author observations, MANETs used on Exercise, Norway, March 2022.

[24] Nick Reynolds, 'Getting Tactical Communications for Land Forces Right', *The RUSI Journal* (Vol. 166, No. 5, 2021), pp. 64–75.

[25] Author observation of a MANET system under examination from an EW baseline, US, October 2021.

[26] Sunil Kumar Verma, 'Security and Privacy Issues in Wireless Ad Hoc, Mesh, and Sensor Networks', *Advance in Electronic and Electric Engineering* (Vol. 4, No. 4, 2014), pp. 381–8.

Another limitation of the MANET system is power. In order to transmit a radio must generate a spike in energy. Under the old hierarchical system radios were often kept off except for key transmission windows. Having fewer radios meant that across a section batteries could be carried to keep the radio working for an operationally relevant period. In a MANET system there are many more radios. Each requires power to both transmit and process what it is receiving. Moreover, the mesh depends upon all of the nodes collaborating and therefore the power draw is constant. There is therefore a significant limit to how long a MANET can function or else the batteries on personal radios need a means to be recharged. A further challenge is that the bandwidth of the network (how much data it can carry) is determined in part by the power each MANET component can generate. More power means shorter battery life. MANET systems therefore have practical limits to how much data they can bear before they are saturated and – as sensors increase in fidelity – the size of data packages that forces want to pass is increasing. It is increasing faster than the capacity to transmit it.

The challenge of power can be mitigated in part by a hybrid network that combines two MANET architectures. The first is the dismounted network which is optimized for voice and low-bandwidth data transmission, and the second is that between vehicles which can use the engine to generate drastically more power and can carry a larger antenna. If data can be moved from the dismounted to vehicular network, then this can go some way to managing power consumption. In practice however, there is a need to compress data packets at source, a need to ensure that only relevant data are prioritized and a limit to how much can be passed to the centre. To maintain a robust MANET architecture therefore it is clear that current force design must change to support a new signals structure, distribution of skills in units, and training and awareness of risk management as communications architectures evolve. It is also apparent that while a restructuring of military communications can help to realize aspects of the panopticon, reality is never likely to meet the vision. A force that fails to modernize communications risks being dominated by the enemy's situational awareness and agility. But truly centralized battlespace management is unrealistic. This is especially the case when one considers the havoc that can be wrought on communications by enemy activity.

Making a mess of the EMS

Electronic warfare may be divided into three broad functions: electronic intelligence (ELINT), electronic protection and electronic attack. The first concerns the locating of electronic signatures through the monitoring of activity in the electromagnetic spectrum, aimed at pinpointing bearings for signals known to correlate with subjects of interest. The second comprises the application of electronic countermeasures to disrupt enemy effects targeting friendly forces. The third is to emit energy into the spectrum with the intention of disrupting enemy communications, frustrating enemy ELINT and radar and damaging systems by overloading their circuits with electrical energy. For much of the twentieth century the EMS was dominated by military activities. In many austere environments, military communications would be one of the very few sources of emissions. Civilian infrastructure meanwhile operated within limited bands of frequency that could be carefully regulated.[27] Today, things are different. Civilian demand for bandwidth is exceedingly high and increasing. The explosion of wireless communications, remote control systems and the importance of networks for controlling civil infrastructure mean that background activity in the spectrum is noisy, complicated and diverse. This both increases the detail of surveys necessary to have a useful baseline for an operating environment and restricts military training because it has become harder for militaries to employ EW effects on training areas without disrupting civilians. As militaries also seek to make use of 5G and other civilian networks, there is also an increasing tendency for military units to try and hide their signature in the surrounding noise.

It is occasionally suggested that a future great power conflict would see so much activity in the EMS that between fratricidal communications and enemy jamming all parties will be denied access to most of the useful bands in the spectrum and will revert to fighting unplugged.[28] Although this situation may arise, it is unlikely to do so for a sustained period. Wide area jamming of multiple frequencies demands a great deal of power. A vehicle with a large antenna and a dedicated generator might deny a range of frequencies out to around 20 km in the right kind of terrain, for as long as its generator has fuel.[29] An artillery deployed jammer – which might be around the size of a champagne bottle – may suppress communications out to 200 m but will only do so for a short period of time because of its limited internal power supply. Beyond limited power there is the problem of detection. A jammer actively emits energy and a dirty jammer – one that is untargeted but simply jamming a large band of frequencies in all directions – is readily detectable. It can therefore be struck. Nor can such a jammer easily be moved while it is having its effect because a sufficiently large antenna is difficult to support while driving. Between the short life expectancy of dirty jammers therefore, and the limited endurance of artillery deployable systems or man-portable jammers, denial of the EMS is an effect that can be created for a limited period across a limited geography. For the period in which it is being delivered, it is likely exceedingly disruptive. In the opening hours of Russia's invasion of Ukraine, for example, jamming against Ukrainian air defence radar was highly effective.[30] If one side is disproportionately dependent upon EMS access, such temporary denial may make a force uncompetitive at the vital moment. But commanders will need to make careful judgements as to when they emplace such a capability and understand its relative impact on opposing forces. A decision to create such an environment is also a decision to sever a commander from the capacity to direct or influence the battle for a limited period.[31]

[27] Peter Roberts and Dave Hewitt, 'Episode 29: Electronic Warfare and Cumulative Risk', Western Way of War, RUSI podcast, 17 December 2020: https://rusi.org/podcasts/western-way-of-war/episode-29-electronic-warfare-and-cumulative-risk, accessed 3 November 2021.
[28] Igor Sutyagin and Bill Hix, RUSI Land Warfare Conference, London, 19 July 2017.
[29] Author observation of Russian EW capabilities deployed in Ukraine, June 2022.
[30] Author interviews, Ukrainian air defence specialist, Ukraine, April 2022.
[31] Indeed, the reversion to wide area jamming by Russian forces in June 2022 in Ukraine reflected their vulnerability to precision munitions rather than their dominance on the ground, author observations, Ukraine, June 2022.

Electronic attack does not need to deny the spectrum to prove highly disruptive, however. Against a rigid architecture working on a limited range of frequencies – which characterized most land forces communications at the conclusion of the Cold War – it is eminently feasible to both identify the location of key nodes through their emissions traffic and then jam the frequency associated with the target network along the bearing of the command post. Because the jamming is targeted and directional, a much smaller power level can achieve drastically greater range. A comparable power source for a dirty jammer producing an omnidirectional effect out to 20 km may produce an effect on a narrow band of frequency along a 20 m corridor out to 400 km, though in this it is constrained by the curvature of the earth.[32] In practice, line-of-sight limitations mean that except on specific terrain and the use of elevated antenna, this effect will only target aircraft or satellites at that range. Nevertheless, that the effect can travel that far also means that the jammer can be kept further from harm, potentially having enough time to be alerted as to an incoming threat and move.

Historically the game between communicators and jammers was driven by manual adjustment. A network could switch frequencies on a pre-agreed schedule or sequence and thereby evade the jammer, whose crew would then need to survey the spectrum to find the new frequency and then adjust their jammers to effect it. Today this manual evasion is insufficient. The impact of software-defined radar, radios and EW suites, combined with machine learning, outlined in the previous chapter, means that surveying the spectrum can be done constantly, while adjustments to a jammer to follow specific points of emissions can happen rapidly. This is the crux of the problem facing current militaries. Against an enemy that has modernized their electronic warfare and communications architectures, they can disrupt legacy kill chains and suppress their functioning through sustained targeted jamming, while passing information within their own force along agile networks. The system does not need to function as seamlessly as corporate marketing implies. It simply needs to function at the speed of relevance and if it can do that one force will impose disproportionately accurate and responsive effects upon the other. Militaries therefore must not see their communications as a support function like plumbing that is built and can then be relied upon. Instead, they must be equipped – with both the tools and knowledge – to fight to be heard and contest the enemy's capacity to exploit the EMS. They must contest and win in the electromagnetic spectrum at the tactical level. The proliferation of sensors like AESA radar among tactical units means that more and more systems on the battlefield can be used as jammers. Systems used for electronic detection are increasingly deployable as electronic attack assets. In this context, understanding how to employ these effects will be critical.

An additional dimension to the contest for the EMS is the relationship between electronic warfare and cyber-attack. Growing awareness of cyber vulnerabilities has caused an over-reaction in much military discourse.[33] While a mesh network allowing remote access can theoretically be penetrated by a cyber-attacker, the mesh should

---

[32] Technical examination of Krasukha-4 EW complex, Ukraine, June 2022.

[33] Jack Watling and Justin Bronk, 'The Slow and Imprecise Art of Cyber Warfare', *Necessary Heresies: Challenging the Narratives Distorting Contemporary UK Defence* (London: RUSI, 2021), pp. 11–23.

be monitored, and assuming that rudimentary safeguards are in place attempted intrusions should be detected and severed.[34] Tactical cyber effects will be limited in the scope and scale of their impact. At the tactical level the greater value of cyber-attacks is in gathering intelligence about enemy systems long before hostilities, except where cyber capabilities complement electronic attack. The distinction between electronic warfare and cyber-attack may be understood as activity that is concerned with transmission of data as compared with activity concerned with the contents of data. Nevertheless, if the process by which a system translates a transmission into data is understood, then it becomes possible to push energy at the system in such a manner as to trip reactions within both its software and hardware that either lead to data being lost, misidentified or the system shutting down. In order to do this it is necessary to have a deep technical understanding of the system. This can be developed through provoking the system and measuring its reaction, or by penetrating enemy networks in peacetime using cyber-attacks and exfiltrating data about the system to design highly precise EW capabilities. The result is that very low energy electronic attack can have a dramatic effect on a given sensor or receiver, either generating a false positive or jamming the link. The use of cyber-attack in competition to develop precise electronic attacks against specific systems to be employed in war also allows the attack to have a very low signature and therefore be difficult to detect and counter. Although much more efficient and effective than standard electronic attack, these techniques are not transferable between devices. If the vulnerability is identified, the enemy can often change it. Using such a capability therefore risks not being able to employ it a second time. When to employ such capabilities is therefore a key decision for commanders as to when it offers the greatest advantage.

A final consideration as regards disrupting the enemy through the electromagnetic spectrum is spoofing. At its simplest spoofing can comprise the emission of signatures associated with known objects in order to create false positives for enemy sensors. In practice, this has become much harder as the fidelity of sensors has improved. In order to emplace effective spoofing it is necessary for the false emitter to mimic the behaviour of friendly actual emitters. It is also necessary for the emission to mimic what the adversary has recorded in their data libraries as the signature of specific systems. This therefore requires long-term intelligence preparation to be credible, and to have electronic warfare specialists who understand how the combined arms formations they are mimicking operate so that they are integrated into the planning process and can use their expert judgement to apply their tools appropriately and dynamically.

There is a more complex form of spoofing, which is also arguably more effective. As sensors become enabled by machine learning – which seek to establish unique identifiers – and information management becomes protocol driven, so that particular signatures are given a higher priority for transmission through a network, it becomes possible to spoof the technical architecture in ways that are difficult to repeat at scale against a human operator. If the protocol for how a system will interpret or react to a given signature is known, then this signature can be replicated to cause significant

---

[34] Author observations, live defensive cyber capability demonstration of a MANET, July 2021.

disruption to an automated system. Consider, for example, the machine-learning algorithm designed to identify puppies which was able to reliably distinguish dogs from most objects but could not readily distinguish between golden retrievers and cookies.[35] If one knows how an automated system works, a signature can be presented to it that is very different to the actual signature but without contextual understanding the system will still misclassify it. This is therefore easier for an electronic warfare team to do because they no longer need their emissions to replicate those of the forces around them, reducing the need for them to maintain a common operating picture with the forces they are supporting. A further advantage of such approaches to spoofing is that because it emits the unique signatures that automated systems are programmed to respond to, it does not require a massive amount of power. Very small power levels can produce the effect, which are in turn difficult for the enemy to identify and respond to, especially under stress. Imagine, for example, that a system associates a particular signature with a ballistic missile launch and that this information is automatically given the highest priority of bandwidth access to move this notification to ballistic missile defence systems. Upon receiving the alert, the track data are insufficient to provide any cuing information for the defences. The ballistic missile defenders will know that they are being spoofed. But so long as the system believes what it is detecting is a ballistic missile, it will continue to push this useless data over the system at the expense of other transmissions. This further complicates the ability to communicate, identify the source of the problem and respond. The humans may know it is bogus but preventing the system from treating it as genuine may be time consuming, stressful and create enough space for an actual ballistic missile to be launched without the enemy being able to respond appropriately within a relevant timeframe. The defender must therefore be able to override their systems to separate signal from the noise.

The signal from the noise

As military digital systems become increasingly connected, the prioritization of bandwidth becomes critical to their functioning effectively. There are too much data in the battlespace for it all to be available across the network. Hard-baked into the algorithms managing the flow of traffic on the network therefore must be prioritization. What a force prioritizes will determine where it is responsive and where it is not. Software patches can refine the prioritization, and different priority stacks could be encoded on the network for fighting different opponents. Nevertheless, how the communications architecture is programmed to prioritize signal from noise is a key command and force design decision that must match how the force is structured to fight.

While data mission files could be distributed across a network to assign priorities appropriate to an adversary and theatre, it is harder to make the prioritization context specific. For example, for a company in contact the absolute priority is available bandwidth for clear voice transmission. For the company's bandwidth to be reassigned

---

[35] Alan Brown, RUSI Land Warfare Conference, London, 5 June 2019.

to other tasks would be unacceptable. Preventing this from happening however requires that a defined group are able to switch their systems from being an open route for the wider network to a closed constellation within it. This places the burden of switching setting to the company and creates a training burden for the unit to understand how to set themselves up as a group within the network. Having this capability within the system comes with other dangers too. Suppose that all units in contact simultaneously firewall themselves from through traffic. Suddenly a belt of relays throughout the contact zone become unavailable, significantly constraining access to bandwidth for the recce screen. While this may individually make sense for the troops in contact, it also risks higher echelons remaining unaware and therefore being unable to shape what is immediately approaching them.

The building of priority stacks for assigning bandwidth can come with additional challenges. In short, higher echelons can specify certain returns as higher priorities for specific systems – such as hostile air detections being passed to air defences – but this can also enable the adversary to use probing attacks with aircraft to saturate the network. Furthermore, it risks surprise if the volume of contacts within the high-priority stack prevents reconnaissance units flagging threats that had not been foreseen centrally. The alternative is for prioritization to be based upon the judgement of the reconnaissance screen in which pushing information with an assigned priority determines the allocation of bandwidth. This risks the centre receiving very different data sets from different parts of the battlefield and, while it means that surprises and outliers are likely to be detected, it will also suppress the accumulation of routine reporting at the centre in such a way as to limit situational awareness and the ability to make accurate assessments as to the trade-offs between the threats being indicated.

The need to manage bandwidth may lead certain parts of the force to continue to field bespoke communications channels to bypass and avoid interference with the general communications traffic of the force. Bespoke channels must be made robust and difficult to detect since a small number of transmitters and receivers necessitates beyond line-of-sight communication and cannot consequently hide in the noise of the force. One example of this would be to utilize free-space optical communication, to either a relay node, aircraft or satellite,[36] which can give tactical units at the edge gigabytes per second of bandwidth with almost no capacity for detection or interception.[37] The downside of this system is that alignment over considerable distance means that the emitter and receiver must be mounted on a gyroscope and therefore be based on a vehicle. It also degrades considerably in dense cloud, fog, rain and other climactic conditions and smoke. Reversionary communications such as HF would also be necessary with the resultant constraints on bandwidth, vulnerability of detection and

[36] Kevin Chilton and Lucas Autenried, 'The Backbone of JADC2 Satellite Communications for Information Age Warfare' (Washington, DC: The Mitchell Institute, 2021): https://mitchellaerospacepower.org/wp-content/uploads/2021/12/The_Backbone_of_JADC2_Policy_Paper_32-ver2.pdf, accessed 20 July 2022.

[37] Capability briefing and demonstration, Qinetiq, UK, May 2021; Brian Perrett, 'Guiding Light: How Lasers Can Inform Military Operations', *Qinetiq*, 19 November 2020: https://www.qinetiq.com/en/blogs/how-lasers-can-inform-military-operations, accessed 20 July 2022.

complexity for the user. Satellite communications present a more reliable reversionary means of pushing data but introduce latency into the transmission.

The challenge for the future of command and control is not a lack of data. Data are plentiful on the future battlefield. But accessing the relevant data within a relevant timeframe will remain a major obstacle. In overcoming that obstacle commanders must determine what information they value, what access to information they wish to assure and where they wish to take risk. Commanders must be able to judge when to broadcast, when to connect and when to unplug. They must treat electronic warfare support as part of their combined arms formation and communicate clearly to these operators when they are prepared to fight for bandwidth, and when they are able to support others.[38] Ensuring that the signal can be found amidst the cacophony of battle demands that forces approach communications and the electromagnetic spectrum as a plane that they must manoeuvre through and actively fight for advantage in, rather than a supporting function that is simply available to varying degrees of degradation. The question of when a commander requires situational awareness, and when they need to be able to answer narrow, specific, but detailed questions, may lead to force design decisions that shape how the wider force fights, where it can pursue competitive advantage over the enemy, and where it accepts that the enemy has the opportunity to sense and communicate. Finally, conventional hierarchical communications are neither sufficiently robust, nor are they able to handle a sufficient volume of data to support modern competitive forces. But as networks become more complex and flexible, they also impose a higher training demand on the user and expose the force to the risk of cyber penetration. Cyber-attack is rarely decisive and relatively simple to counter. But failure to adhere to discipline in basic procedures makes the threat far more acute. What is clear is that if armies do not modernize their communications, they risk being left deaf and blind.

---

[38] Author interviews, Alec Bain, Warminster, January 2019.

3

When protection is an illusion

Tactically, there is the revelation that firepower invalidates the doctrines in force. Morally, the illusions with which we had armoured ourselves are swept away in the blink of an eye.[1]

Charles de Gaulle

In the autumn of 2021 several teams from 40 Commando, Royal Marines, spread out across the high desert of southern California in light vehicles as part of a warfighting exercise. To their north was a fully enabled and mechanized USMC Regiment, tasked with seizing an objective to the South. A comparison of relative combat power would have suggested that the Commandos could be brushed aside. Instead, as USMC elements manoeuvred they were engaged by fires, suffering heavy casualties. If they dispersed, they found their combat power dissipate across their frontage. If they concentrated, they found themselves blunted by artillery. Over the course of five days of fighting the USMC were attrited until combat ineffective. The Commandos meanwhile suffered around a dozen casualties.[2]

The idea of a light infantry company having the capacity to fix mechanized battalions would have been ludicrous for much of the twentieth century. In 1950 Task Force Smith – an infantry battalion supported by artillery – attempted to halt the advance of a North Korean force spearheaded by a platoon of armour. The armour pushed straight through the position while North Korean infantry enveloped the unit.[3] Today, by contrast, heavy forces attempting to push through screens of light infantry are routinely attrited. What is more, heavily armoured vehicles tend to be picked off first, owing to their high signature and high priority. The reasons for this change are multifaceted, but foremost among them are that a small number of people today can rapidly bring to bear a disproportionate weight of fire from neighbouring positions, while also staying harder to detect than the forces trying to punch through them. The implications of this change pose fundamental challenges to the foremost principle of mechanized warfare, which is the concentration of force. This chapter will unpack why this shift between lethality and protection has come about, and the problems this poses for manoeuvre elements.

[1] Charles de Gaulle, *La France et son Armée* (Paris: Tempus Perrin, 2016), pp. 244–5.
[2] Author observations, MWX22, Twentynine Palms, October 2021.
[3] Max Hastings, *The Korean War* (New York: Simon and Schuster, 1988), pp. 15–22.

The paradox of armour: Too much and never enough

The design of armoured vehicles is often described as a set of compromises between protection, lethality and mobility. While trade-offs between these properties are inherent in the design of armoured fighting vehicles, they exist within a hierarchy. The transformative effect of armoured vehicles on the battlefield was fundamentally a result of mobile protection, rather than firepower. The ability to move through barbed wire and across trenches without falling victim to fire from a concealed enemy was critical to breaking the positional deadlock of the Western front. Equipping tanks with cannon – rather than just small calibre weapons – became a priority for two reasons: the need to defeat other tanks, and the need to defeat dug in artillery with armoured gun shields.[4] These were priorities because if the tanks could not be defeated then they would dislocate the armour from their supporting infantry, and because if anti-tank artillery was not knocked out then the armour would be rapidly destroyed. The growth in firepower on armoured vehicles therefore was fundamentally driven by the need to protect the vehicle and its enablers. AFVs meanwhile that were built around firepower at the expense of protection were doctrinally separated from tanks in the Second World War.[5]

Once tanks were expected to fight one another, this created a race between firepower and protection that has continued for the last century. In general, this saw a staggered parallel progression. From the 76mm gun of the Sherman Firefly, NATO moved to the 105mm and thence the 120mm. The Soviet Union similarly moved from 85mm on the T34-85 to the 100mm of the T-55, 115mm on the T-62 and thence to the 125mm. Protection similarly evolved, becoming thicker, harder and heavier, and also more complex with spall liners to prevent internal fragmentation killing the crew and reactive plates mounted externally to prevent single round penetration.[6] With the current competition between anti-tank-guided weapons (ATGWs) and active protection systems – designed to intercept projectiles before they reach the tank – it may seem that this parallel progression of protection and firepower is set to continue. It is not. Today improvements in lethality are increasing exponentially. Improvements in protection by contrast have begun to advance logarithmically with smaller gains requiring ever-greater resource to achieve. This has far-reaching consequences for how militaries think about and design their fighting systems. The traditional hierarchy of priorities is no longer sufficient. To explain why it is necessary to explore some principles in armoured vehicle design.

Military vehicles may be divided into wheeled and tracked platforms. Although there have been great improvements in the cross-country mobility and survivability of wheeled platforms, they remain fundamentally more vulnerable than their tracked counterparts because even light artillery will shred their tyres and so significantly

---

[4]   Guderian, Achtung Panzer, pp. 178–87.
[5]   Harry Yeide, *The Tank Killers: A History of America's World War II Tank Destroyer Force* (Newbury: Casemate, 2010).
[6]   Jeremy Black, *Tank Warfare* (Bloomington: Indiana University Press, 2020).

reduce their mobility. This does not mean that they are worse, but it does mean they are less robust. We will therefore begin by focusing on tracked vehicles. Tracked vehicles are constrained in their dimensions by civilian infrastructure. They must be loaded onto and off ships, railways and equipment transporters. Designed for off-road mobility, tracked vehicles wear out quickly if forced to move on roads over long distances. Railways, tunnels, bridges, lorries, cranes and other infrastructure are optimized to support the unimpeded passage of standard ISO containers, which have a width of 2.44m and are usually carried by vehicles with a width of around 2.6m.[7] Most infrastructure is optimized for passage of vehicles narrower than 3.15m. Although wider vehicles can be moved on specialist equipment transporters, they will be limited in the routes they can take by the availability of infrastructure that can support them. Although some infrastructure can support widths of up to 4m, any increase above 3.15m will begin to impose significant constraints upon vehicle mobility.[8]

The manoeuvrability of tracked vehicles relies on the interaction between their two tracks and the distribution of weight across them. If the length of the track in contact with the ground is less than 1.5 times or greater than 1.8 times the distance between the two tracks, then the vehicle's mobility will be severely impaired.[9] The hull will extend beyond the contact surface but cannot do so by a long way without impeding the ability of the vehicle to transition onto and off slopes. Thus, one would expect the overall length of the hull of a fighting vehicle to be less than 8m. The width of the track itself is also critical to a vehicle's mobility. Too narrow and the tracks will cut into the ground. Wider tracks are preferable. The width is limited however by the need to have a turret to host the main armament, and a crew. Simply put, the larger the turret, the larger the gun it can carry. If a vehicle has a remote turret – which does not have a basket extending into the hull – and places the crew fully inside the vehicle hull, then the width of the hull needs to be a minimum of two people wide. Although this allows a larger turret to sit on a hull with comparably wide tracks, it also increases the height of the hull, thereby increasing the surface area needing to be protected and consequently reducing the relative protection for the same weight of armour.

The observant reader may have already noted that most modern armoured vehicles – while adhering to the ratios outlined above – are wider than 2.44m. The Leopard 2, M1 Abrams and Challenger 2 are all above 3m wide. Designed in the 1980s, these tanks were optimized for a fight on the North European Plain where they were kept close to the expected area of fighting. As such operational mobility was not a

---

[7] Bruce Jones, *To Rule the Waves: How Control of the World's Oceans Shapes the Fate of the Superpowers* (New York: Simon and Schuster, 2021), pp. 93–166.

[8] Note that civilian infrastructure in Europe has been optimized for civilian freight with EU standardization placing little or no emphasis on military requirements, leading to deviation from Cold War governments paying closer attention to NATO STANAGS, Council of the European Union, 'Directive (EU) 2015/719 of the European Parliament and of the Council of 29 April 2015 Amending Council Directive 96/53/EC Laying Down for Certain Road Vehicles Circulating within the Community the Maximum Authorised Dimensions in National and International Traffic and the Maximum Authorised Weights in International Traffic', *Official Journal of the European Union* (L115/1, 6 May 2015).

[9] T. W. Terry, *Fighting Vehicles* (London: Brassey's, 1991), p. 117.

foremost priority in their design. Survivability and firepower were paramount.[10] The NATO tanks above – with their full protective loadout – sit above 70 tonnes. At this weight they were sufficiently protected to have rounds from Iraqi T55s and T72s fail to penetrate in 1991 and 2003.[11] The cost came in mobility. All must travel on specially widened rail carriages. They are severely restricted on which routes they can traverse. Movement through populated areas moreover risks inflicting widespread damage to sub-surface infrastructure such as reticulation and power and telecommunications cables.[12] Large areas of ground will struggle to support their weight, canalizing their movement. Collectively, these limitations make the platforms difficult and expensive to project, maintain and to deploy for exercises.[13] The T-72 and its derivatives, coming in at just over 50 tonnes distributed over a comparable area, are easier to move, but given the mobility constraints of modern armour it is perhaps unsurprising that the T55, at 36 tonnes, remains the most widely employed tank around the world today.

Given the mobility constraints already experienced by Main Battle Tanks in the 70-tonne weight bracket, and the fact that infrastructure prevents armoured vehicles becoming significantly larger to spread their weight over a larger area, we may assume that protection cannot be achieved by layering more armour onto platforms. The aim therefore has been to pursue better armour within established weight categories. Active Protection Systems attempt to catch anti-tank-guided weapons before they reach the vehicle, increasing the number of shots required to destroy a tank.[14] Reactive armour aims to nullify the explosive force of a warhead, therefore requiring a tank to be hit multiple times.[15] Statistical armour around less protected parts of a vehicle attempt to reduce the reliability of incoming munitions detonating.[16] Electrical armour seeks to disrupt the ionized jet created by shaped charge projectiles. As armour becomes specifically aimed at types of projectile however it is clear that this approach adds significant cost and complexity while offering limited and highly contextual protection.

In the 1980s the loss of mobility was made up for by the protection afforded. Today, however, it is less clear that the gain in protection is sufficient to meet the threat. Whereas protection is capped by weight, and gains are therefore becoming ever-more incremental, lethality is increasing drastically because of three lines of development: precision, range and energy. To begin with precision, the reduction in the size of

---

[10] Malcolm Chalmers and Lutz Unterseher, 'Is There a Tank Gap?: Comparing NATO and Warsaw Pact Tank Fleets', *International Security* (Vol. 13, No. 1, 1988), pp. 5–49.

[11] Author interviews, multiple tank crews from both conflicts, UK, US, 2019.

[12] Which was one reason why the US Military strongly opposed Abrams tanks participating in President Trump's quasi-military parade in 2019, author interview, G4 for the event, Washington, October 2019.

[13] Consider, for example, the number of MLC70+ bridges in Eastern Europe; see Jeff Milhorn, RUSI Waterways, Conference: Obstacles and Opportunities, London, 27 April 2022.

[14] 'TROPHY® Active Protection System for AFVs', Rafael: https://www.rafael.co.il/worlds/land/trophy-aps/, accessed 20 July 2022.

[15] V. Madhu and T. Balakrishna Bhat, 'Armour Protection and Affordable Protection for Futuristic Combat Vehicles', *Defence Science Journal* (Vol. 61, No. 4, 2011), pp. 394–402.

[16] Jon Hawkes, 'Primer: Statistical Armour', *The Institute of Tankology*, 5 March 2022: https://www.tanknology.co.uk/post/statistical-armour, accessed 20 July 2022.

processors combined with novel technology like 3D printing of circuitry means that precision guidance is now possible on much smaller rounds and is also becoming cheaper to manufacture. Combined with the greater fidelity of target data derived from modern sensors, it becomes possible to guide munitions along optimal attack vectors towards a target, as well as reliably strike the most vulnerable point. On an armoured vehicle this includes areas like the radiator and the engine deck. The need to have an exhaust and a radiator means that there must be a path between the exterior of the tank and the engine. Generally, these components are accessible through the rear engine deck, requiring a munition to strike from above and behind to approach the vulnerable point. Against traditional direct fire systems these points on the vehicle are unexposed but as more munitions gain a top attack capability, irrespective of whether they are ground or air launched, the likelihood is that munitions will strike the parts of a vehicle that cannot be physically protected by armour. This has a secondary implication, which is that while a strike to this area may not destroy the vehicle, it has a very high probability of destroying its engine and preventing it from moving. Armoured vehicles that are unable to manoeuvre may be recovered if they are part of an attacking force but can also be overrun if the enemy advances. Historically the loss of immobilized or damaged armour has often accounted for more vehicles than those destroyed by direct fire.[17] The fact that such munitions are going after areas of an armoured vehicle that cannot be heavily protected reduces the explosive payload they need to carry and therefore makes them lighter, cheaper and easier to fire over considerable distances.

Precision is also an increasing feature of direct fire systems. While ballistic calculators have been highly accurate for some years, tracking a target with a turret has still ultimately relied upon the skill of a vehicle's gunner. The recalibration and offset required to bring main versus coaxial armaments to bear have required a great deal of experience.[18] When under the threat of lethal return fire, the probability of an accurate follow-up shot diminishes. In order to be able to keep the weapon aligned while the vehicle manoeuvres dynamically there is a need for a very substantial training burden that few militaries meet. The widespread employment of remote weapons stations during the war on terror, combined with the integration of digital fusion already discussed in relation to sensors, however, alters the pressure on the gunner. Monitoring the feeds from a vehicle's sights, it becomes possible for the gunner to classify objects as hostile, friendly, or neutral and to assign a priority to them. The targets can then be engaged on command, with the weapon system automatically tracking the target. Combined with improvements in ballistic calculators this is significantly extending the range and hit probability of first and follow-up shots. For small arms that a human operator would be expected to use with precision at 300–500m, remote weapons stations are reliably carrying out precision engagements at 700–800m in trials.[19] For high-calibre cannon range is more likely to be constrained by line of sight within

---

[17] Ben Wheatley, 'Surviving Prokhorovka: German Armoured Longevity on the Eastern Front in 1943–1944', *Journal of Intelligence History* (Vol. 1, No. 1, 2020), pp. 1–87. https://www.tandfonline.com/doi/abs/10.1080/16161262.2020.1750841?journalCode=rjih20.

[18] Author observation, tank crew operating, Salisbury Plain, June 2021.

[19] Author observation, Exercise Autonomous Warrior, Salisbury Plain, November 2018.

terrain rather than weapon range. However, the ability to have very accurate secondary shots allows for lower-calibre weapons to achieve much higher probability of kill against heavily armoured targets because of the reliability with which follow-up shots will strike the same section of armour as the first, nullifying reactive armour and other defences. Indeed, the speed and accuracy of the second shot enabled by auto-tracking opens more reliable multiple stage engagements whereby – for instance – an airburst or high explosive round is employed to destroy a vehicle's sensors or to set off reactive armour, followed by a kinetic energy penetrator. At present the aim for first hit kill is partly reflective of the drop in accuracy for the second shot. Most passive protection is measured in its effectiveness against a single strike because human gunners have not reliably achieved second shots into the same area. However, testing demonstrates that remote weapons stations can reliably put bursts of five 30–60mm cannon rounds into the same armour plate at combat relevant ranges within the time that a main armament can fire once. This repeated strike nullifies a range of defences.[20]

The significance of precision in direct fire systems is of secondary importance to the precision of beyond line-of-sight munitions because of the extended range of modern weapons. Loitering munitions are increasingly achieving ranges between 40 and 150km. MLRS will be delivering effects between 120 and 150km and heavy howitzers are reaching out to 70km with precision munitions and out to 40km with unguided shells. The introduction of gliding munitions – which have doubled the range of mortar bombs – could see a similarly significant increase in the range of tube artillery. Long-range fires like this will not be principally concerned with groups of vehicles, though sensor-fused sub-munitions are a threat to groups of vehicles and can be fired out to 70km. Munitions designed to engage single-armoured vehicles are also seeing a significant increase in range, with many anti-tank-guided weapons having an effective range of 20–32km. Even systems that can be carried by dismounted infantry are achieving ranges of between 4 and 10km. This transforms the threat picture for armoured vehicles in several ways. ATGWs have posed a disproportionate threat to armour since their invention but they have tended to be limited in number and have had a limited time within which to engage. Because a missile takes longer in flight than a direct fire weapon, the operator stands in considerable danger of being killed before their munition engages its target. ATGWs with a short range also tend to be present in small numbers at the point of attack, while rapidly advancing armour can close the distance.[21] Using smoke and other techniques armoured vehicles have often sacrificed some tempo to essentially waste rounds from enemy ATGW firing posts. Although highly effective against isolated armour, ATGWs have historically afflicted attrition but not stopped determined armoured thrusts.[22] Moreover, when engaging a target in direct fire range, an armoured vehicle that is immobilized but not destroyed can still often contribute fire in support of their comrades.

[20] Author interviews, KMW R&D Team, Munich, October 2020.
[21] John Matsumura et al., *Lightning Over Water: Sharpening America's Light Forces for Rapid Reaction Missions* (Santa Monica, CA: RAND Corporation, 2000).
[22] Ancker Clint, 'Whither Armor?' *Military Operations* (Vol. 1, No. 2, 2012), pp. 4–8.

Longer-range munitions change the dynamic decisively for three reasons. Firstly, more firing posts are able to engage a manoeuvre element simultaneously, thereby negating the advantage of the concentrated force attacking a limited sector. Secondly, by extending the threat to beyond line of sight ATGW operators will be able to fire multiple rounds and guide them in without the pressure of being under direct threat, increasing their accuracy and the volume of fire through which armoured vehicles will need to fight. They will also have time to be more discerning in which targets they engage – prioritizing mobility support and engineering vehicles because the direct fire systems no longer pose an immediate danger. Thirdly, by pushing the threat back, the necessary level of lethality required of munitions decreases. The immobilization of an armoured vehicle 10km from the front line takes it out of the fight; it can no longer materially affect the outcome in the direct fire zone. Even if a long-range strike simply breaks up the reactive armour and smashes the sensors of the armoured vehicle, it has been rendered far less competitive as it attempts to close and becomes more susceptible to destruction by the first round on target. Range allows for the infantry and engineers to be targeted.[23] Tanks ultimately chaperone infantry onto objectives. But if the infantry fighting vehicles are targeted and destroyed before they get into contact, then the tanks cannot exploit or hold what they roll onto. Increased range therefore allows an adversary to break apart the combined arms formation. Finally, increased range enables salvos to be fired in progressive engagements. An initial wave of small, slow, loitering munitions may not make it through active protection systems but since hard-kill active protection systems have a very limited magazine capacity and take time to reload, the vehicles would then be highly vulnerable to a second salvo of ATGWs. On the other hand, if the APS does not engage the loitering munitions, then they will potentially immobilize and likely damage the sensors and defensive systems on the vehicles.

The third element is the increasing lethality of munitions themselves. 30mm Armour Penetrating Fin Stabilised Discarding Sabot (APFSDS) rounds can achieve penetration of over 140mm against rolled homogeneous armour.[24] The cumulative effect of five such rounds striking an armoured section of a vehicle is more than most vehicles can withstand. Those vehicles in the 70-tonne range can survive such strikes, but only if struck on the most heavily armoured parts of their hulls. Against a 125mm or 120mm kinetic penetrator reactive plating and misdirecting the energy of the round after penetration can enable a vehicle to survive the first hit. Almost no vehicle, without pushing above 80 tonnes can survive a second. Against a high explosive (HE) or airburst round the nullification of passive layers can be achieved across a wide area, making the probability of kill from the follow-up shot easier. Indeed, against most modern armour a two-stage engagement from a 105mm gun firing airburst followed by APFSDS will likely be sufficient to destroy even the most heavily armoured of targets.

---

[23] Ground-launched Brimstone, for example, was found to be particularly effective in Ukraine because it caught Russian IFVs and APCs while they still had crew inside with the target vehicles on the move, author interviews, Ukraine, June 2022.

[24] Capability demonstration, KMW R&D team, Munich, August 2021.

APS systems are not able to effectively protect vehicles from the effects of the initial HE or airburst round and are usually rendered incapable of interfering with the follow-up round because of the effects of the first on the APS's sensor suite. Beyond direct fire systems there has also been a step change in the efficiency of explosives, so that comparatively small warheads as on Brimstone, can reliably penetrate even the thickest armour fielded on main battle tanks.[25] Thermobaric explosives meanwhile have a significant effect on infantry, and especially infantry in cover, and are increasingly available in comparatively small-calibre munitions. They can also kill tank crews if hatches are left open.

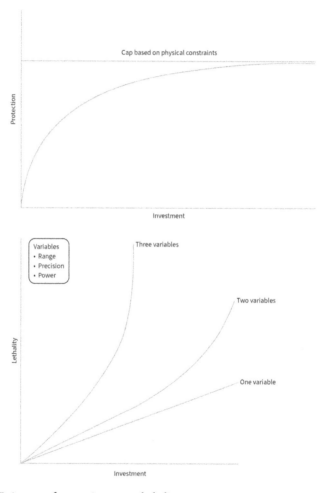

Figure 1 Trajectory of protection versus lethality.

[25] Capability demonstration, MBDA, UK, November 2020.

The rapid increase in lethality, compared with the logarithmic growth in protection, should cause a fundamental shift in the prioritization of attributes for military vehicles, and has several implications for the concepts of how such vehicles are organized, deployed and fight. To begin with the individual vehicle we may draw several conclusions. Firstly, EW and other passive protective capabilities need to be managed across a system of platforms and not on a platform by platform basis. The integration of a full suite of defensive systems on every vehicle drives up weight and cost to a point where the level of protection gained is inefficient compared with the cost of simply expanding the number of munitions fired. Secondly, passive protection against heavy machine gun fire, mines and indirect fire effects still imposes a significant resource issue in the enemy's ability to knock out the vehicle. Protection against 30mm and 60mm rounds where possible adds significantly to the vehicle's survivability. However, the level of protection required to adequately defend against 105–125mm fire carries the weight of a vehicle beyond what is logistically supportable, while the additional armour does little to make the sensors that allow the vehicle to fight any more survivable. Without them such a vehicle can be mission-killed and destroyed at leisure. Thus, there is very little reason for the level of armour on a vehicle to increase above approximately 54 tonnes.[26] Any weight above this sees a significant decrease in protection gained for mobility sacrificed. If individual vehicles are becoming more vulnerable however, and protection must be managed systemically across a formation, then this leads to fundamental changes in tactics for armoured forces. These trends do not mean that armoured forces are obsolete or that infantry become vastly more survivable. Infantry cannot carry sufficient volumes of anti-tank weapons to defend themselves from armoured vehicles except in very dense terrain and are disproportionately vulnerable to fragmentation indirect fire when moving. Armour still brings pace to the battlefield. But it is far more fragile and must therefore fight differently.

An imposed loss of concentration

Moving to the formation level, the increased effectiveness of modern weapons achieved through range, precision and lethality, combined with the fidelity of stand-off sensors, imposes a major hurdle to a second core tenet of mechanized warfare: concentration. Although precision weapons can increasingly target vehicles on the move, they do so within a limited field of regard. A formation therefore can be targeted with a great deal of accuracy, even while on the move, because if the munition's time in flight brings it over the target, it is unlikely that vehicles of the formation will have left the field of regard. The axes of advance of a large group of vehicles are also more predictable. Against small packets of vehicles targeting on the move is more precarious. Munitions tracking targets moving at speed in small

---

[26] This is the rough balance point that consistently emerges in studies whether by KMW in Germany, or KIDA, interviewed in South Korea in April 2022. The main outlier is Israel, though the Merkava can also carry personnel and is not expected to cover significant ground, making its context somewhat unique.

groups must either be navigated to intercept by an offboard sensor, or fly a course that increases the likelihood of intercept within the limited field of regard of their onboard sensors. Munitions that depend upon external guidance are reliant on a kill chain to achieve precision that can be targeted and interfered with. While viable against sub-peer adversaries these kill chains are not robust in a peer conflict, as outlined in the preceding chapter. Therefore, the effective targeting of small packets of moving vehicles with precision munitions – and especially if it requires a layered attack – is likely to be inefficient. Against larger formations however precision allows devastating effects at considerable ranges. This forces dispersion. Dispersion however is limited by the importance of systemic protection against longer ranged attacks, since if vehicles are dependent upon other vehicles to carry effecters against specific threat vectors, then they cannot be separated from that protection. Dispersion therefore has a minimum viable level that must be determined. The inability to initially concentrate limits tempo, combat power and the ability to roll enemies from prepared positions. Thus, there is a need for units to operate dispersed, but to be able to concentrate at the right point in time and then to disperse once again.

This is not how current formations are equipped, trained or organized to fight. For instance, during British Army testing of dispersed operations using existing orders of battle manoeuvre was viable until attrition was suffered. The limited availability of medical and engineering support meant that units had to stop moving and wait for those limited assets to reach them.[27] Across a dispersed formation this could be over a considerable distance. Across the intervening space it was often necessary to escort and protect the engineering and medical vehicles, but this then brought a point of concentration when the engineering and medical vehicles arrived at the dispersed element. They could therefore be targeted. In this way, sections of enemy personnel were able to fix large units and undermine the tempo of manoeuvre of an opposing company. Conversely when the Royal Marines attempted these tactics with integrated support elements down to the team level, the framework proved robust.[28]

The risks of concentration become especially severe in canalizing terrain. Take, for example, a gap crossing operation. Suppose that fires, amphibious reconnaissance vehicles, and air or riverine assault infantry have managed to secure the far bank and establish a perimeter to provide a stretch of bank where a bridge can be emplaced. Historically attriting forces crossing the bridge would demand a concentration from a battery of artillery, which would need to be in range of the crossing. This battery could be suppressed by counterbattery fire or pushed out of range. Today however a single vehicle with a set of precision munitions could remain in a hide within range of the area screened by the crossing. Stand-off sensors could wait until there was movement across the river, giving the indicated point of the emplaced bridge, and thereby cue on a set of precision strikes to destroy the bridge. A counterattack could then press in upon the cordon which, as it fell back and therefore became concentrated, would also become more vulnerable to fires. This is not an entirely hypothetical scenario. In May

---

[27] Author observation, Strike Experimentation Exercise, Scotland, April 2019.
[28] Author observation, MWX22, Twentynine Palms, October 2021.

2022 Russian forces attempted a crossing of the Siverskyi Donets River. They emplaced a pontoon bridge, only to be located by a UAV. In the subsequent artillery strikes the Russians lost almost an entire battalion tactical group.[29]

To consider a different scenario, suppose a battlegroup were conducting a traditional armoured attack along two parallel axes across a 6-km frontage. At this point they may be sufficiently dispersed to reduce the indirect fire threat. However, the axis of advance would be eminently apparent from GMTI and acoustic sensors. Suppose the enemy were to drop a fire mission of scattered mines in front of one of the axes. The targeted company multiple could either slow down its tempo to clear its way through or divert onto the other axis. In the first instance the slowing down of the company would allow reliable engagements against its vehicle with precision effects, over a longer period and would also dislocate the attack, since one axis would culminate before the other. If, on the other hand, the targeted company multiple were to divert onto the other company multiple's axis of advance this would suddenly double the concentration of targets, rendering both susceptible to a layered strike.[30]

The second example is especially useful in highlighting the problems with the methods employed in mechanized warfare because the only thing preventing the targeted company multiple from shifting onto a third axis outside of the 6-km frontage is that soldiers are expected to remain within their unit boundaries assigned to them during planning and would not shift into a neighbouring unit's area of responsibility. This is generally sensible if boundaries deconflict effects, but the process of applying boundaries is often highly problematic as forces disperse and more and more effects are in range. Concentration in one sector is now likely to draw cross-boundary fires from adversary units. Dispersion also drives a tendency towards mutual penetration and the intermingling of the lead elements of a force. If units adhere rigidly to their boundaries, therefore they tend to disregard threats or opportunities on their flanks,[31] and in a context where enemy may remain on the flank having been bypassed by a neighbouring unit this can rapidly dislocate manoeuvre. This has been repeatedly demonstrated in wargames and simulations involving dispersed forces. The problem is often not that the threat cannot be mitigated but that units trained to divide the battlefield into unit boundaries fail to guard against such threats. Unit boundaries are not irrelevant in future operations. However, what they indicate and how they are drawn must be re-examined.

It still comes down to the infanteer and their rifle … or radio

So far this chapter has been focused on the survivability of vehicles and groups of vehicles. The reason for this is straightforward. Vehicles give formations mobility and

[29] Howard Altman, 'Debacle on the Donets: How Russian Forces Got Obliterated Trying to Cross a River', *The Drive*, 12 May 2022: https://www.thedrive.com/the-war-zone/debacle-on-the-donets-russian-forces-got-obliterated-trying-to-cross-a-river, accessed 20 July 2022.
[30] A wargamed scenario with the King's Royal Hussars, Salisbury Plain, June 2021.
[31] A phenomenon witnessed on multiple occasions at ascending echelon from company to full brigade. The latter during an exercise on Salisbury plain in January 2018.

are therefore critical to their offensive combat power and survivability. They allow forces to concentrate rapidly and exploit breakthroughs, as well as bring heavier weaponry to bear. But operations ultimately depend upon the taking and holding of ground, and since a force that is losing the mechanized confrontation will seek to level the playing field by withdrawing to terrain unfavourable for vehicles it follows that many fights must culminate in infantry engagements. The most obvious example of this phenomenon in recent years is the defence of urban centres forming the final phase of campaigns, whether that be Islamic State's falling back to Mosul and Raqqa as they became overwhelmed in open country,[32] or the Armenian attempt to retain Shusha in the war for Nagorno-Karabakh.[33] Therefore, the survivability of infantry bears examination.

Dismounted infantry units are highly survivable when static by virtue of being resource intensive to detect. Although personnel need food and water the logistics tail of a dismounted infantry unit is drastically smaller and therefore less conspicuous than any mechanized force. Dug into complex terrain behind multispectral camouflage, dismounted infantry can effectively evade detection unless subjected to sustained observation. Sustained reconnaissance can detect dismounted infantry and over time can enable a unit to be attrited; however, the detection and elimination of infantry units absorbs a great deal of ISR. The destruction of infantry in prepared positions is often even more resource intensive. While a precision munition is often economical for targeting a vehicle, it is less so for targeting a person. Infantry are often dispersed and are not deployed in a manner that makes multiple kills per strike achievable. Consider, for instance, how long it took Syrian forces backed by Russia and Iran to retake urban strongholds in Syria, the Iraqi Army backed by US airpower, or Ukrainian separatists and Russian forces at Donetsk Airport to dislodge comparatively small numbers of dismounted infantry from urban centres.[34] Consider, moreover, the vast quantity of munitions required to achieve these effects. Grozny too – often cited as an example of the speed of assault achievable through ruthless tactics[35] – was a highly inefficient campaign in terms of the volume of munitions required to eliminate a small opposing force.

A further dilemma presented by dismounted infantry is that so long as they have communications even a single infanteer is a highly capable sensor. Given the

[32] Mosul Study Group, 'What the Battle for Mosul Teaches the Force', September 2017: https://www.armyupress.army.mil/Portals/7/Primer-on-Urban-Operation/Documents/Mosul-Public-Release1.pdf, accessed 20 July 2022.

[33] John Spencer and Harshana Ghoorhoo, 'The Battle of Shusha City and the Missed Lessons of the 2020 Nagorno-Karabakh War', *Modern War Institute*, 14 July 2021: https://mwi.usma.edu/the-battle-of-shusha-city-and-the-missed-lessons-of-the-2020-nagorno-karabakh-war/, accessed 20 July 2022.

[34] Amos Fox, '"Cyborgs at Little Stalingrad": A Brief History of the Battles of the Donetsk Airport, 26 May 2014 to 21 January 2015', *Association of the United States Army*, May 2019: https://www.ausa.org/sites/default/files/publications/LWP-125-Cyborgs-at-Little-Stalingrad-A-Brief-History-of-the-Battle-of-the-Donetsk-Airport.pdf, accessed 20 July 2022.

[35] Anatol Lieven, *Chechnya: Tombstone of Russian Power* (New Haven, CT: Yale University Press, 1998).

concentration of munitions and effects that must be applied to drive infantry from dense terrain, it must be noted that if enemy fires are available beyond that terrain feature, even very small numbers of infantry can disproportionately attrit a force by calling in fire. While high-bandwidth transmission, necessary for ISR and precision fires, is difficult to guarantee in a contested electromagnetic spectrum, the passage of simple fire missions rearwards can be quite robust. Thus, infantry in dense terrain represent a major obstacle, not only because they themselves are hard to dislodge, but because of the extent to which supporting assets beyond the position must be suppressed, displaced or destroyed if a force is to concentrate sufficiently to efficiently clear infantry.

What infantry offer in defensive tenacity they lack in offensive capacity. Infantry that are manoeuvring are less detectable than vehicles, as they do not tend to kick up dust, can pass through obscuring terrain and produce very little acoustic signature. Ground penetrating radar is able to track moving dismounted infantry because of the metal equipment they carry, but this is at significantly reduced range compared with vehicles and is harder to distinguish from clutter. Thermal imaging represents the most effective means of rapidly acquiring dismounted infantry as they manoeuvre. Once located however infantry are exceedingly vulnerable. Out of cover, infantry units can be rapidly killed by artillery and unlike vehicles they move at a slower rate, allowing a slower kill chain to still bring effective fire to bear.

Historically the approach to infantry in well-defended positions has been to attempt to bypass them, since without supply they must move and once moving can be rapidly defeated if dislocated from their supporting arms. Clearing infantry from isolated pockets has been made easier by the fact that once infantry have been effectively bypassed and severed from supply, many cognitively accept defeat and surrender before being killed. The tactical dispersion of radios and the extended range of fires shift this calculus, however. Since small numbers of infantry do not need significant quantities of supplies, UAS and other methods can be used to sustain them. This is also easier because the battlefield is becoming more porous as militaries are forced to disperse to survive. Unless being directly attacked therefore dispersed infantry can remain survivable for a significant period. Cognitively, so long as supply continues it is far from inevitable that they will surrender or collapse. Russian operational analysis demonstrates that it takes twenty platoons of conventional forces to locate a single platoon of infiltrators.[36] Even if we argue that technology will reduce this, the capacity of infantry in the rear to call in fires and thereby coordinate effects disproportionate to their organic combat power means that merely bypassing pockets of infantry presents significant dangers. This therefore poses a serious challenge to traditional armoured tactics that seek to punch through positions and manoeuvre in depth. It swings the calculus from manoeuvre isolating defended positions to defended positions being able to reliably dislocate manoeuvre.

One of the consequences of the miniaturization of precision is that considerations that were previously relevant at formation level become significant in sub-tactical

---

[36] Igor Sutyagin, 'RUSI Land Warfare Conference 2017 – Session 7', 19 July 2017, 21:54–48:00: https://www.youtube.com/watch?v=_EcrrD1dBhg, accessed 20 July 2022.

engagements. In a world where dismounted infantry sections have the equipment to deliver precision effects using UAS delivered 40mm grenades but can only carry a limited number of these effects, employing such munitions against individual firing posts is inefficient.[37] Again, however, movement demands coordination and therefore requires key leaders of an adversary force to come together. In Nagorno-Karabakh, overhead observation allowed Azerbaijan to target tactical groups of platoon commanders and their section leaders as they came together to coordinate. This demonstrates how forcing movement, even at the platoon level, presents opportunities to achieve disproportionate effect. The efficient elimination of infantry therefore increasingly requires pressure to force movement alongside the capability to target that movement at the speed of relevance. Concentration to clear infantry therefore is not simply a case of concentrating mass but is enabled through the layering of effects.

Mastering illusions

This chapter has highlighted several challenges to critical tenets of manoeuvre-based mechanized warfare. Concentration remains necessary to overcome strongpoints and seize vital ground, but concentration is also easier to punish. Movement is central to manoeuvre, but manoeuvre also makes key parts of the force more vulnerable. Armour meanwhile is offering diminishing returns in terms of the cost of increasing the passive protection on platforms.

There is another pertinent trend however that has been implicit throughout this chapter. The destructive power of modern weaponry requires complex, layered effects to maximize its efficiency. This requires the concentration of effectors and is also expensive. A section with ATGWs may pose a greater threat to armour than previous generations of infantry, but the number of rounds available to them will be limited. If they employ their ATGWs against the wrong kinds of target, armies will struggle to maintain a high volume of them throughout the battlefield. In this context, protection is best achieved not by giving every platform as much armour as possible. Instead, forces must use ambiguity and misdirection, signature management and deception, to cause their adversary to employ their weapons systems inappropriately. In short, the protection offered by armour may be illusory, but it is in casting illusions that armies can regain survivability.

The ambiguity that armies must strive for, discussed in the first chapter of this book, is the first building block to casting a protective illusion. Given the contested nature of the electromagnetic spectrum, as outlined in the previous chapter, remote control will be increasingly difficult for any beyond line-of-sight effect. Autonomy is therefore necessary in remaining competitive. Autonomous systems however unless drawing upon hugely expensive arrays of sensors and carrying data far beyond what would be economical or safe to store on board a munition are not contextually aware. They look for specific returns and strike them. What returns a munition seeks varies. Munitions

---

[37] Jack Watling and Nicholas Waters, 'Achieving Lethal Effects by Small Unmanned Aerial Vehicles', *The RUSI Journal* (Vol. 164, No. 1, 2019), pp. 40–51.

may track outlines using an electro-optical sensor, they may use a millimetric radar, seek thermal signatures, or radiation. More capable munitions use several indicators. The generation of false signatures has often been seen as a means of deception. It can be, but in many contexts deliberate reconnaissance capabilities will see through such ruses unless they are resourced to achieve high-fidelity false positives. Against munitions however false positives are more problematic. An anti-radiation missile approaching a formation with two radar, for example, will struggle if the radar alternates between being on and off, while moving. At a certain range the field of regard of the warhead will lose its target rather than transition from emissions sources. An electro-optical sensor can suddenly lose the ability to approach a target if it runs into multispectral smoke. Sensors are also susceptible to saturation and in this way can be attacked through either EW or directed energy effects. A laser does not need to destroy the munition. It simply needs to dazzle the sensor. Across a formation, such techniques, if appropriately applied, can significantly extend the life of the formation's components. Furthermore, by reducing the efficiency of enemy capabilities the formation may exhaust key types of effect and then use the freedom generated by the reduction in the number of threat vectors to gain advantage.

This is best illustrated by way of an example. Consider a company of medium vehicles in a patch of complex terrain. Across the company there are a full range of sensors distributed across the various vehicles. A couple of the vehicles have kinetic air defence capabilities. Another couple of vehicles have multispectral smoke dispensers. Two have directed energy weapons. Two more have EW arrays. The company also has long-range precision fires in the form of loitering munitions and a couple of orbits of organic ISR assets. The formation has many thermal sights and is well positioned with dismounted ATGW firing posts and machine guns covering the main approaches.

Attacking such a formation by any single means is difficult. Concentrating sufficient artillery to conduct a saturation bombardment of the area may be ruled out because such a large number of guns coming together with their associated ammunition may be detected by GMTI and then be attacked by loitering munitions from the target company and adjacent formations. A concentrated thrust by armour would suffer heavily from the ATGWs. Loitering munitions risk being disorientated by the directed energy weapons or disrupted by electronic attack. ATGWs or active seeker munitions can be defeated by the dispensing of smoke. Preventing the target company from realizing these are coming could be achieved by knocking out the formation's radars with anti-radiation munitions, but if the radar pulse on and off then successfully defeating them may be unreliable. Simply firing enough munitions for long enough to overwhelm the defensive capabilities could work but would be very inefficient. It might lead to the company being defeated, but then leave the force with insufficient munitions to attack the next objective.

Suppressing the systemic protection comes down to the sequencing of multiple effects. Firing anti-radiation munitions that cause the radars to switch off may deny the directed energy weapons situational awareness, creating a window of opportunity within which a successful set of strikes can penetrate the systemic defences efficiently. If we envisage these successful strikes knocking out some of the capabilities of the targeted company, then follow-up attacks could exploit the part of the system that was no longer operable and so the system would break down. The defenders could counter such sequential attacks through a range of appropriate tactics. The use of a decoy to lure anti-radiation missiles for instance could render the attempt to suppress the radars ineffective. This competition between attack and countermeasures however is dependent upon situational awareness. Where one side gets the sequence wrong, they could become vulnerable. Thus, the prerequisite for achieving sufficient concentration to defeat a defended position becomes the capacity to whittle down its defences through a series of appropriate layered attacks. Defeating these layered attacks is achieved by denying the attacker sufficient information, or else too much ambiguous information, to apply the appropriate effects. A formation therefore must distribute its capabilities, spread its vulnerabilities, but be able to provide mutual reinforcement between platforms. Such an approach necessitates robust tactical communications, at least sufficient to coordinate the mutual support from constituent capabilities within a formation.

In conclusion, therefore, when it comes to the survivability of ground forces, and their offensive capacity, it is apparent that the new era of warfare is seeing a fundamental shift from passive protection to active protection. Camouflage and armour are not irrelevant but they are insufficient to protect an individual platform from either detection or damage. However, active tactics that create ambiguity, that reduce the time available to acquire a target, active systems that counter a range of threats across a defined area, can all shift an engagement from being highly economical to uneconomical. On the future battlefield commanders are likely to have the means to destroy targets they prioritize. But if they prioritize the wrong targets in the wrong order, they are liable to find that they expend key munitions and resources and so begin to suffer more and more for the progress they make, until the balance of forces shifts in favour of the adversary. How forces are to ensure that they have the range of capabilities necessary within their formations is a key question when designing combined arms formations of the future.

4

When the tail needs teeth

What did we determine? That we needed to fight outnumbered and win, and that we needed to defeat the second echelon.[1]

Lt Gen Eric Wesley, Director,
US Army Future Concepts Centre

The reclamation of most of Nagorno-Karabakh by Azerbaijan from Armenia in the autumn of 2020 gave insight into a number of important changes that are underway in the dynamics of combat. The Nagorno-Karabakh region – recognized as Azeri territory – was occupied by Armenia in the 1990s and fortified.[2] Intermittent skirmishing persisted for the best part of three decades, but in 2020 Azeri forces launched a major offensive, seizing most of the region in six weeks. Despite securing some key villages in the first days of fighting the Azeri advance initially stalled as Armenian mobilization reinforced their defence lines. Two weeks later, however, Armenian resistance began to crumble, and, despite a determined defence of many strongpoints, Armenia was rapidly rolled back in the South until its supply lines in the Lachin corridor were threatened by artillery and risked being cut. The reason for the collapse in Armenian combat power is instructive. Throughout the conflict Azeri UAVs, loitering munitions, long-range artillery, electronic attack and Special Forces targeted and broke up Armenian reserves, replacements and resupply, as well as targeting command and control infrastructure, air defences and other key assets.[3] Thus, as munitions at the front were consumed, and troops began to tire, little was getting through to replenish them. Of the 240 Armenian T72 tanks destroyed in the conflict, most were struck out of contact with Azeri forces.[4] In and of itself the destruction of the enemy in the deep through stand-off strikes and

[1] Eric Wesley, Day Three Opening Remarks, AUSA Global Force Symposium, Huntsville, 28 March 2019: https://www.dvidshub.net/video/668339/ausa-global-force-symposium-day-3-opening-remarks-and-keynote-speaker, accessed 20 July 2022.

[2] Michael Kambeck and Sargis Ghazaryan, *Europe's Next Avoidable War: Nagorno-Karabakh* (London: Palgrave Macmillan, 2013); Ohannes Geukjian, *Ethnicity, Nationalism and Conflict in the South Caucasus: Nagorno-Karabakh and the Legacy of Soviet Nationalities Policy* (London: Taylor & Francis, 2016).

[3] https://cast.ru/news/vyshla-kniga-tsast-burya-na-kavkaze.html, accessed 20 July 2022.

[4] Oryx, 'The Fight for Nagorno-Karabakh: Documenting Losses on the Sides of Armenia and Azerbaijan': https://www.oryxspioenkop.com/2020/09/the-fight-for-nagorno-karabakh.html, accessed 20 July 2022.

air power is not conceptually new. Comparable to AirLand Battle it was reminiscent of the defeat of the Iraqi Army from the rear forwards during Operation Desert Storm in 1991.[5] But the Azeris achieved this affect while spending $2 billion a year on defence, reflecting the extent to which it has become realistic for weaker states to strike the deep.[6] For major powers the ability to deliver long-range firepower is far greater.

On the face of it this appears to be the same challenge as already described in the first and third chapters of this book, namely that sensors and shooters can find and strike targets long before they reach the direct fire zone, preventing surprise and concentration. So far, however, this book has focused on the effects of these dynamics on the combat arms. The outcome of warfare, however, is equally determined by logistics. The fighting power of the Taliban was not drastically superior to many Afghan National Army formations. But because the ANA could not sustain itself, its capacity to resist without NATO's support was essentially limited to the length of time that its units had ammunition.[7] The impact of these changes on combat service support is not only distinct because the viability of historical approaches to logistics is increasingly questionable, but also because the changes imposed by the threat environment on the combat arms alters what they need from their logisticians. As the combat arms disperse to survive the battlefield becomes increasingly porous, there is an increased likelihood of mutual penetration, and therefore of meeting engagements between the forward elements of enemy combat units and logistics troops. This chapter therefore considers three key challenges presented by emerging capabilities. Firstly, it considers how logistics are currently managed by militaries and the problems that emerging threats present to these practices. Secondly, the chapter examines how combat service support can adapt to become more survivable. Thirdly, the chapter examines how combat service support can best meet the demand of the elements it is supporting.

Inverting the pyramids

The balance between combat, support and service support arms within a military has shifted over time, reflecting the technological complexity of a force and therefore its greater or lesser dependence upon technicians, mechanics and a diversifying array of materiel.[8] The balance has roughly shifted from a comparable distribution of combat

[5] GAO, 'Operation Desert Storm: Evaluation of the Air War', July 1996: https://www.govinfo.gov/content/pkg/GAOREPORTS-PEMD-96-10/pdf/GAOREPORTS-PEMD-96-10.pdf, accessed 20 July 2022.

[6] Jack Watling and Sidharth Kaushal, 'The Democratisation of Precision Strike in the Nagorno-Karabakh Conflict', RUSI Commentary, 20 October 2020: https://rusi.org/explore-our-research/publications/commentary/democratisation-precision-strike-nagorno-karabakh-conflict, accessed 20 July 2022.

[7] Jack Watling and Nick Reynolds, *War by Others' Means: Delivering Effective Partner Force Capacity Building* (London: RUSI, 2021), pp. 45–61.

[8] John J. McGrath, *The Other End of the Spear: The Tooth-to-Tail Ratio (T3R) in Modern Military Operations* (Fort Leavenworth, KS: Combat Studies Institute Press, 2007), pp. 42–7.

and support arms during the First World War, to almost two-thirds of the force providing support functions during the War on Terror. These figures are often concealed in the reliance upon non-uniformed contractors making up a large proportion of the latter roles.[9] In any event, military forces in counter-insurgency have tended to operate from hub and spoke logistics bases enabling vast quantities of supplies to be amassed in theatre and distributed to enable company-sized elements to manoeuvre on the ground. In warfighting, the structure of a force can be represented by two pyramids forming an hourglass. The base of the bottom pyramid constitutes the front, where the majority of combat arms are concentrated, with reserves grouped behind. These then taper backwards to the artillery lines, brigade support areas, divisional support areas and corps support areas. Most higher echelon supply depots, maintenance workshops, field hospitals and other support functions become increasingly concentrated as they get further from the front, since centralized supply allows for materiel to be efficiently massed, ordered and thereafter distributed to the dispersed units. This process of concentration reaches the peak of the pyramid at the highest tactical echelon relevant to the campaign. In the Falklands conflict for example the divisional logistics hub sat at Ajax Bay.[10] However, once one hits the highest tactical echelon an inverted pyramid begins with supply being progressively amassed through the operational echelon from international supply lines. Multiple factories producing shells, replacement parts, refining fuel or packaging food send their materiel forwards to be amassed. Shipped from multiple points the theatre sustainment command must aggregate and sort the sinews of war so that they can be pushed forward to the tactical echelon.

A second aspect of this double pyramid is the push and pull factors. Strategic and operational echelons will set objectives that will determine the priorities for production and therefore push output to the tactical echelon. Tactical commanders will amass this resource and allocate it against lines of effort. But at the lower tactical edge most armies will use their equipment unevenly. Some will expend disproportionate quantities of ammunition; others will use up more fuel, and yet more will run into shortages of specific spare parts. Requests for resupply will therefore work their way backwards up the chain. There is therefore a second intersection between two pyramids between push logistical processes and pull logistical processes. Some armies trade resource efficiency for logistical simplicity by having a push system to the lowest levels. This was the Soviet approach. However, such a system leads to a much greater quantity of logistics support close to the enemy. Given that a force wants as much of its capacity available for fighting as possible, there is considerable advantage to be gained by ensuring the efficiency of logistics structures. This leads to logistics vehicles requiring small crews with as much of their load carrying potential dedicated to carrying supplies as possible. They tend, therefore, to have very limited protection. There is also a desire to minimize the maintenance burden of the logistics fleet so that maintenance capacity does not become fixed supporting the support arms. This leads to logistics fleets

9   Peter Singer, *Corporate Warriors: The Rise of the Privatised Military Industry* (Ithaca: Cornell University Press, 2007).
10 Kenneth Privratsky, *Logistics in the Falklands War* (Barnsley: Pen & Sword, 2014).

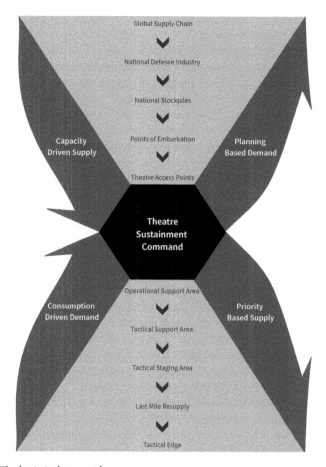

Figure 2 The logistical pyramids.

having limited cross-terrain mobility, since tracked cross-terrain platforms impose a higher maintenance burden. In consequence, much of the high-volume logistics until the 'last mile' – referring to the final movement of materiel to the unit that will employ it, rather than to a specific distance – will be constrained to move on prepared ground, tracks or road. Resupply therefore is harder to conceal than fighting elements that are able to freely manoeuvre across country.

A further critical point about the dynamics of logistics in mechanized warfare concerns how the need for resupply sets tactical imperatives. For a force on the offensive the need to concentrate to break through an enemy defence usually leads to penetration of enemy territory across a narrow front. Having broken through the penetrating force will seek to drive as deep as possible to sever supply lines and thereby isolate enemy forces to either side. This causes the greatest level of dislocation. However, a unit that has penetrated a frontline also has exposed flanks and a limited amount of fuel and ammunition. The reserves must therefore surge into the breach to widen it and to secure the line to create a saliant. The enemy meanwhile will seek to blunt the offensive from getting deeper and counterattack on the flanks to sever the penetrating force from its supply lines and thereby impose a hard limit on its endurance and the potential length of its advance. This dynamic has been repeated throughout the era of mechanized warfare. The need to secure ground lines of communication to maintain momentum therefore has been a key component of determining the force ratios necessary to execute a successful offensive operation.

On a battlefield where the effective range of artillery is around 21 km while reconnaissance is primarily achieved through human observation the survivability of logistics units behind the frontline was sufficient to allow the dynamics described above to characterize operations. By contrast, on the battlefield described in the preceding chapters, such a logistics structure begins to look exceedingly fragile. The extent of that fragility was proven in July 2022 when Russian forces – operating in a manner consistent with the traditions of mechanized warfare – came under attack by an enemy with access to satellite imagery and long-range precision fires. Within three weeks over 100 of their artillery stockpiles and command and control nodes were destroyed.[11] The points of acute fragility are outlined below, but the cumulative impact is that the logistics structure for mechanized warfare is unable to offer assurance that a force can be sustained. This strikes at the heart of a key tenet of mechanized warfare: tempo, the idea that by operating quicker than an adversary a force can build momentum as it degrades an enemy in detail. In Russia's case the effect of Ukrainian GMLRS strikes was to stall a renewed offensive, preventing momentum rolling over from its successes in Severodonetsk.[12] Tempo is undermined because once a force is disconnected from its logistics, it can only sustain operations for a short period, and the faster it seeks to operate the sooner it will come to a halt. Indeed, once it has expended its ammunition, it not only halts but stops being a force in being. So long as the tails of the opposing forces remain mutually vulnerable therefore – so long as the enemy can break the intersection between the two logistical pyramids – the force that will prevail is likely the one that can best conserve its strength and ammunition rather than the one that can operate faster. Before considering the consequences for how the force must adapt to this challenge, it is first useful to explore in more detail where the specific points of friction lie for the logistics structures: specifically persistent signature patterns, large targetable footprints and the soft nature of the target.

As has already been explored combat arms can disperse and conceal themselves to avoid detection. The organic firepower of combat arms also makes finding them a risky endeavour. While certain activities inevitably produce a signature, combat arms can often produce levels of ambiguity as to their whereabouts, size or composition. This is substantially harder for logistics, medical and maintenance units. In the first instance all

[11] Dan Lamothe, 'As Ukraine Pounds Russian Targets, U.S. Sends More Artillery', *The Washington Post*, 22 July 2022: https://www.washingtonpost.com/national-security/2022/07/22/ukraine-artillery-russia/, accessed 20 August 2022.

[12] Natalia Zinets, 'Ukraine Says It Has Destroyed 50 Russian Ammunition Depots Using HIMARS', *Reuters*, 25 July 2022: https://www.reuters.com/world/europe/ukraine-says-it-has-destroyed-50-ammunition-depots-using-himars-war-with-russia-2022-07-25/, accessed 12 December 2022.

of these functions struggle to operate efficiently without a high level of communications traffic. What spare parts are required? What medical treatment is needed? What type and how many vehicles are in need of repair? Furthermore, because combat arms manoeuvre and must be aware of units moving into their areas of responsibility to avoid friendly fire, while supporting arms do not know where casualties will be taken, there is a need to communicate to establish rendezvous points. While manoeuvre can be synchronized ahead of time, vehicle break downs and casualties cannot, so that these functions must necessarily be performed at irregular intervals and at unexpected locations. A force that expends an unexpectedly high quantity of ammunition is likely not having its activities go to plan and therefore must be resupplied if it is not to stall but must therefore communicate this need. This traffic is difficult to mask in the electromagnetic spectrum. It is the kind of traffic that necessitates a significant volume of communication in both directions and often – because a vehicle has broken down, or casualties cannot be readily moved – cannot pursue standard procedures for moving having unmasked. Russian airstrikes on medical facilities in Syria have often been directed by the electromagnetic signature of the location.[13]

The signature of logistics is also significant for enemy radar, electro-optical sensors and penetrating reconnaissance units. Most logistics vehicles are road bound. Their lines of movement are persistent, not only because of the mobility constrains of the platforms but also because the volume of materiel that must be moved imposes a significant burden on road traffic management. If this goes wrong large traffic jams ensue, as Russia demonstrated as it attempted to resupply its forces attacking Kyiv.[14] The result is a need for logistics convoys to remain on time and to follow designated routes. The even spacing, regular groupings and uniformity of these convoys make them highly distinguishable from civilian traffic, while tracking the points of origin and destination of these convoys rapidly reveal areas of interest for more intensive scrutiny where combat arms must be gathered or else support areas situated.

Support areas are in themselves difficult to protect for several reasons. Firstly, support areas are by definition filled with materiel that is being amassed and waiting to be moved. The materiel therefore is not mobile and once established these sites tend to become fixed. Second, the quantities of materiel necessary to sustain a large combat formation for any period take up a very considerable area of ground. These sites also require large entry and exit points to enable a flow of traffic in both directions. Increasingly there is also a demand for power. Nor can the critical sites be easily concealed. In armoured warfare – as outlined in the previous chapter – many vehicles in combat are immobilized or otherwise damaged, without being destroyed. Often the force that will win is that which can repair these vehicles and keep them fighting. Changing engine blocks and other major maintenance tasks however requires

[13] Kareem Shaheen, 'Russia's Long History of Bombing Hospitals', *New Lines Magazine*, 11 March 2022: https://newlinesmag.com/newsletter/russias-long-history-of-bombing-hospitals/, accessed 20 July 2022.
[14] 'Why a Huge Russian Convoy Remains Stalled North of Kyiv', *The Economist*, 4 March 2022: https://www.economist.com/europe/2022/03/04/why-a-huge-russian-convoy-remains-stalled-north-of-kyiv, accessed 20 July 2022.

purpose-built or makeshift cranes. For any operation at scale the footprint of these sites makes them difficult to conceal. Whereas in previous conflicts maintenance yards were usually far beyond the effective range of the enemy, other than raids by air forces which could be deterred by air defences, the increasing range and precision of artillery can now reach out and strike these locations. In Ukraine strikes on repair workshops have pushed maintenance several hundred kilometres from the front.[15]

The impact against support functions is made even more severe by the inherent vulnerability of support vehicles and supply depots. Islamic State achieved some spectacular results using small UAS to detonate Syrian military ammunition dumps in Deir Ez-Zor.[16] The Russian military repeatedly achieved the same effect against Ukrainian forces around the Donbas.[17] Iran and its Houthi partners have demonstrated the ability to achieve highly precise effects in terms of both the accuracy of the munitions and the timing of strikes, to target bases with ballistic missiles. In the case of the Houthis this has mainly involved targeting airports when key personnel are transiting through them, but there is no reason why such an approach could not be used to break the back of an adversary's logistics effort for sustaining a theatre. Finally, logistics personnel themselves are often lightly armed, spend less time training for close combat and are dispersed. This combination makes them vulnerable to attacks by Special Forces conducting direct action. Around the world militaries are expanding the number of deep reconnaissance units in their orders of battle, suggesting that the threat against logistics convoys in the rear area is increasing. Where special forces are often overmatched by conventional units and must use surprise to overcome isolated positions,[18] against logistics forces as currently constituted many special forces units have superior firepower.[19] This is amplified by the availability of man packable loitering munitions, thermobaric launchers and other weapons typically found among units tasked with interdiction operations. Finally, because efficiency encourages logistics personnel to group types of materiel and move it in the largest practical volume, while a logistics formation may be very large, targeting specific types of logistics vehicle can have a disproportionate effect on the force they are supporting. The obvious example is fuel bowsers which are specialized vehicles, often easy to distinguish and highly vulnerable to damage because of the nature of their cargo.

A final point to consider is the changing requirements of units as regards the types of materiel being consumed. The most important shift is a drastically expanding demand for electricity at all echelons. All sensor arrays demand power. Communications systems demand power. Increasingly personal weapons and protective equipment demand power. For vehicles power can be generated by the engine. But as the demand

[15] https://www.youtube.com/watch?v=ktJNrw6dxwo&list=LL&index=2, accessed 20 July 2022.

[16] 'Syria: Footage Shows Islamic State Drone Blowing Up Stadium Ammo Dump', *ABC News*, 25 October 2017.

[17] Kyle Mizokami, 'Another Ukrainian Ammo Dump Goes Up in Massive Explosion', *Popular Mechanics*, 27 September 2017.

[18] William H. McRaven, *Spec Ops: Case Studies in Special Operations Warfare Theory and Practice* (Toronto: Random House Canada, 1995), pp. 4–11.

[19] Alan J. Levine, *The War against Rommel's Supply Lines, 1942–43* (New York: Praeger, 1999).

for electricity becomes constant, this also means that vehicles running their engines will require resupply at regular intervals even if they are static. Furthermore, with the increasing ability to detect vehicles through acoustic and thermal signature there is a strong incentive to avoid keeping engines running indefinitely. The consequence is likely to be a proliferation of auxiliary power units or batteries. Individual personnel too have become highly dependent upon large quantities of batteries which are both heavy and must be stored and handled with care. For battery packs in vehicles there is also likely a need to be able to replace these when they receive battle damage. Damaged batteries have a tendency to combust, are complicated to repair and will affect the functioning of systems.[20] It is occasionally suggested that novel power generation – using solar panels for example – will allow units to meet these new demands. This is unlikely. In the first instance many novel power generation technologies that have anything approaching the necessary level of efficiency have a high signature. In the second instance if units must charge their own batteries, then this will severely shape the tempo of operations, forcing units to go static for periods. Thirdly, complex electrical capabilities are unlikely to be repairable in the field and the personnel qualified to repair them will be expensive and scarce assets that armies will be reluctant to risk by pushing them forward. The conclusion therefore is that at the same time as logistics and maintenance units are seeking to reduce their footprint and obfuscate their signature there is an increasing requirement to be able to repair, maintain and recharge an increasingly complex range of equipment. While organic power generation will help, the inevitable consequence of these trends is an increased dependence upon civilian power generation in rear echelons.

Becoming a hard target

The foremost requirement in ensuring that the fight can be sustained is in reducing the efficiency of enemy engagements against the logistics system. This can be achieved in three ways: increasing the number of munitions necessary to achieve an effect against service support arms; increasing the resource commitment to finding service support arms; or increasing the risk in targeting service support elements.

Increasing the munitions necessary to degrade service support can firstly be increased by concentrating support areas further from the front line. Increasing the range must necessarily reduce the proportion of enemy munitions – and increase the value of those munitions – that are able to reach the support areas. Furthermore, by increasing the distance beyond the range of conventional fires this method either encourages the use of fewer kinds of less capable longer-range systems, which are susceptible to hard counters, or the use of munitions that deliver overkill against the target. As a practical matter any artillery system firing beyond approximately 40 km will

---

[20] Diego Lisbona and Timothy Snee, 'A Review of Hazards Associated with Primary Lithium and Lithium-Ion Batteries', *Process Safety and Environmental Protection* (Vol. 89, No. 6, 2011), pp. 434–42.

begin to see a very considerable variation in the circular error probable of its effects.[21] For that reason, effective engagements beyond this range must use some form of guidance and this means that they comprise a class of complex or precision munitions that are never cheap. The withdrawal of corps and divisional support areas from the indirect fire zone is far less disruptive than the extension of the brigade support area. Nevertheless, it seems inevitable, given the scale of the threat, that maintenance areas and supply hubs are pulled back in order to survive, to an approximate depth up to 100 km.

Another means of driving up the number of munitions needed to engage support areas is the use of a larger footprint combined with force protection engineering, or the exploitation of natural protection. The combination of creating negative space, combined with putting containerized supplies in scrapes, or placing them in structures, significantly increases the volume of munitions necessary to destroy the supplies because it firstly requires each and every strike to directly hit a target in order to damage it, and secondly ensures that one munition can at best damage one target, rather than having large quantities of materiel in one location where incidental damage to a range of materiel is achieved with each strike.[22] There is also considerable advantage in reducing the number of critical points of failure in the service support system. This can be achieved by laying ground cables to draw off the civilian power grid as well as running generators.

A further means of reducing efficiency is the creation of ambiguity. If almost all supplies are containerized, all containers in logistical support areas are covered in tarpaulins or other obscuring materials, or otherwise concealed, and the supporting infrastructure for logistics sites like power supply is obfuscated by laying extended ground cables from the civilian grid or dispersed generators, then it becomes exceedingly difficult for the adversary to know what supplies are valuable and which supplies are therefore worth prioritizing for the limited number of munitions that are in range. There is also a need to remove patterns of life that assist in targeting. For instance, inflating a large fuel bladder inside an industrial building will prevent the tell-tale footprint being observable by satellite. However, this is no use if the carousel of vehicles stopping and refuelling in front of the building reveals its contents. The nature of the site could be obfuscated by having a couple of different refuelling hoses stretching to different tents or buildings, so that vehicles that are refuelling are filled away from the site and the pattern of

---

[21] Extensive testing by the Finnish military concluded that there was little point seeking to extend the range of 155mm howitzers beyond 40 km; author interview, senior Finnish artillery officer, Seoul, May 2022; this is also demonstrated in the resort to precision munitions for fire missions from the US experimental 60 cal 155m howitzer, see Michael Evans, 'US Army Supergun Breaks Record with Direct Hit on Target 70km Away', *The Times*, 24 December 2020: https://www.thetimes.co.uk/article/us-army-supergun-breaks-record-with-direct-hit-on-target-70km-away-80vwdd586, accessed 20 July 2022.

[22] Note the catastrophic effects achieved against Russian air bases by Ukrainian forces because of the VKS's habit of storing fuel and munitions in close proximity to each other and aircraft, see Dan Sabbagh, 'Russian Airbase on Western Coast of Crimea Damaged in Explosions', *The Guardian*, 10 August 2022: https://www.theguardian.com/world/2022/aug/09/russian-airbase-on-western-coast-of-crimea-damaged-in-explosions, accessed 25 November 2022.

life is broken up across several locations where the nature of the activity inside cannot be observed. Breaking up the pattern of life of EMS traffic can also increase the resources necessary to distinguish between elements. This may simply mean having communication nodes offset from the units to which they belong and moving them intermittently so that as the enemy becomes more familiar with the individual signatures of units within the area of operations, the distinction between static and mobile elements is kept unclear. Another aspect to this function is that there are likely to be significant numbers of civilians in the rear area who will film convoys from their balconies and share this kind of information on social media. Preventing this is practically impossible. The best means of protecting against it therefore is to have footage of vehicle movement and to flood social media with old activity, misleading activity, or other videos and pictures that prevent the enemy from relying on this as a reliable or efficient source of targeting information. There is also a need to monitor what is appearing online and to engage with the civilian population to discourage certain behaviours.

One of the advantages of increasing the distance between support areas and the indirect fire zone is that it forces the enemy to traverse more ground to achieve an effect against the support area. This is true of missiles as well as raiding troops or aircraft. In the first instance the distance to be traversed can enable defensive systems to receive early warning and be prepared to intercept the threat. Similarly, air defences distributed throughout the battle area may engage targets trying to reach the support area. Beyond increasing the risk to the threat, range also allows soft defeat options for logistics elements like the opportunity to relocate key assets while a cruise missile system – for example – is in flight. This is only achievable if logistics elements have a common air operating picture and an understanding of the threat along with established training, tactics and procedures. As such there is a need for logistics and maintenance personnel to work more closely with those elements of the force who can offer them protection, through either point defence or situational awareness.

While expanding the distance may be advantageous in providing air defence, it creates significant problems for protecting the ground lines of communication from raiding and interdiction. In Afghanistan British forces found that up to half of their force on major operations could be sucked into protecting GLOCs, with limited success.[23] As the gap between the fighting echelons and the support areas expands, this means that logistics and reserve units must traverse a considerable distance under threat to keep the force fighting. They are therefore exposed to greater risk as they approach the front, and on a permeable battlefield offer the enemy many opportunities to strike. Ensuring that confronting these elements is dangerous and comes at a cost is – as already mentioned – important, but how to achieve this depends upon how the logistics effort is organized and moved.

---

[23] Nick Reynolds, 'Learning Tactical and Operational Combat Lessons for High-End Warfighting from Counterinsurgency', *The RUSI Journal* (Vol. 164, No. 7, 2019), pp. 42–53.

Traversing the impact zone

As logistics, maintenance and medical elements traverse the distance from the support area to the fighting echelons, it is evident that they will need protection. Providing sufficient dedicated protection is likely resource prohibitive. The first requirement therefore is using synchronization to provide an incidental wrap. For instance, if the movement of logistics packets forward is synchronized with offensive action, with a large air strike package, or other mission, then the enemy must choose whether to assign assets to interdict the logistics packets or to blunt the offensive effort. The pursuit of the logistics effort must necessarily drive up the risk to friendly elements. Another means of providing incidental protection is to synchronize movement with other fighting assets like attack aviation. If we envisage attack aviation moving from the support area to a forward refuelling point, then there is an opportunity for that aviation to provide overwatch for logistics packets. The protection of critical infrastructure and choke points meanwhile can be facilitated by placing reserve units in positions that have overwatch of these positions, preventing these areas from being occupied by enemy infiltrators. There is a need here for the logistics elements again to sequence their movements with the rest of the force so that the time and place of their traversing key points are known by the units holding them, thereby reducing the risk of friendly fire.

Despite these measures it seems most likely that there will be long stretches of road where service support packets will be moving without substantial escort. In the first instance making sure that the logistics vehicles themselves have basic ballistic protection to protect their crews from shrapnel and small arms is desirable. It must also be assumed that if they are engaged by infiltrators, their attackers will do this from prepared positions and will therefore have substantial cover. For this reason, logistics units must have a sufficient volume of heavy weapons to suppress such targets. Furthermore, since they are likely to be engaged while moving, it is highly desirable for fire to require limited precision, making weapons equivalent to Heavy Machine Guns firing.50 BMG with Mk.211 ammunition, or Mk.19 40mm GMGs an appropriate capability. The specific armament is less important than the effect. The aim should be that for a force trying to interdict a logistics unit they should anticipate coming under a high volume of effective fire. Knowledge of this consequence will cognitively shape planning and narrow the options.

If infiltrators are deterred from using the light weapons available to them for direct engagements against logistics units, then the fallback will be the use of mines and stand-off munitions. Assuming that air defence screens and EW prevent saturation of routes with loitering munitions however, it must be assumed that such effects will be limited in quantity. The priority therefore is not sustained defence but the capacity to rapidly evade and bypass small numbers of these threats. Having convoys led by a vehicle with a plough and other means of defeating scattered mines may help a logistics packet maintain momentum. Similarly, having the ability to pop multispectral smoke may provide sufficient cover to prevent a loitering munition accurately striking its target, so that a logistics convoy can avoid being struck precisely and then accelerate through the area where the infiltration party can coordinate effects.

Logistics convoys can further increase the resources necessary to degrade them by continuing to operate in small packets. If we assume that the air and missile defence system and the countermeasures on the vehicles have a saturation point that must be overcome before significant attrition is achieved, then by reducing the size of the packet the defender ensures that the same level of resource must be committed for the smallest possible reward once the saturation point is reached. Furthermore, by obscuring the types of cargos and increasing the number of packets, the enemy may be able to track the movement but cannot reliably prioritize what is targeted. They must either expend greater effort to find out what is being carried in each packet, or risk expending a high level of resources to achieve unpredictable results. Moreover, unless they achieve a considerable effect against a critical mass of vehicles, the unpredictability of what has been destroyed creates a challenge in assessing the flow on consequences for the supported combat arms. This forces more resource to be committed in battle damage assessment, or the continuation of planning with a greater band of uncertainty underpinning core assumptions, or analytical paralysis.

The final point of the logistics packet is that they must not accumulate large quantities of stores at the end point or go static for long enough to allow the packets to converge as one unloads and others arrive. This calls for rapid unloading of materiel. Given that these packets are unlikely to manoeuvre to forward positions because of their own lack of protection and the risk of exposing the positions that they resupply, there is likely a need for palletized packages within a containerized vehicle that can individually be carried by smaller vehicles organic to the combat arms. Either the container itself can be dismounted from its carrier and camouflaged as a cache, or the pallets should be removed and cached. These caches can thence be concealed and await pickup shortly thereafter by the supported element. In instances where different kinds of materiel are located in different caches, this information must be passed to the forward element. For manoeuvre elements palletized caches already comprising mixed loads of their regular consumables and immediate specialist packages are likely most practical. For fires elements – by far the most resource-intensive part of the force in terms of volume of materiel required – the caching of supplies can be integrated into their hide rotations for the carrousel system. For instance, a gun line that is rotating from hides to firing positions and to secondary hides can have its ammunition carriers on an adjusted cycle to approach the cache point so that their carrousel brings them by rotation onto the drop-off point for the logistics tail. This is made easier by the fact that fires elements will almost always be positioned slightly back from the combat arms. Getting resources from cache to the combat arms however becomes a problem for organic logistics arrangements among those forward forces.

The breakdown in a continuous front owing to diminishing force density at the edge leads inexorably to the comingling of forces. This disrupts the traditional notion of a support company shuttling materiel through the last mile to resupply troops in contact. Rather than being reliably behind the line of contact, last mile resupply increasingly appears to be a tactical move that would potentially come into contact with enemy forces. We may therefore instead envisage a need for these units to have a mobile supply group able to cycle from the cache through the contact zone to link up with those further forward to distribute supplies. Similarly, rather than a dedicated medical evacuation chain which must necessarily expose nodes at echelon, we may envisage the exchange of supply for casualties and damaged vehicles so that these can be cycled back and thence picked up from hide positions, with the convoy that resupplied a cache thereafter picking up that which had accumulated at the hide position for movement rearwards. The point of departure from current practice is that the mobile supply group in this context must be a fighting element, likely drawing on the reserves of the supported units forward. There has been speculation that this function of last mile resupply may see the employment of autonomous systems. Autonomous mules may provide a technological means of minimizing the manpower commitment to the supply group by making a higher proportion of manpower available for force protection. However, UAVs and UGVs must be set up and supported. Their paths must also be planned in accordance with the tactical laydown of the unit being supported. The need for a coordinating function that is more closely integrated with the fighting echelon remains.

Orchestrating the future

There is a conceit widely held among combat arms that they choose the objective and how they want to fight and that it is the role of logistics officers to come up with an ingenious scheme to make the materiel flow fit the plan.[24] Higher echelon formations are almost always commanded by officers from the combat arms. Divisional headquarters see themselves as directing the fight. This conceit even makes its way into force design processes. When the British Army was designing its Future Soldier construct during the 2020 Integrated Review, no logistics officers were in the compartment. When asked why, a senior officer overseeing the process explained that the team could reach out to specialist expertise when it was needed.[25] The preceding chapters have described a battlefield in which higher echelon headquarters will have a limited number of choices that they must make about the conduct of the fighting, albeit those choices are likely to be exceedingly important. The perpetual struggle for sensor dominance will be decided by the tactical proficiency of reconnaissance and screening troops. The fires and counterfires battle will be decided by decisions that must be made too quickly to have an extended kill chain synced with a regular higher echelon planning cycle. The close fight will be determined by the convergence of effects across the combined arms formation in contact. The struggle for information will largely be determined by decisions about priorities and architectures made long before contact. The objectives will likely be determined by the political echelon. Indeed, a higher headquarters trying to exert control over these things will likely cause its subordinates more grief than it will offer them help. As a tactical commander put it in interview,

---

[24] Delves, *Across an Angry Sea*, p. 235.
[25] Author interview, senior officer in the Embankment team, UK, March 2021.

I had my teams in their kill boxes malletting the enemy. Where exactly they were in their assigned battlespace was something I did not know and didn't want to know, since finding out would have forced them to keep on terrain where they had communications with me and therefore limited their movement while exposing them in the EMS. The headquarters meanwhile was perpetually reaching down to me to find out where people were. The only way I could have satisfied them was to go static and set up a communications node, which would have gotten me killed in short order. I had enemy behind my position. In the end I had one of my NCOs set himself up to the rear and feed them whatever we could get to him. It was bad information, out of date by the time it reached the headquarters. But it made them feel like they knew what was going on. What was mad was that the need to feel in control meant that the pressure was on blue force tracking. My priorities for the net where the risk of illuminating was justified was reports on enemy positions, calls for fires, and battle damage assessments. In informational terms the headquarters ate like an elephant and shat like a mouse. We didn't get anything the other way in terms of useful situational awareness.[26]

This dynamic has arguably been exacerbated by the War on Terror where even cabinet members have become habituated to receiving live video from operations.

The key points of judgement for the higher headquarters as regards combat will be where to apply their limited number of penetrating ISTAR assets to understand the enemy deep, where to apply long-range fires to shape the enemy, and when the balance between sensors and fires has met the conditions for committing a concentrated force. By contrast, if the higher headquarters fails in the protection of its support area and the management of logistics within its battlespace, it will lose the fight shortly thereafter. The ability to get resupply right will determine the future. It is often said that higher headquarters should think about the fight tomorrow. This has usually been understood to mean planning for the next engagement. Increasingly, as forces are contacted in depth, it suggests that the capacity to fight tomorrow must be won today.

The pressures on logistics described in this chapter cannot be met by logistics officers alone. Nor can the issue of maintaining supplies to the front be seen as a road traffic problem to be handed off to the military police. Instead, it requires a constant planning and synchronizing of movement that is highly cognizant of the activities of combat and support arms operating behind the contact zone. In short it becomes a major planning task for which the horsepower of higher headquarters is invaluable and essential. The establishment of support areas, imposing discipline to prevent the detection of key stocks, analysis of what materiel must be prioritized, where to impose control measures to avoid fratricide while traversing the battlespace, selection of cache points and the provision of overwatch are all critical tasks. They require a level of situational awareness and integration of functions that goes well beyond the realm of logistics and maintenance.

The burden of planning created by the pressures on resupply is in some ways less dramatic for the character of fighting as the effects on tempo. Historically the aim has

---

[26] Debrief of a tactical commander immediately after a prolonged field exercise, US, October 2021.

been to accelerate resupply to keep pace with troops after they have broken through to exploit the opportunity and seize as much ground as possible. There may be limited periods where the coherence of the enemy has been disrupted sufficiently to allow a more traditional approach to logistics to be survivable. Nevertheless, the risk is that this will encourage more mass to be surged forward than can be sustained once signature management and protection reimpose a cap on the flow of supply to the front. Limited supply must place limits upon the distance that can be covered in an assault. This reinforces a trend towards a positional dynamic in warfare in which incremental shaping makes the assault onto a key position possible. Once in place to punch onto the objective however a force must build up the munitions and forces to be able to take it. This may be incremental. In the first chapter a situation was described in which a logistics unit and a manoeuvre element move together to conceal one going static. Such techniques could be used to allow the logistics element to halt and unload without being detected. However, it could also be used to move and build up manoeuvre forces from the reserve to the staging area for an eventual assault, to be launched when the reconnaissance and fires battles have created the opportunity for concentration. This gradual positioning of forces similarly requires higher-level orchestration, providing another example of how a higher headquarters might set the conditions for the next phase of operations through the coordination of the force's support system.

The overall impact on tempo is of a series of bursts of acceleration to seize key positions preceded and followed by slow manoeuvre for advantage. The narrative that militaries often use – regularly citing John Boyd's OODA Loop – is of constant pressure with the aim of each force being to outpace the other. Constant high tempo activity however is precisely the behaviour that leads to the pursuit of the most efficient approach which creates vulnerability through pattern setting and predictability. In an environment where predictability is a cause of rapid attrition, the key question is the capacity of the force to accelerate and decelerate. Moreover, if periods of acceleration can be made unpredictable through the obfuscation of logistical build-up, then a force can establish the potential energy to dislocate its adversary by pre-empting an opponent's acceleration. The ability of higher headquarters to use their distance from the fighting to understand trends in adversary activity and thereby time actions to disrupt adversary planning becomes a critical responsibility that determines initiative and therefore shapes the capacity for success for subordinate units.

Central to this conception of manoeuvre establishing the conditions for the seizure of key positions is that sufficient mass can be brought to bear to secure the objective. Much debate in military circles has focused on whether warfare is positional or manoeuverist,[27] just as there has been a debate about whether forces should optimize for rural or urban operations. This is to miss the criticality of both. For various reasons elaborated upon at length in previous chapters – from the improved opportunity for

---

[27] Amos Fox, 'A Solution Looking for a Problem: Illuminating Misconceptions in Manoeuver Warfare Doctrine': https://www.benning.army.mil/armor/earmor/content/issues/2017/Fall/4Fox17.pdf, accessed 20 July 2022.

access to infrastructure, ready concealment and protection – the strongpoints that are likely to constitute the inflection points between periods of manoeuvre and positional assault will be centred on either significant terrain features or, more often than not, urban centres. The challenge with urban warfare is that many of the developments in capability described in previous chapters apply differently in urban environments, producing requirements on the force that are not aligned with a force optimized for operations outside of urban spaces. A key challenge therefore for militaries is how they successfully manoeuvre to isolate cities, and then transition to operating inside them. This question is the principal subject of the next chapter.

5

Blood in the streets

I don't need reinforcements. I need buildings to fight from.[1]
Call-sign 'Vortex', Battalion commander
during the battle for Severodonetsk

The precise number of Islamic State fighters defending Mosul is hard to pin down. Membership of a terrorist organization does not mean that an individual was a fighter, and some of those defending Mosul fought out of fear of sectarian reprisals or to retain property seized from opposing tribes, rather than through loyalty to the group. Nevertheless, estimates of between 5,000 and 8,000 fighters appear reasonable.[2] The attacking force comprised more than 100,000 troops, of which around two-thirds were employed in screening the city and then holding captured ground. The remaining third largely comprised Divisions of the Iraqi Army and Federal Police, who would rotate their brigades into seizing and clearing parts of the city, spearheaded by companies from the Iraqi Counterterrorism Service (CTS).[3] Before the assault a detailed picture of the populations' sentiment had been built up, which contributed to the prioritization of districts targeted.[4] Overhead the international coalition provided pervasive and constant intelligence, surveillance and reconnaissance, with ubiquitous fast air on stand-by. The intelligence soak on Mosul had been conducted over the preceding years. Despite the overwhelming numerical and technological advantages of the attackers the subsequent siege lasted 252 days. Potentially up to 8,000 Iraqi

---

[1] Catherine Philp, 'Severodonetsk's Last Stand: Brilliant Manoeuvre or Reckless Waste of Life?', *The Times*, 1 July 2022: https://www.thetimes.co.uk/article/severodonetsks-last-stand-brilliant-manoeuvre-or-reckless-waste-of-life-6hzp733hc, accessed 20 July 2022.
[2] John Spencer and Jason Geroux, 'Case Study #2: Mosul', *Modern War Institute*, 15 September 2021: https://mwi.usma.edu/urban-warfare-project-case-study-2-battle-of-mosul/, accessed 20 July 2022.
[3] Michael Knights and Alex Mello, 'The Best Thing America Built in Iraq: Iraq's Counter-Terrorism Service and the Long War against Militancy', *War on the Rocks*, 19 July 2017: https://warontherocks.com/2017/07/the-best-thing-america-built-in-iraq-iraqs-counter-terrorism-service-and-the-long-war-against-militancy/, accessed 20 July 2022.
[4] Author observations, preparations for the assault on Mosul, Iraq, September–October 2016.

security personnel were killed,[5] and 10,000 civilians died,[6] with potentially up to 3,000 killed by airstrikes.[7]

There is a tendency in some quarters to look at Mosul and describe it as an outlier. The willingness of Islamic State fighters to act as suicide bombers demonstrated a level of fanaticism that is rare, and other adversaries might not have fought to the last. Other adversaries however would likely have been equipped with more advanced anti-tank and high explosive weaponry, obviating the need to rely on suicide bombers as mobile ordnance. And though the final days of fighting were costly, the battle would not have looked much easier if the final remnants of Islamic State had surrendered. Far from being an anomaly, Mosul was consistent with a trend observable in both low- and high-intensity conflicts. Once one side wins sensor dominance and fires dominance, which in turn disproportionately punishes enemy movement and therefore allows their units to be fixed and defeated in detail, the losing side collapses back into complex terrain where they are protected from the adversary's advantages.[8] Furthermore, as the centres of economic activity cities are often the political objectives around which conflicts revolve. Thus, in Syria government forces supported by Russia and Iran quickly dominated parts of the countryside, only to face sustained and attritional fighting to capture rebel cities like Aleppo. In the opening years of the Russo-Ukrainian war, Russian forces spent a considerable period besieging Donetsk Airport.[9] Where defenders lack advanced weapons and attackers are therefore free to array massed fires against an urban area – as in Grozny during the Second Chechen War or Mariupol during the Russian offensive against Ukraine in 2022 – urban areas can be dominated more quickly.[10] But in these instances it still took over a month and left most of the city in rubble. There are also examples where the collapse of a defence can accelerate victory, as in the 2020 war in Nagorno-Karabakh, which saw the battle for the strategic

[5]   Brett McGurk, 'Press Conference by Special Presidential Envoy McGurk in Erbil, Iraq', *US Department of State*, 4 September 2017: https://2017-2021.state.gov/press-conference-by-special-presidential-envoy-mcgurk-in-erbil-iraq/index.html, accessed 20 July 2022; the CTS suffered 40 per cent casualties through the siege, see Office of the Secretary of Defence, 'Justification for FY 2018 Overseas Contingency Operations: Counter Islamic-State of Iraq and Syria Train and Equip Fund', *Department of Defence*, May 2018: https://comptroller.defense.gov/Portals/45/Documents/defbudget/fy2018/fy2018_CTEF_J-Book_Final_Embargoed.pdf, accessed 20 July 2022.

[6]   Susannah George, Qassim Abdul-Zahra, Maggie Michael and Lori Hinnant, 'Mosul Is a Graveyard: Final IS Battle Kills 9,000 Civilians', *Associated Press*, 21 December 2017: https://apnews.com/article/middle-east-only-on-ap-islamic-state-group-bbea7094fb954838a2fdc11278d65460, accessed 20 July 2022.

[7]   Ibid.

[8]   King, *Urban Warfare in the Twenty First Century*.

[9]   Amos Fox, '"Cyborgs at Little Stalingrad": A Brief History of the Battles of the Donetsk Airport, 26 May 2014 to 21 January 201', *Association of the United States Army*, May 2019: https://www.ausa.org/sites/default/files/publications/LWP-125-Cyborgs-at-Little-Stalingrad-A-Brief-History-of-the-Battle-of-the-Donetsk-Airport.pdf, accessed 20 July 2022.

[10] Anna Politkovskaya, *A Dirty War: A Russian Reporter in Chechnya* (London: Harvill Press, 2001); 'As It Happened: Ukraine Facing "Crucial" Period as Russia Focuses on East', *BBC*, 4 April 2022: https://www.bbc.com/news/live/world-europe-61032786, accessed 20 July 2022.

town of Shusha become a pivotal moment in the campaign.[11] Shusha was a small town, and it is worth noting that the Azeris chose to sign a ceasefire rather than invest the much larger city of Stepanakert, just as the Israelis chose to negotiate a Palestinian withdrawal rather than fight their way through Beirut.[12] In short, therefore, the ability to seize cities is a critical capability for any force that wishes to credibly contest ground. This can be anticipated to remain the case over the coming decades.

A useful illustration of the operational significance of capturing Urban centres as the consequential measure of progress in conflict can be seen in the 2015 Yemeni Civil War. In the Spring of 2018 Emirati-supported forces made a drive up the western coast backed by air and armour. They effectively displaced the Houthis from the countryside on the approaches to the port of Hodeidah,[13] but international outcry over the humanitarian impact of urban fighting led them to halt.[14] The result was that none of the gains they made translated into any additional leverage over the Houthis, and eventually the area between Hodeidah and Mocka – their urban base of operations further South – transitioned back to contested ground. Conversely the Houthis conducted a deliberate and methodical advance on the city of Marib over the course of 2021.[15] Where the capture of Hodeidah would have given the anti-Houthi coalition a finger on the windpipe of supply to the Houthis, the fall of Marib would see a critical mass of the country's natural resources fall into Houthi hands and likely collapse any capacity for a continued opposition to Houthi rule in northern Yemen.[16] While the Houthis had developed an effective tactical doctrine however, and were able to persistently win encounters in the hills on the approaches to Marib, they failed to translate this tactical success into an operational gain. This was because the final stretch of terrain before the city is exceedingly open, and the vigilance of Saudi aircraft prevented the Houthis from getting a critical mass of fighters into the urban space. In this instance, the inability to win the fires fight meant that they could not sustain an assault on Marib itself. Russia suffered the same fate in 2022. Without seizing

[11] John Spencer and Hirshana Ghoorhoo, 'The Battle of Shusha City and the Missed Lessons of the 2020 Nagorno-Karabakh War', *Modern War Institute*, 14 July 2021: https://mwi.usma.edu/the-battle-of-shusha-city-and-the-missed-lessons-of-the-2020-nagorno-karabakh-war/, accessed 20 July 2022.

[12] Richard Gabriel, *Operation Peace for Galilee: The Israeli-PLO War in Lebanon* (London: Hill & Wang, 1984).

[13] Bruce Riedel, 'In the Face of Hodeidah Assault, Yemen Is on the Brink', *Brookings*, 13 June 2018: https://www.brookings.edu/blog/order-from-chaos/2018/06/13/in-the-face-of-hodeidah-assault-yemen-is-on-the-brink/, accessed 20 July 2022.

[14] https://documents-dds-ny.un.org/doc/UNDOC/GEN/N18/455/86/PDF/N1845586.pdf?OpenElement, accessed 20 July 2022.

[15] Ned Price, 'The Houthis Must Cease the Assault on Marib', *US Department of State*, 16 February 2021: https://www.state.gov/the-houthis-must-cease-the-assault-on-marib/, accessed 20 July 2022; 'Houthi Attacks Reporting Monitor, Volume 1', *Embassy of the Republic of Yemen to the United States*: https://www.yemenembassy.org/wp-content/uploads/2022/03/Harm.pdf, accessed 20 July 2022.

[16] Alkhatab Al-rawhani, 'Marib: Local Changes and the Impact on the Future of Yemeni Politics', *LSE Middle East Centre*, 29 March 2017: https://blogs.lse.ac.uk/mec/2017/06/23/marib-local-changes-and-the-impact-on-the-future-of-yemeni-politics/, accessed 20 July 2022.

Kharkiv, Kyiv and other urban centres, occupying the surrounding country was not operationally sustainable.

That urban operations are likely to remain pivotal to the capacity of a force to seize the key objectives of their campaigns poses a serious challenge for land forces because the requirements imposed on the force by urban terrain are different to the equipment, training, structure, tempo and tactics that changes in technology are driving in fighting outside of the city. As outlined in the preceding chapters the future-operating environment is seeing a level of sensor density that makes concealment difficult, preventing forces from achieving operational surprise; a contested EMS where forces must fight for access to their networks; a volume of long-range precision fires that prevent concentration; and in consequence a severe limitation on the tempo that can be maintained because of the constraints the preceding changes place upon logistics. Urban terrain restores the capacity for surprise because of the density of cover available. Fixed communications infrastructure is abundant, meaning that defenders do not need to fight for communications in the same way. Concentration remains dangerous, but the nature of urban terrain also makes it less important. Logistics in cities are survivable and can therefore be persistently accessed. The dispersed, networked, mutually supporting structures that have been described as necessary to reach the city are therefore sub-optimal in penetrating it. The conclusion – as heralded by the importance of Iraq's CTS in Mosul – is that urban operations are a task for which generalist units can prepare, but for which some specialist capability must be maintained. The fundamental aspects of urban operations that create distinct requirements include its unique battlefield geometry, its human and virtual terrain, the degrading environment and the impact of a dense civilian population on operational tempo. These challenges shall be considered in turn.

The urban battlespace

Many of the challenges posed by Urban operations stem from its almost unique characteristics as a battlespace.[17] The first characteristic of urban operations is that it collapses engagement ranges from 200 to 600m for infantry in open ground, to 5–100m. Short-range engagements in open country clearly occur, just as longer-range sniping occurs in urban fighting, but the distribution of engagements comes closer. Closer engagements mean that it takes less time to acquire and engage a target once it has been identified. Unlike dense forest, where despite similarly close engagements, targets appear from a limited number of positions, the regular geometry of urban spaces means that an individual moving through it must continuously scan many more potential sources of threat than the defender. At a basic level a room may have four corners but only one door, meaning that someone in the room must monitor one potential source of threat while someone entering the room must scan four. This only gets more complicated as we consider – for instance – stepping into a street overlooked

---

17 Liam Collins and John Spencer (Eds.), *Understanding Urban Warfare* (Havant: Howgate Publishing, 2022), pp. 17–124.

by windows, which presents potential sources of threat at multiple elevations as well as at different bearings. Another aspect of urban environments that differs considerably from woodland is that woods impede movement. Underbrush and uneven ground all make quiet manoeuvre through them hard, though concealment easy. Urban areas by contrast are designed around flows of people and so movement through buildings is very easy for dismounts and can be achieved rapidly. But this is usually through a small number of routes. If we consider a block of flats, for example, there are easy routes up and down and in and out of the building, but there are also only a couple of them. This canalization by design means that movement through urban spaces can be rapid but is often predictable. The combination of these factors significantly favours units on the tactical and sub-tactical defence. They know the ground behind them and have proved the area they are defending. They can therefore move with greater certainty and therefore speed and assurance. They have an advantage in contact because they can predict where the threat will come from, whereas the attacker must first find the target.

A second and important impact of the canalization of tactical engagements in urban terrain is the effect this has on mass. The narrow movement corridors in urban terrain tend to limit the number of personnel that can engage a position simultaneously. Flanking a position does not necessarily offer an opportunity to engage it. In consequence it becomes very difficult to bring mass to bear. Much has been written about urban operations being mass intensive.[18] While it is true that commanders have often used large numbers of personnel in urban operations, the number of those personnel actually able to engage the enemy at a given time is very restricted. This means that defenders tend to fight multiple successive engagements at close to a parity in mass. As an illustrative example it makes little difference to a defender at the top of a staircase whether there are five or fifteen people on the floor below. So long as there is only one approach to the staircase, this likely means they have to fight one or two attackers at any given time, which is likely manageable. Much mass in urban operations meanwhile is less useful in breaking through the enemy than in assuring that a large amount of unoccupied space is in fact secure.[19]

Overcoming these challenges requires novel and specialized tactics to generate the uncertainty and multiple dilemmas that allow the advantages of the defence to be circumvented. At the level of individual teams methods of room entry that allow all corners of the internal space to be scanned as quickly as possible demand close teamwork and therefore repetitive training. This can be assisted through the use of grenades and other tools like stun grenades to dislodge or seize the initiative from defenders. Shorter barrelled weapons and increased protective equipment can also allow for faster and safer room entry. All of these tactics and equipment however require repetitive training to be employed successfully. Above the level of the team there is the need to expand the geometry of the battlespace through the use of

[18] Christopher Lawrence, *War by Numbers: Understanding Conventional Combat* (Lincoln, NH: Potomac Books, 2017), pp. 256–64.
[19] US Government Accountability Office (GAO), 'Report to Congressional Committees: Securing, Stabilizing, and Rebuilding Iraq: Iraqi Government Has Not Met Most Legislative, Security, and Economic Benchmarks', GAO-07-1195, September 2007, pp. 46–7.

explosives, ladders, deployable bridges and dynamic entry tools to create additional avenues of approach.[20] Blowing through walls and floors can disrupt the arcs of fire of the defenders and directly harm them, but also creates sudden multiple points of entry, flipping the uncertainty onto the defence.[21] Simultaneously attacking buildings from the ground floor and from the roof down can similarly fix an enemy into a static set of positions that can then be cleared with grenades and thermobaric explosives. Again, there is a heavy training burden to be able to use these entry methods quickly and to avoid fratricide with explosives in close proximity to friendlies. Finally, if a concentration of enemies can be fixed within an identified structure, and the structure does not serve any advantage if captured intact, then the application of heavy firepower to collapse it can obviate the need to commit troops.

Although the techniques outlined above can enable forces to seize urban terrain from a defender, the process is exceedingly resource intensive, psychologically and physically exhausting for the personnel involved, and often destroys much of the urban environment that is liberated, with a high rate of civilian casualties.[22] This process is prohibitively expensive to execute systematically across an urban expanse, and it is not necessary to do so since the size of urban areas vastly exceeds the available number of defenders in any army in the world. Most of the environment therefore is undefended. The problem is that because urban terrain obscures so much of the battlespace from observation, it is exceptionally difficult to determine where is and where is not occupied by defenders. The capacity for defenders to move under cover and rapidly reposition further exacerbates this problem. The reinfiltration of cleared urban areas is often relatively easy given that the force that was originally in the city can prepare subterranean and other concealed pathways and has the advantage of being intimately acquainted with the terrain prior to the onset of fighting.[23]

At the unit and sub-unit level the urban environment imposes support requirements that are less useful in open ground. Wide area coverage from radar, acoustic sensors and EW for example are of very limited utility in a highly cluttered environment. High-fidelity electro-optical sensors are also vulnerable because in an environment where ranges are reduced such assets are liable to be seen and damaged. Stand-off and elevated sensors can offer prolonged surveillance but will by necessity have no practical coverage inside buildings or behind them. On the other hand, there are numerous shorter-ranged systems that, while impractical in the field, have considerable utility in cities. Micro-UAS for example often have insufficient range and are too vulnerable to adverse wind to be depended upon in open country.[24] Given the

[20] Alec Wahlman, *Storming the City: U.S. Military Performance in Urban Warfare from World War II to Vietnam* (Denton, TX: University of North Texas Press, 2015).
[21] Eyal Weizman, 'Walking through Walls: Soldiers as Architects in the Israeli–Palestinian Conflict', *Radical Philosophy* (Vol. 136, 2006), pp. 8–22.
[22] ICRC, 'New Research Shows Urban Warfare 8 Times More Deadly for Civilians in Syria and Iraq', news release, 1 October 2018: https://www.icrc.org/en/document/new-research-shows-urban-warfare-eight-times-more-deadly-civilians-syria-iraq, accessed 2 January 2021.
[23] Nick Reynolds, 'The British Army and Mass in Urban Warfare', *The RUSI Journal* (Vol. 166, No. 4, 2021), pp. 1–14.
[24] Author observations trialling micro UAS on Salisbury Plain and in the US in 2018, 2019 and 2021.

short distances and sheltered environment within urban areas however these systems offer immediately relevant situational awareness.[25] These capabilities might be split into two kinds: those supporting fires and screening and those conducting route proving for units moving through the terrain. Another higher echelon capability relevant to urban operations is engineering support. Although engineering is of considerable importance in traversing non-urban terrain, urban environments impose particular constraints upon these assets. Firstly, buildings restrict movement, limiting the size of vehicles that can be employed. Protection must also be from enemies firing from elevated positions. The destruction of obstacles can also lead to rubble falling onto vehicles in a way that is less likely in obstacle breaches in open ground. Given the complexity of these tasks and the need for small vehicles remote control becomes highly desirable, even if this limits the distances over which vehicles can operate. Both micro-UAS and remote vehicles however are dependent upon communications, which urban environments make complicated.

The layers of material blocking line of sight in urban spaces renders point-to-point communication patchy at best. Remote links to robotic vehicles are notoriously difficult to maintain in urban environments, which have led to the failure of these systems when deployed by Russian forces in Syria.[26] Given the relatively short distances over which much equipment must operate, one option is wire-based remote control, which cannot be jammed and can function around corners. Assuring communications with units meanwhile can be achieved through the distribution of relay points over the operating environment. Again, micro-UAS can prove useful in this by landing on elevated positions and thereby providing nodes that are difficult to find. While such a method would often be prohibitively expensive across a large geography, it becomes viable in urban areas where distances are reduced. Nevertheless, these functions require different equipment skills, stores and procedures among troops. This is even more the case when it comes to considering how forces interact with the virtual infrastructure that permeates cities and the population.

Human and virtual terrain

Cities exist as physical spaces, but also as virtual archives.[27] Planning permission and modern architectural software mean that governments hold repositories of designs, while the maintenance of public utilities like sewage, electricity, communications and roads demands continuous monitoring and therefore data collection on the location and status of components. Modern billing for energy consumption meanwhile provides real-time pattern of life data for whole communities. Mobile networks in

---

[25] Conclusion of force-on-force testing in Twentynine Palms by Royal Marines, January 2019.

[26] 'Большая часть техники на Параде Победы прошла боевые испытания в Сирии' (Most of the equipment at the Victory Parade passed combat tests in Syria), RIA Novosti, 6 May 2018: https://ria.ru/20180506/1519978275.html, accessed 20 July 2022.

[27] David Kilcullen, *Out of the Mountains: The Coming Age of the Urban Guerrilla* (London: Hurst, 2013).

towns – because of the close proximity of phone masts – provide highly accurate real-time location data on a majority of the individuals within them. These data are rarely available in a single repository or accessible for a single user. The fidelity of such data varies by country. Moreover, war must necessarily see the degradation of this supporting infrastructure combined with significant changes in people's pattern of life. The virtual terrain of urban environments does not offer a perpetual panopticon of a city and its inhabitants. But it does offer a huge amount of useful data for intelligence and planning purposes.[28]

Detailed structural information about a city offers military planners the ability to brief their forces in detail as to the terrain into which they are advancing and the key tactical points of concern that they will likely need to overcome. The ability to plan in detail is greatly aided if operational echelons can penetrate repositories of information and push it forward to units anticipated to operate within an urban area. Another aspect of this planning must be an appreciation for how a city's infrastructure is routed. This may make certain buildings – especially where fibre optic cabling and other systems branch – key objectives. Other buildings may need to be marked as hazardous because of the consequences of the destruction of their contents, or because they comprise critical support systems for the civilian population.

Beyond the use of archived data for planning there is the question of how much of a city's infrastructure can be exploited in real time. Cities often have concentric circles of surveillance systems from public cameras to building security systems, to private camera systems on doors and cars. Many of these systems rely on commercially available architectures against which standardized exploits can be developed and therefore deployed by cyber teams supporting units. Street lights and other utilities are increasingly remote controlled.[29] In theory this could allow militaries to hijack communication links to share their own data, or to stimulate and thereby control such infrastructure. Other examples include exploitation of subterranean infrastructure which can enable concealed movement through an urban space. These passages can be used by friendly forces. Alternatively, entrances – which are not always obvious – can be identified and denied or secured to prevent enemy infiltration.[30] Life support within these systems can also be used to deny the enemy if ventilation and filtration systems can be identified and manipulated.

It is worth noting that militaries seeking to exploit these systems are best advised to leverage reserve specialists who come from the relevant sectors in their civilian work. Not only will many of them know the architectures involved but they will also be able to speak with local civilian administrators with a level of nuance and precision that

[28] Ishida, T. et al., 'Digital City Kyoto: Towards a Social Information Infrastructure', Klusch, M., Shehory, O. M., Weiss, G. (Eds.), *Cooperative Information Agents III. CIA, Lecture Notes in Computer Science* (Vol. 1652, 1999), pp. 34–46.

[29] M. S. A. Muthanna, M. M. A. Muthanna, A. Khakimov and A. Muthanna, 'Development of Intelligent Street Lighting Services Model Based on LoRa Technology', *2018 IEEE Conference of Russian Young Researchers in Electrical and Electronic Engineering (EIConRus)*, (2018), pp. 90–3.

[30] John Spencer, 'Underground Warfare in Israel and Gaza', *Modern War Institute*, 28 May 2021: https://mwi.usma.edu/underground-warfare-in-israel-and-gaza/, accessed 20 July 2022.

helps to avoid mistakes and misunderstanding.[31] And there will be civilians. Although some civilians may flee in anticipation of a conflict, even where evacuations have been enforced, many conspire to remain. In most contexts civilians remain dispersed throughout urban battlespaces. They are a significant complicating factor for militaries. Where they are hostile to a force – as much of the population was in Mogadishu towards American units – they can seriously impede operations by assisting in the erection of obstacles and in acting as spotters for the enemy.[32] They can also engage in acts of resistance like taking down or changing road signs and participating in information operations against occupiers.[33] Alternatively – as with the Dutch at Arnhem – they can provide medical support and supplies and guide forces through a town, increasing their operational endurance, independence and survivability.[34] Civilians may have an array of protections under international law but they are very rarely neutral to what is happening around them.[35] Armies must be able to speak with, gather information from and mitigate the risk posed by civilians within their area of operations. Understanding the social structure, cultural distribution and hierarchy of local institutions within an urban environment is critical to the terrain analysis that should inform planning before moving into an urban space.

In any urban space where intense fighting occurs, civilians will die, likely in large numbers. Others will be displaced. Internally displaced people require care while civilians will also put pressure on the logistical and medical capacity of a force. Without robust procedures for handling civilians militaries can place them at risk and can have disproportionate resources fixed in providing for their needs, which can affect the force's combat effectiveness.[36] Moreover the perception of how civilians are treated by the forces fighting within an area can shape human flows through the environment. On the one hand, a force that treats civilians poorly is likely to find the population turn hostile or at best be uncooperative. A force meanwhile that treats civilians well and has a reputation for it will more than likely benefit from their cooperation. However, that force is also likely to be sought to provide medical assistance and flows may go towards areas under their control. They are consequently likely to bear a disproportionate burden in meeting their humanitarian obligations.

[31] Paul O'Neill, 'A First-Rate Second Echelon', Jack Watling (Ed.), *Decision Points: Rationalising the Armed Forces of European Medium Powers* (London: RUSI, 2020), pp. 63–78.

[32] Mark Bowden, *Black Hawk Down* (London: Penguin, 1999).

[33] Something that happened in Kuwait, across Ukraine, and in Mosul and Raqqa, see Mike Stevens, 'Resistance and Information Warfare in Mosul and Raqqa', *The RUSI Journal* (Vol. 165, No. 5, 2020), pp. 10–21.

[34] Anthony Beevor, *Arnhem: The Battle for the Bridges, 1944* (London: Penguin, 2019), pp. 126–40; 172–93; 334–52.

[35] And armies often do not respect their protections; see Reiner Salverda, 'Beyond a Bridge Too Far: The Aftermath of the Battle for Arnhem (1944) and Its Impact on Civilian Life', Jane Fenoulhet, Gerdi Quist and Ulrich Tiedau (Eds.), *Discord and Consensus in the Low Countries, 1700–2000* (London: UCL Press, 2016).

[36] Margarita Konaev, 'The Future of Urban Warfare in the Age of Megacities', *Focus Stratégique*, No. 88 (Paris: IFRI, 2019), pp. 34–46.

A new facet of the human terrain through which forces manoeuvre when conducting urban operations is that they are often globally connected and can increasingly shape the perception of forces both among the local community and internationally. Anthony King has written about not only how urban operations produce a disproportionate volume of video and material shared on social media, but how political perceptions of conflict and the behaviour of other actors around the world become linked to the struggles for urban symbols.[37] Another feature of this phenomenon is how – as Matthew Ford and Andrew Hoskins have explored – civilians actively shape the narrative in real time through the information they collect and disseminate.[38] In this way they are increasingly participants in urban operations and can cause parties to be disproportionately punished for how they conduct themselves in an urban space. This is usually on a highly partisan basis, rather than judging forces against an objective standard. The use of what civilians collect and disseminated through the monitoring of communications and social media also blurs the line between neutrality and participating in fighting, exacerbating ambiguity over the targeting of 'spotters' that has occurred in previous conflicts. In Ukraine civilians were deliberately integrated into the defensive ISR net.[39] In confronting this challenge militaries entering urban areas need robust information warfare procedures, must be able to monitor and shape the collateral from their physical activities in the virtual dimension, and be proactive in framing perceptions of their campaign.

One of the curious aspects of urban operations is that because the number of people who populate an area dwarf the size of the military forces operating within them, fighting can be exceedingly intense in one part of a city while life continues with a high degree of normality in other districts. This means that many civilians can comment upon and actively participate in the shaping of the information environment. However, the extent to which a semblance of normality can be maintained often shapes how a conflict is perceived. In Mosul – for example – the slow pace of the advance meant that life in much of the city continued while fighting was on the outskirts. The fighting however steadily worked its way through the districts and because the defenders continued to contest ground, block by block, more and more of the city was destroyed until in the aftermath Mosul appeared to be largely reduced to rubble. It is worth contrasting this with how Russian, Iranian and Syrian propaganda framed fighting in Damascus. While much of the city was similarly damaged, other districts remained largely untouched. The regime worked hard to portray a contrast between areas under rebel control and its own, and to thereby terrify opposition-held areas with the consequences of resistance while also promoting the normality in

[37] King, *Urban Warfare in the Twenty First Century*, pp. 182–98.
[38] Matthew Ford and Andrew Hoskins, *Radical War: Data, Attention and Control in the 21st Century* (London: Hurst, 2022).
[39] Drew Harwell, 'Instead of Consumer Software, Ukraine's Tech Workers Build Apps of War', *The Washington Post*, 24 March 2022: https://www.washingtonpost.com/technology/2022/03/24/ukraine-war-apps-russian-invasion/, accessed 20 July 2022.

regime-controlled areas to foreigners who were prepared to spread their message.[40] This was possible because the insurgent rebels were largely constrained in their ability to penetrate neighbourhoods in a highly sectarian civil conflict. In conflicts without this dynamic however the speed at which armies can bypass the non-contested space must necessarily determine the proportion of the city that is fought over. If a force can bypass parts of a city and instead focus on key terrain, then the positional struggle for key areas can avoid the systemic destruction that characterized fighting for Aleppo, Raqqa and elsewhere. This is important because the level of destruction directly impacts the extent to which an urban area can be leveraged after capture if it is a waypoint rather than the ultimate objective in a campaign.

Rubble, ruin and restoration

The Battle of the Somme, in 1916, opened with one of the most intense artillery bombardments in history. This had surprisingly little impact on the battlefield, however. German shelters were dug too deep to be damaged by the modest calibre guns firing at them. The barbed wire remained largely intact despite the high explosive employed against it. The foremost effect of the impact fused shelling was the redistribution of a considerable quantity of topsoil.[41] From the First World War to today artillery may be the foremost cause of death on the battlefield, but outside of the urban environment it tends to have a transitory effect on terrain. Its impact on the urban environment is different. Cities degrade rapidly under fire. This tends to occur in stages. First the glass is blown out of the windows. Then the facings of buildings fall into the streets. The streets themselves become rubble strewn and pocked with craters that sever utilities. Eventually the skeletons of buildings are brought crashing down to leave jagged mounds or masonry and metal. And yet – beneath the rubble – pockets of structures will often remain standing. The initial stage of fighting in a city is often one of precise movement into and out of buildings. The higher the intensity of the fighting, the sooner the battlefield becomes a chaotic wasteland above ground and an unpredictable labyrinth beneath it.[42]

If the process of rubbleization usually suggests that a defender is coming under a punishing volume of fire, its aftermath often makes the attacker's task exceedingly difficult. Movement in a rubbleized city is made hazardous because there is no predictability to the environment and the utility of pre-war mapping is diminished. A tenacious defence will often see an attacker revert to fires as a means of avoiding attrition, only to return to gruelling offensive operations to clear the depleted enemy

---

[40] This was evident early in the conflict, see https://www.youtube.com/watch?v=-FDG9kBcWII, accessed 20 July 2022, and has continued, see https://twitter.com/MaxBlumenthal/status/1170688827779964928, accessed 20 July 2022.

[41] Keegan, *Face of Battle*, pp. 200–13.

[42] Richard Spencer, David Charter, Felix Light and Sebastian Mann, '90% of Buildings in Mariupol 'Damaged or Destroyed', *The Times*, 17 March 2022: https://www.thetimes.co.uk/article/us-to-send-800-million-in-military-hardware-to-ukraine-885r9f68q, accessed 20 July 2022.

from the smouldering ruins. If fires are used to dislodge an enemy, then they must be followed by assault rapidly or else the enemy will likely recover and dig in. Localizing fires – rather than delivering them against a wide area – can help to limit the disruption to axes of advance.

A further aspect of rubbleization is that urban areas usually comprise objectives because they are logistical hubs, political centres and provide a support system for protracted enemy resistance. The latter of these can be addressed through the city's destruction. The first two, however, indicate the desire to exploit the terrain once it is captured, and here rubbleization prevents that exploitation. An urban area can hardly act as an effective logistics hub if the critical infrastructure has been destroyed. Far from enabling the attacker to take advantage of an urban area, rubbleization both denies the use of the space and is likely to create a humanitarian catastrophe, further absorbing resources from the attacker as they seek to manage displaced people. Whereas in Kherson, for example, Russia captured a functional port and centre of local government, in Mariupol the destruction far exceeded the capacity of the Russian state to repair while under sweeping sanctions.

Although rubbleization is an inevitable consequence of protracted fighting, its implications need to be carefully considered as a force determines where and how to fight for an urban environment. Most cities were not designed from scratch but instead grew from the merging of multiple villages. Other cities revolve around key terrain features, from fortified hills to ports. Cities often comprise a cluster of sub-environments ranging from the commercial, the civic, the industrial and the residential. Furthermore, these sub-environments not only vary in their operational features – cover and movement through industrial buildings differ to residential ones for example – but are also often separated by open spaces, main supply routes or terrain. Key questions for a military therefore are whether they can isolate these sub-environments, which are essential for the future exploitation of the environment, where can be rubbleized and therefore constitutes preferred killing areas for the enemy, and where can the enemy be fixed and ignored. The defender will have a considerable say in which key positions they prioritize for defence, but here the use of feints, fixing actions and information operations can help to draw an enemy into parts of the city that can then be isolated from operational targets. Cities do not necessarily have to be occupied to be controlled.

Another consideration for the attacker is the disproportionate utility of precision weapons in an urban environment. In open ground area effect is an effective means of punishing enemy concentration. In an urban environment, where the defender does not necessarily need to concentrate to maintain numerical parity on key axes, area effect artillery can be extremely resource intensive – creating a logistical target outside the city that may prove vulnerable – and rubbleize a much larger area creating a greater problem than the number of enemies killed. Precision munitions, by contrast, can keep the extent of rubbleization proportionate to the damage inflicted on the enemy force.

While isolating the key parts of a city, containing the fighting where possible and the use of precision munitions can all limit rubbleization, it must nevertheless be recognized that the degradation of a city's habitability and key support infrastructure means that a key part of future operations will be how quickly a city can be restored. Historically, this has been looked at primarily through the lens of post-war reconstruction.[43] However, if we are today envisaging cities as the operational objectives and waypoints in a campaign, fortified areas from which forces can pulse and withdraw, and therefore necessary to turning progress in the open into secure gains, then a force is not just aiming to take a city but to subsequently operate from it. By way of example, Russian forces in Ukraine did not target Ukrainian rail links until surprisingly late in the conflict because for much of the first month they hoped to seize Ukrainian cities and then exploit the rail infrastructure for their own logistics purposes. This proved a major mistake by Russian planners. Nevertheless, it highlights how a key part of capturing any city – in terms of meeting both the human security responsibilities of a force and the military utility of the captured infrastructure – is the speed at which critical transportation, energy, communications and other infrastructure can be restored after fighting.

A further impact of this tension between the importance of firepower in reducing strongpoints and the disadvantages of rubbleization is the allure of novel weaponry and the hazard of prohibited weaponry in such an environment. In Syria, for example, the use of chlorine gas as a means of disrupting the defence became normalized, while nerve agents were also utilized to break the will of the civilian population to resist.[44] Deterrence has so far discouraged Russia from employing such techniques in Ukraine. However, whereas chemical weapons are generally inefficient in rural areas – especially so against dispersed forces[45] – they may be attractive to less scrupulous adversaries in urban areas because they offer the opportunity to drive an enemy from key terrain without damaging it. Another tactic increasingly in use to achieve a similar effect is the prosecution of sieges with the aim of starving the defence.[46] For those more concerned about international law there are nevertheless a range of non-lethal weapons that may become increasingly prevalent in urban fighting. Sonic weaponry, for example, may offer a means of driving defenders off-target positions. High-power microwave weaponry – developed currently for defensive purposes – offers little offensive potential in dispersed operations given its limited range and high signature. In an urban environment, however, it too might provide a means of displacing a defence.

Putting aside the deliberate use of novel or prohibited weapons in urban environments the process of rubbleization creates second-order consequences that impact upon the capacity to hold urban terrain. Fire and its associated smoke – which is often additionally toxic in urban environments – is the most obvious second-order hazard to troops. The destruction of water piping and the flooding of subterranean infrastructure, the damage to gas piping and chemical storage in industrial areas

[43] Antonio Sampaio, 'Before and after Urban Warfare: Conflict Prevention and Transitions in Cities', *International Review of the Red Cross* (Vol. 98, No. 901, 2016), pp. 71–95.

[44] Hamish de Bretton-Gordon, *Chemical Warrior: Syria, Salisbury and Saving Lives at War* (London: Headline, 2020).

[45] Dan Kaszeta, *Toxic: A History of Nerve Agents, From Nazi Germany to Putin's Russia* (London: Hurst, 2020).

[46] Nils Hägerdal, 'Starvation as Siege Tactics: Urban Warfare in Syria', *Studies in Conflict & Terrorism*, (2020), DOI: 10.1080/1057610X.2020.1816682.

releasing ammonia and other substances or the respiratory effects of dust from destroyed structures all impede combatants in urban environments. Robust nuclear, chemical and biological defences and training, experience in how to mitigate these threats and fight in the relevant equipment are all factors for units seeking advantage in an urban environment that are arguably less important for manoeuvre forces in open country.

The impact of a degrading environment is complex and cannot be entirely controlled. Nevertheless, there are strong imperatives for both sides to limit it if possible. The key function of whether rubbleization becomes extensive is time, and this creates a further interesting dynamic in urban operations that should be a driver in force design and encourages the use of specialized assault units for urban attack and defence.

Time between the towers

The description of the challenges facing land forces in the preceding chapters highlighted how the notion of a high-tempo concentrated assault was likely to lead to operational failure in the face of layered modern sensors and fires. The conclusion is that fighting in non-critical environments will likely be slower, with lower force densities engaged in highly lethal engagements that are nevertheless small in scale. As one side gains sensor dominance they may accelerate and concentrate sufficiently to push into the urban area. But here, as outlined in the previous section of this chapter, there is an imperative to dominate the vital ground quickly. There is a considerable risk in urban fighting that it becomes protracted, fixes the force to a predictable set of targetable MSRs and ultimately leaves it vulnerable to operational counterattack as achieved against Axis forces outside Stalingrad by the Red Army,[47] or against the Russian Army outside Kyiv in 2022.[48]

Conversely, the belief that urban areas are impregnable is dangerous, as is the comparison between modern urban warfare and medieval sieges. Medieval sieges functioned as they did because castles defended key terrain, could house individuals who were politically indispensable and often the centre of gravity in a feudal society, and yet had small numbers of defenders. A small garrison could therefore hold out for a long time.[49] As the balance between attackers and the civilian population has changed, the logic of siege and urban warfare has shifted. In the classical era urban populations were large compared to the armies attacking them. This meant that isolating cities was rare.[50] Hannibal dominated the Roman countryside, for example,

---

[47] Anthony Beevor, *Stalingrad* (London: BCA, 2005), pp. 239–65.
[48] Jack Watling and Nick Reynolds, *Operation Z: Death Throes of an Imperial Delusion* (London: RUSI, 2022), pp. 2–7.
[49] Jim Bradbury, *The Medieval Siege* (Woodbridge: The Boydell Press, 1998), p. 1; pp. 48–152.
[50] Consider the number of towns stormed during the year of the four Emperors for example; see Gaius Cornelius Tacitus, *The Histories*, Kenneth Wellesley (trans.) (London: Penguin, 2009).

but could not isolate Rome.[51] He therefore could not translate tactical victories into operational success. When cities in the ancient world fell, they tended to fall to storm. Similarly in the early modern era when artillery made towns penetrable even if it was resource intensive, the main question was how long a town could delay an attacking force and thereby obstruct campaign progress within a season.[52] Today the dynamic is somewhat different. A force that has achieved sensor dominance outside of a city may be able to isolate it through the application of fires and interdiction without placing a complete encirclement around the town. If this is achieved, then time very much works in favour of the attacker. The defender can only continue to resist so long as food, water and ammunition continue to be available. The isolation of parts of a city can limit the impact of such tactics on the civilian population. For less scrupulous armies, however, the colocation of the opposing military with a large civilian population may in fact reduce the endurance of an isolated defence by increasingly the consumption rate of critical supplies. On the other hand a town that is not isolated can continue to function effectively and provide a safe logistical hub from which raids and strikes can be conducted. In this way a town that is not isolated can in fact project-influence into its rural periphery. For the attacker this means that becoming fixed in urban spaces that have not been isolated can rapidly see time work in favour of the defender, since they retain freedom of movement.

A further aspect of time in urban operations is that as fighting protracts the civilian population is either likely to become displaced, to become increasingly dependent upon the force controlling the area they are in or become increasingly hostile to the military in their city. These factors mean that the longer a force remains fighting in an urban area, the more resource intensive it is likely to be to maintain a presence. Once the adversary is driven from the environment on the other hand and supply and local government can revert to civilian control, cities can become highly efficient areas in which to hold forces. It is therefore in the interests of the attacker to rapidly achieve their objectives once they commit to attacking an urban area. Fighting at high tempo requires specialization, and this therefore strengthens the case that urban operations should be spearheaded by specially equipped and trained units.

Although – as political and economic centres of gravity – armies will struggle to avoid fighting in urban areas in the future, it is also important that armies do not optimize for the urban fight at the expense of reaching the urban area. The challenge is the relationship between urban and rural, with rural operations shaping the conditions for decisive operations in the urban. Similarly, for the defence the urban provides the cover from which shaping and disruption can be sustained in the rural periphery. Whereas historically armies have optimized for rural operations and pushed into cities as it has become necessary, today these constitute two halves of almost any successful operational design. And yet, as the tactics and equipment for these two environments

---

[51] Titus Livy, *The War with Hannibal: The History of Rome from Its Foundation Books 21–30*, Aubrey Selincourt (trans.) (London: Penguin, 2004).

[52] Andrew Wheatcroft, *The Enemy at the Gates: Habsburgs, Ottomans and the Battle for Europe* (Oxford: The Bodley Head, 2008).

diverge, there is also the question of how these different operational elements are commanded, how are they planned and how do the force elements train to be able to successfully cooperate across their operating environments. In some respects the challenge from a planning and command point of view resembles that between maritime and amphibious forces. Each force must obey conflicting logics of operation, and yet once the amphibious force has landed they remain dependent upon the maritime force being able to sustain and protect them.[53] Victory is illusive without the amphibious force being successful on land, but defeat at sea can doom the operation. Each force is managing different and in some ways competing risks.

---

[53] Timothy Heck and B. A. Friedman (Eds.), *On Contested Shores: The Evolving Role of Amphibious Operations in the History of Warfare* (Quantico: Marine Corps University Press, 2020).

Part Two

The arms of the future

6

The geometry of the future battlefield

*Soldiering has always been about evolution, and successful armies have always
adapted to changing threats and technology. And given the unrelenting pace
and acceleration of change today, the Army stands on the cusp of another such
transformation. Possibly – possibly – the most significant one since mechanization in
the 1930s, 1940s.*[1]

General Sir Mark Carleton-Smith

Standing around a folding table in an armoured vehicle shed in Tidworth, Southern
England, the officers of the Royal Welsh battlegroup poured over the map of an
urban landscape. In the wargame they were to defend a dense urban area besides a
critical bridge, which they were tasked with denying to an advancing enemy force.
Unfortunately, they had run into a problem. They and their sister battlegroup had each
been given a defensive area separated by a main road. This main road ran through
the middle of the town and led directly to the bridge each battlegroup was supposed
to defend. The division of responsibility was intended to give each force an area in
which they had freedom to plan and manoeuvre, with a clear boundary. Crossing the
boundary without notifying the other battlegroup could risk friendly fire. The question
was who was responsible for the road between their formations. This was especially
problematic because it was assessed as most likely that the enemy's main effort would
push directly along this axis.[2]

The concept of battlefield geometry relates to how commanders divide up, measure,
manage and conceive of the battlespace. Since Airland Battle was promulgated in the
1980s, the battlefield, for NATO armies, has been divided into the rear, close and
deep.[3] The rear connotes the area behind a force in which support functions can be
safely situated and which the force should protect from the enemy. The close may be
understood as the battlespace occupied by the enemy force with which the commander
is currently engaged. The deep may be understood as comprising the space within

---

[1]   Mark Carleton-Smith, 'Land Warfare 2021: Welcoming Remarks and Opening Keynote', RUSI Land
     Warfare Conference 2021, London, 2 June 2021: https://www.youtube.com/watch?v=JhcGUoNo6Hk,
     15:00, accessed 20 July 2022.
[2]   Author observations, Exercise Urban Lion, Tidworth, July 2021.
[3]   US Army Training and Doctrine Command (TRADOC), 'FM 100-5 Operations 1982', 1982.

which the enemy force holds its support area, and through which subsequent enemy formations must pass to reach the fight. The concept of deep battle – at the heart of Soviet doctrine from 1936[4] and subsequently absorbed into Western military concepts – argues that by penetrating the close on a narrow frontage and then spreading out to disrupt the deep, the enemy in the close will be starved of resources and likely collapse. The close, deep and rear geometry may also be viewed as temporal rather than special blocks, as articulated by General Don Starry in his concept of the extended battlefield.[5] The close comprises today's fight, the deep is the next fight. The security of the rear is what enables the next fight. In this context using artillery and other methods to delay enemy forces in the deep can mean they lose combat power before entering the close, or can increase the time available to win the close fight. Battlefield geometry also has lateral temporal and special considerations. Units are assigned 'frontages' in military planning for which they are responsible. The boundaries between frontages represent control measures so that units do not commit fratricide or impede one another. When units must move in front of, behind or through one another, these movements must be planned and coordinated, so that flows of vehicles along roads and around terrain features do not lead to traffic jams and present easy targets for the enemy.

An example of the disastrous consequences of failing to properly account for battlefield geometry can be seen in Russia's defeat in the battle of Kyiv, where multiple Russian units sought to simultaneously manoeuvre along two main supply routes (MSRs), becoming stuck and wasting their fuel in idling, waiting for the road to clear, at the mercy of Ukrainian artillery. The challenge troubling the officers of the Royal Welsh was that the brigade staff to whom they reported had devised an incompetently drawn scheme for the battlefield geometry. By putting the most likely main axis of enemy advance between the formations the brigade had hamstrung the commanders of the two battlegroups from having a clear and unified command and scheme to counter the primary threat. Precise battlefield geometry, therefore, is vital if a force is to understand the tasks assigned to it and to be able to execute them effectively. How a battlefield is understood holistically by a commander is critical to understanding how they wield the combined arms elements that they control.

The previous section of this book concerned itself with defining the problems facing the tactics, force structures and concepts underpinning mechanized warfare in a new age of informatized warfare. Chapter 1 argued that armies will find it increasingly difficult to achieve operational surprise in the face of persistent and high-fidelity sensor coverage. The second chapter highlighted the need for new communications architectures to handle an increased volume of traffic if forces were to remain competitive. Chapter 3 examined the implications of an inability to concentrate in the face of long-range, precise and highly lethal fires. The fourth chapter argued that operational tempo has become increasingly disjointed by the threat posed to logistics, necessitating a more deliberate process of infiltration, rather than rapid thrusts to break up enemy formations. And yet, as argued in Chapter 5, operational success

---

[4] *Vremennyy Polevoy Ustav RKKA 1936* [Provisional Field Regulations for the Red Army 1936] (Moscow: People's Commissar for Defence of the USSR, 1936).

[5] Don Starry, 'Extending the Battlefield', *Military Review* (March, 1981), pp. 31–50.

requires that the force achieve concentration to rapidly seize urban areas once the shaping battle had been won around towns.

This part concerns how armies need to structure themselves to be competitive in this future-operating environment, how they should be equipped and trained and how they will need to be commanded. This chapter, and the four that follows it, will set out the combined arms operations of the future in relation to four interrelated combined arms systems, that of manoeuvre, fires, assault and support. Before delving into each of these in turn, however, it is first necessary to unpack the implications of the dynamics of warfare described over the preceding section on battlefield geometry. This provides a framework within which the four combined arms systems described later operate as a whole. Most importantly, understanding the geometry of the future battlefield provides a breakdown of military tasks and effects that the future force must be able to deliver.

The geometry of manoeuvre in positional warfare

That battlefield geometry is changing has been widely acknowledged in militaries. In Russia the idea of the fragmented battlefield,[6] in which forces expect to fight with exposed flanks, protecting themselves by denying ground with fires and electronic warfare, reflects a recognition that the idea of a forward line of own troops or frontline is not consistent with how modern militaries deploy.[7] In China the idea of the battle of annihilation through systems destruction envisages defeating the enemy from the back forwards, using network targeting and joint firepower campaigns to break up command and logistics hubs to paralyze enemy combat forces and destroy their will to fight.[8] This may be seen as an evolution of airland battle, extending operational depth to integrate ballistic and cruise missile ranges, and envisaging a battlefield that revolves around key nodal points, rather than lines of control. The US military had long recognized theoretically that lines were increasingly arbitrary. In the post-Cold War era the United States increasingly envisaged its adversary as a series of connected nodes, with the ability to find and strike the correct nodes in sequence leading to the enemy's collapse.[9] This was encapsulated in concepts of network-centric warfare, though the concept was increasingly captured by an emphasis on the targeting cycle,[10]

---

[6] Lester Grau and Charles Bartles, 'Russian Future Combat on a Fragmented Battlefield': https://www.benning.army.mil/infantry/magazine/issues/2021/Fall/pdf/5_Grau_txt.pdf, accessed 3 December 2022.

[7] Ministry of Defense of the Russian Federation, 'Очаговая Оборона' [Fragmented Defence], Военная Энциклопедия [*Military Encyclopaedia*], Volume 6, (Moscow: Voyenizdat, 2002), p. 214.

[8] Jeffrey Engstrom, *Systems Confrontation and System Destruction Warfare: How the Chinese People's Liberation Army Seeks to Wage Modern Warfare* (Santa Monica, CA: RAND Corporation, 2018).

[9] David S Alberts, John J Garstka and Frederick P Stein, *Network Centric Warfare: Developing and Leveraging Information Superiority*, 2nd edition (Washington, DC: DoD C4ISR Cooperative Research Program, 2000), pp. 88–93.

[10] Charles Faint and Michael Harris, 'F3EAD: Ops/Intel Fusion "Feeds" the SOF Targeting Process', *Small Wars Journal*, 31 January 2012.

driven by the need to break up non-state actors during the global war on terror. The wars in Iraq and Afghanistan allowed for an unparalleled level of air and ground integration rather than deconfliction and the United States has sought to retain the advantages this offers in peer warfighting. The threat posed by Chinese and Russian capabilities has been theorized in the United States as comprising a problem of 'layered stand-off', with the idea of multi-domain operations developed as a counter to this threat.[11] Within MDO the United States envisages warfare as a cycle in which the force competes, penetrates, disintegrates, exploits and recompetes. In essence, battlefield geometry is determined by enemy long-range systems. The force must penetrate their threat rings and once inside break up the components, allowing the force to then transition to a more traditional ground-fight, exploiting the gaps in enemy systems. MDO is largely envisaged as being applied at the corps echelon and above. The divisional warfighting concepts behind it are still being refined, while the actual tactics employed by units look much more conventional. Although MDO does recognize a significant shift in battlefield geometry therefore, it does not provide a scheme that can be applied to tactical actions. Another feature of all the concepts so far outlined is that they remain enemy centric and do not articulate the positional character of warfare. Furthermore, while network-centric warfare and MDO both outline what is to be done to the enemy, they do not explain how the force mitigates the same threat against itself. These concepts are largely offensively focused and their explanation of battlefield geometry does not – as deep operations and airland battle did – explain how both sides may interact.

In articulating a new battlefield geometry for tactical echelons therefore it is first necessary to acknowledge that warfare may continue to depend upon outmanoeuvring the enemy force in tactical engagements but has becoming operationally positional,[12] with campaign progress determined by the capture of vital ground, which likely comprises urban nodes.[13] Whereas the deep, close and rear emphasized the enemy force, it did not ascribe any particular importance to geographically static objectives. The starting point for the new battlefield geometry therefore is to acknowledge that a force likely has a base of operations from which it is projecting – and which is partially protected from long range precision fires – and an objective. These are fixed points determined by the available infrastructure and political context of an operation. They remain true until either the base of operations is rendered non-viable and overrun, or the objective is taken and secured. At this point the objective may become a new base of operations and a new objective may be sought.

As identified in Chapter 5, seizing an objective needs to be achieved quickly and requires concentration of forces. As outlined in the first chapter, concentration is only viable outside of the range of enemy stand-in sensors that allow for accurate targeting. We may therefore describe the battlespace as comprising three zones: that of opportunity, of contestation and of risk. The zone of opportunity may be understood

---

[11] US Army, 'The US Army in Multi-Domain Operations 2028', TRADOC Pamphlet 525-3-1, 6 December 2018.
[12] Amos C. Fox, 'Manoeuvre Is Dead?', *The RUSI Journal* (Vol. 166, No. 6, 2021), pp. 10–18.
[13] Amos C. Fox, 'On Sieges', *The RUSI Journal* (Vol. 166, No. 2, 2021), pp. 18–28.

as the battlespace that is not covered by enemy stand-in sensors and therefore offers the opportunity to concentrate. The zone of contestation may be understood as the battlespace covered by friendly and hostile stand-in ISR and massed fires. Here concentration is lethal and dispersed forces are likely to find themselves intermingled and in direct firefights, fighting to blind one another. Beyond the range of friendly stand-in ISR and the range of friendly massed fires lies the zone of risk, where the enemy has the opportunity to concentrate and practise deception.

Sound military concepts must be simple. The theory of victory in AirLand Battle was essentially that a force must manoeuvre to defeat the second echelon.[14] In short, by fixing in the close and striking in depth a force could break up, destroy and isolate an enemy force into unsustainable elements that could be defeated in detail. If the cohesion between echelons could be broken, then the enemy would culminate early, while friendly forces would maintain the freedom to concentrate a full combination of arms against each enemy formation in turn. The theory of victory in the era of informatized warfare is equally simple. The force should manoeuvre to bring the objective into the zone of opportunity. By blinding the enemy, defeating its reconnaissance elements, striking its artillery, jamming its communications and pushing forward friendly ISR and strike assets, the force may shape the enemy to disperse and cede ground until the axis of advance onto the objective is secured for an assault to be initiated. This geometry also

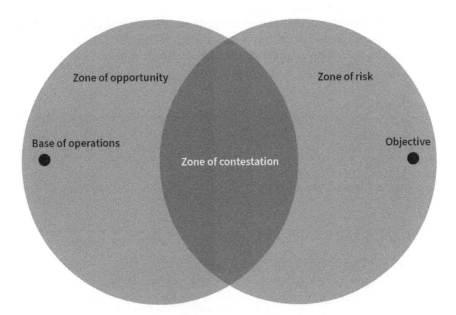

Figure 3 The new battlefield geometry.

[14] Eric J. Wesley, 'AUSA Global Force Symposium: Day 3 – Opening Remarks and Keynote Speaker', 28 March 2019: https://www.dvidshub.net/video/668339/ausa-global-force-symposium-day-3-opening-remarks-and-keynote-speaker, accessed 26 May 2019.

has a temporal as well as a spacial component. If the spacial dimensions of the zones are bounded by how far the enemy can see, communicate and shoot, the temporal dimensions relate to the duration of effects that may disrupt any of these variables. For example, the enemy may be temporarily unable to deliver effects against an area because electronic warfare is applied to disrupt the communication of firing solutions, UAV orbits are brought down and space-based systems are jammed. Conversely an area may become safe for concentration for a limited time because enemy artillery has been forced to relocate or has had its ammunition resupply disrupted. The creation of temporary opportunities for concentration can – in positional warfare – significantly alter the balance of advantage locally, locking in advances by manoeuvre elements and so pushing back the enemy's area of effect. Bringing a range of effects together is resource intensive and requires planning. Forces must therefore judge when they orchestrate these temporary windows of opportunity. If denial of enemy capability allows for the demarcation of zones to be temporarily altered, another is where a commander decides to prioritize and task their stand-in sensors. If we accept that these are limited in number then the decision to task them – and where they are pushed into the zone of risk – may open up additional areas to precise and responsive fires and thereby disrupt enemy concentration. Conversely, since by definition this means pushing into uncertainty, it could mean the attrition of crucial sensors and therefore the contraction of the area that a force is able to contest, enabling the enemy to move forward fires and reconnaissance assets.

Sound battlefield geometry should be applicable at ascending echelons, at least within tactical formations. Concepts at operational echelons may differ considerably. Nevertheless, it is worth considering the span or distances involved in a concept

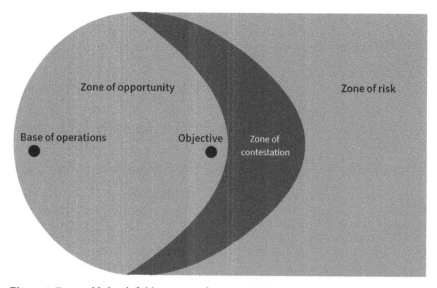

Figure 4 Favourable battlefield geometry for operational success.

because the area to be covered by a force must drive certain requirements as to its size. Within the traditional close, deep and rear battlefield geometry the object was to concentrate as much combat power as possible at the decisive point. To that end, there was a maximum level of concentration that was viable for a given size of force before units lacked room to manoeuvre. Thus, a brigade frontage in the attack was often concentrated to an optimal minimum of around 6 km. Greater concentration than this – while sometimes necessary – would produce diminishing gains in combat power as the number of vehicles in the formation could not all manoeuvre and cooperate, but instead were liable to foul one another's lines of sight and advance.

The new battlefield geometry is premised upon the initial phases of an operation having dispersed forces, while depths are shaped heavily by the field of regard of sensors, the viable distance over which communications can be maintained and the range of fires. It is worth articulating the relevant distances because these provide a rough guide for how much terrain a single tactical formation may have to be responsible for, and therefore may offer insight into the size and composition of future tactical formations. To begin, therefore, with fires a distinction must be drawn between unguided area effect, guided area effect and long-range precision fires. The first is cheap, with the primary constraint on the number of times it can be drawn upon being resupply. The second and third are expensive and so can only be drawn upon a limited number of times by a force. For unguided munitions ranges beyond 48 km are unlikely to have a sufficiently small circular error probable to target military formations reliably. Given size and weight constraints, most unguided fires are unlikely to reach beyond 40 km. Area effect munitions in particular must usually dispense sub-munitions at a sufficient altitude to achieve a spread and for those countries that adhere to the Oslo Convention, sub-munitions must be at a sufficient height to scan for targets. Since unguided munitions fly on a ballistic trajectory, this means that most area effect munitions will be most effective at a maximum range of 28 km for tube artillery and 38 km for rockets. Guided area effect capabilities are temporally rather than spatially constrained. Any strike on a moving target must cover the distance between launch and delivery point without the target escaping the searchable area of the munition. At present these variables constrain the viable range of these munitions to below 100 km if they are to be tactically useful. Additionally complex seekers might push the useful range to 150 km but this would increase cost and complexity. Long-range precision strike meanwhile is unconstrained by range insofar as tactical echelons are concerned as munitions can reach beyond operational depth. LRPF strikes however must hit their intended target directly to reliably achieve effect and so are best used against static targets or high-value targets with very specific characteristics that make the complexity of an active seeker munition with such range a reasonable economic trade-off. The constraint therefore on LRPF is largely reconnaissance and certainty of an identified target. The constraint on precision area effect munitions is principally the stockpile of available munitions which will always be realistically constrained. Another consideration is the ability to layer attacks. It is possible to achieve precision at ranges beyond 500 km with comparatively cheap munitions like loitering munitions.[15] However, these capabilities – while they can hold soft targets at risk – can be defeated by quite simple defences if they are the only threat. They become drastically more dangerous when employed in combination with other fires, because they often force a defender to manage conflicting imperatives to optimize their survivability.[16]

The importance of these range considerations is that they determine some minimal spacial requirements for a force. If the aim of manoeuvre is to bring the objective within the zone of opportunity, then we may conclude that the axis of advance to the objective must not be in range of enemy-unguided area effect artillery. This would require a screen to be in place with a frontage of up to 80 km, straddling the axis. Assuming there is an intention to have some space to manoeuvre towards the objective therefore it is reasonable to articulate a requirement for a force to maintain a reconnaissance and screening force across a frontage of 100 km. In practice terrain will prevent the enemy from threatening the force across such a wide area in many regions. In Estonia, for example, there is only 60 km of frontage available along the northern axis from Russia. A similar distance is the maximum frontage between major water obstacles on the Karelian axis into Finland. Thus the force may not be persistently dispersed to 100 km, but this is a reasonable training and capability benchmark. This does not protect the axis of advance from guided attack, and so preventing destruction of the force from these capabilities requires the suppression of the shooters, depletion of relevant ammunition during the shaping phase of operations or degradation of kill chains sufficiently to create a temporal opportunity.

Range also outlines the realistic depths of the different zones and how they relate to one another. If we assume that artillery will remain to the rear of a defensive screen, not least because of the vulnerability of its logistics, then unguided artillery is likely to practically hold an area at risk of around 30 km. Beyond this distance concentration remains risky if not accompanied by deception and other protective measures out to ranges of 90 km from the enemy screen. Ahead of the screening force the depth penetrated by enemy reconnaissance, and thus a force's vulnerability to precision strike, largely depends upon the vigilance and progress of the screening and counter-reconnaissance battle. We may therefore understand a contested zone of around 30 km in depth, and thereafter a fade of around 60 km from contest to opportunity dependent upon the progress of the reconnaissance and screening battle. If we further assume that the axis to assault an objective must be protected from indirect fires, then it follows that a force must be able to push its screen approximately 30 km beyond an objective, and that sustainment efforts will need to project across that space. There is, therefore, a need to push resupply and pull casualties in a tactical posture of distances of around

[15] Henry Thompson and Jack Watling, 'Assessing Dynamics of Control through Iranian Technology Transfer to Yemen's Houthis', *The RUSI Journal* (Vol. 167, No. 4, 2022), pp. 64–77, DOI: 10.1080/03071847.2022.2148557. https://www.tandfonline.com/doi/abs/10.1080/03071847.2022.2148557.

[16] Justin Bronk with Nick Reynolds and Jack Watling, *The Russian Air War and Ukrainian Requirements for Air Defence* (London: RUSI, 2022): https://static.rusi.org/SR-Russian-Air-War-Ukraine-web-final.pdf, accessed 3 December 2022.

60 km. These dimensions, therefore, determine the battlespace that must be managed within a realistic operational framework.

A further aspect of the future battlefield geometry to consider is the decisions that it presents for commanders. Within the rear, close, deep geometry the key decision points for the commander were the selection of the axis for a concentrated breakthrough, when to commit reserve forces to blunt either an enemy attack or counterattack, or to exploit the breakthrough via a forward passage of lines with the first echelon, and when key assets could be released from the close fight to affect a higher echelon's area of responsibility. The latter was a key question in resource allocation. When, for example, might an attack helicopter squadron be released from assisting the brigade close in order to plan and prosecute targets in the divisional deep.

Within the new battlefield geometry outlined above the commander has different decision points. The first key decision point is the rules of engagement given to fires capabilities relying on stand-off sensors alone. This is significant because expansive rules of engagement without positive identification of targets by stand-in sensors could significantly increase the depth at which enemy systems are held under threat and therefore expand the zone of contestation and limit the enemy's zone of opportunity. However, relaxed rules of engagement for fires relying on stand-off sensors also risk falling victim to enemy deception and the wastage of a considerable volume of munitions, including potentially scarce precision munitions if such engagements are prosecuted at considerable range. Relaxed rules of engagement could thus expand the zone of contestation for a limited period, only to see the enemy's zone of opportunity suddenly expand as the availability of precision munitions is exhausted.

The second key decision point for a commander is the axes that must be prioritized as regards protection from enemy fires. Crucially this is very different from determining which axis is the priority for a breakthrough because it means the dedication of forces elsewhere. The selection of key routes from the base of operations to the objective will determine the distances that must be screened by the manoeuvre force, and the key allocations of defensive systems to protect axes of approach. There is a direct tension between the desire to have a simple plan with a limited commitment of forces as compared with the ambiguity generated by fighting across a wider area. The more focused a force is on securing a specific route, the simpler the task for the enemy to identify this intent and to disrupt it. Moreover, since the routes selected will become critical once the force begins to seek to seize the primary objective, early identification of approach routes may enable the enemy to optimize the defence of the objective against the impending assault.

The third decision point is when a commander commits their assault forces against the objective. This is likely the decisive point in the operation and, given that this force cannot be readily extracted, reformed and recommitted, must bring about either the success or failure of the endeavour. It is also an effort that is likely limited in its duration and as outlined in the previous chapter, one in which ensuring a short battle is highly desirable if the objective is to be rapidly converted into a base of operation. A further requirement for informing this decision is accurately judging whether the enemy has been shaped sufficiently to enable concentration. Whether through pattern of life analysis, key indicators, battle damage assessment or reconnaissance, a headquarters must be able to accurately determine when the objective falls within the zone of opportunity. Conversely a key deception priority for the defender is to convince the enemy commander that concentration is safe when it is not.

Finally, a commander faces a key decision point as to when they can advance their base of operations. Attempting to do this too early risks the destruction of scarce sustainment assets and the collapse of an advanced force. Failure to move up the base of operations by contrast leaves a long and vulnerable supply chain that risks leaving the force inside an objective vulnerable to counterattack and isolation if the enemy can bring the MSRs into the objective back within the zone of contestation. The decision to advance the base of operation also requires an understanding of civilian sentiment as regards the permissibility of an objective, weighed against the human security demands that might require sustainment functions being brought forward.

Critical tasks and effects

The positional battlefield geometry outlined above brings with it a range of critical tasks that a military force must be able to perform if it is to be relevant to the future-operating environment. These critical tasks must be identified because a force's ability to execute them provides a framework for assessing the suitability of the force. The foremost tasks include reconnaissance, counter-reconnaissance and screening, shaping, destruction, assault, blunting, sustainment, stabilization and preparation. It is worth considering the dynamics of these tasks in turn.

Reconnaissance has always been a critical military function. Historically reconnaissance has primarily been aimed at locating the enemy and surveying terrain in order to inform friendly manoeuvre. The capacity for detailed stand-off terrain analysis has significantly reduced the requirement for physical terrain reconnaissance. This task now largely comes down to confirming and assuring stand-off collection rather than discovery. Similarly, tracking enemy force movements is now possible from stand-off ISR, and so finding the enemy is less important than providing positive identification and protection from enemy deception. Although reconnaissance has been a means of setting up precision strike, the volume of responsive fires that a reconnaissance team can now bring to bear means that active reconnaissance is a viable means of hunting and breaking up enemy formations. It is therefore now an aggressive combat function, and one that should be used to proactively expand the zone of contestation and limit the enemy's zone of opportunity. Reconnaissance forces are therefore an enabler of shaping by fire, which in turns makes the elimination of reconnaissance forces critical to the protection of the force.

Counter-reconnaissance and screening protects the force from observation by enemy stand-in reconnaissance and thereby shields it from fire. Historically screening has predominantly involved placing a skirmish line to disrupt enemy forces from impeding or dislocating an axis of advance. The concept of screening here, however, is predominantly concerned with countering infiltration, while counter-reconnaissance aims to blind the enemy by knocking down stand-in ISR and thereby denying battlespace to the enemy. The latter task also involves the dispersal of air defences. The aim of the screening forces should be to cover as much battlespace as possible, thereby providing the means by which the force demarcates and expands its own zone of opportunity. Screening units therefore must operate inside the contested zone.

Shaping may be defined as coercing the enemy to adopt a disposition of forces that is conducive to enabling an operation. The foremost method by which the enemy is shaped is through the application of fires. Holding parts of the force under threat – or convincing the enemy that they are under threat – will force dispersion. Dispersion necessarily dissipates combat power. Another aspect to shaping is convincing the enemy to withdraw systems that cannot be concealed and thereby extending their lines of supply or restricting the coverage of defensive systems like air defences. This shaping function becomes critical to the protection of main supply routes and axes of advance towards objectives. Convincing the adversary to either withdraw from holding key terrain under threat, or else to accept attrition of key systems, is a means by which a force can create opportunity for friendly concentration and therefore favourable force ratios within an area.

Destruction of enemy high-value targets or concentrations of enemy troops is the threat that most acutely achieves shaping. However, at times, the aim will be the destruction of the enemy force, which means deceiving the enemy into concentrating or exposing high-value systems when they believe it is safe to do so. This means concealing the manoeuvre of key fires assets and the obfuscation of stand-in sensors to give the false impression of an opportunity. Luring the enemy to expose themselves to unsustainable levels of attrition is a means by which the enemy can be denied a route to operational success, as destruction of key assault units will likely make the seizure of objectives non-viable.

Assault is a function that requires concentration and is therefore enabled by the enemy having been shaped away from the axis of advance towards an objective, which must be effectively screened. Assault may be understood in positional terms as the application of combat power to drive the enemy from vital ground. It is likely to be limited in duration as the intensity of operations necessary for successful assault can rarely be sustained for a prolonged period. Assault actions constitute the decisive phase of any offensive operation.

Blunting may be necessary for two reasons. In the first instance a blunting operation may arise as the defensive counter to an enemy assault if the enemy concentration cannot be destroyed by fires. This defensive blunting activity may be understood as an attempt to extend the time of an assault to the point where it exhausts the sustainment operation supporting it and therefore loses intensity and tempo. Conversely a blunting operation may immediately follow an assault. An assault onto vital ground, in which the approaches to the objective were effectively screened, will leave a force vulnerable to counterattack if defensive systems have not been moved forward. There will be a window of opportunity in which the assault force is tired, defensive positions have not yet been established, the force will be vulnerable to fire as the positions it is occupying will be known, and friendly fires will not have had the freedom to advance sufficiently to prevent strikes and counterattacks on the objective. Here, blunting operations must again slow a counterattack sufficiently for reconnaissance and fires functions to render its sustainment non-viable, forcing the enemy to withdraw forces from the objective area.

Sustainment is an essential component to all operations, concerning the provision of food, water, ammunition, fuel, spare parts, replacement personnel and medical care across the force. Logistics are a constant enabler in warfare. However, for much of history logistics activities have primarily been seen as supporting combat operations. Increasingly the risk that can be taken with sustainment is a critical command decision and the fight to sustain the force will require significant tactical innovation. Dispersion of forces also means that in many instances combat troops will need to support sustainment operations rather than be supported by them, to ensure the safe passage of supplies through the zone of contestation. The base of operations constitutes the positional heart of the sustainment effort. A further key decision point therefore is when the base of operations can be moved forward. In order to do this it is necessary to set the conditions for the safe basing of sustainment operations upon captured objectives.

Stabilization of objectives once captured comprises a number of interrelated activities, but fundamentally enables the advance of the base of operations to sustain the force against subsequent objectives. Stabilization includes the repair of critical infrastructure, liaison with local civilian authorities, information operations aimed at securing support among the local population, the management and distribution of key supplies to ensure human security, the systematic assurance of rear area security within a secured objective and the suppression of enemy collection within the objective area. Stabilization is not just an obligation but vital to securing a seized objective and rendering it exploitable by the force. If liaison with the civilian population is particularly successful, stabilization activities can also significantly reduce the commitment of forces in rear areas and thereby expand the force's capacity for further offensive manoeuvres.

Preparation draws upon many similar capabilities to stabilization but with a different intent. If stabilization is principally concerned with ensuring that an objective is brought back to normal functioning after combat operations, preparation concerns altering the environment to harden an area in advance of blunting activities, or the emplacement of additional military infrastructure including key sensor sites, air defences, semi-permanent bridges, forward arming and refuelling points, emergency landing zones and other enablement to allow for the rapid resupply or manoeuvre of friendly troops within the zone of opportunity. There is often a tension between stabilization and preparation in that the latter likely disrupts the free movement of civilians and could necessitate the requisitioning of houses to turn into strongpoints.

Understanding the key tasks comprising a successful operation it becomes possible to begin to frame a force structure that is capable of performing them. One of the distortions that can arise from the use of vignettes in military concepts, and especially in military PowerPoint presentations replete with CGI, is that the number of tasks that can be performed by a given number of personnel is exaggerated. It is not uncommon, for example, for autonomous vehicles to be shown engaging armoured targets with anti-tank-guided weapons, then defeating infantry with cannon, UAS with lasers, and finally enemy aviation with anti-air missiles.[17] This tendency is partly a narrative device – limiting the number of characters or objects that an audience must track to understand the art of the possible. Arguably it is something that is subliminally reinforced by both films and video games. The need to limit the number of characters, and vary the player experience, encourages directors and game designers to carry an infeasible array of weaponry, and for the work of small teams to have effects disproportionate to the scale of the capability they bring to bear. If a film revolves around a section, for example, and one of the characters has an anti-tank weapon, it is to be expected that they come across a tank and successfully knock it out. Rare is the film in which they come across a company of tanks and lack the ammunition to counter the threat. The point is that these tasks must be tackled by groupings of units and each unit must be task-organized, trained and equipped. Functionally there must be divisions of labour and a concentration of assets to tackle specific threats at the appropriate echelon, and under the right command. For example, if screening requires that UAS are interdicted from penetrating the friendly area of opportunity, how many air defence systems does this require, and how many reloads can be accommodated on each vehicle, without either making each vehicle prohibitively expensive, or requiring so many vehicles as to make dispersed deployment impossible? Before tackling the questions of what capabilities fall to each task it is first important to outline how the tasks might be grouped, and how they might be commanded.

The four combined arms systems

There is never one way to task-organize a force. What follows therefore should be understood to be indicative rather than prescriptive, serving as a demonstration of the distribution of capabilities needed across a combat formation. Broadly speaking the tasks outlined in this chapter fall into four very distinct systems, demarcated by the capability, command and control and training requirements for their execution. These systems might be labelled manoeuvre, fires, assault and support. Although each of these systems is integral to one another's capacity to fight an operation, architecturally they are distinct. Collectively we might envisage these four systems coming together to form a future Division, often defined as the tactical formation able to independently execute operations against an objective, bringing together the full combined arms capabilities of a force.[18] It is worth briefly explaining why these systems are distinct and the tasks they must each perform.

---

17 Sean MacFarland, 'TRADOC Mad Scientist 2017 Georgetown: Welcome to Day 2 w/ LTG Sean MacFarland', 9 August 2017: https://www.youtube.com/watch?v=Cp3NqSzSnTg, accessed 20 July 2022.
18 General Sir Nick Carter – RUSI Land Warfare Conference 2016, 28 June 2016: https://www.youtube.com/watch?v=K_MRagWu8p4 06.15-06.40, accessed 7 September 2021; William Slim, *Defeat into Victory* (London: Macmillan, 2009), p. 7.

The manoeuvre system includes troops responsible for reconnaissance and screening. Traditionally reconnaissance enables manoeuvre forces. However, on the future battlefield, it is the advance of sensors that allows the force to manoeuvre by fire, shaping the enemy to enable positional assault. The reason for reconnaissance and screening being a combined function is that these demand that a force operate across a wide area in a dispersed posture. Such a force must be able to move in self-supporting small packets, must have a limited dependence upon engineering and other mobility support and must have a communications architecture that allows a dispersed force to maintain mutual situational awareness in the face of electronic warfare. This includes a method for deconflicting a dispersed force to avoid fratricide. The force must have personnel comfortable with operating in isolation, with exposed flanks, and trained to call in, direct and deconflict fires and other airspace considerations like UAS. This system is the custodian of the stand-in sensor fleet. The manoeuvre system must also have a means of managing resupply that does not give away its position and allows it to avoid concentration. The manoeuvre system requires an array of sensors and the means to power them. Lacking significant mutual support it must hold significant organic lethality to avoid becoming fixed in contacts. This also prevents the enemy from pushing through the screen in small packets. The means by which the manoeuvre system is protected from a concentrated breakthrough is its relationship with the fires system, with which it must maintain robust communications.

The fires system is distinct from the manoeuvre system because the need to shoot and scoot to ensure survivability, the need to deconflict fires from air and aviation, the need to set up and defend key sensors and the high rate of supply needed all lead to very different parameters in force structure and deployment. Fires capabilities are likely to remain dispersed behind the screening element of the manoeuvre system. The tasks undertaken by the fires system include the shaping and destruction of the enemy. The threat of destruction of enemy force concentrations protects the manoeuvre force from breakthrough, while the relationship between reconnaissance and fires is what delivers shaping. The fires system may comprise close support fires, long-range precision fires, medium- and long-range air defence and the stand-off sensor screen. The force may also take under command capabilities like strike aviation or hold limited penetrating stand-in sensors for the purpose of target acquisition. The fires system should be supported by robust, low-latency data sharing between the control nodes for these capabilities. Although the speed of engagements and windows of opportunity necessitate control to be delegated to the lowest practical level within the fires system, the management of supply and the allocation of fires in support of the manoeuvre or assault system mean that centralized command of the fires system is ideal. This also allows for the stand-off sensor picture to be fused to allow for prioritization decisions. Finally, the centralization of command for the fires system also makes it the docking point within the land force for integration and deconfliction with air operations.

The assault system is responsible for high-intensity close combat over objectives and is therefore tasked with both assault and blunting operations. The separation of the assault system from other functions is essential for a number of reasons. Firstly, conserving its combat power until the environment has been shaped appropriately is critical. Secondly, the assault system must be able to plan and prepare for a specific problem, requiring a staff that is aware of but not drawn into command of the shaping battle. Thirdly, where the manoeuvre system is concerned with operating across a wide area at a sustained tempo, winning meeting engagements and skirmishing, the assault system is concerned with fighting at high intensity for a limited period in a tightly bounded area. The command and control requirements are also different. The assault system is likely to need to exercise control over units fighting in close proximity but not in line of sight, over subterranean operations, and in a battlespace full of civilians. The specialist training, equipment and psychological preparation necessary for the assault force to be successful is distinct. Another crucial point is that there is a mutual dependency between the fires and manoeuvre systems for much of an operation. The recce function within the manoeuvre system supports the long-range precision strike function within the fires system. The close support fires the serves the screening function within the manoeuvre system. Once the assault system is committed however, both manoeuvre and fires systems must align in support of the assault.

The support system should be responsible for sustainment, stabilization and preparation. Commanded from the base of operations the support system is required to arrange the supply of materiel into the battle area, its protected and concealed storage, and distribution to mutually agreed handover points with manoeuvre, fires and assault systems. The support system also holds the responsibility for liaison with the civilian population, force protection engineering, rear area security, assuring key communications infrastructure and point defence of critical nodes. The active planning of resupply and fighting to safely deliver supplies to and extract casualties from the manoeuvre system requires distinct training and battlespace management. The support system will need to routinely traverse other system command boundaries and must therefore establish and manage control measures to avoid fratricide. The support system is also likely to host the operational commander.

Having considered the geometry of the future battlefield, its operational logic and the tasks that a force must carry out, as well as how these tasks might be grouped, it becomes finally possible to match equipment to formations, and the scaling of formations to the necessary range of equipment. Alongside articulating the challenges presented by emerging technology, the first part of this book assumed that new technologies would be fielded by militaries, without outlining in what formations and density these capabilities could or should be maintained. The next four chapters consider each of the combined arms systems above and begin to match capabilities with their responsibilities. As this book moves from concepts to the more tangible focus on how future forces might be structured and equipped, there is a risk that it comes across as prescriptive. It must be stated from the outset that just as a force may organize other than in the four systems described above, it is equally not a hard and fast rule that a section should comprise twelve people or that an artillery battery contains six guns. Nevertheless, when examining where militaries will need to adapt to integrate new capabilities, where they will need to retain legacy systems, and which capabilities they can discard, the complexity and implications of fielding equipment are best assessed by mapping out the force structure requirements in detail. The resulting structure therefore is not prescriptive, but a guide that if well evidenced will highlight a range of proportions and dependencies which armies can manipulate as they pursue asymmetric advantage, but that they will contradict at their peril. It is precisely by outlining these challenges that we may understand, for instance, how many UAVs are realistically threatening a formation, and thus what capacity a viable defensive system must have to deal with simultaneous threats. Some adversaries may use more UAVs, and others fewer, but that choice will still fall within a range determined by the number of support vehicles and crews necessary to launch, pilot and recover the UAVs. The following chapters therefore consider the combined arms systems outlined above in turn, structuring them in relation to the tasks identified in this chapter.

7

The manoeuvre system

Whether for the sake of deities, doctrinaires, or just grand old traditions, there appears to be an immovable fixation upon Attrition theory within the U.S. Army, at times approaching the madness of the Aztecs' flowery wars in its application. The priorities found in doctrinal manuals, in schools, in combat units, and most important, in the souls of our leaders often appear to be aimed at destroying rather than defeating, at fighting fairly rather than stealing every possible advantage over the enemy, and at pursuing perfection in method rather than obtaining decisive results.[1]

Robert Leonhard

The manoeuvre system – as described in the previous chapter – is tasked with reconnaissance, counter-reconnaissance and screening, aggressively blinding the enemy, enabling fires and expanding the friendly zone of opportunity. The force must keep an area of up to 100 km in breadth under observation, though it will often be operating across a frontage of closer to 60 km. Since the aim of manoeuvre is to bring the force's objective into the zone of opportunity, it follows that the manoeuvre forces must envelop the objective. In doing so it will be divided on three axes: the left and right axes and one that closes on the objective. For this reason the manoeuvre system should be comprised of at least three command nodes. Each axis, meanwhile, must comprise three elements, the reconnaissance element, the screening element and a support element. Reconnaissance and screening are very different tasks. The former requires the ability to infiltrate the enemy. The latter demands a capacity to maintain wide area situational awareness and deny enemy infiltration. There is also an intimate relationship between the two functions. The reconnaissance forces protect the screening troops by using fires to prevent the enemy from concentrating enough combat power to break through the screen. Conversely, the screening element provides a backstop that allows the reconnaissance element to be bypassed without revealing its position and can support the reconnaissance element if it is actively hunted. The overriding driver for the design of the force is that it must be able to function in a dispersed posture, as it is to be expected to manoeuvre within range of and under threat from enemy fires. This chapter will first outline how the components of this force might be structured,

---

[1] Robert Leonhard, *The Art of Maneuver: Maneuver Warfare Theory and Airland Battle* (New York: Random House, 2009), p. 4.

the balance of old and new capabilities they might field and the support and personnel necessary to sustain these capabilities in the field. The chapter then considers how such a force might be fought on the defence through a tactical vignette. The chapter goes into a significant but uneven level of detail. This is because the detail showcases the components necessary to make new capabilities sustainable within a fighting structure.

The reconnaissance force

In 2013 the Finnish Army ran an experiment. The Finnish defence concept at the time envisaged light reconnaissance forces providing a skirmish screen in depth that would coordinate fires to slow down and break up invading Russian forces.[2] The reconnaissance troops were organized into three-man groups and were assigned areas of responsibility. The experiment saw the Finnish-armoured corps form up to imitate a Russian Motor-Rifle formation and attempt to penetrate the defence line. Pekka Toveri, who commanded the enemy force for the exercise, told his troops to keep their vehicles tightly packed and drive at full speed along their chosen axis of advance. The Finnish tankers got rolling and punched straight through the skirmish screen. They were moving too quickly for the skirmishers to call in fires to catch them. Moreover, having concentrated on one axis the defenders found that most of their troops were much too far away to reach the enemy armour before it was assaulting the objective. Most of the defenders found themselves running through dense wood, trying to catch up with tanks. The few Finnish defenders who confronted the armour were out of position and outnumbered. They did some damage, but far too little, and much too late.[3]

For reasons already outlined in this book, Pekka Toveri's tactics would be unlikely to succeed on the future battlefield. The Finnish military did not conclude from the experiment that a reconnaissance in depth was not important. However, they did conclude that if a force was to conduct reconnaissance and to harass an enemy, it needed to be more mobile than their main combat formations. Dismounted reconnaissance is a skill set that is highly important for reconnaissance troops – and will remain so – if they are to infiltrate positions to overlook key objectives. But the decision to proactively dismount to reduce signature does not mean that reconnaissance troops should begin dismounted. These forces must have organic mobility.

The question arises what this mobility should comprise. During Exercise Cold Response 2022 the Royal Marines sought to land reconnaissance teams at night on a defended shore. UK Commando Forces retain organic medical, engineering and artillery elements, and because there is a need to ensure that all parts of the force remain trained to conduct landings, the landing included 105mm light guns, their gun tractors and a BV-10 carrying a UAV team.[4] The results of this strange force

---

[2] Author discussions, Finnish general officer, Helsinki, November 2021.
[3] Author discussion, Pekka Toveri, London, April 2022 – highlighted previously by analysts from Finland's National Defence University, in discussions with the author, Helsinki, November 2021.
[4] Author observations, Exercise Cold Response, Norway, March 2022.

package – produced by exercise requirements rather than tactical judgement – nevertheless proved interesting. The large, noisy and slow-moving landing craft necessary to deploy such a force package was detected by the German OPFOR. Nevertheless, at the beach the reconnaissance party and BV-10 managed to slip away without getting caught and rapidly pushed inland. The artillery meanwhile ran into an enemy platoon and were unable to proceed with their mission, while the field ambulance ran into an enemy patrol and its crew were shot. The BV-10, despite clearing the beach, subsequently became stuck in some rough ground and was similarly removed from play. The German defenders felt quite pleased with their nights work. But they remained unaware that the reconnaissance party was now manoeuvring behind their lines. This rather strange set of occurrences highlights some interesting implications of working with vehicles in a reconnaissance role. Firstly, vehicles that are likely to work independently must operate in pairs. Without engineering support it is mission critical that vehicles can be recovered by one another. Reconnaissance vehicles must therefore be light. It is also imperative that they can be inserted quickly and subtly. This is not feasible for vehicles significantly larger than a civilian 4x4. Adhering to the rough dimensions of a civilian 4x4 meanwhile offers the capacity to create ambiguity for enemy stand-off sensors as to the nature of any signature they may detect. Similarly, large numbers of vehicles must necessarily attract attention. If two light role vehicles can fit into a support helicopter, for example, and most missions are ideally flown in pairs, then two support helicopters can deploy four vehicles. This is probably the largest force package that can realistically manoeuvre with a light signature. A vehicle of the proportions of a civilian 4x4 can carry upwards of five people, but with the volume of specialist equipment used by reconnaissance troops and the need for stretcher space in the event of a casualty, or the capacity to redistribute personnel if a vehicle is lost, we might posit three per vehicle being ideal. Thus, the approximate size of a reconnaissance section may be assessed at twelve personnel distributed across four vehicles, able to break into two teams of six for tactical manoeuvre.[5]

This rough baseline is important because it determines the number of specialisms and quantity of equipment that a reconnaissance section can carry. In terms of requirements the section's primary task is to locate the enemy and direct effects against them. The distribution of sensors and communications is therefore critical. Secondly, the section must have sufficient skills to be able to manoeuvre over terrain with limited support. Thirdly, the section must be able to hold the enemy at threat irrespective of what it runs into, though this is first and foremost to inflict damage and break contact rather than defeat the enemy. We may therefore envisage a section comprising a commander supported by a signaller qualified to call for and direct fires, and a sniper pair similarly qualified. This ensures that each pair of vehicles has the capacity to call for fires. The section must also have a medic, and an engineer, able to assist in overcoming obstacles and in conducting demolitions. The section might also contain an anti-tank-guided weapons operator, a MANPADS operator, a qualified UAS

---

[5] This rough grouping has been confirmed in multiple exercises and experiments to be optimal. Specific requirements may produce variation but as a planning assumption this is robust.

operator, a machine gunner and two reconnaissance troopers able to act as assistants to the MG and ATGM operators.

As regards equipment the section would ideally have a mesh network-enabled radio for their own communications, and a couple of additional means of reach back communications. The commander's vehicle, for instance, might have a 50-foot extendable mast with an electro-optical sensor and laser receiver and emitter at its top.[6] This would allow free-space optical communications while in woodblocks directed to the screening force to the rear. The section might also employ a satellite communications link to ensure that they could relay calls for fires to the fires system, with the dish off-set from their position and directionally shielded by terrain.[7] The spotter in the sniper pair would ideally have a thermal scope. The ATGM clue would likely include a powerful thermal imager. The UAV operator would ideally have a fixed wing UAS with a modular payload but would likely carry an electro-optical sensor. Collectively this would mean that each vehicle would hold one piece of heavy equipment: the mast, ATGM and reloads, MANPADS and reloads and UAS, respectively. Each vehicle might also have a length of metal on its flank that, once connected between vehicles, could allow the troop to cross small obstacles. Each vehicle ought to be equipped with a multispectral camouflage net deployable as a canopy from its roll cage or roof. It would also be advantageous for the vehicles to be hybrid electric drives so that they could run quietly for a time if manoeuvring close to enemy positions.

To consider the reconnaissance section as regards its capabilities therefore, each pair of vehicles would field a thermal and electro-optical sensor. In the case of the UAV this could be used to look beyond ridge lines to protect the force as it moves. It could also be used to interrogate an enemy unit without exposing the position of the reconnaissance team. Similarly, the mast could be used to look over tree lines or ridges and extend the line of sight of the force. The ATGM operator and spotter could similarly identify enemy infantry and vehicles using their thermal optics. Each vehicle pair would also be able to call for fires. From a defensive point of view each vehicle pair could deliver suppression, through sniping and the machine gun, respectively, and each could destroy medium weight vehicles or helicopters using the ATGM and MANPADS. One vehicle pair could destroy a tank. The other could threaten fast air. Between the range of their sensors and the fact that the section was tasked with infiltrating, and therefore moving through rather than blocking enemy units, one could envisage each section having up to 6 km of frontage, though normally it would be covering closer to 3 km. Six sections would thus cover up to 36 km of frontage. In reality, impassable terrain would almost always reduce the area over which the force operated. In addition, just as the reconnaissance screen would primarily draw upon fires for its effect, so too would it be tasked by the stand-off sensors controlled by the fires and screening forces, so that the focus of the

---

[6]   The author has had extensive experience deploying such a mast for observation rather than communication. It can be raised in around forty seconds and stowed along the length of a civilian car.

[7]   The use of this technique under enemy EW threat was observed to be successful when employed by Ukrainian reconnaissance forces on operations in June 2022.

reconnaissance force would be much more limited, directed at confirming returns. Even if spreading this force over 36 km would be unusual, it is worth considering the number of personnel necessary to cover the maximum required distance. Laying up by day under multispectral screens to observe the enemy, and moving by night, such a force would be the mainstay of the stand-in sensors available to the commander of the reconnaissance force.

The foremost limitation on the effect of these forces is their supply of fuel and therefore electricity to power sensors and communications, and thereafter food, water, spare parts and ammunition. The former constraint is what limits the volume of new capabilities that can be integrated into these units. Food and water for up to eight days may be carried on the vehicles. This could be extended to twelve at the expense of other equipment. There is, however, a direct correlation between the intensity at which the force depends upon its sensors and its endurance. Since the team is likely to remain in hide positions during the day, the use of solar panels may extend the endurance of key batteries in certain environments. Nevertheless, the assurance of resupply is critical to the endurance of the force. Although resupply is likely to be projected from higher echelons, control measures to manage the link-up between recce units and supply must be coordinated. This requires a detailed understanding of where the recce troops are, which is difficult if they are concealing themselves, moving frequently and minimizing their communications signature. It is also disruptive if small recce teams must arrange to meet with resupply vehicles. For this reason it makes more sense to have a separate node able to assure communications with higher echelons and make these arrangements. We may therefore envisage a vehicle pair supporting each pair of sections to form a reconnaissance platoon. This vehicle pair would work forwards of the screening force, organizing the drawing forward and caching of supplies for reconnaissance teams to collect. To do this it is vital that this team can certify that an area is not under observation, and it therefore makes sense for them to have a passive sensor array. The most dangerous detection method is likely from UAS and so this passive sensor array would also usefully be able to eliminate UAS. A mast, for example, with an acoustic, passive radar and electro-optical system would passively detect UAS, and could then use an RF jammer to isolate the system and high-energy laser to burn out the UAS's sensor payload.[8] The other vehicle pair would likely need to carry the platoon commander, a communicator and medic, while the C-UAS platform could carry a systems operator, the platoon sergeant and a mechanic trained to conduct basic field repairs on the standard reconnaissance platform.

Finally, the reconnaissance force must also be tied into the planning of wider operations. If platoon commanders can direct their sections to pursue updated priorities for stand-in reconnaissance, informing higher echelon planning requires significant time communicating and therefore under greater exposure. Above the

---

[8]   Destruction of UAS-borne sensors effectively denies the capability but requires drastically less power than the destruction of the UAS. Such a system also has a high volume of possible shots and because of the comparatively low power necessary can be made small enough to sit atop a mast.

three reconnaissance platoons aligned per axis, therefore, ought to be a command post behind the protection of the screening force able to liaise with the platoon commanders about the current operating picture and answer the queries of higher echelons as well as coordinate bringing resupply forwards. This would constitute the company command post. We might envisage this comprising two sections, each comprising a command vehicle, an ambulance and two utility vehicles. These would see the commander and company NCO have a primary and secondary command post, each with the ability to organically move up supplies with a vehicle pair if urgent, or to recover casualties. The reconnaissance company envisaged here, therefore, would comprise 114 personnel mounted in 38 light utility vehicles.

The screening force

While reconnaissance units proactively shape the enemy by finding, identifying and calling in fires, this is only sustainable so long as the reconnaissance sections can be resupplied. It also only achieves progress if the space the enemy vacates as a result of shaping can be occupied or otherwise denied to reinfiltrating enemy. If the reconnaissance force will routinely allow the enemy to bypass its positions, it is vital that these enemy units run into a hard backstop. The fires system should prevent enemy forces concentrating above the size of the company group. This, therefore, is the size of force that the screening force must be able to outmanoeuvre and fight, while also engaging in a sustained counter-reconnaissance battle. Given the area that must be screened, this cannot be effectively achieved by occupying a continuous line. Instead, forces must maintain nodes at intersections, bridges, villages and high points while maintaining sensor coverage of the spaces in between and the capacity to manoeuvre to defeat enemy-penetrating groups. Furthermore, this force must be able to defeat enemy aviation and armour, tasks that demand heavier systems than can be carried. The force must therefore be mounted. For those units seeking to hold key terrain they are likely to come under indirect fire. Protecting these personnel from fragmentation is therefore important. As these units are also expected to confront enemy vehicles, they are also liable to come under direct fire and should therefore be armoured. Unlike the reconnaissance force, which aims to avoid confrontation, this force seeks it.

Although this force will need to carry highly lethal armaments and have some protection, its mobility remains paramount and given how far into the contested zone it must operate it cannot maintain a large support force. The force will often need to operate in small packets, likely around four vehicles, though these packets will likely converge upon enemy forces so that up to eight vehicles may be involved in a particular engagement. This is important because it sets organic mobility and recovery criteria that limit the weight of the platforms and therefore places upper limits on protection and firepower. For example, unless the force is to be supported by assault bridges, it will likely need to be amphibious, placing an upper weight limit of around 32 tonnes on the platforms, and unless the vehicle is to have an extremely large signature, likely closer to 26 tons.[9] This kind of weight is also recoverable by civilian utility vehicles and is compliant with much rural infrastructure. However, at 32 tons it is unrealistic to achieve protection above Level 3 STANAG 4569, broaching Level 4 at key points. Without a requirement for amphibiosity the primary constraint is infrastructure, creating a maximum viable weight of approximately 42 tons and a more optimal weight closer to 38 tons,[10] allowing a vehicle to have Level 4 protection up to Level 6 on key points. A 26-ton vehicle is likely better, but understanding the upper limit is useful. Vehicle design in either category may reduce the risk to the crew even if it cannot prevent the vehicle being mission-killed by larger calibre fire. One key requirement – irrespective of the decision on amphibiosity – is the need for a modular payload in order to enable a single vehicle type to fulfil the span of required roles. This is to minimize the logistics and maintenance burden of a dispersed force. Such a vehicle may be wheeled or tracked, though tracks are clearly preferable offering greater tactical mobility and greater survivability and endurance. Although the mobility of wheeled vehicles has improved considerably in recent years, wheels remain vulnerable to fire and there is a considerable logistic burden in transitioning between tyre types for different surfaces. Rubber tracks, meanwhile, overcome most of the issues of damage to road surfaces caused by metal tracks and offer reliability across the 48 by 70 km relevant to the area of responsibility for this formation.[11]

The screening force may be understood to comprise two types of unit: those tasked with occupying points and those tasked with manoeuvring, creating a hammer and anvil. To deal with the latter type, there are two further sub-types: those that seek direct engagement and those that seek indirect engagement. Given the limitations on protection it is necessary for the force to be able to converge effects without concentrating and therefore engage beyond line of sight. To deal with the indirect group first, the capacity to break up an enemy unit must depend upon bringing multiple threats to bear simultaneously so as to overcome defensive systems. ATGMs for example are inefficient if used against enemy vehicles with active protection, but area effect weapons to break the sensors upon which an APS depends, followed by ATGMs will likely succeed. Working on the basis that the force works in packets of four, and always aims to keep in pairs to enable peer recovery, we can argue that the indirect fires capability should comprise unguided and guided weapons and that the unguided weapons will need a higher volume of fire and therefore should be more numerous than the guided weapons. The force must also be able to threaten aircraft as a key part of its screening function. Thus we might envisage four vehicles, one

---

[9] Author interviews with R&D team at KMW, Munich, August 2021; author interviews, USMC Battle Lab, US, October 2021; note that the USMC ACV is not just amphibious, but intended for ship to shore movement and is therefore a larger platform.

[10] Council of the European Union, 'Directive (EU) 2015/719 of the European Parliament and of the Council of 29 April 2015 Amending Council Directive 96/53/EC Laying Down for Certain Road Vehicles Circulating within the Community the Maximum Authorised Dimensions in National and International Traffic and the Maximum Authorised Weights in International Traffic', Official Journal of the European Union (L115/1, 6 May 2015).

[11] Jon Hawkes, 'Primer: Composite Rubber Track (CRT)' Institute of Tankology, 17 January 2022: https://www.tanknology.co.uk/post/__crt, accessed 20 July 2022.

carrying four to eight ATGMs able to engage beyond line of sight out to 10–25 km depending on type,[12] two vehicles each carrying something equivalent to a 120mm mortar or recoil dampened 105mm howitzer, and a vehicle mounting four to six semi-automatic command to line-of-sight (SACLOS) anti-aircraft missiles with a range of 6–8 km and critically, the ability to engage at medium altitude. SACLOS systems offer no warning to the aircraft being engaged other than the missile launch itself and are highly resistant to countermeasures. If the air defence vehicle also uses a thermal and electro-optical camera to identify and classify air threats, then this can be used to maintain both situational awareness against infiltrators and detect aircraft without revealing the position of the air defence system. The automated guidance of an identified target can also eliminate crew error as a cause of inaccuracy in guidance. The two mortar or howitzer vehicles might also carry UAVs to be used to organically correct their fall of shot, further enabling the force to detect infiltrators without moving too much and thereby revealing the force to GMTI or other enemy stand-off sensors.

The direct fires group, by contrast, must be able to confront enemy vehicles and infantry. The threat from ATGMs means that these vehicles likely require hard kill APS. Without this capability the force would be vulnerable to infiltrators steadily attriting its vehicles. With an APS by contrast the group would likely survive the volume of ATGMs that an infiltration party could bring to bear and thereafter destroy them with direct fire. This counter-reconnaissance function also demands that the direct fires group have powerful sensor capabilities. The obvious requirement is for a powerful thermal sight and commander's thermal optic. If the latter were mounted on an extendable mast, with a laser emitter and receiver, this would enable a wide area to be kept under observation while hull down and would also support free-space optical communication with the reconnaissance forces. Operating in two pairs of two vehicles, the direct fire group could have one vehicle in each pair equipped with such a mast and the other with an acoustic board, enabling passive detection of vehicle movement from beyond line of sight. As regards firepower they ought to be able to defeat Infantry Fighting Vehicles in direct fire and thus carry a main armament of between 30 and 60mm, with both programmable air-burst and armour piercing ammunition. If this armament were mounted on a remote weapon station, it could be programmed to adjust its sighting for different kinds of targets, allowing destruction of UAS and helicopters as well as ground targets. It may be possible to mount a 105mm smoothbore cannon to such a vehicle, but this is likely unnecessary, and enemy main battle tanks ought to be engaged by the indirect group. As regards communications the vehicles would have sufficient power – which could be accessed for a sustained period through the use of an auxiliary power unit – to run a strong mesh network between themselves and act as a relay for the recce screen to the fires group. Another useful capability

---

[12] Successful examples of such a capability include Azeri forces employing Spike NLOS in Nagorno-Karabakh and Ukrainian forces employing ground launched Brimstone on the southern front in May 2022, author interviews, Ukrainian officers, June 2022.

is Identify-Friend-or-Foe (IFF) enabling rapid dispersed manoeuvre without rigid control measures to prevent fratricide.[13]

Both direct and indirect groups should have vehicle crews of four people. Militaries around the world have been experimenting extensively with reduced vehicle crews of sometimes two people.[14] While this works in short experiments it is sub-optimal on operations. Within the assault force this may be viable. Within the manoeuvre force it poses challenges and often reduces the capacity to exploit advances in technology. There are two reasons for this: fatigue and cognitive load. To begin with fatigue, the screening force must function in a dispersed posture. To operate the vehicles systems effectively it requires at least two people. One, for example, can monitor the sensors while another drives, or engages in other tasks like communicating with other elements. For many tasks – especially those involving maintenance or extracting the vehicle from terrain, it will take more than two people. Thus, for much of an operational period three people must be active, and the minimum is two. It therefore follows that with a crew of three crews will struggle to get sufficient sleep and their performance will deteriorate significantly over time. The issue of cognitive load is different. The driver will have their attention taken up driving the vehicle. The gunner will be identifying and engaging targets. The commander is theoretically responsible for coordinating with other vehicles and keeping situational awareness to direct where the vehicle should be going and which targets it should prioritize. This division means that there are tanks – like Russian T-series and the South Korean K2 – that function with a crew of three. When the system comes under stress however it becomes harder for three crew to cover all relevant tasks. Consider, for example, a vehicle trying to reverse at night, engage a threat to its front and coordinate an indirect engagement against the target. Working out the route by which it should reverse is easier with an extra pair of eyes, just as it may be exceedingly useful to have a fourth person to monitor the squadron net and keep an eye on additional threats.[15] Putting aside whether the extra capacity is useful during intense activity, one can quickly see how a fourth member of crew is essential if the vehicle is to exploit additional sensors or capabilities. If vehicles have UAS for example, who is to get out, launch, pilot, monitor and recover the UAS without reducing the capacity of the vehicle to fight.[16] Insofar as technology allows crews to integrate more systems this is a good thing, but it does not necessarily drive down the advantage of having a full crew compliment. Vehicles in the indirect fires group – because the cognitive burden is less outside of the direct fire zone – might

---

[13] Tactics for vehicle-mounted IFF are significantly developed in South Korea, author observations of 28 Battalion, ROKA, South Korea, May 2022.

[14] As with the Israeli demonstrator of a next-generation armoured vehicle: https://www.youtube.com/watch?v=ZJgvhsgTzCc, accessed 20 July 2022.

[15] Author experimentation regarding cognitive load from the commander's position of a Challenger 2 on Salisbury Plain, June 2021, contrasted with observations of T-series tanks being operated in Iraq, October 2017.

[16] In the 1991 Gulf War, US cavalry reconnaissance troops in Bradleys used a fourth crew member in the back for a range of additional tasks, see Mike Guardia, *The Fires of Babylon: Eagle Troop and the Battle of 73 Easting* (New York: Casemate, 2015).

realistically function with a crew of three, but this will likely increase to four if these vehicles are supposed to utilize additional sensors.[17]

Finally, there is the infantry to hold key points. These troops should have protected mobility. Four such vehicles per platoon, with a driver, section commander and seven additional dismounts would field a platoon of thirty-two infantry and four mounted personnel. This would allow for three eight strong sections, each with a machine gun and anti-tank weapon. The platoon would also include a platoon commander, platoon sergeant, medic, signaller, a sniper pair and MANPADS team. The drivers could enable resupply shuttles. These troops would provide the ability to control key terrain, interact with the local personnel and act as the anvil against which the enemy must advance, only to be fixed and thereafter struck by the hammer provided by the direct and indirect fires groups. Thus, the force would hold a squadron of cavalry, comprising three troops of eight vehicles and twenty-eight to thirty-two personnel each, and a company of mechanized infantry comprising three platoons of forty personnel and four vehicles each. If cavalry troops and infantry platoons were linked up, this would create a multiple with three elements – infantry, cavalry and supporting fires – which could be coordinated by a command group comprising an additional four vehicles and crews containing a command and control vehicle with driver, vehicle commander, multiple commander and signaller, an ambulance with driver, commander and two medics, an engineering vehicle with a crew of four and a logistics vehicle with a crew of four, including the senior NCO.

Mapping out the exact number of personnel and vehicles, their rough weights and armament are useful because it highlights what is required to actually field future technologies. The force described above, for example, would be able to deploy in twelve groups of four vehicles commanded as three multiples. Each multiple would be able to generate six UAS, would contain two vehicles with acoustic arrays able to detect vehicles out to 10 km, two elevated thermal cameras, a further eight mounted thermal cameras and two dismounted thermal cameras, and an ability to passively track and identify air targets. At maximum dispersion therefore the force could maintain acoustic coverage of an area 45 km in breadth and maintain that entire frontage under continuous multispectral observation. When combined with the early warning gathered by the reconnaissance force and with its screening reinforced by stand-off sensors, infiltration against this force would be difficult. Infiltration in sufficient force to engage the multiples, moreover, would make the enemy vulnerable to fires. Early warning through stand-off sensing and stand-in reconnaissance meanwhile would allow the force to prepare for enemy attack.

The support force

The forces outlined above must be sustained in the field. They also need other classes of support held organically to the formation. These support functions should be

---

[17] Vehicles like the Patria NEMO can operate with three crew, as have Stormer SHORAD vehicles in the past, but the manual and cognitive load on these vehicles is high already, even without additional sensors and capabilities, as observed inside both vehicles, the former in October 2019 and the latter on Thorny Island, UK, in July 2021.

outlined. They include, command and control, mobility and counter-mobility support, logistics, medical and mechanical functions. To begin with the logistical requirements, each multiple in the screening force requires fuel, ammunition, food and water and spare parts. We may therefore envisage four vehicles – a fuel bowser and three supply trucks – being assigned to each multiple. These groups could move behind the screening force on a carrousel system, so that the groups from the screening multiple can link up with the resupply vehicles in small packets. The other support functions across the screening force should be task-organized rather than assigned to specific units. Each multiple, for example, already holds an engineering vehicle in support. However, some engineering challenges will require a surge in resource. Thus, an additional three engineering vehicles should sit in the support force. Since engineering activity of this nature will require being in place for some time, this grouping should also have an air defence platform assigned to it of the same type as allocated to the indirect fires group in the screening force.

The same may be said for electronic warfare support. When it comes to direction finding – the reconnaissance function within electronic warfare – targets need to be triangulated. This requires three points of bearing for highly accurate targeting. Thus, another grouping of four vehicles comprising the electronic warfare baseline in three and an air defence vehicle as escort would similarly manoeuvre to monitor the enemy. The final air defence vehicle in the formation would thus sit with the command group for the screening force, comprising a vehicle for the principal planning group, a vehicle for the wider staff and a communications vehicle responsible for beyond line-of-sight satellite and radio frequency communication with higher echelons. The formation's backup command post of a C2 vehicle and communications vehicle would sit with the force's medical facility, comprising an ambulance and a second medical vehicle. Finally, the force would need a fitter group comprising four vehicles: two mounted workshops and two recovery vehicles, able to deal with damaged vehicles. The burden on this group would be reduced by the capacity of the force to conduct peer recovery across its platforms. Nevertheless, fitters are essential to maintain a force that must necessarily suffer mechanical failures over the course of an operation.

The command and control of the manoeuvre force would cover three essential functions. Firstly, it would maintain situational awareness of where reconnaissance and screening forces were deployed, the status of their resupply by the support force and what they were observing on the ground. Second, the command group would need to understand the operational priorities of the higher command and thereby disseminate intent to the company commanders to be able to execute effective reconnaissance, and to the multiple commanders as to where to prioritize as their vital ground. Another important function of the overall command of the manoeuvre system would be to accumulate battle damage assessment and assess enemy strength, dispositions and losses, to be able to present a coherent J2 picture to higher command from the sum total of stand-in reconnaissance collection. The most important aspect of this assessment would be to judge where had been rendered safe from enemy fires through shaping and which routes might fall within the zone of opportunity.

The totality of the force thus far described would comprise three battlegroups, one covering the left, another the right, while the third closed around the objective. Each battlegroup would comprise four companies: a reconnaissance company, a mechanized infantry company, a light cavalry company and a support company. Having considered how such a force might be structured and equipped, we can now examine how these elements might cooperate in the fight.

Fighting the manoeuvre system

Having described the potential components of a future manoeuvre system it becomes possible to describe how a force might function as a combined arms formation. There are, of course, many types of mission and permutations of how they might be executed. However, an indicative vignette can illustrate how such a system overcomes the challenges in the future-operating environment described in the first chapter. It also highlights where the limits of such a system of fighting lie and therefore its dependencies on other formations. In establishing this vignette it is assumed that the fires system will shape the enemy into forces no larger than company group in the attack, and that the company group must be halted by a sector of the recce screen and a multiple from the manoeuvre force. The attacking company is to operate in a manner consistent with current tactics but fielding advanced systems augmenting its usual order of battle. For this defensive vignette it is assumed that an enemy company is tasked with seizing a village on an intersection with a main supply route (MSR).

The enemy company group comprises four main battle tanks and eight infantry fighting vehicles, supported by a pair of reconnaissance vehicles, two air defence vehicles, two attack helicopters, a UAV orbit and available call-down fires from a supporting artillery battery. The force advances along the edges of the MSR towards the village in the early hours of the morning. The axis of advance is detected initially by GMTI radar held at higher echelon and this allows one of the recce teams to bring the force under direct observation using a UAV. The UAV is shot down by one of the air defence systems; however once the force's identity has been confirmed, it can be tracked by GMTI. The recce section that had launched the UAV sets up further along the MSR and, as the recce vehicles and helicopters pass, fire their MANPADS at the second helicopter, downing it, before pulling back through a woodblock to avoid pursuit. The enemy throws up a UAV to track them, but this is engaged and blinded by the recce platoon's CUAS vehicle. The second helicopter manoeuvres to find cover, while the enemy reconnaissance vehicles move to screen the flank of the company against the recce section.

As the enemy company slows at a pinch point in the road, their acoustic sensors light up to warn of incoming fire. Six 120mm mortar bombs fall in a line along the formation, shredding aerials and damaging the radar for the active protection systems on some of the vehicles. Seconds later four long-range ATGMs crest the treeline and dive onto the column. An MBT and an IFV are hit, one ATGM misses and the fourth is intercepted by an APS. The supporting enemy battery send counterbattery fire against the heavy mortar, but it has already displaced. Simultaneously another six mortar bombs land along the road, fired by the second mortar vehicle. This time the bombs catch some infantry who have dismounted, and mission kill another IFV. Not wanting to be caught in a killing zone and fearing the depletion of combat power the enemy commander orders the force to maintain its momentum and accelerate. Around the corner they see a rolling approach to the small village that constitutes their objective, around 5 km distant.

As the remaining enemy force begins to shake out and close the distance, an ATGM comes in from the recce troops, still working from woodblocks to the flank. This hits another MBT that had suffered damage from the mortar fire, crippling the vehicle. Four kilometres from the village two ATGM launches are detected from the houses and the attacking force pops smoke, while the helicopter overhead begins to work forwards to engage the ATGM firing posts. It fires TV-guided missiles from dead ground, but the ATGM teams in the village have displaced. As the enemy continues to advance, another salvo of four long-range ATGMs comes in from the flank. Two are caught by APS but the last two knock out the remaining tanks. The helicopter also finds itself hit by cannon fire from the right as four armoured vehicles emerge from a woodblock and engage the infantry fighting vehicles with their rapid-fire cannon. The enemy by this point dismounts its infantry to seek cover. They manage to fire an ATGM, but it is caught by the APS of the advancing vehicles on their right. Sniper fire begins to come in from the recce section to their left and machine gun fire from their front. From the right 50mm airburst shells begin popping above the infantry and as they seek cover twelve further mortar rounds come arcing in. Having suffered heavy casualties the force begins to withdraw.

Everything may have gone right in the vignette above, but the engagement as described is consistent with outcomes observed in Nagorno-Karabakh and Ukraine, and the lethality of the ATGMs described above is lower than that achieved in Syria where the probability of kill was often as high as 0.7.[18] Although ATGMs are described as doing the killing in the above vignette it is important to understand that they are not – by themselves – sufficient to produce such an outcome. The ability to rapidly interrogate indications from GMTI while the enemy is still some kilometres from line of sight enables a mobile force to dynamically set up the killing area. It also allows synchronization of effects between blast and ATGM engagements, which together account for the lethality.[19] The mobility and communications of the defenders were also vital to allowing manoeuvre to optimally counter the attack. ATGM teams alone would have been insufficient or else highly inefficient. Without the blast effects enemy APS would have been more effective. Without salvos of coordinated ATGMs the Pk would have been reduced. Finally, the ability to shoot down enemy aviation and UAVs was critical to giving the manoeuvre force freedom to break contact. In short,

---

[18] Jacub Janovsky, 'Seven Years of War – Documenting Syrian Rebel Use of Anti-Tank Guided Missiles', *Bellingcat*, 4 May 2018: https://www.bellingcat.com/news/mena/2018/05/04/seven-years-war-documenting-syrian-rebel-use-anti-tank-guided-missiles/, accessed 20 July 2022.

[19] A similar scenario at shorter ranges played out in 2003 when a company of the Household Cavalry mounted in CVRT came into contact with an Iraqi Tank Battalion, knocking out the armour as it sought to advance over a series of berms, only to be engaged by Swingfire missiles. Author interviews with British officers involved in the engagement, Warminster, January 2019 and London, August 2021.

such a concept depends upon an interdependent set of capabilities. A larger attacking force of course would pose a significant challenge to the screen, requiring either other multiples to be drawn into a concentrated defence or – preferably – the fires system to break up the attack. The interrelationship between the manoeuvre system and fires system is crucial to understanding how such a small force can remain combat effective, and also how the manoeuvre force can conduct offensive operations. The fires system, therefore, is the focus of the next chapter.

8

The fires system

Anti-tank missiles slowed the Russians down, but what killed them was our artillery. That was what broke their units.

A senior adviser to General Valerii Zaluzhnyi[1]

Throughout the twentieth century fires caused the majority of casualties in combat.[2] In the twenty-first century the lethality, range and accuracy of fires have all increased. Range has also given fires the opportunity to field much more complex enablement, allowing for the exploitation of far-reaching technological capabilities that transform their employment on the battlefield. In the previous chapter the structure of the manoeuvre system was influenced more by the threat from fires than by technological advances fielded by the manoeuvre forces themselves.[3] Capabilities like artificial intelligence offer more flexible main armaments – able to target air and ground targets dynamically – and the integration of multiple sensors on a vehicle. For the fires system, however, such capabilities can be more widely leveraged than in manoeuvre forces. The primary purposes of the fires system, as outlined in Chapter 6, are the shaping and destruction of the enemy. In outlining the possible contours of a future fires system to understand its impact on how the force can fight, this chapter breaks the fires system into four components: command and control, target acquisition, lethal fires and non-lethal fires. Having outlined what these might include the chapter explores how the fires system, in conjunction with the manoeuvre system, can conduct offensive shaping.

Directing the storm

Operation *Guardian of the Walls*, in which the Israeli Defence Forces conducted an extensive bombardment of Gaza in retaliation to a barrage of rockets fired by Hamas

---

[1] Author interview, a senior advisor to the commander of the armed forces of Ukraine, conducted in Ukraine, April 2022.

[2] Robert Whalen, *Bitter Wounds: German Victims of the Great War, 1914-1939* (New York: Ithaca, 1984), pp. 41–2; Phillip Karber, 'Lessons Learned from The Russo–Ukrainian War', Potomac Foundation, 8 July 2015, p. 17.

[3] The most extensive theorizing of this relationship and the transformative effects on manoeuvre warfare are contained in Guy Hubin, *Perspectives Tactiques* (Paris: Economica, 2009).

in early 2021, revealed a great deal about the future direction of fires.[4] Above Gaza Israeli UAVs maintained layered surveillance of the strip. Along the boundaries of the blockaded enclave Israeli reconnaissance personnel peered through their binoculars. Unit 8200 meanwhile maintained a constant watch on Palestinian communications. Whereas historically these disparate elements of the force would have either fed into a targeting cycle that would subsequently direct a fire control headquarters to task artillery and aircraft onto target, or else in the case of the reconnaissance troops require assigned guns in support of units,[5] the IDF managed fires onto Gaza through a unified system. Fireweaver, an Israeli software package, allows multiple ISR feeds to populate targets to be prosecuted dynamically by available shooters.[6] Targeting data can be as simple as a smartphone photograph, which the software can stitch from the vertical plane into the horizontal plane of a satellite image to convert pixels into coordinates. The result was rapid and devastating for the Palestinians.

Israeli fires in Gaza represented the practical application of capabilities that have been widely theorized and pursued by other states. In the United States, Joint All Domain Command and Control aspires to build an expeditionary capability to similar ends. US Naval Integrated Fire Control-Counter Air already manages real-time cooperative engagements though against a narrower set of targets. The PLA meanwhile observed Israeli operations with considerable interest, hoping to leverage AI to similarly realize their concept of a Joint Firepower Campaign.[7] Russian modernization has also aspired to build a unified digital fires architecture,[8] though it has not yet materialized in practice. There are major hurdles to realizing the Israeli model more widely. Israel faces an adversary with minimal EW capability and controls the communications infrastructure surrounding the battlespace. A similar advantage helps the US Navy: it is connecting a small number of platforms, mainly within line of sight, that each has a large amount of available power.[9] It is therefore useful to explore how far such a system can be created – and what is required to deploy it – for a future expeditionary land formation.

An effective fires headquarters must be able to understand where friends and enemies are on the battlefield in real time if it is to appropriately allocate fires. Historically, fires have usually processed and responded to calls for effect by supported

[4] Anna Ahronheim, 'Israel's Operation against Hamas Was the World's First AI War', *The Jerusalem Post*, 27 May 2021: https://www.jpost.com/arab-israeli-conflict/gaza-news/guardian-of-the-walls-the-first-ai-war-669371, accessed 20 July 2022.

[5] Ronen Bergman, *Rise and Kill First: The Secret History of Israel's Targeted Assassinations* (New York: Random House, 2018); process observed during an exercise in the Negev, July 2019.

[6] 'FIRE WEAVER ™ – A networked combat system (urban scenario)', Rafael, 4 April 2019: https://www.youtube.com/watch?v=gJHjcukNbpw, accessed 20 July 2022.

[7] Sam Cranny-Evans conducted a study of PLA discussion of Operation Guardian of the Walls, August 2021.

[8] Sam Cranny-Evans, 'Introducing the Russian Radio-Electronic Fire Strike Concept', *RUSI Defence Systems*, 5 January 2022: https://rusi.org/explore-our-research/publications/rusi-defence-systems/introducing-russian-radio-electronic-fire-strike-concept, accessed 20 July 2022.

[9] Jack Watling, 'More Sensors than Sense', Jack Watling and Justin Bronk (Eds.), *Necessary Heresies: Challenging the Narratives Distorting Contemporary UK Defence* (London: RUSI, 2021).

elements of the force. This, however, gives few options for senior commanders to prioritize targets. Instead, the prioritization decision is largely a product of to whom control of the relevant guns is assigned and the munitions allocated to each mission. Because increased range allows the same guns or launchers to support multiple lines of effort, it is important that commanders can assign their fires dynamically. The capacity to proactively direct this storm demands access to multiple data feeds for the purpose of target acquisition. It is worth outlining these feeds, their characteristics, the tasks necessary to exploit them, and thus the command and control laydown relevant to a future fires formation. Each feed of data entering the fires control headquarters has its own analytical logic and latency issues. Some feeds are constant, others are periodic. The feeds must therefore be fused to accurately confirm the identity of tracks and to then track the identified objects in real time, to direct accurate fires against legitimate targets.

At the outer edge of the fires architecture, therefore, are constant feeds. These might include GMTI, electromagnetic spectrum activity and the common air picture. The GMTI feed will be available so long as there is a connection with the collection platform. Each of these feeds requires different analysis. A GMTI feed requires pattern recognition against known speed, signature and formation characteristics of targets. It also requires marking where identified tracks go still and therefore disappear from the feed, so that those objects can be reacquired once they start moving again.[10] Much of this analysis can be conducted by AI, which can measure the distribution between groups of vehicles and compare it with historical patterns to assess the level of confidence that identified movement belongs to a particular class of object. Such a process of classification, however, requires monitoring by a human, to approve or correct AI judgement and to determine whether the data have been corrupted. Left unsupervised there is a risk that false data could be fed into the fusion process and thereby corrupt wider identification and assessment. EMS activity is similarly well suited to AI analysis. AI can both assess the alignment of detections – direction finding – and pinpoint the pattern of emission to a particular platform type, and potentially even down to a particular vehicle or operator, depending upon the fidelity of its catalogue.[11] The common air picture is likely contributed to by radar controlled by the air defence group within a force, but also received from friendly air assets either from their radar, or their blue force tracking. The latter is especially important to avoid friendly fire, especially against aircraft returning from sorties. Each of these feeds likely requires three operators, one to monitor the feed and approve the classifications by the software, one to manage communications either from a feed contributor, or to answer queries coming into the fire control headquarters relating to the feed they oversee and one on stand-down recovering from a period of concentration.

[10] T. Kirubarajan and Y. Bar-Shalom, 'Tracking Evasive Move-Stop-Move Targets with a GMTI Radar Using a VS-IMM Estimator', *IEEE Transactions on Aerospace and Electronic Systems* (Vol. 39, No. 3, 2003), pp. 1098–103.
[11] David Adamy, *Introduction to Electronic Warfare Modelling and Simulation* (London: Artech House, 2003).

The tasks for periodic feeds – including imagery, signals intelligence, metadata harvesting and reporting – are quite different. Imagery may comprise call-down satellite images – both electro-optical and synthetic aperture radar – which could have a latency of within twenty minutes for any location on earth if the right commercial solutions are available,[12] and SAR imagery taken by radar bearing assets, to images captured and pushed back by forward units. Assessment of images has historically been a slow and laborious process but once again AI is enabling the rapid identification and classification of objects, with Fireweaver being a good public example of this capability. The tasks for conducting image analysis, therefore, include tasking image collection against unknown detections or locations of interest. This requires analysis of other feeds and communication with assets and likely requires two people. It is also necessary to then receive the images and to monitor their classification by the AI to ensure that objects are not mislabelled, and that any machine learning process is not thereby corrupted. Given the number of images and the slow speed at which humans classify these objects, this too might be assigned to two people. Two people, therefore, would ideally be on stand-down to enable rotation.

Signals intelligence collection is closely related to EMS mapping but concerns the contents of messages. SIGINT will often be collected by national means and thereafter shared downwards. Alternatively, it may arise from capturing signals at the tactical level. There are several latency issues involved. Firstly, the information about movements, units or the location of equipment may be captured in clear or encrypted communications. If it is the latter it must be decrypted before it can be analysed, and the level of encryption will determine the length of time necessary to decrypt the signal. This can take hours. Once decrypted the content must be analysed and then shared with the appropriate target acquisition headquarters. Signals intelligence therefore will build up in pieces at a disjointed tempo. Like imagery, it must be time stamped to the time of capture, but as SIGINT may concern what the enemy intends to do – as well as what they are doing – it may also produce tasks for imagery collection to plot enemy intent and confirm whether they are executing as intended. It is not realistic for detailed SIGINT decryption and analysis to take place in a target acquisition and fire control headquarters. But there is nevertheless a need for analysis as to what to do with the information that SIGINT provides.[13] To this end the minimum workforce appears to be six analysts: two to communicate with and plot what is received from higher national authorities, two to communicate with and integrate what is received from organic EW assets and two to assess future trends and flag opportunities or tasks to those directing stand-in reconnaissance. These tasks, because they are likely to be intermittent rather than constant, should allow analysts to stand-down at irregular intervals, meaning there is less of a need to have a rotation.

[12] Florence Cross, RUSI Waterways Conference: Obstacles and Opportunities for Manoeuvre, London, 27 April 2022.
[13] Richard Aldrich, *GCHQ: The Uncensored Story of Britain's Most Secret Intelligence Agency* (London: HarperCollins, 2011).

Metadata harvesting presents different challenges from the other feeds because it does not concern independent collection by military systems but rather the interaction of military systems with wider civilian infrastructure. Essentially it involves two lines of effort, monitoring connections to the web or cell network, and pinging devices of interest to establish their location. A third function is tying open-source information to these connections by devices. The requirement is for a connection to the internet, therefore. This exposes this group to cyber penetration or at least to location detection via the same methods that the team uses to find targets. This function is critically useful, however, as it is likely to provide both information on enemy movements, but also information on civilian concentration and displacement that should guide the application of fires. Metadata harvesting will largely be conducted by higher echelons and relevant data pushed down to a target acquisition and fires control headquarters, but the headquarters may also wish to assess the environment based on its own immediate planning requirements. AI-assisted analysis can allow for visualization of flows and the isolation of targets of interest within metadata, with systems produced by companies like Palantir providing rapid network analysis that supports real-time targeting, refined during the War on Terror. The minimum staffing for this function within a target acquisition and fires control headquarters is likely to be three people: one to assess the broad trends in the environment, one to track high-priority targets and one rotating out. Metadata analysis is periodic in that updates to locations only occur when a device connects to the internet or cell network. For high-priority targets this may be very irregular. Other targets however will remain almost constantly connected and therefore able to be tracked in close to real time.

Finally, there is communications. This is simply the collection and plotting of reports from subordinate units, including contact reports, routine situation reports and calls for fires. Plotting these reported detections allows for visual confirmation by the manoeuvre system to confirm or improve upon assessments made by stand-off target acquisition. Such reports are periodic and must be time stamped. It is also likely laborious, requiring regular data transfers from many nodes. This may take up to six people, therefore, four on and two off.

The final function within the target acquisition system is fusion. If each of the feeds described above constitutes a layer of data, by fusing and overlaying these layers it becomes possible to have multiple continuous tracks on data points which can then have periodic confirmations of identity overlaid onto the map, with several layers of redundancy. AI can help to fuse these layers and to tag identifications to tracks when they meet in space and time.[14] AI can also assist in recognizing when there is a break in a track, and the period between identification data reduces the confidence in the identity when a track is re-acquired. This requires careful monitoring, however. The fusion team – likely requiring six people – essentially monitors the overlays to ensure that the target acquisition teams are giving the fire controllers the best assessment of the truth on the ground. Additional layers – which should not be merged – may

---

[14] Preventing accidents like those that led to the attack on the USS Liberty in 1967, see Michael B. Oren, *Six Day of War: June 1967 and the Making of the Modern Middle East* (Oxford: Oxford University Press, 2002), pp. 263–9.

comprise the picture of the battlefield at variable confidence intervals. For example, there may be one version of the battlefield that is populated by positively identified targets with a validated live track, another with previously positively identified targets for which there is a validated live track, a layer for assessed identified targets for which there is a live track, a layer for live tracks and a layer for identified and assessed targets for which the track has been lost.

Once the target acquisition group outlined above has established a fused picture of the battlefield, this can be provided to the fire direction group, which may be broken into two: a proactive and reactive fires cell, each directing subordinated assets. The former must plan and direct the movement and positioning of fires assets and the prosecution of strikes against the priority target list. The reactive fires cell must ingest and approve air defence weapons release, counterbattery fire and close support fire missions.

The fire control headquarters, therefore, may be understood to comprise a target acquisition group of eight cells, and a fires direction group of two cells. Each of these cells constitutes groups of between three and six operators who must be supported by computers. It therefore makes sense for each cell to be mounted in a non-descript truck, each with a cargo equivalent to a shipping container on its back. It might even be possible to have these containers droppable and recoverable, but this is not essential. The point is that this headquarters of ten vehicles is a high-priority target for the enemy and must minimize its signature. It is precisely what enemy long-range precision fires will be prioritized against and will be a key collection priority for enemy stand-off and stand-in reconnaissance. In the first instance this group of vehicles is best deployed as dispersed as possible, ideally under cover: either in a woodblock or underground car park or similar hardened structure. It is also important that the electronic signature of the headquarters is minimized. This is difficult because the volume of data moving around this structure requires high-bandwidth, low-latency communications. The best way of achieving this is likely ground-laid fibre-optic field cable, and so a vehicle carrying these cables, able to rapidly run the connections between the vehicles, is advisable. The headquarters could also fall back on something like free-space optical directional links, which would also allow greater dispersion, but field cables are cheaper and easier to maintain and repair. The formation must also be able to send directions to its various subordinate batteries, and to make enquiries of the screening force, and to receive data from its stand-off reconnaissance assets and from high echelons. The receivers need not generate a signature as they can be passive. The emitters however will be detectable and targetable. Furthermore, even if the emitter does not provide an enemy with a targeting solution for fires, it could provide the enemy with a bearing to focus electronic warfare against the receivers, thereby severing the headquarters from its data feeds. For the receivers it is likely ideal to have two, mounted on dedicated vehicles with masts. These can be located fairly close to the headquarters as they are passive and connected by fibre-optic cable. Having two receiver masts reduces the risk from long-range jamming. The emitters are more problematic. Fortunately, the headquarters is not seeking to push a high volume of data out, but simply coordinates and fires orders, along with occasional queries. For satellite connections it is possible to have a directional antenna with limited detectability. RF communications are harder to conceal. The key is to have several antenna and to locate them away from the headquarters. This, therefore, is probably the longest stretch of field cable, or else could justify a free-space optical link to a receiver to allow a long jump between the antenna hub and the location of the headquarters. The restriction of emissions to fires direction and enquiries should also shield the headquarters from detection by appearing comparable to much of the other kinds of traffic moving between units. Nevertheless, setting up the antenna likely takes two vehicles and an appropriate link. The final challenge for the fire control headquarters is power. Power in the field demands fuel and means keeping engines running, which produces a heat signature. Given that the fires direction headquarters can be some distance from the front, however, it is also possible that the vehicles could plug into the mains, so long as there was the capacity to shield the spike in consumption rates from being detected and associated with a specific location. If this is not possible then the flow of fuel bowsers to this formation will need to be carefully managed to avoid compromising the location, while generators should be set up under multispectral camouflage or hard cover.

Traditionally, the fire control headquarters outlined above would likely be held at the corps level. The problem with this is that fires supported by this level of

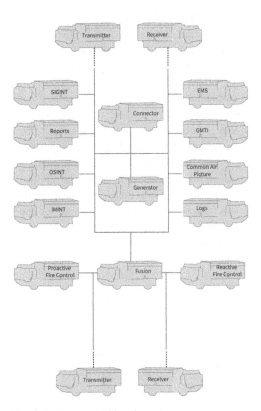

Figure 5 Fire control headquarters.

coordination will defeat fires without it, irrespective of echelon. This, therefore, is the competitive footprint for a fires headquarters, irrespective of the size of the force that it is supporting. Its capabilities may need to be scaled up as more fires assets are brought under command, but the types of analysis necessary remain relatively constant. This is perhaps an example therefore of how the traditional echelon structure is collapsing, since irrespective of the scale of the operation some capabilities bring with them an irreducible footprint and in the case of fire control the above is indicative of what such a footprint might look like.

Target acquisition

Some of the feeds drawn upon by the target acquisition group outlined above are inorganic to a ground combat force. Space-based infrastructure may be national or commercial assets while the common air picture is likely enabled by the Combined Air Operations Centre (CAOC). SIGINT feeds may partly arise from organic EW but will more often be furnished by national collection assets. Nevertheless, there were capabilities that the fires system should command organically, including the ability to sustain GMTI, SAR, UAS orbits for target identification and an EW baseline. It is worthwhile building out what is indicatively required to field these capabilities below.

To begin with GMTI radar, these are most effective when airborne. At a height of 5,000 feet a radar can track targets out to 150 km.[15] At that altitude there are rotary and fixed wing solutions, but as such a radar must continually emit, and given its importance to the target acquisition process it must also be able to evade enemy air threats. Although such a long-range system can stand-off sufficiently to gain some protection, the ability to rapidly descend offers a means of defeating many of the most potent threats like longer-range surface to air missiles. Rapid decent to landing makes a rotary platform more survivable, though a fixed-wing platform offers greater fuel efficiently. Ideally a force could sustain three platforms aloft, both to ensure coverage across the frontage of the force and to have redundancy if one is forced to land or the enemy employs jamming against the system. On the assumption that one platform is being recovered and refuelled and another may be receiving further maintenance for each that is airborne, this leads to nine platforms in a battery across the force. There is no particular requirement for these assets to be crewed. They can also remain in an orbit above their ground station. A directional link can push data to the ground station reliably. It could even be possible for the platform to have a tether to its ground station to ensure consistent data transfer, though this would limit the platform's manoeuvrability. These would be necessarily large platforms. Not only would an appropriate radar be heavy, but it also has significant power demands, requiring a large engine comparable to that used in a light helicopter. Each would likely need to be transported on a truck and have a dedicated operation and maintenance crew of at least four people. These platforms would also be able to conduct SAR imagery by dedicating a proportion

---

[15] As per radar range equation.

of their emitters and receivers to SAR and moving perpendicular to the target at a slow speed.

Using UAS for target identification is rather different. The aim is to have long-range UAS able to fly to bring targets under direct observation or to correct the fall of shot. Smaller and shorter ranged systems for this purpose have already been described as being fielded by the manoeuvre system, but it also makes sense for there to be an organic capacity in the fires system. These UAS should be cheap, rugged and easily replaced. Fixed-wing systems with a modular payload have the best range. They should be flyable above the MANPADS ceiling to ensure survivability. They could carry electro-optical, EW or metadata harvesting equipment, or communications relays.[16] Ideally the flight path would be preprogramed with optional updates, rather than actively flown, but the data pushed back live. If we envisage the need to maintain three directions – one against the objective, one against the left flank and one against the right – and assume a rotation of assets from that which is deployed, that which is being readied, and that which is being recovered or prepared, then we may envisage nine UAS per battery with three batteries supporting the fires system, with resupply of UAS available as they are destroyed. Alternatively these orbits could be combined so that a full suite of capabilities – EO/IR, EW, Comms – can all be brought to bear above a target of primary interest. We may envisage each three UAS being launched from a catapult and recovered by parachute, moved in a vehicle pair, each carrying an operator, technician and communicator. Thus, a battery would comprise nine platforms and eighteen personnel, moved in six vehicles. Three batteries across the fires system would offer sufficient coverage and redundancy to query multiple targets of interest simultaneously. Note that the loss rate of UAS will be high.[17]

Electronic warfare baselines have already been described as part of the manoeuvre system. A trio of more capable collection platforms may be held within the fires system, capable to standing off further from the frontline. The collection process for these systems is fairly straightforward. Mast-mounted arrays should enable spectrum monitoring with the three vehicles in a line allowing for effective direction finding to locate enemy units. These vehicles may also facilitate ELINT and limited SIGINT collection since the captured waveforms of enemy signals could also be pushed to the fire control headquarters for decryption and analysis. The EW battery would ideally be divided into six vehicles, three for collection and three for offensive EW effects. Again, the fires system as a whole would ideally hold three batteries to keep alignments against the three axes of the manoeuvre system, and to ensure redundancy and avoid suppression. The offensive EW baseline constitutes non-kinetic fires to be considered subsequently.

---

[16] The latter has been found to be critical to survivable UAS operations in Ukraine for target acquisition because the relay UAS can prevent the location of the ground control station, and without EW suppression of the station's receivers it becomes difficult for the enemy to prevent the transmission of video, author interviews, Ukrainian UAS technician supporting the General Staff, Ukraine, August 2022.

[17] Ukrainian forces found that UAS loss rates approached 90 per cent within the period of two months of fighting, author interviews, Ukrainian General Staff J7, Ukraine, August 2022.

Non-lethal fires

Electronic attack over long distances presents a number of challenges for battlespace management. Firstly, it may affect all targets on the bearing of its antenna. It can therefore jam friendly systems as well as enemy ones. Secondly, such high-power emissions have a large and distinct signature, meaning that these effects cannot be employed persistently without drawing fire. They should not be co-located with other high payoff targets. These constraints collectively mean that it is often more effective to jam enemy systems with shorter ranged and lighter platforms pushed forwards. As already described as part of the manoeuvre system, the distribution of EW effects for targeting the control of UAS at platoon level makes considerable sense. However, there is value in the fires control headquarters being able to conduct long-range electronic attack for both offensive and defensive purposes. Offensively the application of long-range electronic attack can open up windows of opportunity for other capabilities. For example, suppose an enemy attack commences and the fires control headquarters wishes to break it up with artillery, but is concerned about a large number of enemy guns that remain unlocated and are feared to be positioned for counterbattery missions. Instead of taking the risk, the fire control headquarters could request its EW screen to confirm the location of enemy counterbattery radar and then direct an electronic attack against these radar, preventing them from identifying the location of friendly guns and thereby freeing friendly artillery to fire and move. Another example is in support of air defence. Long-range jammers can be used for more sophisticated attacks too. Suppose that the commander has determined to commit the assault force against an objective and that just as the force begins to mass an enemy-airborne GMTI radar turns on. Rather than delaying the concentration to knock down the radar a long-range jammer could conduct a protocol-based electronic attack to flood the GMTI radar with false returns, sending a cascade of false information through the enemy fire control headquarters and thereby delaying their ability to identify the axes along which forces are converging to conduct the assault.

EW can also be used defensively to protect the force by interfering with the targeting or navigation systems of incoming munitions, or denying access to key navigational systems. This kind of effect – especially if it is conducted over an area – must be coordinated with other fires and ISTAR capabilities because it may conflict with the friendly employment of UAVs or precision munitions and likely requires cuing on from other sensors. This is why such capabilities should be under the control of the fires system.

The exact number of offensive EW platforms necessary to perform specific tasks will vary considerably, but three seems to be the minimum for long-range effects. This gives the fire control headquarters the capacity to have one effecting a system, one preparing to do so and one repositioning, thereby enabling a carousel of electronic attack to maintain a persistent effect. Alternatively, it allows one to be delivering an effect and one remaining poised to be used reactively and defensively, with an attrition reserve. We may envisage each vehicle to comprise a large antenna system with a generator, equivalent in size to a military truck and with a crew of three to four personnel, thereby able to drive, set-up, communicate with the fires control headquarters and operate the system. Such systems can also be used for brute force attacks against penetrating enemy UAS as an area defence asset.

Shorter ranged jamming is also a non-lethal effect. The jammer ought to be a short-ranged deployable pod, capable to prevent the receipt of communications within a short radius, appropriate for suppressing command posts or key enemy defence systems for a limited period, determined by the battery life of the jammer. Such a jammer ought to be programmable so that it can be set to deliver protocol-based effects against specific systems prior to launch. The means of delivering these jammers, however, ought not be a bespoke non-lethal system but, since it concerns projecting a physical object to the enemy, should be delivered by the same means as lethal payloads. The delivery mechanism, therefore, will be considered in the next section of this chapter.

It is briefly worth outlining some capabilities that should not sit within the fires system, because NATO armies in particular have made a serious conceptual error in their force organization that needs to be corrected. It has become standard practice to group information operations and cyber capabilities into a 'joint effects' cell and have them coordinated as part of the fires systems.[18] Many units have experimented with various configurations of joint effects and invariably run into the same two fundamental problems. Firstly, information operations and cyber capabilities work to a long tempo and the time on target, or timing of the effect, is not easily controlled. In any planning process an unpredictable and slow set of activities will almost always be relegated to secondary importance as compared with kinetic fires that must be executed within tight timeframes and therefore demand constant and immediate attention. Thus, cyber and information effects – which require very careful design – are often starved of command attention. Secondly, cyber and information effects depend upon constant activity, whether that be output or probing enemy cyber systems. Attempting to synchronize a continuous process with a fires process usually leads to cyber and information products being treated like high payload munitions as regards permissions for release, and this means that they are stifled by the staff process and rendered uncompetitive.[19] Both cyber and information capabilities are very important to modern operations, but they sit within the support system, not the fires system and will therefore be detailed in Chapter 10.

---

[18] Thomas G. Bradbeer (Ed.), *Lethal and Non-Lethal Fires: Historical Case Studies of Converging Cross-Domain Fires in Large-Scale Combat Operations* (Fort Leavenworth, KS: Army University Press, 2018), pp. 203–9; Commander Cornelis van der Klaauw, 'Joint Effects: Integration and Synchronisation of Lethal and Non-lethal Activities', *Three Swords Magazine* (Vol. 36, 2020), pp. 74–8: https://jwc.nato.int/application/files/8216/0523/5268/issue36_15lr.pdf#:~:text=Joint%20Effects%20is%20the%20integration,strategic%2C%20operational%2C%20and%20tactical, accessed 20 July 2022.

[19] Author observations of ineffective joint effects cells within headquarters on both exercise in September 2021 and on operations in March 2022. It is worth noting that where non-kinetic effects did take out staff time, it had a detrimental impact on the efficiency of lethal effects within the staff process, as observed on exercise in January 2019. Indeed, the subordination of non-lethal fires to a joint effects architecture is so inefficient that the author observed the defeat of a divisional formation in the information space by a team of four people in an exercise. Against four individuals with appropriate permissions a staff of several hundred found themselves overmatched by the volume, speed and effectiveness of effects. This lesson is consistent with the centralized intent and decentralized execution that has characterized effective Ukrainian information operations during 2022.

Lethal fires

The lethal effects that the fires system must deliver comprise shaping the enemy, and the destruction of key targets. Shaping may be defined as holding key systems at risk to constrain their employment and being able to break up concentrations of forces above the size of the company group. Destruction may be defined as kinetically destroying high-priority systems and fixed enemy forces. We may divide the effectors needed to achieve these missions into three kinds of platform: rocket systems, gun systems and loitering munitions. Rocket systems have the range and accuracy to hold the enemy at risk over a large area, but cost limits the number of targets these systems can engage. Gun systems offer shorter range but more economical capabilities that can therefore be repeated. Loitering munitions meanwhile allow for long-range sophisticated attacks against vulnerable targets. By fielding these layers of threat the fires system complicates the enemy's ability to counter them, as methods for constraining gun systems, for example, are often vulnerable to targeting by rockets, and defensive systems able to intercept rockets are often vulnerable to loitering munitions. By posing a layered threat, the fires system shapes the enemy into choosing the limited number of areas they can afford to defend.

The necessary number of platforms can be determined by the task. If the MLRS battery must be able to break up a concentrated battlegroup-sized formation, then this could be understood as a requirement to destroy approximately eighty vehicles. If we assume a probability of kill for a sensor-fused sub-munition of 0.5, which is consistent with trials conducted by Finland and other states,[20] this means that 160 sub-munitions must be distributed above the formation. The Oslo Convention prohibits a munition to have ten or more sub-munitions,[21] and so if we assume that each rocket dispenses eight active seeker explosive penetrators and one electronic attack payload able to scramble defensive radar, then this requires twenty rockets to be launched to break up the formation.[22] An enemy brigade may contain three such battlegroups, so this means that across the force it is desirable to have sixty rockets ready to fire in a salvo. If each vehicle carries twelve rockets, then this requires five MLRS platforms to remain ready to fire. If we assume that there should be some attrition reserve, and that it may be desirable to take shots at smaller concentrations of vehicles – like the company group described in the last chapter – then six MLRS platforms carrying seventy-two such rockets seems like a sensible level of firepower to effectively hold the enemy at risk, and therefore shape them into a dispersed posture.

---

[20] Trials were conducted in Lapland by Finnish artillery while testing a range of sensor-fused 155mm sub-munitions. This data tracks with US trials. Author interview, senior Finnish artillery officer, May 2022.

[21] 'Convention on Cluster Munitions', United Nations, 2008: https://treaties.un.org/doc/Publication/CTC/26-6.pdf, accessed 20 July 2022.

[22] There are relatively few historical cases of sensor-fused munitions being employed in combat, but where they have, they have proven highly effective, as in Iraq where two CBU-105s broke an Iraqi tank attack; see Chris Osborne, 'Sensor Fused Weapons Aid Combat in Iraq', *CNN*, 19 August 2003: http://edition.cnn.com/2003/US/08/19/hln.terror.sensor.fuzed/, accessed 20 July 2022.

Shaping the enemy into a dispersed posture may prevent the enemy from concentrating to attack, but it does not prevent the enemy fires system from imposing similar constraints upon friendly forces. Finding and striking the enemy fires system is an intensive process because it requires key targets to be found and struck without incoming munitions being intercepted, or the target moving while the munition is in flight. Targeting the wrong systems can become very munitions intensive. Nevertheless, it is often necessary to strike a key threat system to force it to move, and then potentially its supporting radar so that even if it sets up again, its eyes are having to move and it cannot therefore receive target data. This suppression of a threat system can create windows of opportunity for concentration. A further aspect of such harassing long-range shots is how they open up opportunities for other attack vectors. For example, if a rocket attack targeting critical infrastructure encourages the enemy to turn on key radar in order to intercept the strike, these radars become vulnerable to radar homing loitering munitions and other capabilities. In any case, there is a persistent need for these shots when targets are found. If we assume 24 available rockets with deployable jamming payloads, able to effectively suppress and confuse defensive systems, and 120 ready rockets for precision strike, this would come to 144 rockets, fitting in 12 launchers. In order to spread risk and opportunity we might envisage the area effect rockets already described being distributed across all of the launchers, rather than concentrated in six, so that overall, the force fields eighteen MLRS launch platforms each loaded with four area effect rockets, one electronic warfare rocket and seven precision strike rockets. Working in six groups of three vehicles, so that one can fire, one can remain on standby to take over firing as the first vehicle displaces, or to conduct counterbattery fire, and the third repositions or reloads, then this allows the force to disperse. Each group might also be accompanied by a logistics vehicle carrying reloads and a communications vehicle, so that it can receive and send information without giving away the position of the launchers. Each vehicle would have approximately three crew. To maintain sufficient reach to shape the enemy deep across the frontage of operations described in Chapter 6, a force would ideally field two such MLRS battalions, totalling thirty-six launchers.

Long-range rocket artillery may be able to destroy high-priority targets and shape the enemy into a dispersed posture but it is poorly suited to destroying infantry or engaging smaller formations. Given the desire to hold MLRS rounds ready to punish concentration – and to protect the capacity to do this to shape enemy deployments – using guns for smaller scale tasks is preferable. If we assume an effective range for area effect munitions fired from self-propelled artillery of 28 km,[23] then this requires twelve groupings of guns to keep the entire frontage under risk in support of the manoeuvre system.[24] If the target set for a fire mission is groupings

---

[23] This is roughly the effective range for top attack sensor-fuzed munitions fired from 52 calibre 155 mm howitzers, author interviews, 228 Battalion ROKA and Hanwha Defence officials, South Korea, May 2022.

[24] This assumes that howitzers are held approximately 7 km back from the screening force, meaning that at maximum offset they can deliver area effect fire 12 km beyond the screening force, unguided impact or proximity fuzed fire at 21 km ahead of the screening force, and guided proximity or impact fused fire at 42 km.

below the battlegroup, then it becomes possible to outline a rough requirement as regards the number of guns. Casualties will generally be inflicted in the first minute of a bombardment, before the target is able to get into cover. The number of rounds necessary to achieve effect across the area occupied by a concentrated platoon is approximate twelve to eighteen rounds, while a mechanized company group will usually comprise ten to twelve primary combat vehicles. With an autoloader modern self-propelled howitzers can achieve a rate of fire of up to nine rounds per minute.[25] If we assume eight rounds per minute, then two howitzers can deliver sixteen rounds onto target within a minute, and within 28 km can land the first six rounds simultaneously. Against mechanized targets, firing sensor-fused explosive penetrators could produce approximate eight mission-killed vehicles from this salvo. Working on the basis that one gun pair is delivering the effect, another is ready to deliver counterbattery fire and a third is repositioning, while twelve gun-groups are required to cover the frontage of the formation, the force should therefore have at least fifty-four guns organized into three battalions, each fighting in three six-gun batteries of three gun-pairs. If each vehicle carries forty-eight rounds and each pair has an ammunition vehicle assigned to it, then the force can conduct twelve fire missions per gun pair, and thirty-six fire missions across each battery before needing to be resupplied. Each battery of six guns would also require a command vehicle and back-up command vehicle to receive and direct fire to the guns.

The third layer in the lethal fires mix is loitering munitions, able to increase the threat vectors against the enemy system and hold high-value targets at risk. There are certain misconceptions about the use of loitering munitions. Firstly, they are assumed to be cheap when the sensors necessary to make them effective are expensive. Secondly, they are often envisaged as being used en-masse. The problem with massed salvos of the same munition is that they become vulnerable to hard counters, like high-power microwave defences. These slow-flying systems are effective precisely because they are fired in limited salvos that are hard to optimize against. We may envisage three kinds of engagement. First there is the sequential engagement, in which loitering munitions converge on a target from multiple vectors to overwhelm it. Experiments by the Israeli Defence Forces have found that four loitering munitions can overwhelm almost any point defence system.[26] Since point defences are necessarily sectored, knocking out two systems should clear the path to a target. A salvo of twelve loitering munitions, therefore, should be able to knock out the defensive systems and the high-value target they were protecting, with the final strike following sequentially at a brief interval from the effects against the point defences. The second attack profile might be understood as a collaborative engagement. Here, one loitering munition acts as a decoy, likely employing an electronic warfare payload to suppress or dazzle defensive systems, creating an opening for other munitions to strike. The final attack profile would be a simultaneous strike, best employed against packets of enemy platforms that

---

[25] Author observations, Hanwah Defence, South Korea, May 2022.
[26] Author interview, IDF officer, February 2020; and has been confirmed through technical examination of capabilities like Pantsir-S1 conducted in Ukraine, June 2022.

lack defensive systems. The greatest lethality for such an attack would strike logistics convoys. As military packets rarely exceed four vehicles, however, and convoys would rarely exceed twelve vehicles, it makes sense that salvos are organized at this scale. The rough laydown of a loitering munition capability therefore would be a quad-packed launcher on each vehicle, with a launch group comprising three launchers and a command and control vehicle. Three launch groups provide enough ready rounds across the force to enable break-in against defended targets. Thus, the loitering munition component constitutes three batteries of nine launchers, each able to launch four munitions, providing 108 ready rounds across the force. As demonstrated in Nagorno-Karabakh, loitering munitions are not in and of themselves transformative, but when used to open a path for other capabilities – whether artillery or air – they can have a devastating effect in combination with other components of the fires system.

The final lethal fires component is medium-ranged air defence. Distributed MANPADS and SHORAD in the Manoeuvre System hold enemy air at risk as it tries to enter the contested zone, complicating planning and constraining enemy air operations. It also offers self-defence to those elements most isolated from support. The fires system, by contrast, should aim to force the enemy to conduct suppression or destruction of air defence operations if they wish to use airpower against the force. The air defence system also offers the capacity to intercept cruise missiles if they are not employed with appropriate enablement. The result is to force the enemy to commit decisive quantities of equipment to achieve an effect with high lethality systems and thereby constrain the number of times such capabilities can be brought to bear. For instance, US modelling of corps aviation found that against an enemy with layered air defences, enablement reduced the number of viable missions from a battalion attack being repeatable nightly, to a force generation cycle of seventy-two hours because of the additional enablers needed.[27]

Medium-ranged air defence may be understood as holding aircraft under threat between 40 and 70 km. Assuming 70 km range, the battlespace described in Chapter 6 would require four batteries to effectively screen the frontage of the force. With each battery comprising four launchers each carrying eight ready to fire missiles, a command and control vehicle, and a target acquisition radar these batteries would be able to offer mutual protection and overlapping radar coverage. The system could be rendered considerably more effective if augmented by a passive air defence platform equivalent to that supporting the manoeuvre force, to provide point defence against low flying threats or loitering munitions, and a long-range missile with 120 km reach in order to hold at risk enablers and other aircraft that might try to support the strike package. A good example here would be a dedicated jamming aircraft, which against a system with 70 km range may be able to push the range down to a point where aircraft can enter into striking distance of the system.[28] With a longer-range missile – likely reducing carried missiles – however, the jamming aircraft becomes a target even as

[27] Author interview, US Corps J3 and J5, Deep Effects Symposium, Gloucester, January 2022.
[28] Author interview, USAF EW Operator, Sweden, September 2021; Finnish air defence officer, Helsinki, November 2021.

it pushes down the range on the bulk of the munitions. The passive point defence capability, meanwhile, offers a pop-up threat that could be positioned ahead of the battery to complicate pressing home an attack if the battery radar stops illuminating. The overlapping coverage is critical because it enables a battery to reposition or stop illuminating without opening the airspace to a strike package.

Manoeuvre by fire

Having mapped out the capabilities of the fires system it is possible to outline how it can be employed in conjunction with the manoeuvre system to shape the enemy. Suppose an enemy battalion were in defensive positions around a hamlet of some eighty homes, overlooking a key junction on an MSR, lying beneath a hill that offers a good vantage point for surveying the surrounding country. The enemy mechanized infantry battalion, supported by a howitzer battery, MLRS battery and an air defence battery, is deployed with one company occupying the hamlet, another with its vehicles on the reverse slope of the hill, concealed along a treeline, and the third in reserve off the MSR.

Advancing slowly at night, the recce section advances in two teams, eventually laying up in two woodblocks. Wearing anti-thermal clothing they move in sight of the edge of the wood, dig observation posts and begin watching the hamlet. Further back the vehicles raise their masts, peeking above the treeline, while UAS are launched from dead ground to gain observations from different directions. Initially the enemy throws out patrols. One finds itself engaged by the recce section's sniper, taking a casualty and withdrawing after being fired at by the recce section's machine gun. Another passes behind the recce section's positions in a pair of vehicles, but is intercepted by the screening force's manoeuvre group and destroyed. After these incidents the enemy keeps its patrolling closer in, where its units can mutually support. The recce section catches movement that suggests enemy sniper teams might have pushed forwards to keep the approaches to the village under observation.

Over the following twenty-four hours the recce section notes several patterns. A particular house has several people enter and exit at irregular intervals. The UAS start to note cuts in the ground leading to points in the woods which are marked as hides for enemy vehicles. Retroreflective sensors also manage to identify several firing posts. The recce section's efforts are augmented by stand-off observation. Satellite imagery similarly reveals track marks leading to hides. Electronic warfare detection overlayed with the observations from the recce team suggests that the building from which personnel periodically emerge is likely a command and control node. There is also a strong communications emissions pattern from behind the hill, assessed as the likely communications relay for the air defence battery. Based on this information a UAV orbit is tasked to investigate. As the UAV approaches the village it notes camouflage netting between two of the houses, marked as a likely hide for a mortar team. Suddenly, as it approaches the hill there is a massive spike in the EMS, the air defence radar having turned on, and the UAV is shot down. The launch point is detected by radar and the TELAR tracked using GMTI as it repositions into a new hide, which is marked by the fires control headquarters.

Twenty minutes later another UAV appears. This time, when the air defence radar illuminates it struggles to lock the target, whose signature appears to expand and retract as its electronic attack payload is activated. As the radar operators seek to achieve a lock three more UAVs suddenly cross the radar horizon and come diving for the radar. A point defence system opens fire, destroying two of the UAVs, but the third hits home. Again the point of origin for the fires is caught by the wide area stand-off radar and tracked as the point defence system displaces. Once it stops moving two precision rounds come in, along with a rocket, targeting the TELAR, point defence system, and command and control node, respectively. Upon the air defence radar being struck the hostile counterbattery radar illuminates and, after ninety seconds of the precision rounds being fired, three enemy guns open up with a salvo of counterbattery fire. The targets had packed up in the interim, and as it takes seventy-four seconds for the rounds to travel to their target, they displace in time to avoid the fires. The point of origin of the counterbattery fire is logged, the guns tracked with GMTI radar as they displace, and then struck as they go static.

While the artillery duel develops, the manoeuvre group within the reconnaissance battalion begins to move back and forth, beyond direct fire range from the village. At the same time the 120mm mortars start to fire between the buildings, displacing after each couple of shots. Having suppressed the enemy artillery the guns begin to prosecute strikes on the identified hides. Slowly the manoeuvre group works forwards, keeping out of ATGM range from the village, but using their thermal sights to search for the enemy recce pickets. One enemy recce group fires an ATGM, but as an isolated launch it is caught by the APS and responded to with 50mm cannon fire. Realizing they risk being combed out the recce pickets begin to fall back. More UAS begin to be thrown up, with another orbit appearing over the radar horizon, no longer threatened by air defences. As the number of enemy personnel moving increases, so too is their accumulation in strong points in the village logged. As key buildings are identified to contain a critical number of personnel, it is only a matter of time before a rocket comes bursting through the roof. Casualties begin to accumulate, but it is clear to the defending commander what will happen if they try to reinforce the village or recover their wounded. The artillery threat effectively seals the approaches to the village. Although the defender has numerical superiority, its harassed reserves are fixed, too far from the village to defend it, and unable to counterattack without falling victim to concentrated fires. Although most of the company in the village are intact, it is evident that without artillery support they will be progressively attrited.

The infantry platoon from the recce force begins to advance on foot, moving in bounds through dead ground and into woodblocks, until they are within direct fire range of the village. Here they come under fire, with the defenders mortars unmasking. 82mm mortar bombs begin to fall, only to be responded to with 120mm fire. Sniping breaks out between the village and the advancing infantry. The platoon is advancing against a company, and so is quickly suppressed. Nevertheless, as the defenders reveal the positions of their machine guns, long-range ATGMs begin to arc in, crashing through windows and killing the defenders in detail.

The challenge for the defending commander in this developing battle is not that they cannot hold the village. With so little mass, the attacker does not have the capacity to carry the area by assault. But having lost fires dominance the defender is also unable to hold it without suffering a steady rate of attrition and cannot manoeuvre freely. The village can be isolated and shaped into the zone of opportunity where the attacker can eventually concentrate and clear them out. The defender therefore is likely to be defeated in detail or to withdraw their force. In either case they are shaped into sub-optimal decisions. The effect of the fires system, in conjunction with the manoeuvre system, therefore, is to progressively constrain the enemy by persistently confronting them with the necessity of ceding ground to minimize losses. Although operationally withdrawal from a position that has become isolated may make sense – as demonstrated in Severodonetsk during Russia's campaign in the Donbas – political judgement may cause a commander to dig in. Similarly, while garrisons of individual villages might be withdrawn, many population centres will be vital ground that must be defended. While shaping can isolate such an objective in the manner described above, it cannot be stormed by these means. To actually seize a defended objective it requires an assault force, the composition of which is the subject of the next chapter.

9

The assault system

The commitment of forces to an offensive must be conditions based, and the determination as to whether the conditions are appropriate is a judgement that is the responsibility of the commander.[1]

Lt Gen Mykhailo Zabrodksyi

The number of personnel involved in urban fighting often suggests that the engagements themselves are large. In fact, urban fighting usually revolves around very intense engagements between small numbers of people, and the environment effectively prevents the participation of more. By way of example, although the Battle for Donetsk Airport saw 242 days of combat, the number of Ukrainian defenders rarely exceeded sixty personnel, who were circulated and replaced at intervals as the build-up of casualties or tempo of attack allowed.[2] Donetsk Airport highlights several important challenges in urban warfare, namely that success or failure as regards seizure and control of ground is often determined by interactions between sections and platoons of personnel. Significant gains are won through sub-tactical engagements. Secondly, because of the rate of attrition, and exhaustion brought about through the intensity of engagements, there is a continued requirement in almost all urban fighting to control and traverse the urban–rural interface. Forces must be able to be reinforced from outside of the urban environment. Building a system for assaulting and repelling the assault of urban areas, therefore, must be built around a robust force structure at the platoon level, and thereafter build outwards to map how forces at this scale are supported and rotated. If the fires system had to be understood in its entirety to appreciate its effect, and the manoeuvre system had to be understood in terms of the complementarity between reconnaissance and screening elements, the assault force must be understood in terms of its core combat element and the combined arms enablement and sustainment that allows them to take ground in a complex environment, secure it and stabilize it for the civilian population.[3] This chapter, therefore, begins by mapping the structure of the assault platoon. The chapter then examines how the capacity to assault an urban

---

[1] Lt Gen Mykhailo Zabrodksyi, Author interview, Ukraine, August 2022.
[2] Author interviews, defenders of Donetsk Airport, Ukraine, February 2022.
[3] The overlayed nature of these problems is captured in Charles Krulak, 'The Strategic Corporal: Leadership in the Three Block War', *Marines Magazine* (1999).

sector can be translated into the isolation of sectors and thus the control of urban pathways. Thirdly, the chapter considers the support necessary to project a force onto the objective and to secure what has been captured. Finally, the chapter will explore a vignette to show how this force might execute an assault.

Assaulting the sector

The basic building block for urban manoeuvre must be the number of people who can move through a gap. In practice, it is rare that more than three people can enter a room at the speed of relevance. A fourth is also important to remain outside, able to hold a corridor, for example, once a team entering a room announces their presence to the rest of a building by opening fire. The basic team, therefore, comprises four people. The basic structure looks something like two assaulters, a grenadier and machine-gunner, ideally with a constant recoil system to allow for accurate suppressive fire while standing, since the transition to fighting prone is not always viable in urban spaces. Although four people can have a wide set of specialisms it is more resilient and efficient to have them supported by additional specialists. The most important specialist in urban manoeuvre is the breacher – an engineer able to enable a team to chart its own course through the urban landscape, rather than follow the path mapped out by architects.[4] While in a counterterrorism context a single breacher may carry sufficient explosives for a mission, in conventional conflict it is likely necessary for breachers to work in pairs, both to carry sufficient materiel, and so that tempo can be maintained, with one prepping charges and the other placing them. It also provides resilience to the unit. A further principle is that most buildings have two directions moving from any point. If a team of four covers an interior axis, this leaves them vulnerable from other directions. There is also value in teams being able to leapfrog one another to maintain momentum. Thus, it makes sense to have two teams per section. If one team fixes an enemy in an interior axis, then the other can work with the breachers to create a new axis and thereby outmanoeuvre the defenders. Coordinating these teams, both internally, and with supporting elements, is a complex task that is best executed by someone screened by these fighting elements, who is thereby given the cognitive space to visualize the environment in three dimensions. It therefore makes sense to have a separate section commander.

One of the challenges of the urban environment is that the compression of distance and the opacity of walls mean that units risk perpetually being ambushed, and have very little time to react. Modern technologies allow for an unprecedented degree of pathfinding by disposable means in an urban environment, significantly reducing the risk to personnel. Small Uncrewed Aerial Systems (UAS) offer the most flexible means of scouting. There are two relevant kinds. The first is the small quadcopter with a centre-mounted camera. By climbing to its maximum altitude, these offer the ability

---

[4] Eyal Weizman, 'Walking through Walls: Soldiers as Architects in the Israeli–Palestinian Conflict', *Radical Philosophy* (Vol. 136, 2006), pp. 8–22.

to look over walls and behind buildings, tracking enemy movements and providing situational awareness. The capacity to drop grenades also allows enemies to be held at risk from multiple, simultaneous directions, increasing cognitive load and stress on the enemy.[5] Another use for these UAS is as communications relays if they are fitted with a radio rather than a grenade. Sitting above two buildings, they can allow a mesh network to be maintained between two sections that are no longer in line of sight owing to urban structures. These additional links in networks can be used to build resilience into communications but also to recover from network breaks. Like the grenades, the ability to drop the radios, or rather place them on high objects, can reduce the enemy's ability to suppress the links, while freeing the UAS for other taskings.

The second kind of UAS is smaller and designed to fly laterally through structures. These are modified racing UAS, able to fly along corridors and into rooms. The ability to fly into buildings is exceedingly useful both for finding and for distracting an enemy. At a basic level, a quadcopter with its rearmost rotors shielded by a guard but its foreword rotors open can precede a team into a room and fly at the eye level towards its occupants. Even though the threat is primarily lacerations very few people can avoid being distracted from having a rotor blade fly quickly towards their face. This psychological effect can be expanded if the UAS can carry and trigger a grenade, stun-grenade or shotgun shell. The ability to accurately place grenades inside rooms not only offers an opportunity to stun enemies defending an entrance, but also offers a precise medium range lethal effect that can bypass cover. Both of the UAS described above require practice to fly effectively in a cluttered environment. They also require an operator to be looking at a screen or into a set of goggles, rather than out at the world. To this end, a UAS operator in each section seems sensible to allow someone to focus on this task. This also allows the operator to carry back-up UAS to allow them to be used as munitions when appropriate.

There is a paradox in urban operations; on the one hand, fighting at close quarters favours moving quickly. Moving quickly – especially through windows, breaches and between levels – favours being light. At the same time urban operations are intensive in their demands for ammunition, especially for charges and grenades. Finally, there are a range of types of equipment that, while occasionally essential, are also heavy, bulky, and therefore poorly suited to being carried organically by a unit. For this reason there is considerable utility in each section having a mechanical mule, carrying spare ammunition, and also some specialist equipment such as a ladder, a ballistic shield, a short range anti-tank weapon, a stretcher and a shoulder launchable thermobaric weapon suitable for clearing strongpoints and bunkers. Historically, such a system would constitute a driven vehicle and would therefore be large and confined for the most part to the street. Automating such a mule, however, while inappropriate for reconnaissance forces lacking maintenance support, is ideal for urban operations where distances are short and the utility high. The attachment of an autonomous ground system therefore, able to carry a pallet of equipment, or a stretcher, navigating

---

5   Jack Watling and Nicholas Waters, 'Achieving Lethal Effects by Small Unmanned Aerial Vehicles', *The RUSI Journal* (Vol. 164, No. 1, 2019), pp. 40–5.

point to point as directed over the network by whoever has logged in as its operator, offers considerable utility in enabling a unit both to carry key equipment, and to be resupplied without needing to expose personnel to risk by having them run back and forth across open ground.[6]

Three sections of twelve, each with their mules, ought to constitute an assault platoon. Each assault platoon ought also to have some additional enablement. There is the commander; the platoon non-commissioned officer; a medic and an assistant; two communicators, trained to coordinate joint effects and carrying radios with larger antenna, able to find a location higher up to maintain links between the sections and those outside of the immediate vicinity; two engineers, not tasked with breaching but with assessing the environment and coordinating the influx of engineering support when specialist vehicles are pushed forwards; and a sniper pair. Where in a reconnaissance section snipers are primarily tasked with ISR and carry weapons optimized for long-range precision, in an urban context this pair likely carries an anti-material rifle, suitable for engaging targets through structures at medium range. The assault platoon, therefore, is a large infantry force of some forty-six people, which in a range of recent conflicts is roughly equivalent to the force concentration that has been found necessary to occupy a given urban objective.

Although around fifty personnel have often been the maximum viable or necessary concentration on an urban objective, preventing the isolation and therefore defeat of that force has required the ability to punch onto and through adjacent urban areas, so that if one platoon assaults or holds the objective, and another is held in reserve to blunt an enemy counter-assault onto an objective, a third is free to disrupt approaches to the objective or to move to isolate it. Thus, three platoons form a company, with additional support elements forming a company group.

Some of the support elements will be explored later, but one that is of immediate tactical relevance is fires support. In the first instance the assault system will be supported by the fires system when it is committed against an objective. To that end the assault system has access to significant volumes of high lethality fires. These, however, cause widespread damage in an urban environment and are inefficient in this environment because they either approach at a high angle of fire that is not suitable for hitting targets precisely on lower levels of buildings, or at a low angle of fire in which case there will often be obstructions on its arc of travel. Tactical fires in direct support of urban operations, therefore, require a fires company supporting the assault companies. These capabilities can sacrifice range for precision and payload. There are several key tasks for this fires support. First, it must be able to lay down multispectral smoke to screen axes of advance to allow the assault force to punch across exposed terrain into the dense urban area. Secondly, it must enable the precision engagement of identified firing posts or occupied structures. Thirdly, it must enable the destruction of high-value targets or threats, which may be moving. The most sensible delivery platform may be a short-

---

[6] TheMIS being an example of such a platform: 'Milrem Robotics' THeMIS Combat Unmanned Ground Vehicle on Display at DIMDEX', *Milrem Robotics,* 20 March 2022: https://milremrobotics.com/milrem-robotics-themis-combat-unmanned-ground-vehicle-on-display-at-dimdex/, accessed 20 July 2022.

range loitering munition, able to approach targets with a flight plan, or under guidance. Such a method allows exposure to defences for the shortest possible duration. Unlike the fires system, in which fire control is best achieved with centralized direction, the clutter of the urban environment makes the detection of targets with stand-off highly problematic. It is better therefore that the fire controllers and sniper teams organic to the infantry platoons call for and direct fires by identifying coordinates and the feature of a building that is to be targeted. As regards the delivery mechanism we may envisage each assault company being supported by three launchers, comprising a vehicle and trailer with the trailer holding up to eight munitions on rails. The vehicle should carry a signaller, a fire controller and two additional personnel. The control systems for the UAS should be able to be used from the vehicle, or offboarded. Similarly, the antenna for controlling the loitering munitions should be removable from the vehicle. Thus, this system may park the trailer in an alley or garage, and have the control unit in a basement, with the antenna mounted on a rooftop, connected by cable. This separation of the location of the antenna and controller, from the launcher, in an already-cluttered urban environment, should prevent effective detection and engagement of the crew or launcher.[7] By launching from within urban clutter horizontally and climbing out of the street, the munition should be able to separate its launch from where it begins to appear on enemy detection systems. The system ought to be autonomously navigable to a point for strike, to a holding area where it will loiter until it receives an update instruction from an appropriately keyed controller or fly under command. It ought to have three warheads, with a modular weapons bay to allow the appropriate fit to be pre-loaded onto the trailer. The warhead options should include a multispectral smoke dispenser or white phosphorous round, a thermobaric warhead and a tandem-shaped charge. In this way the assault company should be able to draw upon sufficient numbers of precise, high-impact strikes, to dislodge strong points that are fixing them, disrupting tempo or proving costly to crack.

The assault battalion therefore comprises three assault companies, a fire support company and a support company. The latter ought to comprise a medical section, a combat engineering section, a signals section and two platoons of logistics troops tasked with resupplying the assault companies. Three such battalions would be the core of the assault force.

Securing the sector

The urban environment is juxtaposed between dense structures, and barren canyons. Roads can create sight lines that run for miles. Perhaps more importantly, they create open ground that can be denied, and which divides up a large urban space into a series of smaller operational challenges. At the most extreme there are rivers, with bridges

---

[7] Strikes on ground control stations of UAS has been widespread during the war in Ukraine and has often proven effective. Author interviews, Ukrainian J7 from the General Staff, Ukraine, August 2022.

becoming vital points over which forces fight for control. This dynamic has been consistent, from Arnhem to Mosul. But divides are also found along key avenues, or even between city sectors with different types of structure. The US walling in of Sadr City in Baghdad demonstrates how a city can become a series of isolated problem sets,[8] just as the distinct phases of the Battle for Hue in Vietnam were separated by the peculiar features of the Citadel.[9] In both instances the divide was both architectural and a reflection of human terrain. For any force wishing to hold an urban area it is necessary to be able to punch across these open spaces and to deny them to the enemy. The control of crossroads, and the ability to hold firing positions on them, allows a force to cover the flank of an assault by preventing the enemy from manoeuvring forces between sectors. Had the Russians – for example – been able to cut and hold the road to Donetsk Airport, rather than just putting it under artillery threat, the duration of the defence would have been considerably curtailed.[10] The process of denying such spaces – which are necessarily exposed to a considerable number of threat vectors – means taking and returning fire. It is therefore a task for which armour is best suited, albeit armour with different characteristics to that outlined as an element of the manoeuvre system.

The characteristics of armour for the manoeuvre system emphasized mobility and sustainability. The characteristics for armour optimized for enabling the urban break-in and dominance of urban canyons must prioritize protection, sensing in a cluttered environment, and mobility over short distances and in constrained spaces. We may align the force against three necessary tasks: contestation, clearance and control. In practice these three tasks require cooperation between parts of the force, but the platforms necessary for each differ considerably.

To begin with contesting urban canyons, the characteristics of an optimized platform are protection and compactness. The minimum size of a platform for the screening function was largely constrained by the minimum crew requirement, which was previously identified as four because of the need to manage cognitive load and to sustain a tempo of operations at reach. The sustainment issue in an urban context is of less significance since the short distances involved open opportunities to replace either vehicles or crews. Here, therefore, we may envisage a platform with three crew being optimal. Given the prevalence of hardened cover and the exposure of vehicles, where the manoeuvre force may wish to control UAS and other systems from under-armour to maintain tempo, in the urban context most of these tasks are better off being carried out away from the vehicle to avoid concentrating functions in a target. Finally, sub-surface urban infrastructure is liable to be damaged by heavy armour, and so light armour that can avoid destroying the infrastructure over which it passes is desirable. The result is a vehicle optimally less than 54 tonnes, with a three-person

---

[8]   John Spencer, 'Stealing the Enemy's Urban Advantage: The Battle of Sadr City', *Modern War Institute*, 31 January 2019: https://mwi.usma.edu/stealing-enemys-urban-advantage-battle-sadr-city/, accessed 20 July 2022.

[9]   Alec Wahlman, *Storming the City: U.S. Military Performance in Urban Warfare from World War II to Vietnam* (Denton, TX: University of North Texas Press, 2015), pp. 181–236.

[10] Author interview, officer who commanded the late defence, Ukraine, February 2022.

crew, mounting an active protection system and with armour prioritized for frontal and vertical kinetic attacks.[11] There has been some debate about the impact of active protection systems on supporting infantry in an urban environment. Testing by Germany and Israel however shows that although APS does pose a threat to infantry, the risk is lower than that posed by allowing the incoming ATGM to strike its target.[12] Finally, an abundance of external cameras, especially for the driver, has significant merit in a vehicle optimized for urban operations. Although susceptible to damage, this is less true of cameras to the rear, and whereas a commander may guide a tank in reverse in open country, opening hatches and other ways of improving situational awareness more readily compromise the survivability of the tank in urban areas, where grenades dropped from above and short-range engagements with RPGs are much more common. Optimizing the driver to function with hatches down is therefore important.

As regards armaments, high-velocity kinetic penetrators have considerable value because of the high probability of kill against enemy vehicles, while offering a competitive advantage against ATGMs because of the time spent in flight for the latter. However, smoothbore cannons optimized for defeating armour are less well suited to engaging structures. First, they tend to either pass through doing little damage or else destroy structures entirely. Secondly, the side blast from these weapons makes them dangerous to fire in close proximity to friendly infantry that by necessity has pushed forwards of the vehicle, along its flanks, to clear nearby buildings. Third, long barrels constrain movement in urban terrain. There is utility in engaging bunkers and other hardened targets with HESH rounds. In practice, however, most tanks rely heavily on secondary armaments for urban fighting. Finally, there is the fact that urban fighting often requires high angles of fire, and the recoil from large cannons places practical limits of around 30 degrees on viable elevation. Lower calibre cannons by contrast can elevate to 60 degrees, enabling engagement of targets on rooftops or of UAS using airburst ammunition. This suggests a need for two variants: one vehicle equipped with a smoothbore cannon of 105mm or 120mm and a second with a 30–60mm cannon. In either case it is desirable for each vehicle to have a separate machine gun – ideally two – mounted on the remote weapons station. It has been persistently demonstrated that attackers fighting vehicles in urban environments tend to cognitively correlate the tank's area of interest with the alignment of its main armament and fail to recognize the facing of RWS which can, therefore, engage targets to the flank, rear or above.[13]

Working in pairs to enable peer recovery, a platoon ought to comprise six vehicles: two vehicles armed with 120mm cannon to provide overwatch, and two pairs of two 30–60mm vehicles to contest the canyon. Historically the size of armoured platoons has been constrained to 3–4 vehicles because of the limitations on viable span of control for a platoon commander. The combination of identify-friend-or-foe and real

[11] The value of lighter tanks has been persuasively argued through operational analysis by Jim Storr, *Battelgroup!: The Lessons of the Unfought Battles of the Cold War* (London: Helion, 2021).

[12] Author interview, IDF and industry representatives, Israel, July 2019, and German defence officials, Germany, August 2021.

[13] Author interview, US armoured officer conducting lessons learned study, US, December 2021.

time blue force tracking across a mesh network, however, enables a commander to extend their viable span of control.

If a sector likely has two crossroads or intersections on separate axes, then it follows that three such platoons of vehicles – two fighting, one in reserve, make up the company that ought to collaborate with the assault company contesting a sector. Identifying and suppressing enemy firing positions and establishing overwatch are pre-requisites to enabling assault forces to push between sectors, and as the infantry move through the buildings, the successful contest of the urban canyon creates the opportunity to begin clearance operations either along the axis of movement or between buildings. The aim should be to create movement corridors for friendly manoeuvre, and to displace obstacles onto, or else erect obstacles upon enemy lines of advance or to obstruct enemy sight lines into a target sector. These are all tasks that ultimately depend upon engineers.

Clearance first demands that axes for friendly movement or resupply be secured once the buildings have been cleared. This may require the removal of mines, barbed wire, rubble, emplaced obstacles, vehicles and the filling in of holes and gaps in the road surface. Armoured engineering vehicles, with dozer blades, hydraulic arms with buckets and winches are key tools. They are likely to be employed for a short period and then moved under cover. Consequently, they do not need a large crew as engineers can be rotated into and out of the platform if it must be employed for a sustained period. A pair of such vehicles is the basic unit of action. Secondly, there is the requirement for armoured bulldozers able to move large and heavy objects, not least steel-reinforced concrete barricades. The lack of available sand or earth in an urban environment means that HESCO-type gabions are not a reliable means of emplacing defences. Wire gabions containing rubble may work. ISO containers filled with rubble or concrete may also be effective. In extremis, T-Walls and other large barriers can be brought into an environment. Thirdly, the clearance of nuisance minefields, the placement of demolitions, and the emplacement of anti-tank mines, razor wire and force protection engineering, including the rapid erection of simple screens from enemy observation – sometimes overhead as used by Islamic State in Raqqa[14] – all require personnel able to climb through the terrain and interact with it. A pair of protected mobility platforms carrying engineer sections is also a compliment to this force. Again, the need for this work to be conducted on two axes around a target sector means that three groups of these six vehicles ought to support operations against a target sector.

The final part of the trio of tasks outlined above is the ability to control movement corridors once they have been successfully contested and cleared. This is essentially a case of screening. Whereas in rural environments the screening force is best crewed, as it must rapidly and fluidly move between multiple complex tasks, the geometrical constraints of urban terrain and the close proximity, means that platforms can be specialized and – therefore – there is a greater opportunity to employ autonomous systems. There are three advantages to autonomous systems in this context. First,

---

[14] Mike Stevens, 'Resistance and Information Warfare in Mosul and Raqqa', *The RUSI Journal* (Vol. 165, No. 5, 2020), pp. 10–21.

lacking a crew they can be smaller and harder to detect. Secondly, whereas the crewed systems for contesting the urban canyon will move and present a fleeting target, maintaining long-term observation of an axis demands remaining static. The likelihood of being eventually identified and struck is therefore high. Avoiding the loss of personnel in this role is an advantage. Thirdly, autonomous systems can detect and engage targets against a complex background far quicker and more accurately than crewed systems.[15]

The basic unit of action for autonomous elements ought to comprise three protected mobility utility vehicles and three autonomous platforms. The protected mobility utility vehicles would tow the Robotic Autonomous Systems (RAS) into the area of operation. Each vehicle would carry four crew, with a RAS operator and mechanic in each vehicle. The unit would also have a signaller, a sniper pair, a UAV operator equipped in the same manner as those in the assault teams and a MANPADS pair. Having selected a vantage point for the RAS, the MANPADS team would seek elevation, prioritizing air threats but also capable of engaging vehicles if necessary. The signaller would seek to maintain links with the assault company that the RAS unit was protecting, in order to establish arcs of fire and control measures. The UAS operator would seek to establish overwatch to maintain situational awareness for the unit off the arc to be covered by the RAS, thereby protecting the unit from enemy infiltration. The mechanics would be responsible for setting up the RAS, while the operators would be responsible for monitoring the feeds from their weapons systems and sensors.

As regards the RAS, the basic format would be a tracked platform. One would carry a sensor mast mounting passive acoustic, electromagnetic, and elector-optical and thermal sensors, as well as an active retro-reflective sensor. The use of a laser as an effector could also be used to dazzle enemy optics or UAVs. The mast would be given an axis to cover and could be camouflaged against the broken top of a wall, a lamppost or similar pieces of urban clutter. Using the interplay between these sensors the ISR RAS would automatically flag identified targets, for the operator to approve or decline for targeting. If approved, the target would be handed to the two armed RAS. These would carry an HMG or GMG and ATGM each and, upon receiving target coordinates, could then roll from cover, slew to the bearing and using their own optics acquire the target, with the operator monitoring from cover whether it had correctly identified the target. Because speed would be critical, the operator would be on, rather than in the loop, with the opportunity to veto engagement. The operator could also end an engagement in the event that the system glitched and – for example – engaged the same target multiple times.[16] Three such groups per target sector forms the RAS company.

---

[15] Author observations, experimentation of autonomous overwatch during urban break in, Exercise Autonomous Warrior 2018, UK, October 2018.

[16] Determining the status of a target that has been engaged or even hit can be especially problematic for autonomous systems. Defining the point at which a target is dead as compared with lying down for better cover is not always clear. Rag-dolling dead targets meanwhile is both a waste of ammunition and produces gruesome video that could have a negative impact in the information environment.

The radio frequency detection capability within these units is a particularly important sensor. In a non-urban context, the significant distances involved limits the density of UAS and therefore makes the destruction of UAS a viable means of breaking down enemy ISR. In an urban context – or similarly dense terrain – the drop in distance makes small UAS a pervasive tactical tool. UAS can be downed using air burst cannon or even shotguns carried by assaulters.[17] In some contexts this is both viable and sensible. In many contexts, however, a counter-UAS strategy reliant upon jamming, directed energy effects, or direct fire, is of limited utility in an urban setting. Generally, line of sight will be restricted until the last minute. Distinguishing friendly from enemy UAS will be difficult. Jamming, meanwhile, is highly likely to cause significant fratricide. A more assured approach is identifying UAV control stations or controllers before handing off these targets to be engaged with fires.

In total, therefore the assault system should have an armoured battalion comprising three armoured companies, an engineering company and a RAS company to support assault battalions in the urban environment, and a second armoured battalion of the same composition to dominate and screen the urban, rural interface, ensuring resupply routes into and out of the city.

Controlling the sector

A persistent problem in urban operations is the ability to control what has been seized. Subterranean networks, stay-behind forces and insurgents among the civilian population can all enable the enemy to reoccupy cleared areas. Although much has been written on the combat mass necessary for urban fighting, historically much of that mass has been needed to isolate and then occupy ground rather than conduct the business of seizing and clearing it. Another point is that assault troops make for poor control forces. Troops trained, equipped and psychologically prepared to punch onto defended objectives are likely stressed, violent and lack the equipment and tools to effectively interact with and deal with civilian needs.[18] This, therefore, requires different forces. The key tasks of the control force must be ground holding, managing the civilian population, securing infrastructure, gathering intelligence and sustaining assaulters. Finally, this is the natural place for the headquarters of the assault system to be nested.

Infantry must be at the heart of any control force. There are myriad tasks, from maintaining checkpoints, blocking positions, patrolling and force protection, for which infantry skills are essential. As a structure it makes sense to have three infantry

---

[17] Author interviews, Royal Marine Commandos exploring C-UAS layers, UK, June 2022.

[18] From a mindset point of view, consider the use of assault troops for riot control that led to the events of Bloody Sunday, see *Report of the Bloody Sunday Inquiry* (London: HM Stationary Office, 2010): https://assets.publishing.service.gov.uk/government/uploads/system/uploads/attachment_data/file/279133/0029_i.pdf, accessed 20 July 2022; and there is a long history of successful assaults being followed by periods of intense violence, as in Mosul, see Ghaith Abdul-Ahad, 'After the Liberation of Mosul, an Orgy of Killing', *The Guardian*, 21 November 2017: https://www.theguardian.com/world/2017/nov/21/after-the-liberation-of-mosul-an-orgy-of-killing, accessed 20 July 2022.

companies – structured in the same manner as the infantry companies of the manoeuvre system – able to maintain the perimeter. At the same time, however, it is necessary for infantry to be attached to protect the other functions within the control force. For this, an additional company of infantry is required, but with its sections aligned with the elements they are supporting, rather than formed as a company. This produces nine units of action.

The first necessary function is two medical sections, one to operate and the other to deal with casualties who do not need to be operated on and can be treated in place. Whereas in other parts of the force the medical challenge is dispersed and units require potentially complex treatment but at a small scale, in urban operations there is likely to be a significant number of casualties, and there is also the need to support civilian casualties. Furthermore, distances being moved are shorter and it is often possible to have a hardened structure to use as a field hospital. Concentrating medical capacity is therefore sensible. The medical section ought to work on the basis of two vehicles of equipment that they can unload where they have established the field hospital, with the vehicles then able to function as ambulances, to be taken over by the assigned infantry to extract casualties to the point as they are withdrawn from the line.

A second critical requirement is the management of the civilian population. This involves linking with local notables, clearly communicating with the local population, and the ability to detain and look after both enemy prisoners and civilians who may be assisting the enemy or doing harm to other civilians. For this task the provision of a section of military police is advisable. Another function is intelligence, both to identify enemy sympathisers and recruit friendly agents, but also to leverage the civilian population to identify enemy hiding points, access points for subterranean features, the location of booby-traps, caches and other points of interest. In practice the military police and intelligence sections would likely work in pairs, each requiring a team or sub-section infantry grouping for protection.[19]

The securing and managing infrastructure involves several specialisms. First, there is the need to have structural engineers able to assess damage to and the safety of buildings, responsible for identifying and organizing where can be fortified, where must be repaired, abandoned or demolished. Secondly, there is a need for cyber and signals specialists able to access, control and stabilize key communications infrastructure, to understand what data may egress from a controlled sector and what access points to uncontrolled sectors may have been secured. There is also the need to be able to establish controlled networks for the civilian population and to identify hostile signals activity that may indicate spotters or other nefarious actors within the sector. Thirdly, there is an engineering requirement comprising specialists on public utilities, able to assess the state of, risk to and repair of critical infrastructure, and to make judgements as to the impact on sanitation. Fourthly, there is the need for a CBRN team with firefighting equipment, able to approach and respond to environments that may be contaminated by hazardous materials.

---

[19] Jack Watling, 'Preparing Military Intelligence for Great Power Competition', *The RUSI Journal* (Vol. 166, No. 1, 2021), pp. 68–80.

The final section of specialists comprises mechanical and logistical reconnaissance. A section is too small to actually conduct maintenance or sustainment for the force. Instead, this section would be responsible for identifying areas in a sector that have stores or can be used for storing equipment. They would also identify the routes that supply would need to take moving through a sector and therefore established the priorities for where needed screening or hardening. This advice would also allow the military police to understand where they needed checkpoints and how to redirect civilian traffic so as to keep key military movement corridors clear. The mechanics would likely see what spaces and systems could be commandeered to support maintenance of military equipment and therefore the routes through which damaged equipment would need to be recovered. Both logistics and maintenance personnel could also liaise with the assault force to agree routes for resupply and the recovering of damaged systems, ensuring effective control measures for handover.

The command and control of the assault system is a complex task. Unlike the fires system, which executes real-time control of many of its subordinate systems, there is very little direct control required or possible within the assault system. The intensity of fighting and complexity of sub-tactical actions simply impose too much complexity for management from afar. The task is also distinct from the manoeuvre system. The manoeuvre system relies on reactive coordination of its capabilities in response to what is discovered, but could not conduct detailed planning because the whole point of the manoeuvre system is to push into the unknown. For the assault system by contrast the problem is the objective, which is set before an operation is launched and is therefore known for a considerable period prior to the assault being initiated. Planning for the assault requires detailed terrain analysis and throughout the conflict requires judgements to be made as to when to commit units, which urban canyons to contest, and when, and when to hand over from the assault companies to the control units. Once committed, assets cannot be readily repositioned. The planning staff, therefore, should aim to have a detailed, three-dimensional synthetic environment in which they can assess lines of sight, structural resilience, population concentration and other variables to plan where and when units are pushed forward. This synthetic environment would also need updating as the city degrades. The easiest means of doing this is to have a UAV overfly sectors and then load the video into a generator to render the environment. Reports returning from the control force on the state of infrastructure can allow updates to electricity and utilities data in the synthetic environment. The command group, therefore, requires a communications shop, a planning cell, and operations cell, and an intelligence cell, each likely mounted on a vehicle, enabling the force to maintain an accurate picture of the environment and to push in additional resources as required.

Seizing the objective

Two weeks of manoeuvre had seen the enemy withdraw their artillery from the heights around the city. The reconnaissance screen had fought an intense series of actions to push back the enemy pickets from two key MSRs to the West. There was still an enemy mechanized brigade defending the city, amidst around 340,000 inhabitants. The city straddled a wide river, running north to south. Its civic buildings were concentrated along the river's west bank, with the east bank primarily new-build, middle-income housing. Running southwest from the heart of the city was a ridge of elevated ground, with large, affluent houses on its southern side, and dense low-income housing spreading north, running into industrial estates to the northwest. The ridge steadily descended to the river, where at its tip sat the central train station, north of the civic sector. The MSRs ran south of the industrial sector, and along the southern base of the ridgeline, converging towards the central train station.

For the commander of the assault force there were several important features to the town. First, there was little of logistical or military importance in the east. Secondly, if the bridges across the river could be controlled or denied then this would have the effect of isolating enemy troops in the west. The four key bridges were situated in the civic sector, with an additional railway bridge to the north. Another important feature of the city was that the ridgeline effectively divided the west of the city into north and south. The ridgeline was defensible ground and offered opportunities to call in accurate fires across the south. Taking it, however, looked like a challenge.

In designing the attack, the assault commander decided that enemy forces needed to be fixed in the north and east, while the assault force focused on the south-western axis to seize the civic buildings along the river, penetrating up to the railway station. To achieve this, she instructed the reconnaissance screen to begin to intensify its skirmishing along the eastern perimeter of the town, encouraging the enemy to move its battalion holding the eastern bank further from the river. On the day before the break-in large numbers of vehicles from the support system were instructed to move towards the northern MSR, while the fires system began to conduct preparatory fire missions into the industrial zone. Dropping rounds through the warehouses did little structural damage, simply shredding the roofs of corrugated iron. Nor – given the nature of the structures – was there much likelihood of civilian casualties. Some industrial materials were ignited by the fire, causing dense smoke to billow out. The aim of the bombardment was to draw the enemy north in anticipation of the advance of the mass of vehicles identified by stand-off sensors along the MSR. The screening force was told to vigilantly engage any UAS moving north to positively identify the increasingly concentrated vehicles.

Cyber penetration of the town's electrical substations and the control stations for some of its utilities enabled the infliction of a power cut approaching midnight, blanking out surveillance systems associated with the town's infrastructure. Slowly the assault battalions manoeuvred over the start-line, working their way into positions to the southwest from which they could rapidly conduct the break-in. Just before the attack began, a series of missiles struck the bridges along the river, effectively severing the enemy battalion to the east from the threatened sector. Multispectral smoke was deployed on key points, cutting off sight lines to the avenues of approach to the southwest. Behind these screens, robotic autonomous systems and armoured support moved into identified overwatch positions and began to prosecute pre-identified enemy targets comprising enemy firing and observation posts. Air defence units begin to knock down enemy UAS, as they lifted from the buildings to try and see over the smoke screens. Friendly UAS meanwhile began to inflict jamming on the targeted sector and identified enemy mortar positions to suppress fire missions. More UAS were assigned to hold orbits to observe the lines of communication between the northern industrial and residential sector and the southwestern MSR, cuing artillery fires to prevent the repositioning of enemy forces from the north.

Reconnaissance had identified lines of advance that avoided the belt of mines on the axis of approach. For safety, the assault companies were preceded by engineering vehicles. They did not attack along the MSR, but instead breached the city just below the southern crest of the ridge, and along a wider front to the south of the MSR. This put them immediately into dense and complex terrain, with poor movement corridors on their axis of advance. Using breaching however the companies punched through the buildings, using their training and specialist equipment to cut into the defenders in multiple small, vicious engagements. UAS operators began to find and strike firing posts ahead of the assault teams, identifying and suppressing threats and robbing the enemy of situational awareness. The information they passed forwards enabled the assault teams to keep up momentum, pushing into the urban space against isolated, scared defenders. The defence had been organized to cover the roads and movement corridors with fire. Instead, they found themselves attacked through the walls and unable to mutually support. As in all urban fighting, progress was won at the price of a steady build-up of casualties. Nevertheless, the fact that the defence was isolated and fragmented, its command and control disrupted, and under attack from multiple vectors ensured that as dawn broke, the assault companies had worked their way to the edge of the civic sector.

Behind the assault force came the infantry and engineers. These began turning the houses along the ridge line into strong points, screening the southern MSR from the enemy battalion to the north. More infantry and engineers moved into holding positions to secure the residential sector south of the MSR. With their flanks along the MSR secured the armour began to move in, robotic autonomous systems taking up positions to close down movement corridors that the enemy could use to counterattack. The armour pushed into firing positions to begin engaging targets in the civic sector, while the assault companies regrouped. For the rest of the day the assault force held its positions, moving in more ammunitions, extracting its wounded and inviting the enemy to attack their urban defences. One enemy attempt to move armour south into the civic sector came under attack from UAVs. An infantry assault on the ridgeline started but was beaten back by the fresh infantry that had occupied the ground. Getting rest in the cellars and underground car parks the assault companies slept, ate rations and restocked their ammunition for the second day.

Urban fighting is slow, methodical and destructive. A day-by-day account of a fictional battle is of limited value. What is set out above, however, highlights how a force that can isolate enemy units in a city, can establish greater situational awareness at the tactical level and greater freedom of manoeuvre at the sub-tactical level, can chew through an enemy piecemeal – even in complex terrain – to take it under control. In the above narrative, over several days the force would punch into the civic sector and then north, culminating in the capture of the railway station and from there the isolation of the battalion to the north, with an offer to allow its withdrawal across the river if it abandoned its arms. The other half of the city, lacking vital ground, could then be isolated by the reconnaissance force, its defenders slowly attrited by fires, and fixed by the assault force holding the far bank. The dynamic would become rather like that described in the previous chapter, where although the enemy can retain the ground they can only do so at the cost of steady casualties and cannot exploit it to do anything. Meanwhile, without fires assets, they would be unable to seriously prevent the exploitation of the industrial area or the railway by the attacker, and once severed from supplies would either withdraw or surrender. This sounds very clean, when in reality, like all urban fighting, it would be protracted, bloody, and lead to significant damage to civilian structures and the death of civilians caught between the opposing sides. There would need to be an extensive stabilization effort behind the assault. But compared to the attempt to use conventional forces for the urban assault – suffering mass casualties like the Russian 8th Combined Arms Army in Mariupol[20] – the above vignette indicates how dedicated assault forces can turn the urban defence into a trap, even for a force with technical parity of numbers. Any such multi-day endeavour requires sustainment, as does the reconnaissance force and fires forces that shaped the battlefield to enable the assault. Critical support functions, therefore, are the subject of the next chapter.

---

[20] John Spencer, 'A Firsthand Account of the Battle of Mariupol', *Modern War Institute*, 25 November 2022: https://mwi.usma.edu/a-firsthand-account-of-the-battle-of-mariupol/, accessed 7 December 2022.

10

The support system

We have ten days of ammunition. How much longer we can resist is dependent upon those behind us.[1]

Colonel Bratishko, Commander 95th Air Assault Brigade

The previous three chapters have built forces from the bottom up, beginning with the mission and its associated tasks, and then outlining the constraints on the force and what it needs to bring modern and sophisticated capabilities to bear. This led to projections of the size of specific task-orientated formations. This chapter must proceed differently. With regard to sustainment, the number of trucks needed is entirely dependent upon the size of the force being supported, the intensity of operations it is undertaking and the terrain over which materiel must be transported. Above a certain echelon materiel will be moved in bulk by shipping and unloaded at ports, by train, or by convoys of contractor-operated lorries.

The transition from this bulk shipment to its distribution to tactical echelons requires that materiel is moved from fixed points and then disseminated downwards. In the past there has been a descending order of stockpiles as logisticians move critical materiel into divisional and then brigade support areas, to be moved to tactical units by those formation's organic logistics capabilities as the supply is consumed. As outlined in Chapter 4, this is a model that is increasingly vulnerable. In Ukraine, the ease of finding logistical dumps of ammunition and supply and the range of strike complexes has allowed Ukrainian forces to target and destroy Russian support elements operating according to the conventional logistical methods.[2] The challenge to be addressed by this chapter therefore is less about the overall size of logistical units, but rather the tactical structures necessary and the command and control systems required to move materiel from the fixed and therefore findable hubs where materiel flowing into theatre builds up, to the fighting units. This chapter also deals with other critical support functions, the protection of key hubs, the command and control of the force and the sensing and shaping effects that may enable tactical

---

[1] Colonel Bratishko, Commander 95th Air Assault Brigade, Author interview, Ukraine, February 2022.

[2] Max Hunder, 'Ukrainian Military Strikes with Western Arms Disrupt Russian Supply Lines – General', *Reuters*, 14 July 2022: https://www.reuters.com/world/europe/ukrainian-military-strikes-with-western-arms-disrupt-russian-supply-lines-2022-07-14/, accessed 20 July 2022.

actions but are too cumbersome and operate at too slow a tempo to be directly integrated with tactical actions. Unlike the previous chapters it does not end with a vignette.

Sustainment and enablement

Throughout this book the working assumption is that within the range of enemy artillery, groupings larger than four to six vehicles are highly vulnerable to being found and targeted. Dispersed groupings of four to six vehicles comprise a threshold at which the pay-off between the risk of unmasking and expenditure of ammunition required to achieve an effect does not balance against the reward of destroying the forces being targeted. This presents an immediate problem for logistics, maintenance and tactical functions like bridging. All of these tasks risk the concentration of tactical units and their enablers into a large group of vehicles at a specific location for a long enough period of time to allow for targeting. At the same time, the separation of logistics vehicles from the combat arms limits their available protection, expanding the opportunities for enemy UAVs, reconnaissance teams and other systems to disrupt the sustainment of the force. There are several principles therefore that dictate operations. First, it is desirable that works groups of logisticians, maintainers or engineers and operational groups are not co-located. Second, because they are not co-located, the works groups need organic protection. This protection must guard against small raiding groups, air threats including UAS and potentially light armoured vehicles. The basic security element, therefore, might be best comprised of a pair of vehicles, common with those in the reconnaissance force. One ought to be a short-range air defence vehicle, equipped with a directional jammer and laser capable of blinding UAS and displacing navigation signals to prevent precision targeting, while its missiles might be optimized for SACLOS engagement of aircraft at medium altitude, but with a secondary capability to engage vehicles. The second ought to be an infantry carrier, with a mounted section on board.

The rest of the works group ought to comprise between two and four vehicles, either comprising trucks or fuel bowsers with droppable containerized payloads[3] and MGs or GMGs for self-protection, bridging vehicles, recovery vehicles and fitters, ambulances, or engineering works vehicles. These units of action might then be assigned to a manoeuvre, fires or assault component that they are supporting for an operation. Thus, a resupply for an artillery group, for example, might see a works group comprising three vehicles carrying ammunition and one carrying fuel move into a position and drop their containers, with their escort providing overwatch, and then leave these in place to displace into a secondary location. They would then communicate the location of the drop to the gun group. The two guns, reload vehicle and C2 vehicle comprising the gun group would then move to the dropped containers, reload their ammunition

---

[3]   This was experimented with during an Exercise on Salisbury Plain and proved highly satisfactory, author observations, Salisbury Plain Training Area, September 2022.

and refuel and then move back to hide positions, while the logistics group could then retrieve the containers, and withdraw to the supply base.

Another example might be a bridging operation supporting an assault group seeking to move into positions to approach an objective. The reconnaissance system would use its engineers to conduct the engineering reconnaissance to identify the crossing point. The manoeuvre system would maintain situational awareness around the identified point – potentially by leaving cameras in the area or maintaining overwatch – until the works group was on the approach. At that point the escort pair would establish overwatch and the bridging unit would then emplace the crossing, moving away to allow the assault group to cross the obstacle. Once the assault group was clear the works group could retrieve the bridges and thereafter move away.

Many forces have historically tried to push enablers like bridging to the lowest possible level, with their distribution limited by the number of bridges available rather than a doctrinal desire to centralize such assets.[4] This approach makes sense for rapidly deployable assault bridges aimed at enabling armour to cross small gaps. In practice it is likely that works groups for assault bridging would be assigned to manoeuvre and assault forces and fall under the command of those formations. Bridging wider gaps, however, must remain a higher echelon capability. This is not just because of a scarcity of critical assets, but also because the time it takes to emplace and conduct a crossing leaves the force highly vulnerable to precision strike. In Ukraine, almost an entire battalion tactical group of Russian forces was destroyed when caught by artillery conducting a crossing.[5] In that instance it was a UAV that was used to confirm the location of the crossing despite the measures the Russians took to mask their activity. Protecting a crossing point from this threat therefore required very broad situational awareness and the ability to actively shape the area, just as the manoeuvre system aims at isolating objectives for assault. Bridging units must be held at higher echelon because to conduct a crossing may require the orchestration of the whole force to bring about an opportunity to emplace a bridge.

In terms of scale, the exact size of the sustainment force is highly dependent upon the infrastructure in theatre and the intensity of the fighting. Nevertheless, an indicative scale may be derived from historical trends which have seen sustainment shift from around 40 per cent of the force to two thirds of the force, as the level of mechanical and technical complexity in a force has increased, over the course of the twentieth century.[6] As a minimum it generally takes two logistics companies to sustain a battalion. Based on this approximate rule of thumb, with an expanded demand for sustainment from the artillery batteries, the force described here would

---

[4] The Russian Army having favoured pushing capabilities to the brigade where possible, as outlined by Pekka Toveri, RUSI Waterways Conference: Obstacles and Opportunities, London, 27 April 2022.

[5] Howard Altman, 'Debacle on the Donets: How Russian Forces Got Obliterated Trying to Cross a River', *The Drive*, 12 May 2022: https://www.thedrive.com/the-war-zone/debacle-on-the-donets-russian-forces-got-obliterated-trying-to-cross-a-river, accessed 20 July 2022.

[6] John J. McGrath, *The Other End of the Spear: The Tooth-to-Tail Ratio (T3R) in Modern Military Operations* (Fort Leavenworth, KS: Combat Studies Institute Press, 2007), pp. 42–7.

likely require eight logistics battalions. Based on the number of moving components that may require bridging there is likely a need for up to twenty-two assault bridges and a pontoon bridging battalion. There is also a need for two medical battalions. An additional combat engineer battalion and a force protection engineering battalion are also likely critical components of the support system.

One critical capability within the force that has yet to be discussed at all is aviation. Helicopters have been ubiquitous on modern battlefields and their absence from the reconnaissance, assault or fires systems may strike many observers as odd. Their consideration within the support system derives from both the changing balance of aviation employment likely imposed by the future operating environment and how aviation is sustained in support of the force. Fundamentally, the unique value of aviation is its flexibility and rapid capacity to be rerolled to support different elements of the force that are geographically dispersed. There is therefore considerable value in having it grouped and commanded at higher echelon – in the support system – able to generate units of action to support any part of the force. Secondly, with the expanding range of threat systems combined with the large logistics and maintenance footprint for aviation assets these platforms must rotate to the rear if their availability is to be maintained.[7] While this may make holding aviation in the support system sensible, the change in the threat environment in the air is also likely to reshape the utility of capabilities held within aviation forces.

On a chill desert night in the California desert, a company of US Marines boarded their helicopters and prepared to mount an aviation assault to seize an isolated village defended by the Emirati Presidential Guard. Using the elevation that bisected the exercise area the aviation made it to the designated landing zone but was spotted by a special forces patrol who successfully cued a battery of howitzers to strike the landing zone. Had it not been an exercise, the helicopters and assault company would have been destroyed on the ground.[8] Had this been an isolated incident it might be put down to bad luck. It was not. Throughout two weeks of exercise multiple aviation assaults were attempted. The only one that succeeded was when the umpires prevented it from being struck on landing. Attack aviation fared no better, with a majority of sorties resulting in shoot downs. This is consistent with evidence in Ukraine. Despite using EW and terrain masking to penetrate deep into Ukrainian territory, Russian forces were routinely destroyed on landing in the opening phase of the war, while its attack aviation has suffered massive attrition. Western aviators have widely dismissed the relevance of these losses to their own operations, citing Russian incompetence. In reality, while incompetent Russian aviation missions have been easier to film and therefore tend to be more in evidence, the Russian military also conducted numerous competent aviation operations, and were still routinely downed by MANPADs, cannon fire or ATGMs. Perhaps more important is that despite discussion of terrain

---

[7] Otherwise they risk a similar fate to Russian aviation in Kherson, see Joseph Trevithick and Tyler Rogoway, 'Ukraine Strikes Back: Barrage Leaves Russian-Occupied Kherson Airbase in Flames (Updated)', *The Drive*, 16 March 2022: https://www.thedrive.com/the-war-zone/44780/ukraine-strikes-back-barrage-leaves-russian-occupied-kherson-airbase-in-flames, accessed 20 July 2022.

[8] Author observations, Marine Warfighting Exercise 22, Twentynine Palms, October 2021.

masking, night flying and other tactics obviating risk, Western aviation has proven comparably vulnerable on exercise. On Exercise Cold Response 22 for instance, British helicopters seeking to recce positions were rapidly detected by the defending force.[9] For this reason, Western staffs now assume that mounting major combat aviation missions[10] requires up to three days of preparation to ensure the level of enablement and shaping to assure success. And this is against the current sensor suites on the battlefield. As this book has explored in depth, sensor density and fidelity are liable to increase, further constraining survivability. At the same time, the increasing range and accuracy of ground-based fires is reducing the necessity of mobile aviation fires, since artillery is more likely in range to cover a threatened sector. UAVs too can often achieve the reconnaissance functions without exposing crews to significant risk, and without the cost associated with piloted aircraft. This is not to argue that attack aviation is irrelevant. Rather it is to argue that the balance of utility in aviation is shifting, and that if attack aviation is to be employed then the shaping and enablement necessary for it to survive on the future battlefield means it must be held at higher echelon.[11]

While reconnaissance and attack aviation are becoming harder to employ, there remains a great deal of value in having crewed utility helicopters in the force. Operating behind one's own screening forces, these units are protected from the pervasive pop-up threats in the contested zone. The significance of utility aviation is that it offers a commander flexibility, in the repositioning of either personnel or materiel. The ability to rapidly surge infantry onto a point that has been assaulted, and withdraw exhausted troops or casualties, or to drop off critical supplies of ammunition to hard pressed units all matter. The ability to move specialists – whether they be intelligence personnel, programmers, civil engineers or other experts that may be required – increases the speed at which critical infrastructure or flashpoints with the local population can be managed. The basic requirements for these helicopters are far from revolutionary, spanning light-, medium- and heavy-utility helicopters. As a general rule, helicopter units of action comprise three aircraft. Two will be available to be flown while one is undergoing maintenance. The extensive maintenance that is continually required to keep helicopters flying and their high consumption of fuel and other consumables means that they require a fixed base of operations. Helicopter units may disperse to hubs for short periods, but if this is sustained availability will rapidly drop. The main hub may be moved, but in practice this would take a couple of days, with the new hub ideally being constructed ahead of time to allow for rapid displacement. This centralizing of hubs creates targets. Minimizing the number of enemy munitions able to strike these targets is best achieved by range, leaving the enemy with only a small number of strikes that they can prosecute. This, however, means that helicopters are likely to have longer in transit, making fuel efficiency an important characteristic of

[9]   Author observations, Exercise Cold Response, Norway, March 2022.
[10] Such as the strike on Iraq's radar installations, see Smithsonian Channel, 'Actual Footage of Desert Storm's First Apache Strikes', 22 May 2015, accessed 20 July 2022.
[11] Justin Bronk and Jack Watling, 'Maximising the Utility of the British Army's Combat Aviation', *RUSI Occasional Paper* (London: RUSI, 2021).

future lift. Another consequence is that aviation will need to maximize the efficiency of what it can carry. There is therefore likely a structural bias towards heavy lift helicopters.

Protection

While dispersion has become critical, what is described above demonstrates that there are critical supply hubs, railheads, bridges and airfields that cannot be broken up or easily concealed. Distance is the first means of protection. The Russian military's insistence on using an airfield in Kherson that Ukrainian artillery could conduct raids against saw sustained losses to their aviation for weeks.[12] Such sights must be kept beyond the range of tactical artillery. They cannot be kept out of range of long-range precision strike systems like short-range ballistic missiles and cruise missiles. Nor are they necessarily out of range of slow-flying loitering munitions like those described as belonging to the fires system in Chapter 7.[13] Such missile strikes are limited in their effect by payload. Although it is easier to defeat, another major threat is from strike aircraft, since the volume of munitions they can carry far exceeds that of missile systems. Finally, there is the threat of raiding and sabotage by enemy special forces, something that is especially viable in urban areas where it is easy to go to ground, and there may be an enabling network in a sympathetic civilian population.[14]

There are three broad means of protecting these hubs – passive and active protection, and mitigation – which have force structure and equipment implications. To begin with passive protection the containerization of supply vehicles, outlined above, is not only helpful in allowing vehicles to drop off equipment, but also means that the accumulation of supplies in hubs is very difficult to distinguish as to the types of supplies they contain. For an enemy using a limited number of long-range missiles, this reduces their capacity to plan where to strike. Another element of passive protection is the use of inert munitions for larger explosive payloads, reducing the likelihood of an enemy strike causing a cascading detonation.[15] This is particularly effective in

---

[12] Trevithick and Rogoway, 'Ukraine Strikes Back'.

[13] Nick Waters, 'The Poor Man's Air Force? Rebel Drones Attack Russia's Airbase in Syria', *Bellingcat*, 12 January 2018; or consider the distances involved in striking Abqaeq and Khurais, see Ben Hubbard, Palko Karasz and Stanley Reed, 'Two Major Saudi Oil Installations Hit by Drone Strike, and U.S. Blames Iran', *New York Times*, 14 September 2019: https://www.nytimes.com/2019/09/14/world/middleeast/saudi-arabia-refineries-drone-attack.html, accessed 20 July 2022.

[14] Russia has repeatedly employed this tactic far into the deep, see Andrew Higgins and Hana de Goeij, 'Czechs Blame 2014 Blasts at Ammunition Depots on Elite Russian Spy Unit', *New York Times*, 17 April 2021: https://www.nytimes.com/2021/04/17/world/europe/czech-republic-skirpal-russia-gru.html, accessed 20 July 2022; Martin Farrer, 'Two Russians and One Ukrainian Arrested after Suspected Spying Raid on Albanian Arms Factory', *The Guardian*, 21 August 2022: https://www.theguardian.com/world/2022/aug/21/two-russians-and-one-ukrainian-arrested-after-suspected-spying-raid-on-albanian-arms-factory, accessed 23 August 2022.

[15] As has often occurred when thermite is dropped on ammunition dumps, see *ABC News*, 'Syria: Footage Shows Islamic State Drone Blowing Up Stadium Ammo Dump', 25 October 2017; Kyle Mizokami, 'Another Ukrainian Ammo Dump Goes Up in Massive Explosion', *Popular Mechanics*, 27 September 2017.

limiting what can be achieved with UAVs or saboteurs, because most will not carry a sufficient payload to physically damage all the ammunition in a dump if they cannot trigger a cascading detonation. Limiting damage is also achievable through the use of force protection engineering. Berms and gabions can be built up to divide a large maintenance area or logistics hubs into sections so that a strike on one section does not damage materiel in another.

There is also the need for active protective capabilities. The most complex and expensive component in this protective architecture are long-range air and missile defence systems. These capabilities, in the class of Patriot, David's Sling, HQ-9 or S-400 can cover a large area and have a number of important effects beyond their capacity to intercept threats. The most important of these is shaping. Because enemy strikes have a probability of being intercepted, and any enemy air strike package must be large enough to not only prosecute its mission but also suppress the air defences, these systems massively reduce the sortie rate and efficiency of enemy attacks, since all attacks require multiple missiles to be fired or large strike packages to be brought together.[16] As the size of strike packages expands, so too does their necessary enablement, and that enablement can be targeted by friendly air capabilities to significantly reduce the windows of opportunity within which the enemy can prosecute strikes. Long-range IAMD will need to be connected and subordinate to the fires system, but it is worth discussing in the context of the support system because its role is to protect these fixed points and its siting is therefore determined by the support system.

If long-range IAMD systems represent some of the most complex and expensive weapons system on the modern battlefield, one key protective component is derived from one of the oldest counter-air systems: the balloon. The original barrage balloon was intended to create a physical flight risk for enemy aircraft.[17] This may still have utility in cutting off approaches that are hard to cover with radar. In Ukraine, for example, fast jets have used rivers as protected axes to penetrate defended airspace.[18] The much more valuable use of balloons for defending fixed infrastructure, however, is in their ability to carry payloads.[19] Payloads could include sensors for tracking threats: cruise missiles, for example, are much easier to detect and track with look-down radar than with ground-based defences. Keeping a continual orbit over supply bases of aircraft is resource intensive. Balloons by contrast can have a power connection through their tether and can remain in place for extended periods. Camera payloads can similarly provide situational awareness around hubs to detect infiltrators. Balloons can also carry transmitters and receivers, strengthening communications. During the

[16] James R. Brungess, 'Setting the Context: Suppression of Enemy Air Defences and Joint War Fighting in an Uncertain World', Air University Press, 1994, pp. 1–47.

[17] James Shock, *The US Army Barrage Balloon Programme* (Vermont: Merriam Press, 2006); Franklin Hillson, 'When the Balloon Goes Up: Barrage Balloons for Low Level Air Defence', Air Command and Staff College, 1988: https://apps.dtic.mil/sti/pdfs/ADA192618.pdf, accessed 20 July 2022.

[18] Author interviews, Ukrainian air defenders, Ukraine, August 2022.

[19] The use of aerostats in Afghanistan to maintain situational awareness shows the enduring relevance of this capability, see Shawn Petersen, 'The Small Aerostat System: Field Tested, Highly Mobile and Adaptable', *AIAA 5th Aviation, Technology, Integration, and Operations Conference*, 26–28 September 2005, Arlington, Virginia.

2014–15 fighting in the Donbas, Ukrainian forces found that they could maintain communications in the face of Russian EW by routing coms to a relaying aircraft 160 km from the front.[20] The capacity for free-space optical communication nodes to have a fixed point through which they can transfer large volumes of data potentially overcomes the bandwidth challenge in pushing large volumes of raw ISR data back to a headquarters.

A second payload for protection is electronic warfare effectors. Most modern complex weapons have critical sensors: millimetric radar, visual guidance and GPS receivers.[21] Disruption of a missile's understanding of its location can cause it to miss its target. In Ukraine, Russian forces routinely jammed satellite-based navigation around their own positions in order to offer protection from precision strike. Ukrainian forces found that they could displace the impact point of ballistic missiles by up to 150m using such methods.[22] The advantage of having these effectors elevated is that it places the effector in potential alignment between the munition and its target, while avoiding fratricide with friendly communications on the ground. The ability to hold EW effectors in position and then dazzle, confuse or otherwise disrupt an incoming seeker head is likely especially problematic for UAVs. Although munitions can be made resistant to EW the increase in cost and complexity will limit the size of the opponent's stockpile and so limit how many strikes they can carry out. The third kind of effector would be physical. It is likely unhelpful to have a weapons system mounted on balloons. However, the capacity to release multispectral smoke at altitude could – if triggered by several balloons simultaneously – prove highly effective in shielding an area from enemy strike aircraft or disrupt the sensors on a cruise missile. Although this would not be a capability that could be endlessly repeated, even forcing a strike aircraft to take a second pass drastically increases the risk that it would be intercepted by air defences.[23]

UAS and sabotage groups are less susceptible to these kinds of disruptive measures because they can loiter or persist. Other than ensuring that the perimeters of these sites are patrolled, it is necessary to have CUAS systems as point defences. In many places this would require something equivalent to CRAM as point defences of this kind also provide protection from mortars and similar threats that could be infiltrated close to the base by the enemy. CRAM has a proven track record of being able to engage quite large numbers of incoming munitions. The Russians have used SA-15 in Syria to a similar effect. In addition, the manoeuvre force will have to rotate units from the front in order to allow for rest and recovery. The unit to the rear could

[20] Author interview, Chief of the Ukrainian Armed Forces during the 2014–15 fighting, Ukraine, February 2022.

[21] Sam Cranny-Evans and Sidharth Kaushal, 'The Iskander-M and Iskander-K: A Technical Profile', *RUSI Commentary*, 8 August 2022: https://rusi.org/explore-our-research/publications/commentary/iskander-m-and-iskander-k-technical-profile, accessed 20 August 2022.

[22] Author interview, senior Ukrainian air defence commander, Ukraine, August 2022.

[23] In the Donbass Ukrainian forces found that dropping smoke grenades was highly effective in disrupting laser designation for precision strikes. Author interview, senior Ukrainian EW commander, Ukraine, August 2022.

have its CUAS systems – described in Chapter 7 – assigned to point defence duties. This layered approach ensures that few threats will get through, and those that do will have a limited impact because of the force protection engineering and other passive measures. If they do get through, though, especially against airfields, ports, railheads and bridges, engineer works groups will need to be assigned to quickly repair damaged infrastructure. Between the need for force protection and escorting of works groups it is likely necessary for the support system to hold under command around three battalions of infantry. These units can of course be rotated with those assigned to the assault and manoeuvre systems, allowing for recovery.[24]

A final element of protection is tactical decoys and deception. Operational deception is about shifting an adversary's understanding of one's dispositions and intent. It requires large-scale resourcing and the calibration of the whole force to communicate effectively. Tactical decoys by contrast can be built by a dedicated unit of specialists with the tools to create fake systems – or use damaged or destroyed equipment – and put the right electronic signatures around it so that it is plausible to enemy sensors. The priorities for decoys are command posts, air defence radar and other high-priority targets. Decoys of this kind have a number of effects. First, they slow down the tempo of enemy planning for strikes by forcing the adversary to interrogate target sets to distinguish real from false detections. If the enemy does put the resources in to do this then it also significantly increases the resources they must dedicate to ISR and thereby adds pressure on what are always limited systems. Conversely, if the enemy does not dedicate the resource to the ISR soak then they will expend many more munitions trying to destroy targets because they will waste them on the decoys.[25] The other obvious effect of decoys is that because of either the reduction in tempo or soaking up of scarce resources, they protect the force's actual high-value targets. The location of decoys must be based on an understanding of where the actual assets are and for that reason it makes sense for this capability to be held at the higher echelon to be directed from the force's headquarters. Another use of deception is the disruption of battle damage assessments. Serbian forces, for example, managed to get NATO to repeatedly bomb the same runway by covering it in sheeted plastic each night, suggesting that it was still intact.[26] Conversely, Ukrainian forces photographed and printed the image of destroyed buildings, then stretched them over the roofs of structures that were repaired so that Russian battle damage assessments concluded that functioning targets were destroyed.[27] The effective conduct of deception activities requires skilled personnel at multiple points of presence and likely requires

---

[24] Even with reduced forced densities, mass continues to matter, see Nick Reynolds, 'Doing Less with Less in the Land Domain', Jack Watling and Justin Bronk (Eds.), *Challenging the Narratives Distorting Contemporary UK Defence* (London: RUSI, 2021), pp. 34–48.

[25] 'Strike Me Please: Armenia's SAM Decoys', *Oryx*, 28 April 2021: https://www.oryxspioenkop.com/2021/04/strike-me-please-armenias-sam-decoys.html, accessed 20 July 2022.

[26] Benjamin Lambeth, *NATO's Air War for Kosovo: A Strategic and Operational Assessment* (Santa Monica CA: RAND, 2001: https://www.rand.org/content/dam/rand/pubs/monograph_reports/MR1365/RAND_MR1365.pdf, accessed 20 July 2022.

[27] Author interviews, Deputy Chief of the Ukrainian General Staff, Ukraine, August 2022.

a battalion's worth of troops assigned to the task, though augmenting civilian support may reduce the military headcount required for such work.

Command and control

Placing a force's headquarters – and its commander – within the 'support system' is contrary to both military tradition and historic practice. In many militaries commanders of combat formations are almost always from the 'combat arms' and there is an expectation that those who are directing others into harm's way have a presence on the battlefield. The commander is expected to lead forwards. In the Israeli Defence Force, for example, brigade and divisional commanders are expected to leave their headquarters to be run by their chief of staff, and make their presence felt among their subordinates. It is worth reflecting however, that this type of command as visible leadership is essentially an enabler of the force. The will to prevail matters. This therefore is part of the support system of the force.

The other important reason why the command of the force should be situated within the support system is to increase the gap between command and control. Command and control are very rarely treated separately, and this is a problem, because they are distinct activities and can conflict with one another.[28] A good example of where this becomes an issue is the obsession in much military writing with John Boyd's OODA Loop and the argument that having a faster OODA loop is critical to victory. John Boyd conceived of this concept to describe what was needed for a fighter pilot to prevail in a dog fight.[29] It is worth noting, however, that there is no command decision to be made in this context, just the identification of an optimal course of action. The objective is zero sum and unambiguous. This can be said of the fires system, which is why the structure of the fire control headquarters was laid out in such detail. In counterbattery coordination, seconds can mean the difference between catching an enemy weapon before it displaces and failing to do so. Close and coordinated control is critical. But determining prioritization, balancing resources and setting objectives are not necessarily helped by speed.[30] Ultimately a commander gives their subordinates tasks and battlespace. Their key decision is when thresholds of risk allow or require reinforcements or uncommitted capabilities to be released. This is nonlinear. The key is timing, not tempo. And in order to get the timing right, it is necessary to have access to a high volume of information and to be sufficiently protected so that staff have time to think.[31] Accelerating decision making often risks a headquarters losing

---

[28] Anthony King, *Command: The Twenty-First-century General* (Cambridge: Cambridge University Press, 2019).

[29] John R. Boyd, 'Destruction and Creation', US Army Command and General Staff College, 3 September 1976, p. 1.

[30] The equation of speed with advantage in much military discourse is problematic, see Alberts, Garstka and Stein, *Network Centric Warfare*, p. 89.

[31] Nick Reynolds, 'Performing Information Manoeuvre through Persistent Engagement', *Occasional Paper* (London: RUSI, 2020).

perspective: committing to try and succeed in missions even if it is the operational design that is flawed. Placing the headquarters as part of the support force allows it to have the distance from threats to create this capacity to think, but also access to the greatest accumulation of data spanning the enemy, the status of friendly forces, higher intent and available supplies.

The headquarters must retain some control functions. For example, the logistics system described earlier in this chapter requires a very large number of small packets of vehicles continuously moving around the battlespace. Understanding which unit must move what to where and by what route, especially if this must be sequenced or deconflicted to avoid accidental bunching at choke points like bridges, is a complex task. Here, however, there is a massive intersection between the revolution in civilian logistics achieved through the distribution of powerful computing and the military. Essentially, managing the distribution of logistical works groups is a travelling salesman problem. Historically, military logistics have been paper based, both limiting the availability of detailed logistics data across the force and demanding inefficient if reliable methods of determining consumption and pushing resupply forward. The use of AI, however, theoretically allows for a much more efficient system, so long as that AI tool has access to accurate data representing the system. For civilian systems, the ability to have constant tracking of objects through mobile phones simplifies this issue. For the military, mobile phones are dangerous and insecure. However, the system does not need a live track on all objects to be able to compute solutions. Suppose each container was marked with a QR code and assigned a digital twin describing its contents, location and status. Suppose logistics personnel have a means of scanning the code and annotating changes to the digital twin. This data would not need to be transmitted live. Instead, if each works group had a portable dish for satellite communications, it could be uploaded when the opportunity to upload data arose. Over time, the combination of requests from units for resupply, the ISR data of the enemy's activity, the pattern of consumption rates, and historical data sets should also enable the AI-supported planning tools to begin optimizing works groups in a predictive fashion, managing the movement of materiel so that it is already en route or close to units as they begin to need resupply. This is especially important in a context where the distance from the front to maintenance and supply hubs is likely to be considerable. In Ukraine, for example, both Russian and Ukrainian forces have found it necessary to locate maintenance hubs for tanks several hundred kilometres from the front.[32] If there is not to be a considerable lag between requests for key supplies and their availability at the front, then an element of predictive push logistics will be required.

Such a system would not only provide timestamped location data for an AI to help prioritize and direct works groups but would also provide a highly granular picture for the command team of the distribution and supply status of their units. The same synthetic environment could be used for ticketing work across the support system. The same process with casualty clearing would not only allow for more efficient transfer of wounded troops but would also provide the headquarters with a highly detailed

---

[32] https://www.youtube.com/watch?v=ktJNrw6dxwo&list=LL&index=2, accessed 20 July 2022.

and continuously updated picture of friendly casualty rates. When combined with the ISR data, reporting from units, and feeds from the joint force and national means, it becomes possible for a headquarters to retain an exceedingly high-fidelity picture of the battlefield. Nevertheless, these data are best contextualized by updates by personnel and the discipline among the planning, intelligence and operations staffs to seek to understand the enemy's intent, the logic of engagements, and thereby to refine the operational concept rather than merely see themselves as managers.

Much military theory has emphasized making data available at all echelons. In practice, the complexity and burden of securing appropriately encrypted systems to retain top-secret data makes it hard to push such systems to the tactical edge, where they risk being captured. Much of the raw data is also overwhelming for small staffs. Another important aspect is that for data derived from the air component, space forces or national technical means, it is much easier to have fewer points of contact capable of handling large bandwidth files. The headquarters, and in particular the intelligence staff, will need raw data to manipulate and assess. But for reconnaissance operators – for example – key questions are more specific, such as when they are under satellite observation and when they are not. They do not need to know the types and locations of all the other satellites. This, then, is another sense in which the headquarters should be understood as part of the support force. As the point where data are fused and understood, the headquarters can push fused products to units providing them with vital information. Understanding what subordinate units are doing and what may be helpful is a support function through which the headquarters can enable its subordinates. The distribution of these products into the same satellite accessible cloud should allow units to pull information onto their MANETs periodically when needed. Thus the customer retains control over when they take risk in the EMS.

There is a fourth function that should be situated adjacent to the headquarters. So far we have outlined why the headquarters should exercise command over the force, control over the logistics and wider support system, and should provide a service to subordinates by fusing and sharing relevant situational awareness. The operational headquarters today should also be co-located with the information operations and cyber capabilities of the force. Information operations and cyber effects are produced continuously and their effects are protracted and nonlinear. Unlike fires, where the munition is well understood, in information and cyber operations, all outputs should be bespoke. A fires process therefore struggles to handle permissions for release. Instead information operators need as much flexibility and freedom to release as possible. To be trusted to do this it is important that they understand and appreciate the nuances of the commanders' intent, and therefore are informed by, without being strictly bound to, the headquarters planning process. To freely produce a wide range of products and rapidly disseminate them, this group may need its own works groups to film activity or engage with civilians. It may also need to declassify ISR or Signals data for release. But this must run in parallel with, rather than subordinate to, the kinetic targeting process. The second reason for their co-location with the headquarters is that information operations need to be amplified by and bound to the conversation among the international media and virtual dimension that is not directly in the combat area. This requires access to the internet and other services that are necessarily located some distance from the combat zone. How a force conducts these activities, therefore, is worth detailing in parallel to the discussion of the headquarters' role.

Access and influence

The force as described above – and especially the logistics system – is highly dependent upon digital systems, the security of which must be assured. The first task of the cyber component should be to actively monitor connections to friendly networks and to investigate suspicious attempts at intrusion.[33] A second responsibility is the hunt for and secure ingestion of data from the battlefield. The identification of what data is held within urban and industrial infrastructure and how it can be accessed requires both works groups and centralized databases. This data is important in assessing sentiment and behaviours among civilians, understanding stresses on human support systems and providing the data for detailed operational planning by the assault force. It may also provide valuable targeting information about the enemy. This work, therefore, directly feeds the intelligence cell in the headquarters.[34]

Information operations similarly have a function in supporting a commander's understanding of the battlefield. Monitoring social networks, cell phone activity and connectivity patterns all provide a detailed insight into the locations, attitudes and trends in attitude across the human terrain of an environment.[35] In terms of planning for human security and having a feedback loop of how a force's activities are perceived, this can provide a useful tool for anticipating challenges. It can also be an invaluable source of targeting information as civilians share images of military objects with one another and can allow for friendly units that are identified in this way to be warned to displace.

Both cyber and information operations have an effect function as well as an intelligence collection function. They are also similar in the sense that it is not initially clear how a campaign will develop. Cyber operators will try and find vulnerabilities in enemy systems, either to exfiltrate information, to corrupt data and cause malfunctions or to cause lasting damage.[36] Information operators will identify target audiences and the means of getting information to them. Nevertheless, which vulnerabilities in a network will actually be exploitable is rarely known beforehand. Nor can information operators necessarily predict which messages will take off and which will not. They must test and adapt. This unpredictability means that neither

---

[33] Defensive activity is the core of tactical cyber operations, see 'What Is Security Analysis?': https://www.doc.ic.ac.uk/~ajs300/security/CIA.htm, accessed 21 October 2021.

[34] Scott D. Applegate, 'The Principle of Maneuver in Cyber Operations', 4th International Conference on Cyber Conflict, 2012, pp. 1–13.

[35] When this reconnaissance goes wrong it can have catastrophic effects, see Nick Reynolds and Jack Watling, 'Ukraine through Russia's Eyes', *RUSI Commentary*, 25 February 2022: https://rusi.org/explore-our-research/publications/commentary/ukraine-through-russias-eyes, accessed 20 July 2022.

[36] H. P. Sanghvi and M. S. Dahiya, 'Cyber Reconnaissance: An Alarm before Cyber Attack', *International Journal of Computer Applications* (Vol. 63, No. 6, 2013), pp. 36–8.

can assure the effect they will have, but once they have been given key targets to dedicate their capacity against they will begin to build up options that can be flagged to commanders and activated.

Most information operations will depend upon public figures – think of the prominence of President Zelenskyy in shaping the information environment in Ukraine – while cyber effects will largely draw on critical national means. At the same time tactical activity can in volume create the background noise and thereby set the tone of the information environment. The continued publication of strikes in Nagorno-Karabakh dominated the international perception of the conflict. In terms of effects on the enemy, however, these two activities can be even more closely interwoven. Cyber-attacks against military systems, or the suggestion that these effects might corrupt capabilities upon which an adversary depends,[37] have an attritional effect on the trust an enemy has on their systems, just as leaks of embarrassing information regarding politicians and officials has an attritional effect on public trust in government.[38] The interplay between these two activities can be leveraged for highly tactical success, making small breaches appear significant to the enemy and thereby sapping morale. Again, these capabilities must be held at higher echelon if they are to be executed in a timely fashion because to not only employ tools to penetrate enemy military systems but then to exploit it for information advantage requires permissions to expose the cyber capability and to declassify the operation. Often, cyber penetrations can be designed and delivered against tactical systems via EW capabilities held in the fires system, so that cyber troops design protocol-based electronic attacks that can then be delivered against tactical targets.

Another interesting aspect of information operations is that it is enabled through civilian structures like advertising. Advertising is both the primary reason why the cell phone and internet networks enable the harvesting of such rich data on the human environment, and one of the primary vehicles for pushing content to the intended audience.[39] Advertising professionals are also often the most skilled at producing information campaigns. It is vital that the specialists who work in these fields are led by people familiar with military processes so that they can accurately interpret commanders' orders and communicate their plans during planning. Without that military familiarity external experts in this more conceptual activity can often derail and slow down planning by raising complex issues over which the audience is not empowered to act. However, the limited number of military information operations professionals is best enabled by drawing on personnel whose expertise is primarily

[37] Jack Watling, Justin Bronk and Sidharth Kaushal, 'A UK Joint Methodology for Assuring Theatre Access', *RUSI Whitehall Report* (London: RUSI, 2022).

[38] Sally Walker, 'Into the Grey Zone Podcast: Episode Five – Cyber Power (Part II)', *Sky News*, 3 June 2021, 06:00: https://news.sky.com/story/into-the-grey-zone-podcast-episode-five-cyber-power-part-ii-12212228, accessed 20 July 2022.

[39] Natasha Singer, '"Weaponized Ad Technology": Facebook's Moneymaker Gets a Critical Eye', *New York Times*, 16 August 2018; Anthony G. Greenwald and Mahzarin R. Banaji, 'Implicit Social Cognition: Attitudes, Self-Esteem, and Stereotypes', *Psychological Review* (Vol. 102, No. 1, 1995), pp. 4–27.

communication.[40] To do this, and to empower these personnel with the ability to push out advertising or to purchase critical data, it is necessary that these units have immediately available supplies of a significant amount of money. The trust necessary for pre-authorizing spending that could amount to several million dollars over an operation is another reason why the leadership of these activities need to be closely tied to a headquarters. A final aspect of information operations that fixes their planning and execution to the headquarters is the lead time involved. If information effects are to be prepared ahead of kinetic activity, then it is necessary for the information environment to be shaped proactively before the operation itself is launched. Again, there are difficult issues around operational security in how this is done, and so access for the information operations element to the principal planning group is important.

One critical element of information activities that is harder to control is the media. They are an important vector for communication and also an inherent operational security risk. The basic functions of releasing statements and facilitating embeds is likely to remain relatively unchanged. However, there are some principles in how to do it well that shape the design of the media team. First, some militaries rarely offer comment to the media and do not delegate permissions to engage from senior personnel who are tightly bound in what they can reveal. The result tends to be a highly adversarial relationship with the media that presupposes dishonesty on the part of the Ministry of Defence. Journalists approaching the MoD for comment are more often than not liable to be pumped for information about their story and intended publication plan rather than actually have any questions answered. The protectiveness of this approach is utterly counterproductive. US media personnel by contrast tend to be empowered and exceedingly helpful. At a personal level they go out of their way to facilitate the press and ensure that they provide reliable and timely information. Clearly there are many areas where they decline to comment, but the relationship is often very different. In the above force structure, the ability to move journalists forward via works groups is a key way of showing them that what is being described and briefed at headquarters is consistent with what is happening at the front. Again, just as cyber and information operations follow a distinct logic, the function of public relations should not be a 'posting' taken up occasionally by amateurs but instead be a work stream with professional and corporate knowledge. Just as a headquarters accepts that having assigned a task to an infantry formation the conduct of the close fight should be left to an empowered commander exercising mission command, successful information operations and media relations depend upon a headquarters issuing clear intent and boundaries but trusting its people to manage the relationship.

In summary therefore the support system may be broken down into four components. The first is the large volume of works groups conducting specialist tasks that must move around the battlefield in small packets, connecting the key logistics hubs to the fighting echelons. The second is location-centric protective measures to ensure that the logistics hubs can continue to function despite enemy attempts to

---

[40] Consider the delegation of authorities for information operations by the IDF and the improvement in speed of response that is thereby achieved, see David Patrikarakos, *War in 140 Characters: How Social Media Is Reshaping Conflict in the Twenty-First Century* (London: Basic Books, 2017).

disrupt them. The third is the headquarters element which has a controlling function in coordinating the works groups, and a command function in setting the objectives for subordinate units and judging when to commit resources. For the latter intelligence is critical. Finally, there is the information space, which for several reasons must have access to and awareness of the headquarters and its planning process but is nevertheless an independent function that must be empowered through mission command.

Part Three

The continuation of policy

11

Divergent domains

This vast operation is undoubtedly the most complicated and difficult that has ever occurred. It involves tides, wind, waves, visibility, both from the air and the sea standpoint, and the combined employment of land, air and sea forces in the highest degree of intimacy and in contact with conditions which could not and cannot be fully foreseen.

Winston Churchill[1]

The first part of this book focused on how technology was changing key principles in the conduct of land operations. The second part of this book examined what a force would need in terms of force structure and equipment to bring new technologies to bear, and how it might need to be organized to operate in the threat environment described in the first part of the book. These chapters were overwhelmingly centred on tactical and sub-tactical activity in the land domain. This was necessary, since each domain has its own significant levels of complexity that must be understood before they are examined together. Nevertheless, the purpose of this part of the book is to outline how the changes described already affect how the land domain fits into the other recognized domains of space, cyberspace, air and maritime operations, the choices that armies face in modernizing and how the military instrument is to be employed given the conflict dynamics described. This chapter is concerned with the interplay between the domains.

Much military discussion today is dominated by the US-driven concept of multi-domain operations (MDO).[2] MDO arose from a recognition that to overcome layered stand-off – comprising long-range missile complexes – it would be necessary to increase the cooperation between the traditional domains and to secure and exploit space and cyberspace. This is all very well. Nevertheless, the logic of each domain is distinct and is evolving because of different physical constraints and pressures. As such, while it is widely evidenced that advantage can be gained by attacking targets concurrently from multiple domains, how exactly they intersect and at what echelon this becomes

---

[1] Winston Churchill, *Hansard*, House of Commons, Debate 6 June 1944, vol. 400, cols. 1207–1211.
[2] US Army, 'The US Army in Multi-Domain Operations 2028', TRADOC Pamphlet 525-3-1, 6 December 2018; in the UK It Is Multi Domain Integration, see https://assets.publishing.service. gov.uk/government/uploads/system/uploads/attachment_data/file/950789/20201112-JCN_1_20_ MDI.PDF, accessed 20 July 2022.

relevant for land forces is less clear. This chapter therefore examines the trajectory of military operations and capabilities in each domain and concludes with where the domain activities intersect with land forces.

Space: Assuring the high ground

Five kilometres in front of the forward line of own troops a Ukrainian reconnaissance patrol prepared to launch several UAVs. Russian electronic warfare complexes were known to be situated around 15 km away, and the Ukrainians had turned off their cell phones, refrained from using military radios and set their UAVs to fly on a pre-programmed route rather than under direct control, so as to avoid interference.[3] Before launching the UAVs however, the Ukrainians set up a small satellite dish, masked behind a mound and connected it to a portable generator. This gave them internet access and thereby allowed them to use navigation tools to program the UAVs. The satellites they were connected to were not military but civilian, operated by Starlink.[4]

The ubiquity of civilian satellite coverage in Ukraine is not a new phenomenon. The majority of satellite bearers used by the US military in Afghanistan were also civilian.[5] Nevertheless, Ukraine has demonstrated some of the impacts of where space capabilities are headed. One of the electronic warfare complexes fielded by the Russians is the Krasukha-4, which is designed and capable of conducting electronic attack against satellites. While such a system may have been ideal for suppressing a small number of highly capable military satellites[6] it offered nothing against Starlink. There were simply too many satellites in the constellation for a limited number of Krasukha-4s to effect. The commercialization of space has led to expanding constellations, thereby offering considerable redundancy and therefore protection to infrastructure.[7] Because of this assurance, militaries are becoming more rather than less dependent upon satellites, even as the number of anti-satellite capabilities is also increasing.

While specific kinetic anti-satellite attacks are feasible against specific military satellites under certain conditions, any large-scale attempt to damage a satellite

---

[3] Author observations, Ukrainian reconnaissance patrol, Ukraine, June 2022.

[4] Christopher Miller, Mark Scott and Bryan Bender, 'UkraineX: How Elon Musk's Space Satellites Changed the War on the Ground', *Politico*, 8 June 2022: https://www.politico.eu/article/elon-musk-ukraine-starlink/, accessed 20 July 2022.

[5] Driven by several frictions, see 'Editorial: Bringing Space to Bear in Afghanistan', *SpaceNews*, 25 May 2010: https://spacenews.com/editorial-bringing-space-bear-afghanistan/, accessed 20 July 2022.

[6] A challenge for many military ASAT capabilities, see Brian Weeden and Victoria Samson (Eds.), 'Global Counterspace Capabilities: An Open Source Assessment', Secure World Foundation, April 2020: https://swfound.org/media/206970/swf_counterspace2020_electronic_final.pdf, accessed 20 July 2022.

[7] Kevin Chilton and Lucas Autenried, 'The Backbone of JADC2 Satellite Communications for Information Age Warfare' (Washington, DC: The Mitchell Institute, 2021): https://mitchellaerospacepower.org/wp-content/uploads/2021/12/The_Backbone_of_JADC2_Policy_Paper_32-ver2.pdf, accessed 20 July 2022.

constellation is far less likely.[8] There are two reasons for this. First, the implications of targeting satellites that are widely used by civilians and by other countries have dangerous escalation implications for the state conducting the strike.[9] It is, in many respects, akin to unrestricted submarine warfare in that it is liable to draw others into the conflict, and unlike sinking vessels the effects on the civilian population of states depending upon the space-based infrastructure will be felt immediately. The blowback therefore risks dwarfing any military advantage derived from denying the specific capability. Second, any large-scale targeting of satellites risks bringing about the denial of orbits through the accumulation of debris.[10] In the worst-case scenario this could trigger the Kessler effect where there is a general denial of the space domain through cascading debris accumulation, though this is less likely.[11] Again, the self-harm and international outcry if a state risked bringing this about make it unlikely to be the intentional policy of a state in war. In this context mass provides protection in several ways: it increases the resource required to bring down a constellation, it therefore increases the likelihood of the denial of an orbit and thereby deters the enemy from attempting to target it, and it strengthens and improves the connectivity and coverage of the network. It is ironic that the best means of overcoming the vulnerability of dependence on space among the other domains is to expand the level of dependence on the domain, while diversifying away from dependence on individual satellites.

While kinetic strikes on satellites may be rare, this does not mean that the space domain will be uncontested. First, suppression through dazzling and electronic warfare, delivered from terrestrial and extra-terrestrial platforms, will likely play a key role in the tactical enablement of terrestrial operations.[12] This kind of interference is likely the context in which space operations are most proactively in support of other domain activity, whether it is limiting enemy sensor coverage over a given area for a period of time or disrupting kill chains and communications. This requires space forces to have a presence in other domain headquarters and to both flag threats from enemy systems – offering situational awareness – and proactively offer options and effects to support other domain activity. This then, is perhaps one of the most vivid

8   Alexandra Stickings, 'In Space, No One Will See You Fight', Jack Watling and Justin Bronk (Eds.), *Necessary Heresies: Challenging the Narratives Distorting Contemporary UK Defence* (London: RUSI, 2021), pp. 76–86.
9   Sandra Erwin, 'Report: Industry Has to Face Reality That Commercial Satellites Will Be Targets in War', *SpaceNews*, 23 August 2022: https://spacenews.com/report-industry-has-to-face-reality-that-commercial-satellites-will-be-targets-in-war/, accessed 20 July 2022.
10 Brian Weeden, '2007 Chinese Anti-Satellite Test Fact Sheet', Secure World Foundation, updated 23 November 2010: https://swfound.org/media/9550/chinese_asat_fact_sheet_updated_2012.pdf, accessed 20 July 2022; Brian Weeden and Victoria Samson, 'India's ASAT Test Is a Wake-Up Call for Norms of Behavior in Space', *SpaceNews*, 8 April 2019: https://spacenews.com/op-ed-indias-asat-test-is-wake-up-call-for-norms-of-behavior-in-space/, accessed 20 July 2022.
11 Donald Kessler and Burton Cour-Palais, 'Collision Frequency of Artificial Satellites: The Creation of a Debris Belt', *Journal of Geophysical Research*, (Vol. 83, No. A6, 1978), pp. 2637–46; Steve Olson, 'The Danger of Space Junk', *The Atlantic*, July 1998: https://www.theatlantic.com/magazine/archive/1998/07/the-danger-of-space-junk/306691/, accessed 20 July 2022.
12 Brian G. Chow and Henry Sokolski, 'U.S. Satellites Increasingly Vulnerable to China's Ground-Based Lasers', *SpaceNews*, 10 July 2020: https://spacenews.com/op-ed-u-s-satellites-increasingly-vulnerable-to-chinas-ground-based-lasers/, accessed 20 July 2022.

examples of multi-domain operations. Terrestrial and extra-terrestrial operations are joined together in both their effects and execution. Very often effects in space will depend upon actions carried out on earth. Space is likely to be one of the most closely integrated with other services.

At the same time, the options and effects available to a space force are liable to be determined by the slow competition before hostilities commence. Competition for orbits, ensuring appropriate systems are aloft, and building a sufficient understanding of adversary infrastructure to target the right capabilities with the right effects are all slow and expensive. Although the vast majority of space force officers are liable therefore to work quite separately from the other services, pursuing structural advantage long before conflict breaks out, they will also need to deploy forward in support of the domains to bring those advantages to bear in the fight. In the first instance this means having a presence in the headquarters and fire control headquarters to offer relevant options. It also requires the ability to rapidly push relevant situational awareness to parts of the force so that they can make an informed judgement as to the risk. Finally, for soldiers to know what they are receiving and its significance, and to be able to take appropriate actions in response, there is a training requirement. Since the expertise and data will reside with space forces, they are likely the lead in ensuring that the joint force is domain aware.

A dependency which flows the other way is the importance of Ground Control Stations (GCS) for satellites. Another – potentially interrelated – aspect of space operations is the cyber architecture of the network. Destruction or capture of GCS could have a major impact on the enemy's ability to exploit key constellations and in some contexts may generate critical missions for ground forces. Cyber-attacks, meanwhile, have already emerged as one of the most widely used means of attacking civilian constellations being used for military purposes. Attempts to attack Starlink through cyber penetration did achieve suppression of coverage for a time, until patching resolved some of the issues. Cyber-attacks are likely to persist as a threat to space-based infrastructure, demanding close collaboration between these domain specialists.[13] The capacity to deny or hijack networks without the escalation risks associated with physical destruction make this potentially one of the most consequential targets for cyber operations.

Controlling the air

Air and land integration has been at the heart of joint cooperation for more than seventy years. The close collaboration between the Luftwaffe and Heer was fundamental to German military success in 1940,[14] while close air support has accounted for almost

[13] Juliana Suess, 'Jamming and Cyber Attacks: How Space Is Being Targeted in Ukraine', *RUSI Commentary*, 5 April 2022: https://rusi.org/explore-our-research/publications/commentary/jamming-and-cyber-attacks-how-space-being-targeted-ukraine, accessed 20 July 2022.
[14] E. R. Hooton, *Luftwaffe at War: Blitzkrieg in the West 1939-1940* (London: Midland Publishing, 2007).

80 per cent of NATO's deliverable firepower since the 2000s.[15] Among land forces the narrative of 'multi-domain operations' drives a perception of ever closer collaboration between armies and air forces. Given the firepower that air forces can bring to bear it is understandable why armies would want this to be the case. It also fails to account for the major shifts in the air environment that are likely to see these two domains practically diverge.

One constant in the tension between air and land forces is that while close air support offers the most immediate utility to the ground forces, air forces achieve their greatest effect on an enemy war effort against targets further in depth and of a different character than those that concern land forces. The destruction of industry, critical infrastructure, military logistics and command and control and the enemy air force are all of greater immediate operational importance than attacking ground formations.[16] In permissive airspace there is no immediate cost to the air force in prioritizing support to ground forces. In non-permissive airspace, however, where air forces must justify the risk being taken against their scarce assets, land forces are very unlikely to be the priority. This difference in target prioritization is a long-established tension with air forces,[17] but it is likely to be accentuated by the transformation of the modern threat landscape in the air environment.

The shift in the threat environment is being driven by developments in ground-based air defence. SACLOS munitions may be short ranged but are highly accurate and give exceedingly little warning of their approach. They are also largely immune to countermeasures. At the same time, the expanding array of long-range active seeker munitions is reducing the time that an air defence system needs to illuminate its target. The trend towards the remote control of multiple launchers is also making defensive systems harder to suppress through the exploitation of operator fear. The use of missile canisters is increasingly enabling a single launcher to fire multiple kinds of missile, complicating countermeasures and potentially presenting an aircraft with conflicting imperatives in terms of their attempts to escape.[18] All of these trends in combination are shifting the critical enabling mission for air forces from the suppression of enemy air defences to their destruction, since the lethality of future pop-up threats is too high. A further complication is the impact of long-range missile complexes on enablement.[19] As the range of threat systems increases, their ability to hold refuelling and command and control aircraft at risk creates an imperative for combat aircraft to have the range to cover the distance with enough fuel to execute their mission or contingencies over the target.

---

[15] Justin Bronk in oral testimony to the House of Commons Defence Select Committee, 'Modernising Defence Programme', HC 818, Response to Question 131, 17 April 2018.

[16] Prioritization of command of the air and strategic attack are clear in airpower theory and doctrine, see https://assets.publishing.service.gov.uk/government/uploads/system/uploads/attachment_data/file/668710/doctrine_uk_air_space_power_jdp_0_30.pdf, pp. 25–32, accessed 20 July 2022.

[17] Prioritization and balancing demands being key tenets of airpower doctrine, see https://www.doctrine.af.mil/Portals/61/documents/AFDP_1/AFDP-1.pdf, accessed 20 July 2022.

[18] Justin Bronk, 'Modern Russian and Chinese Integrated Air Defence Systems: The Nature of the Threat, Growth Trajectory and Western Options', RUSI Occasional Papers (January 2020).

[19] Justin Bronk, *The Future of NATO Airpower: How Are Future Capability Plans within the Alliance Diverging and How Can Interoperability Be Maintained?* (London: RUSI, 2019).

The high level of threat places a premium on very low observable aircraft. Combined with the range and performance requirements, this is leading the US Air Force towards the development of exceedingly expensive and highly capable large air platforms like the Next Generation Air Dominance aircraft and the B21.[20] For most other air forces this approach is prohibitively expensive, even if they had the technology to develop comparable systems. In a high threat environment a degree of combat mass to absorb losses is important. The logical route to increasing combat mass while retaining range and payload is to employ uncrewed combat aerial vehicles (UCAVs). UCAVs do not need the weight and complexity associated with supporting a crew. They also do not require the conversion and training fleets or suffer from the wastage of training sorties that limit the readiness and availability of a crewed fighter fleet. Owing to significant vulnerability to command links, however, UCAVs are likely to need to operate in a highly autonomous manner, possible because target sets in the context of DEAD and Air Dominance missions are readily distinguishable from civilian objects.[21]

The increasing use of autonomous weapons systems in the air environment has important implications for ground forces because these capabilities achieve their effectiveness through role specialization. As such, they are not multirole systems that can be dynamically retasked to support ground units. There are therefore two factors that mean that air support for ground operations is in fact likely to become increasingly scarce. First, air forces will prioritize higher payoff targets in a high-threat environment. Second, in order to loiter and identify and strike ground targets air forces will need to conduct a deliberate DEAD campaign,[22] imposing a significant period where providing support to ground forces would pose too great a risk. For air forces that continue to be built around multirole crewed fighters, the need to slowly eat their way through the air defences methodically clearing airspace will likely see the duration of the period where close air support is not a priority to be extended. For air forces that prioritize the DEAD mission and deploy systems optimized for it, the platforms themselves will likely constrain the capacity to provide dynamic support to ground forces.

Once shaping by ground forces or DEAD operations have opened up airspace close air support can either be delivered by traditional multirole aircraft or by medium-altitude long-endurance UAVs.[23] It may also be viable to deliver strikes using long-range air launched munitions if they are identified by ground targets, but they would

---

[20] Joseph Trevithick, 'Next Generation Air Dominance "Fighter" Is Still Being Competed', *The Drive*, 28 June 2022: https://www.thedrive.com/the-war-zone/next-gen-air-dominance-fighter-still-being-competed-drones-farther-out, accessed 20 July 2022; 'B-21 Raider', *Northrop Grumman* https://www.northropgrumman.com/what-we-do/air/b-21-raider/, accessed 20 July 2022.

[21] Justin Bronk, 'Air Forces: Approaching a Fork in the Sky', Jack Watling (Ed.), *Decision Points: Rationalising the Armed Forces of European Medium Powers* (London: RUSI, 2020), pp. 52–62.

[22] An activity that is exceedingly costly in munitions, see Lon O. Nordeen, *Air Warfare in the Missile Age*, 2nd edition (Washington, DC: Smithsonian Books, 2010), p. 230.

[23] Despite the hype over the significance of TB2 performance in Nagorno-Karabakh, using such capabilities in lightly contested airspace was demonstrated to be far more economical than aligning fast air to this task, see 'The Conqueror of Karabakh: The Bayraktar TB2', *Oryx*, 27 September 2021: https://www.oryxspioenkop.com/2021/09/the-conqueror-of-karabakh-bayraktar-tb2.html, accessed 20 July 2022.

need to warrant the allocation of these comparatively scarce assets. Thus, the basic implication for ground forces is that while air forces may deliver decisive levels of firepower in support of ground manoeuvre, they cannot do so in the opening stages of a fight and thus when the enemy has its greatest level of combat power. Ground forces must therefore be able to hold their own in the absence of air support.

Where the narrative around multi-domain convergence becomes both difficult and highly important is in the battlefield interdiction role, targeting enemy land forces that are out of contact in the deep. Such strikes could unhinge an enemy. For example, if ground-based fires have been shaped away from an axis of advance, and the enemy has begun to concentrate their assault force to seize an isolated objective, the opportunity to cripple the enemy's ability to transition from tactical to operational success by striking this concentration may justify taking risk with aircraft. This will require careful planning, however, not just within the air component but also by land forces in understanding what shaping actions or supporting effects they can deliver to help temporarily open the airspace. There is also the fact that large-scale air operations with their accompanying enablement will create a major window of opportunity for land forces to exploit the suppression of enemy defence systems to push land-based ISR forward and strike additional targets outside of the air force's priority target list. The need to draw together a considerable number of supporting assets and align scarce enablers means that large formation air operations will continue to be beholden to the air tasking order and therefore function on a 72-hour process. For land forces to have awareness of planned air operations to exploit contingent opportunity, and to request targets be prosecuted when the opportunity justifies the risk, liaison between the air and land component headquarters will remain important. Perhaps the largest challenge will be the deconfliction of airspace between aircraft seeking to work at low altitude and UAS. In practice, the aircraft will likely gain priority for the airspace forcing UAS to land and thereby imposing risks on tactical land units. The expectation that UAS operators will alert the CAOC or other air component structures to their flight plans is unrealistic and overly burdensome. There is also likely a need to instruct MANPADS operators to hold fire for the duration of the strike. The most likely deconfliction method therefore will likely be the grounding of UAS for a limited period along prescribed routes to benefit from air support. Given these constraints, the relationship between air and land forces is likely to increasingly reflect a need for system compatibility with tactical echelons, and integration at key points, largely at the higher tactical level, but a divergence in routine working.

The maritime flank

A similar divergence is likely to characterize land and maritime cooperation in future conflict. Although there have been theories promulgated about navies adopting more and smaller mission dedicated craft to increase survivability, the reality is that vessels smaller than frigates will have limited endurance and range. Even if larger vessels act as motherships for distributed sensors, expeditionary fleets are likely to continue to be built around large capital vessels able to fight in all weathers.[24]

If navies remain centred around capital ships, the cost of building, operating and crewing them will limit their number. The same dynamic of greater sensor fidelity and coverage, and the range and discrimination of missiles, is making the littoral a perilous environment. Since sensing onto the land from the sea is much harder than the other way about, the effect of the growing density of anti-ship cruise and ballistic missiles is to push navies from contested shores.[25] This is a serious problem for amphibious forces. Contested landings are likely non-viable. For naval power however being pushed away from the coast is less consequential. Sea denial is possible from a considerable distance, while control of the sea and therefore the ability to enact blockades does not require the close blockade of a shore, but rather the control of maritime choke points.[26] The world today sees over 90 per cent of global trade moved by sea and over 90 per cent of global data moved by undersea cable.[27] This is likely to remain the case given population expansion and the efficiency of distributed manufacture. Thus, distant blockade can literally cripple a state, as Ukraine is experiencing in the Black Sea. In this sense land forces may be able to effectively deny navies the capacity to approach the shore, but they cannot prevent navies from crippling a country's economy.

The interaction of naval and land power may therefore be understood to be diverging, except in two areas. The first area is in the use of land forces to establish sea denial over key choke points or from atolls.[28] The limited survivability of Russian forces on Snake Island risks a perception that distributed forces are easily destroyed. Given that Snake Island was in range of conventional artillery from the Ukrainian mainland, it is a poor example. But the use of anti-ship missiles, small minelayers and radar sites able to support friendly naval forces all offer a means of constraining an enemy's maritime options. At its most extreme, the positioning of such systems at chokepoints is likely to make any operation to regain naval access a joint endeavour,

[24] As demonstrated by procurement plans for major navies, see Eric Labs, 'The 2021 Outlook for Navy Shipbuilding Prospects and Challenges in Building a Larger Fleet', *CBO*, 6 January 2021: https://www. cbo.gov/system/files/2021-01/56947-Shipbuilding.pdf, accessed 20 July 2022; H. Sutton, 'Chinese Navy Growth: Massive Expansion of Important Shipyard', *Naval News*, 15 March 2022: https:// www.navalnews.com/naval-news/2022/03/chinese-navy-growth-massive-expansion-of-important-shipyard/, accessed 20 July 2022; National Shipbuilding Office, *National Shipbuilding Strategy* (London: National Stationary Office, 2022): https://assets.publishing.service.gov.uk/government/ uploads/system/uploads/attachment_data/file/1061201/_CP_605____National_Shipbuilding_ Strategy_Refresh.pdf, accessed 20 July 2022; Australian Government Department of Defence, *Naval Shipbuilding Plan* (Canberra, 2017): file:///Users/user/Downloads/NavalShipbuildingPlan_1.pdf, accessed 20 July 2022.
[25] Dennis M. Gormley, Andrew S. Erickson and Jingdong Yuan, *A Low-Visibility Force Multiplier: Assessing China's Cruise Missile Ambitions* (Washington, DC: Institute for National Security Studies, 2014); Sidharth Kaushal, James Byrne, Joseph Byrne, Giangiuseppe Pilli and Gary Somerville, *The Balance of Power between Russia and NATO in the Arctic and High North* (London: RUSI, 2022).
[26] Julian S. Corbett, *Some Principles of Maritime Strategy* (London: Longmans, Green and Co., 1911).
[27] Bruce D. Jones, *To Rule the Waves: How Control of the World's Oceans Shapes the Fate of the Superpowers* (New York: Scribner, 2021), p. 5.
[28] US Marine Corps, 'Expeditionary Advanced Base Operations': https://www.candp.marines.mil/ Concepts/Subordinate-Operating-Concepts/Expeditionary-Advanced-Base-Operations/, accessed 8 September 2019.

even if the land forces finding and striking complexes, supported by the air force, have very little tactical cooperation with the naval component. This kind of operation is fundamentally multi-domain at the operational rather than the tactical level.

The second area of significant interaction is in long-range precision strike and special operations. These are connected because it is the same features of the maritime environment that render them relevant to land warfare. Navies have two key contributions in this space. First, in many states depth, or battlefield geometry, limits the capacity to bring critical targets into range from ground-based fires and constrained vectors of threat assist the enemy in establishing defences and warning. Navies – whose vessels can carry a large volume of cruise and ballistic missiles and can generate large salvos – can reduce the warning time and hold targets at risk by expanding the attack surface to include the maritime flank.

Similar considerations make the sea an important vector for special operations. Infiltrating through enemy ground forces is exceedingly perilous. Aerial insertion in conflict is likely non-viable except in highly bounded circumstances, given the threat to insertion aircraft. While large surface combatants may be vulnerable to coastal defences, however, small surface craft can often conceal themselves while the small size of special operations forces enables sub-surface insertion.[29] The role of special operations by land and maritime forces is not just relevant as an extension of maritime support to the targeting of enemy support areas, but also has a critical role in finding targets for maritime, land-based or air-launched strike.

A final consideration in the trajectory of naval operations is the aircraft carrier. Many have theorized that the aircraft carrier is increasingly vulnerable and will therefore soon be obsolete.[30] There are two reasons to doubt this. First, all navies that aspire to project naval power today are building new aircraft carriers and given the lifespan of these vessels they will therefore be a part of naval forces for the foreseeable future.[31] Secondly, while the proximity of these assets to the shore and thus the ability to project carrier launched air power onto the land may be increasingly limited, airborne sensors

---

[29] Saul David, *SBS: Silent Warriors* (London: William Collins 2021).

[30] In both academic, see John Patch, 'Fortress at Sea? The Carrier Invulnerability Myth', US Naval Institute Proceedings (January 2010); and popular contexts, see Max Hastings, 'Giant Carriers Are Symbols of Our National Delusions', *The Times*, 14 December 2019.

[31] MoD, 'Joint Statement on Carrier Strike Group 2021 Joint Declaration Signing', 19 January 2021: https://www.gov.uk/government/news/joint-statement-on-carrier-strike-group-2021-joint-declaration-signing–2, accessed 20 July 2022; for France, see Elysee, 'Notre avenir énergétique et écologique passe par le nucléaire. Déplacement du Président Emmanuel Macron sur le site industriel de Framatome', 8 December 2020: https://www.elysee.fr/emmanuel-macron/2020/12/08/deplacement-du-president-emmanuel-macron-sur-le-site-industriel-de-framatome, accessed 20 July 2022; for the US, see Congressional Research Service, 'Navy Ford (CVN-78) Class Aircraft Carrier Program: Background and Issues for Congress', 29 September 2021: https://fas.org/sgp/crs/weapons/RS20643.pdf, accessed 20 July 2022; for China, Japan and South Korea, see Felix K. Chang, 'Taking Flight: China, Japan and South Korea Get Aircraft Carriers', Foreign Policy Research Institute, 14 January 2021: https://www.fpri.org/article/2021/01/taking-flight-china-japan-and-south-korea-get-aircraft-carriers/, accessed 20 July 2022; and for Russia, see Paul Goble, 'Moscow's Plans for New Kind of Aircraft Carrier Unlikely to Be Realized', The Jamestown Foundation, 11 March 2021: https://jamestown.org/program/moscows-plans-for-new-kind-of-aircraft-carrier-unlikely-to-be-realized/, accessed 20 July 2022.

and effectors will see organic aircraft remain a vital part of naval situational awareness, self-defence and naval offence. Carriers, however, do not fundamentally alter the dynamics described above as regards the interrelation between land and naval forces. Navies are limited in the size of strike packages they can generate, which combined with the distance imposed by coastal defences, means that air strikes on land from the sea are likely to be fewer than those provided by air forces and thus even less likely to be carried out in direct support of ground forces. Moreover, at the tactical level there is little difference as regards the integration challenge for the land force between aircraft providing support from a fixed or mobile airfield. Thus, although carriers will be critical to the future of naval combat, they are unlikely to determine the interaction between land and naval forces. The trends here described place amphibious forces in a difficult position.[32] Ultimately amphibious forces must decide whether they adapt to prioritize special operations from the sea or whether they become a deployable extension of the fleet, garrisoning land features in order to shape enemy freedom of manoeuvre in the maritime environment.

The implications of this for multi-domain activity are that land forces must closely coordinate with maritime forces at the operational level. At the tactical level, however, the main priorities are that there is shared situational awareness in planning staffs, a means of sharing targeting data between fire control headquarters and the naval component – most likely achieved through satellite connection. Where close working is critical is in assuring theatre access, a requirement critical to both land and maritime forces, likely necessitating joint campaigns and in the case of key choke points potentially a cause in itself of conflict.

War in cyberspace

As described in the previous chapter, cyber defence, reconnaissance and some limited offensive functions are required as part of the land force. However, cyber as a domain is not geographically limited in the same manner as land operations and cyber activity is likely to be an intense component of warfare. Understanding how wider cyber capabilities are likely to be structured and employed is important if the right connections between the cyber domain and land forces are to exist.

The first important character of cyber warfare is that it is slow. The second is that it is unpredictable. It is slow because developing access to defended networks requires a protracted process of reconnaissance, infiltration, payload design, delivery and the development of a mechanism for activation.[33] It is unpredictable because the target can disconnect, patch or alter a network so that either it cannot be reached in a manner

---

[32] Jack Watling, 'Building the Boat while Afloat: UK Commando Forces on Exercise Cold Response 2022', *RUSI Defence Systems*, 5 April 2022: https://www.rusi.org/explore-our-research/publications/rusi-defence-systems/building-boat-while-afloat-uk-commando-forces-exercise-cold-response-2022, accessed 20 July 2022.

[33] Joseph Raczynski, 'Kill Chain: The 7 Stages of a Cyberattack', Thomson Reuters, 12 October 2018.

that synchronizes with military operations, or the payload no longer has the intended effect when activated. The long lead time for cyber operations means that in order to have cyber capabilities emplaced for a conflict it is necessary to conduct a large part of the effort years prior to the conflict starting.[34] This places cyber operations in a unique regulatory position from a military perspective, because while the use of force has a clear threshold marking the boundaries of escalation, everything but the activation of a cyber-attack, and sometimes even that, must be carried out when states are not actually in conflict. Furthermore, cyber operations in warfare are likely to target industrial capabilities far in the enemy's deep, or infrastructure underpinning logistics systems. Even when targeting military systems the vector for access will often be supply chains and sub-contractors. This means that the cyber operations to emplace capabilities in a military context will often target civilian entities. This may be justified by militaries in wartime – especially if the effects do not kill people – but the legality of such actions is more complicated in peacetime.[35]

The features described above make cyber operations culturally and conceptually very different to military operations. Even if cyber operations fall under a military chain of command, the personnel, culture, command and control structure, the decision points on operations and the supporting infrastructure have very little overlap with the other domains.[36] Combined with the target set and when they must be targeted, there is a reason why many states place cyber operations primarily within the intelligence community and not the military. This is accentuated by the targets for cyber-attack that are beyond those of direct interest to the military.

Arguably the greatest impact of cyber operations is in the realm of political warfare. The penetration of personal devices, extraction of personal correspondence and selective leaking of such material can have a devastating effect on politics and on public trust in individuals and institutions.[37] Similarly, the disruption of critical services, or the perception that companies holding personal data are unable to secure it adequately, can cause serious economic disruption. Individually these incidents are less consequential. However, a steady drumbeat of such activities, especially if penetrations are exploited to consistently make specific political or culturally divisive issues prominent in a society's discourse can have an attritional effect on a nation.[38] The critical questions for a cyber organization are the scale of resource dedicated to such efforts. Suppression of adversary narratives online and boosting friendly narratives can similarly shape how political events are perceived, distorting whose message is

---

[34] David Sanger, *Confront and Conceal: Obama's Secret Wars and Surprising Use of American Power* (New York: Random House, 2013), pp. 188–225.

[35] John P Carlin with Garrett M Graff, *Dawn of the Code War: America's Battle against Russia, China, and the Rising Global Cyber Threat* (New York: Public Affairs, 2018).

[36] Nina Kollars and Emma Moore, 'Every Marine a Blue-Haired Quasi-Rifleperson?' *War on the Rocks*, 21 August 2019: https://warontherocks.com/2019/08/every-marine-a-blue-haired-quasi-rifleperson/, accessed 20 July 2022.

[37] Walker, 'Into the Grey Zone Podcast'.

[38] Simon Paterson, 'Sex, Lies and Videotape', *Edelman*, 13 November 2019: https://www.edelman.co.uk/insights/sex-lies-and-videotape, accessed 20 July 2021.

heard, let alone believed. These activities are considered separate from cyber-attacks in support of pure intelligence collection, but overlap heavily with such attacks in support of active measures. Even for states that do not consider such operations ethical or legal, defence against these techniques will be a major task requiring significant cyber threat intelligence, and security structures.

The point of outlining these aspects of cyber operations is that they demonstrate how conflict in cyberspace is by necessity constant. Land forces should not therefore consider cyber operations to be something they direct. Instead, they may articulate areas of interest against which cyber forces can develop access ahead of conflict, but ultimately the cyber force will present land forces with options of the capabilities available at a given time, rather than be directed by a joint targeting process. If cyber forces understand what land forces are attempting to do, they may contribute supporting options. But due to classification and permissions issues it is unlikely that land forces will have a clear idea of what cyber forces have prepared. The wider logic of cyber warfare is fundamentally different to the character articulated in this book. Land operations have been described in this book as operationally positional and tactically manoeuverist. Cyber operations by contrast are fundamentally attritional, except in niche cases where cyber-attacks enable others.[39] They are attritional against society, against its cohesion and its prosperity. There is little conceptual or practical overlap. Moreover the foremost target of cyber operations is the civilian population.

Many military services have in recent years competed for cyber talent both with one another and with the civilian world. This is profoundly unhelpful. The duplication of capabilities limits the scale at which operations can be conducted, while the subordination of cyber forces to officers with limited understanding of the capabilities is a recipe for poor resource allocation. The cultural differences between the communities who populate cyber and land forces also mean that it is better they are separate and mutually respectful, rather than integrated, except in the tactical and security context to provide a bridge between cyber forces and the planning conducted in headquarters. It is for this reason that after much experimentation the US Army has ultimately situated cyber command in Fort Mead as effectively a sub-division of the National Security Agency, and why the UK has created a National Cyber Force which is predominantly staffed by personnel from the Government Communications Headquarters, and only sparsely by the military services. It is also important however that some land force representation exists within cyber forces, because access is much easier if it can be achieved physically rather than remotely, and in some cases the payoff for using land forces to physically access a site may justify the commitment.[40] This is especially true for the landing points for undersea cables and other critical national infrastructure that cyber forces can exploit. Land forces can only facilitate

[39] Sharon Weinberger, 'How Israel Spoofed Syria's Air Defense System', *Wired*, 4 October 2007.
[40] Micah Zenko, *Red Team: How to Succeed by Thinking Like the Enemy* (New York: Basic Books, 2015), pp. 171–83.

these opportunities if they are aware of the requirement, however, and since this requires insight into cyber force planning, classification will limit the proportion of the force able to do this, making liaison a sensible option. The critical area of integration between land and cyber operations therefore is ensuring the cultural compatibility to understand mutual constraints and intent, and to be able to have mutually respectful and informed institutional connections.

What has been described, in surveying the trajectories of the four other warfighting domains, is a future environment in which land forces will become increasingly integrated with space-based capabilities at the technical level, must deconflict and dynamically cooperate with air forces at the tactical and operational level, must coordinate and plan with maritime forces at the operational and strategic level and have a shared appreciation of intent with cyber forces at the strategic and institutional level to inform operational resource allocation.

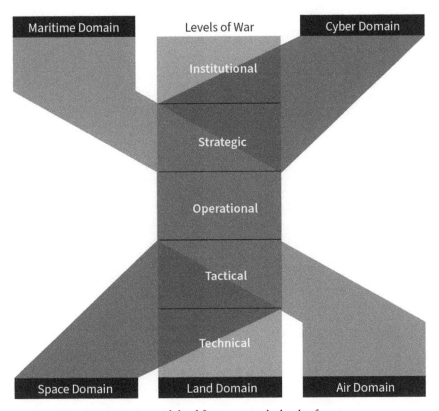

Figure 6 Domain intersection with land forces across the levels of war.

12

Priorities in transformation

How one lives is so far distant from how one ought to live, that he who neglects what is done for what ought to be done, sooner effects his ruin than his preservation.[1]

Niccolo Machiavelli

Almost all the technological capabilities described in the second part of this book already exist. Nevertheless, the force described looks very different in its structure and capabilities to the armies of today. In writing this book I had the luxury of a clean slate, mapping out a force from first principles, optimized for fielding the capabilities identified. For any army, however, they must manage a transition, not necessarily to the force described in this book, but to a force that can overcome the challenges described over the first five chapters. In doing this they must manage the transition from their legacy systems, their traditional structure and existing culture. This is exceedingly difficult because of constrained budgets, institutional inertia, and because ordering new capabilities will not cause them to enter service at the same time. Moreover, this book has only described the force as it is fielded and fights. To take an example of the complexity of bringing such a force to the field, almost all formations described use UASs. Yet how are they trained and certified to use these? Does each unit select and train UAS operators or are they taken on a course and trained separately? If the latter, who is responsible for the course? There is nothing insurmountable about this problem, but in an existing force, which is already heavily tasked, acquiring the equipment, distributing it across the force and certifying personnel from multiple branches is far from trivial. The result is that any transition will be uneven and produce distortionary effects. The question is what should forces prioritize? The purpose of this chapter is to indicate the key priorities and choices that militaries will need to make if they are to implement reforms. Ultimately the chapter argues that there are five areas where armies must prioritize reform – networks, shooters, sensors, urban training and layered defences – and other areas, like lighter armour or the balance of rotary systems, that are of secondary concern. The chapter will examine the priority areas in turn.

---

[1] Niccolo Machiavelli, *The Prince: On the Art of Power* (London: Duncan Baird Publishers, 2007), p. 115.

Networks

The importance of networks as a leading priority in force modernization has been identified by militaries around the world. In the US Army, the Army Network is the foremost priority of Army Futures Command as the critical enabler of Multi-Doman Operations.[2] In the UK, Multi-Domain Integration and the creation of a digital backbone for defence are the foremost priorities of Strategic Command.[3] In Russia, modernized radios and command and control systems in the Akveduk, Akatsiya and Azart networks were critical to the conception of its modernization, while the failure to fully train personnel on the employment of this equipment has been a leading contributor to the gap between Russia's capabilities and performance with strike systems in Ukraine.[4] In China, the aspiration for joint firepower campaigns demands seamless command and control networks for its forces during the opening stages of a conflict.[5]

The approach to network modernization has differed from country to country and service to service. Many countries – including the UK – have sought to build a defence-wide digital backbone, through change programmes seeking to connect the entire battlefield. Such approaches have an abysmal track record both in and out of defence.[6] They lack prioritization, have too many conflicting dependencies and often run into impossible-to-reconcile user requirements. This is in stark contrast to more modest and bounded programmes like the US Navy's Naval Integrated Fire Control – Counter Air (NIFC-CA) programme. NIFC-CA took the approach of defining a problem – initially integrated air and missile defence (IAMD) – and identifying the relevant sensors and shooters associated with that problem. NIFC-CA was not a programme of record but had an office empowered to set data standards for programmes associated with IAMD including the US's Aegis weapons system, special forces communications, E2D-Hawkeye and the US Army's Joint Land Attack Cruise Missile Defense Elevated Netted Sensor System (JLENS).[7] Because the NIFC-CA project office could set data standards for but did not run each of these constituent programmes, it was unaffected

[2]   Army Futures Command, NET CFT: https://armyfuturescommand.com/net/, accessed 20 July 2022.

[3]   UK Ministry of Defence, 'Digital Strategy for Defence', April 2021: https://assets.publishing.service. gov.uk/government/uploads/system/uploads/attachment_data/file/990114/20210421_-_MOD_ Digital_Strategy_-_Update_-_Final.pdf, accessed 20 July 2022.

[4]   Sam Cranny-Evans and Thomas Withington, 'Russian Comms in Ukraine: A World of Hertz', *RUSI Commentary*, 9 March 2022: https://rusi.org/explore-our-research/publications/commentary/ russian-comms-ukraine-world-hertz, accessed 20 July 2022.

[5]   http://www.mod.gov.cn/regulatory/2019-07/24/content_4846424.htm, accessed 20 July 2022.

[6]   The attempt to manage the digitization of the National Health Service as a monolithic project is a good example, see Rajeev Syal, 'Abandoned NHS IT System Has Cost £10bn so Far', *The Guardian*, 18 September 2013: https://www.theguardian.com/society/2013/sep/18/nhs-records-system-10bn, accessed 20 July 2022.

[7]   Assistant Secretary of the Navy for Research, Development and Acquisition and Vice Chief of Naval Operations, 'Updated Responsibilities for Management of Naval Integrated Fire Control – Counter Air (NIFC-CA)', joint memorandum, 11 October 2002.

by the subsequent curtailment of JLENS.[8] However, having proven that data could be passed and utilized between the remaining components, the project therefore had a set of data standards which all subsequent programmes relevant to the system could incorporate and therefore assure compatibility. Thus, F35 or HIMARS integration into NIFC-CA has been comparatively quick to achieve. Today, NIFC-CA not only enables integrated air and missile defence but can coordinate cooperative engagements[9] against ballistic, air and surface targets for a naval task force.

The force described in part two of this book depended upon three critical networks. The first were bounded networks binding tactical formations, with the identified structure being a mobile ad hoc network (MANET) connected by meshed radio links. These would be geographically bounded and forces entering a designated area of operation could join this network to gain local tactical situational awareness. These networks would be relatively low bandwidth, supporting voice, localized blue force tracking and low volumes of data.

The second network identified was a vertical integration of key sensors to the fire control headquarters and from the fire control headquarters to shooters. The bearer identified throughout was free-space optical links. There are other potential bearers, and some are more resilient in adverse weather. Redundancy matters in this context. Few are as low signature or have comparably high bandwidth as free-space optical links. Whatever bearer is selected, high bandwidth and low signature are critical to this network. This system, demanding low latency is best represented by NIFC-CA and for land forces, the critical requirement is establishing clear data standards for the systems that must ultimately plug into this network.[10] Clearly the bandwidth and latency requirements differ considerably from tactical communications. Identifying the platforms for which such a capability is relevant is therefore important, while imposing the requirements of this network on units that do not need it would be to impede implementation.

The third network structure described was a command and control database containing orders, relevant data layers and information support to subordinate units, and unit sitreps. The characteristics of this network are that it is for transmitting finished products rather than raw data and therefore requires a comparatively low bandwidth. The information is also important but less urgent, enabling periodic updates and downloads. Access to this repository was suggested to be achieved through satellite uplink and downlink. The exact architecture for such a network is less important than the standardized training to ensure that items added to and updated within the database are properly encoded and therefore remain trackable through search tools.

---

[8]   Jen Judson, 'Congress Nails Runaway Blimp's Coffin Shut', *Defence News*, 27 May 2016: https://www.defensenews.com/land/2016/05/27/congress-nails-runaway-blimp-s-coffin-shut/, accessed 20 July 2022.

[9]   Johns Hopkins Applied Physics Laboratory, 'The Cooperative Engagement Capability', *Technical Digest* (Vol. 16, No. 4, 1995), pp. 377–96.

[10] Nicholas O'Donoghue, Samantha McBirney and Brian Persons, *Distributed Kill Chains: Drawing Insights for Mosaic Warfare from the Immune System and from the Navy* (Santa Monica: RAND Corporation, 2021).

The principle of a network accessible anywhere also raises security vulnerabilities, especially if a unit is captured. Permissions management is therefore critical, with units only able to access the information directly relevant to their account, and for access to require three factor authentication, while the defensive cyber team must be able to sever a connection. Again, this network differs substantially in its requirements from the fires network or the tactical network.

The three networks described above are not the only viable architectures for a future military. By separating out the requirements for reach, bandwidth, signature and assurance, however, and aligning network architecture to its purpose, it becomes possible to prioritize which platforms must rely on that network and therefore which data standards to apply. Because these standards will need to be common to all future procured systems intended to interface with a given network, it is also important that they are mandated and the IP for the network architecture resides within the military, so that it can be shared with and prescribed to industry contracted to deliver systems that interact with it.

Another reason for consolidating the number of communications architectures and identifying who needs them is that as outlined in Chapter 2, the burden of operating communications is shifting from a small number of signals specialists to all troops. This requires training. However, if troops are trained on systems they subsequently do not use this is both inefficient and leads to rapid skills fade even among specialist signallers. Given that the number of personnel requiring a basic signals competence is likely to increase, militaries will need to begin identifying who needs to be trained on what system and building the training establishments and pipelines as soon as possible. If they fail to do this, then they risk the mistake that the Russian military made in its invasion of Ukraine, where a limited number of trained operators significantly inhibited the appropriate use of modern communications, reducing efficiency and increasing risk to command posts.

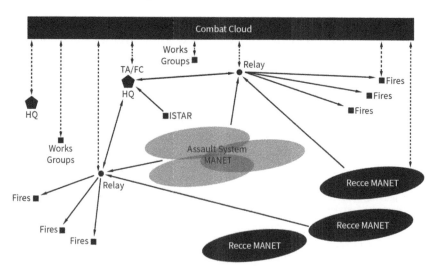

Figure 7 Network structures across the force.

Shooters and munitions

Historically, artillery has been the primary killer throughout the era of industrial and mechanized warfare. The trends identified in this book suggest that its importance and impact are likely to increase in future conflicts. There were five fires systems identified in this book, excluding air defence: 120mm mortars, 155mm howitzers, MLRS, long-range loitering munitions and short-range loitering munitions. Short-range ballistic and cruise missiles were also discussed but not integrated into the force. This is because such systems are a higher echelon capability than the focus of this study, and because they are by necessity scarce and applied for precision strike, rather than as part of responsive fires.[11] The exact specifications of these systems is less important – whether one has a 120mm mortar or a 122mm or 105mm howitzer for example – but the rough range bands and vectors covered by these weapons are all necessary.

For the past thirty years NATO countries have had the luxury of air supremacy and therefore have foregone the logistical challenge of fielding large artillery formations, preferring close air support. Furthermore, the priority for fires delivered has been to minimize collateral damage and therefore most munitions natures that have been prioritized intentionally reduce the lethality of their payloads, meaning that in any warfighting context the greatest expense delivers the least possible effect. As described in the previous chapter, air support is likely to be increasingly scarce in future conflicts. Moreover, as outlined in Chapters 3 and 7, fires protect the force and they do so by having a ready supply of shooters and ammunition. Here it is worth noting that the demand for ammunition in large-scale conflict remains high. In Exercise Warfighter 2020 British forces expended 13,000 rounds of GMLRS and 44,000 rounds of 155mm ammunition in eight days,[12] which vastly exceeds the UK's national stockpiles.[13] In Ukraine, Russia was firing up to 6,000 rounds per 3 km of targeted frontage per day during the height of its attack on the Donbas.[14] Precision reduces the number of rounds that must be fired for a given effect, but Exercise Warfighter in many ways tested the theory of whether it obviated the need for mass and found that mass effect was still essential. Western armies have massively curtailed their industrial capacity to manufacture munitions.[15]

[11] Russia's use of Iskander-M to target TELARs and other tactical targets is a demonstration of poor employment, though it demonstrates that such attacks are possible, see Sam Cranny-Evans and Sidharth Kaushal, 'The Iskander-M and Iskander-K: A Technical Profile', *RUSI Commentary*, 8 August 2022: https://rusi.org/explore-our-research/publications/commentary/iskander-m-and-iskander-k-technical-profile, accessed 20 August 2022.

[12] Brigadier Charlie Hewitt, RUSI Missile Defence Conference, London, 13 May 2021: https://static.rusi.org/302_CR_Precision_Strike.pdf, accessed 20 July 2022.

[13] Lt Gen (Retd) Ben Hodges, House of Commons Defence Committee, 6 July 2021: https://committees.parliament.uk/oralevidence/2496/html/, accessed 20 July 2022.

[14] Author interviews, Ukrainian General Staff Lessons Learned Team (J7), Ukraine, August 2022.

[15] Alex Vershinin, 'The Return of Industrial Warfare', *RUSI Commentary*, 17 June 2022: https://rusi.org/explore-our-research/publications/commentary/return-industrial-warfare, accessed 20 July 2022.

Another reason why munitions and shooters must be a priority is that despite NATO having standard munition calibres, it has emerged that over time there is considerable deviation in the nature of these munitions so that they are in fact not compatible. For example, the transition to smart munitions for tank cannon requires that data be shared with the shell. Yet NATO members have developed proprietary systems for transferring data through their cannon breaches so that these munitions cannot be used across NATO guns of the same calibre.[16] Similarly with artillery munitions while the calibre may be consistent, charge systems and fusing are not, and autoloaders on various platforms have been found to require proprietary ammunition. The result is an alliance with limited national stocks everywhere and an inability to pool munitions anywhere. This is exacerbated by national legal frameworks with different standards for the safe storage and transport of munitions and varying time horizons on their required disposal. Agreeing to standards for these elements is critical if NATO is to have efficient logistics and sufficient stocks of munitions to be ready for future conflicts. Given that shooters are critical to the future of warfare, it is important that the updating of NATO standards is pursued in a manner consistent with the future munition natures identified as necessary, rather than being applied retrospectively to older systems. This standardization also offers the prospect of a larger market for improvements on munition natures, creating an incentive for industry to compete rather than lock in long-term contracts which gain a structural monopoly.

The flirtation with novel ammunition natures and the endless desire to get more sophistication out of munitions is driving up the cost per munition and limiting the scale of any given production run, which in turn reduces the size and consistency of orders and so leads to defence industry reducing the production capacity available. Given the lead times in setting up industrial capacity and producing munitions – especially any munition with a precision payload – armies wishing to transition to the method of warfare described in this book will need to determine a limited set of munition natures and standardize around them. The need to expand the lethality of munitions also requires political leadership, which is why this must be a priority. There are inaccurate narratives about the legality of a range of munitions that pose a serious challenge to properly arming NATO forces. These narratives have counterproductively been pushed during Russia's intervention in Syria, for example. Ensuring that the need for appropriate effective munitions is understood by policymakers will take time.

The one caveat to the need for standardized calibres and natures is loitering munitions. Loitering munitions do require standardization in terms of the control interfaces used, the transport and launch mechanisms that enable them to be fielded. However, UASs can be manufactured cheaply and variation in their form actually makes them harder to defend against. Similarly, modular payload systems are highly beneficial. It is important to standardize the mechanisms by which modules are attached to UASs but allowing for the form and the payloads to be dynamically developed is important in ensuring their long-term relevance. Given the constraints surrounding training with UASs however, certifying the airframes should be premised

---

[16] Author interviews, RBSL CR3 Project Team, Telford, 14 December 2021.

on the characteristics of the controls, flight computer and size, rather than on the exact form. These aspects of loitering munitions, therefore, do require standardization if they are to be fielded across the force and at scale.

Sensors

If the network is the essential enabler, and fires the indispensable effector, then sensors are the third priority that militaries must pursue. They are third because there are already a great many sensors on the battlefield as they were heavily invested in during the War on Terror. What is less plentiful is the means to fuse them, or transfer data from them because of the lack of appropriate networks. Nevertheless, sensors must be a priority in three distinct areas: dissemination, integration and dedication.

To continue with UASs, the present process by which Western militaries train with UASs bears very little relation to how they have used them previously on operations or how they will need to be used in the future. For example, it is not uncommon for UASs to be treated as aircraft. Therefore, for a tactical UAS supporting a reconnaissance section to be put up the section must not only have crews who are trained to liaise with the appropriate air traffic control but the airspace in which the UAS is to be flown must be closed to aviation. UASs being flown autonomously – except under the rarest conditions – often have to be tested in bounded areas, surrounded by nets, in case they deviate from the intended route. The effect of these sorts of restrictions is to limit any training that uses UAS as part of a combined arms force but instead treats them as a sequential serial. It also means that their use becomes limited to those specialists who have the appropriate courses to have obtained approval to fly, rather than being available to anyone able to do so, and massively increases the cost of fielding a capability that needs to be ubiquitous.

As outlined in the seventh-, eighth-, and ninth-chapters UASs of various kinds should be available down to the section level across the force. Clearly there is a training requirement in their tactics. Nevertheless, this should be treated like qualifying a soldier to employ munitions rather than an aircraft. Despite demands for innovation from senior leaders in Western militaries, if the policies and permissions to enable the creative use of these capabilities are not granted then Western militaries will be stymied in their ability to experiment, understand the threat and opportunities and refine the platforms upon which their lives will depend in combat. Excuses about air flight safety are hollow because they simply transfer the risk from training to operations and because in any conflict today UASs are launched by a wide variety of actors who have no clearance to fly and so aircraft will need to adapt to this reality rather than demanding that friendly UASs adapt to them. Easing the qualification burden is also critical if it is to be economical to have these capabilities available across the force. UASs are one example, but there are others, where disseminating sensors widely requires deregulation surrounding their employment. Similar problems bedevil EW force generation.

At the same time sensors are far too often tied to individuals. The notion of one sensor being connected to one operator is being rendered obsolete by the effects of fusing returns from multiple sensors on a single platform using AI. To do this, however, armies must invest in the algorithms and data sets to be able to train appropriate systems. Here it is necessary to separate the hardware from an accompanying software solution. Thus, again, data standards become critical. Propriety packages comprising hardware and software solutions lead to a lack of competition in algorithm performance and slow down the incorporation of updates that may extend capability. Instead, by specifying the required standards for the output of sensors, armies should be able to replace sensors while continuing to ingest and fuse their outputs through separately updated algorithms. Being able to do this requires significant changes to contracting, how competitions are structured, and the commercial governance for military procurement, since militaries are currently often trapped applying platform-centric commercial structures to software, with unsatisfactory results.[17] Appreciating that complimentary sensors, fused by AI, will give a much higher fidelity of picture than a team of operators each examining one sensor is a mindset shift for armies and must be underpinned by operator trust.[18]

The third challenge is that of dedication. During the War on Terror the tendency was to maximize the collect from a given platform. This significantly increased the platform's cost. ISR platforms will always carry a cost because the sensors themselves are expensive. Nevertheless, the desire to do everything with a particular platform has driven up costs. For example, the combination of radar, electro-optical sensing and range on the Watchkeeper is flexible but also highly inefficient. The radar is excellent for taking high-resolution synthetic aperture radar images or conducting GMTI, but to do this the Watchkeeper is best kept at high altitude and a long way from the FLOT. The electro-optical sensor, by contrast, is only useful if the Watchkeeper is flown in to interrogate targets. But as a medium-altitude long-endurance UAS the platform is not survivable in enemy airspace. In short, the platform is confused between the role of a stand-off and stand-in sensor.[19] The dedication of complimentary ISR packages, fused with AI on the platform and thereby offboarding much smaller data packages comprising conclusions rather than raw data, requires sensors to be organized according to task. Especially in the field of stand-in sensors attrition is likely to be high and this means that driving down the cost of the base platforms – even if payloads will remain expensive – is important. Understanding what capability can be neglected on a platform is only possible if its purpose is clearly bounded.

There are also sensors that Western militaries have neglected for decades owing to the adversaries they have been confronting. The most obvious is electronic warfare detection. In the United Kingdom this has shrunk to a single unit in the conventional

---

[17] Jeremy Quinn, RUSI Land Warfare Conference, London, 2 June 2021.

[18] Christina Balis and Paul O'Neill, 'Trust in AI: Rethinking Future Command', *RUSI Occasional Paper*, June 2022: https://static.rusi.org/332_OP_Trust_in_AI_Final_Web.pdf, accessed 20 July 2022.

[19] Jack Watling, 'From Multirole to Modularity', *RUSI Defence Systems*, 10 December 2020: https://rusi.org/explore-our-research/publications/rusi-defence-systems/multirole-modularity, accessed 20 July 2022.

force which is massively over tasked and though a second unit is being stood up, it is unclear where the personnel for it are to come from. In the United States the formation of Multi-Domain Task Forces should bring EW sensors back into the force. Alongside the personnel and sensors, however, it is also important to conduct electromagnetic surveys of terrain to have an accurate baseline. In this space too, there is great scope for AI to massively increase the capacity to accurately detect and locate enemies. In some respects, because there is such little existing capability, it may be easier to expand and proliferate these sensors across the force and generate new doctrine. Armies have the tools to turn the battlefield transparent, but it requires the dedication of resource and discipline in how it is applied.

Layered defences

Layered defence is a capability that has been widely neglected across NATO over the past decades but is now becoming critical as threats to land forces are diversifying, from sub-tactical precision weaponry[20] to ballistic and cruise missiles.[21] Most armies today are chronically vulnerable to enemy fires. The Israeli Defence Forces have a credible layered defensive architecture, but they also have the luxury of knowing the locations they must defend and the capability is not deployable. The United States has many components of the various layers, but as demonstrated by the compromise of a THAAD radar by a small UAV in Korea,[22] has not always combined the layers on deployment. Across NATO there are neither sufficient layers, nor munitions within those layers.

The first priority for armies is CUAS defence. This is a capability that all formations need to possess organically. The challenge posed by UAS is one of economy. Many UAS can find targets beyond the effective cannon range. Though this places them within the range of short-range missile systems, the missile involved is often far more costly than the UAS. In practice, however, the UAS is an enabler for fires, and is therefore a critical component in a much more expensive kill chain. In the economics of missile versus UAS, the cost of not destroying the UAS must also be factored into the equation. The proliferation of uncrewed turrets should – with appropriate programming and ammunition natures – enable many units to have some organic CUAS capability. EW adds perhaps the most effective first tool in targeting UAS. Navigational jamming is a vital tool for disrupting UAS-enabled kill chains, though can also cause problems for friendly capabilities.[23] But the simple fact is that the provision of hard kill capabilities

---

[20] Hubbard, Karasz and Reed, 'Two Major Saudi Oil Installations Hit by Drone Strike, and U.S. Blames Iran'.

[21] Iain Williams and Shaan Shaikh, *The Missile War in Yemen* (Washington DC: CSIS, 2020): https://csis-website-prod.s3.amazonaws.com/s3fs-public/publication/Williams_MissileWarYemen_WEB_FINAL_v2.pdf, accessed 20 July 2022.

[22] Tom Karako, *Distributed Defense: New Operational Concepts for Integrated Air and Missile Defence* (Washington, DC: Center for Strategic and International Studies, 2018), pp. 1–10.

[23] 'Above Us Only Stars: Exposing GPS Spoofing in Russia and Syria', *C4ADS*, 2019: https://static1.squarespace.com/static/566ef8b4d8af107232d5358a/t/5c99488beb39314c45e782da/1553549492554/Above+Us+Only+Stars.pdf, accessed 20 July 2022.

across the force is a requirement in modern combat as a protective measure. The fielding of CUAS capabilities must be carried out in parallel to the arming of the force with UAS, because one of the key skills that units must develop tactics to avoid is how to prevent friendly fire. As there is no realistic means of connecting all personnel to the common air picture or of integrating UAS into it, preventing friendly shoot-downs demands innovative tactics more than technologies.

In addition to UAS it is necessary to field a high density of capable short-range air defence units to both shape the enemy and protect a dispersed force. Although dedicated medium and long-range air defences are important, the distribution of short-range air defence closes down the lanes by which enemy aircraft can approach high-value targets and imposes a significant cost on enemy aircraft, aviation and UAVs that might otherwise bring decisive effect against a part of the battlefield. Distributing short-range air defence capability is also sensible because it introduces significant uncertainty into adversary planning and is hard to suppress or destroy. Unlike active air defence systems a high density of shorter range systems lack single nodes like battery radar that can be targeted. One of the greatest advantages of a layered approach, encompassing short, medium and long-range systems is that it presents enemy aircraft with conflicting imperatives. Gaining altitude to evade short-range systems exposes aircraft to medium-range systems. Being accompanied by the enablers to suppress medium-range systems risks those same enablers being targeted by the long-range systems. The need to layer air defences is not a new phenomenon but it is a critical protection that Western armies have lost and need to regain.

Beyond such big ticket items there is also a need for the distribution of a range of protective suites, from active protection systems on vehicles, to multispectral camouflage screens for vehicles and personnel, which are critical to survival on the future battlefield. These sub-tactical tools are vital in ensuring the staying power of armoured fighting vehicles and the survivability of infantry. Investment in multispectral smoke, defensive lasers and other means of defeating precision-guided weapons must also be a priority to increase the survivability of troops. Beyond survivability these measures have the effect of increasing the effort required for effective ISR and the volume of precision munitions that must be massed to achieve an effect. They are therefore a protection in terms of the probability of surviving a strike, and a protection because they impose choices on the enemy about resource allocation. Ultimately these capabilities are only effective when practised and experimented with. The nuances of employing thermal camouflage, for example, only become apparent when it is used. Ensuring that soldiers at all levels have access to these capabilities, understand why they are necessary and are free to train with them is vital in enabling the force to creatively solve how best to make use of them.

Dedicated urban formations

There is a similar pattern with urban training. When David Kilcullen published *Out of the Mountains: The Coming Age of the Urban Guerrilla* he set off a great deal of speculation in militaries about how to cope with the challenges of the urban environment. Despite widespread acceptance of the issue and a great deal of discussion of its significance at conferences, the acceleration of urban training has been slow coming. Allocating dedicated units and creating specialists in the art of urban warfare is still lagging. Although the United States, France, Germany and Israel all have urban ranges, most exercises in these spaces are either short serials or a small part of a large operation in open country. Units might spend three days in the urban, but are not generally permitted to adapt their structures or equipment to optimize for it. Instead, they usually have to adapt their existing equipment for the urban.

A good example of the importance of urban training is the impact of Iraq's counterterrorism service during the siege of Mosul and previous Iraqi towns. As one of the only parts of the Iraqi military with extensive training and experience of fighting in urban areas they acted as a spearhead for the entire force throughout the siege,[24] suffering around 40 per cent casualties in the process.[25] Russia has similarly fallen into a pattern of struggling with urban operations, setting up storm groups as dedicated urban combat teams to break the impasse, and then discontinuing these structures after the completion of operations. This pattern has been repeated in the Second World War, in Grozny,[26] Syria and most recently Mariupol. The failure to retain this lesson has always been paid in heavy casualties. Among NATO armies, the proportion of the force who are significantly proficient and have regular opportunities to practice in the urban environment are very small; much smaller than Iraq's CTS. It is worth noting that Alec Wahlman, in *Storming the City: U.S. Military Performance in Urban Warfare from World War II to Vietnam*, argues against specialist urban formations, taking the view that it ultimately comes down to the adaptability of the wider force. None of the case studies in his book, however, involved the use of dedicated units. Moreover, even if in practice the wider force must make a prominent contribution to urban operations, the speed of adaptation – and avoiding early costly mistakes – can be aided by a force maintaining a cadre of subject matter experts who have spent sufficient time training in that environment to understand the permutations of how urban fighting unfolds.

Without dedicated units able to adapt their force structure to this environment, many of the transformative tools for urban fighting that are now available will struggle to find an adequate case for purchase and distribution. The effectiveness of robotic autonomous systems, for example, has been amply demonstrated in the urban environment for both logistics and fire support. For units that must transition to the urban these systems have many downsides in terms of their range and endurance, signature and maintenance. In a force that must operate for a sustained period in any environment these capabilities are only ever likely to be augmentations and therefore

---

[24] 'Lt. Gen. Sean MacFarland: Building Better Arab Armed Forces', American Enterprise Institute, 18 March 2019: https://www.youtube.com/watch?v=EWHffWl0DUY, accessed 20 July 2022.

[25] Office of the Secretary of Defence, 'Justification for FY 2018 Overseas Contingency Operations'.

[26] Lester Grau, 'Changing Russian Urban Tactics: The Aftermath of the Battle for Grozny', *INSS Strategic Forum* (Vol. 38, 1995): file:///Users/user/Downloads/1995-07-01%20Changing%20Russian%20Urban%20Tactics%20-%20The%20Aftermath%20of%20the%20Battle%20(Grau)-1.pdf, accessed 20 December 2022.

limited in the extent to which they can be leveraged. Fully integrating tactical UAS, RAS, and bespoke C2 for urban operations requires flexibility in how the force is configured, trained and equipped. Creating the opportunity for more dedicated training and experimentation should therefore build the evidence base to justify the integration of critical emerging capabilities into the force.

Another reason why building dedicated urban formations ought to be a priority is having a part of the force that routinely practices engaging with populations. At present, although human security advisers are distributed across the force, their influence and impact on planning is limited. Their advice may be sought but their concerns are rarely integral to the concept of operation. A force that is dedicated to thinking about how it can operate among the people, by contrast, must build this into their planning and thereby prepare cognitively for a battlefield that is widely observed by the international community and necessarily affecting a significantly greater number of civilians as the population density of cities increases. This also creates the justification for properly establishing and empowering those technical specialists in the force who can access and leverage the information infrastructure of the urban environment.

One challenge in conducting regular urban exercises is that although some countries have impressive urban ranges, these locations quickly become intimately familiar to the soldiers exercising within them. As a result soldiers become highly proficient at gaming the known environment, rather than used to managing the persistent uncertainty that urban spaces tend to confront soldiers with on operations. There are some exercises that require a dedicated range because explosive breaching and other techniques cannot be practiced on functioning buildings. On the other hand, there are many methods of training that are not destructive for the environment and where possible units should train in real urban environments, whether that be to practice exploiting infrastructure or to use abandoned or condemned buildings to train in large multi-storey structures and other features that are prohibitively expensive to build on military training sites. Within a unit's training rotation it is difficult to envisage multiple exercises on urban areas being possible. Again, therefore, assigning specialist units to the role allows for diverse training because their specialism justifies repeated exercises in the urban environment. Some states – like the Baltics – are already good at conducting drills in real urban settings. Nevertheless, for many countries it would require legislative changes and strong relationships between the military and local government.

Legacy systems

The priorities outlined above cover a small proportion of the capabilities that were described earlier in this book. Part two of this book made a wide range of judgements relating to vehicles weights, weapons calibres and for structures that have not been identified above as priorities. It is important to explain why.

To begin perhaps with one of the most controversial conclusions of this book, it essentially argues that the concept of the Main Battle Tank has been superseded by technology.[27] It argues that armour must be made lighter – ideally 54 tonnes – and that while 120mm smoothbore cannon have a place in the force, 60mm cannon are likely of greater utility in a wide variety of circumstances. The book has argued that the best way to destroy tanks is with fires or ATGMs, leaving direct fire systems to prioritize strong points, IFVs and other targets. Future IFVs are given even less attention, the requirements for the protected mobility aligned to several formations left ambiguous. It might well be asked, therefore, why this new generation of IFVs is not marked as a priority. The answer is that while the characteristics described are, in my view, optimal, modern MBTs are by no means incapable of fulfilling these roles. They simply do so inefficiently. For an army like the US Army with an exceedingly large fleet of M1A2 SepV3 Abrams, the cost of acquiring new tanks must be considered in relation to the opportunity cost of putting that resource into delivering the other priorities already outlined. At some point existing armoured platforms will wear out and need to be replaced. As armies design vehicles for the next generation, it makes sense to incorporate some of the thinking outlined in this book. This is likely to confront European NATO members before the United States. The UK's Challenger 3 is likely to need replacing by 2040 while the French and German Main Ground Combat System to replace Leopard 2 and Leclerc will need to be entering service around 2035. Suffice to say many of the current parameters for the MGCS are undoubtedly mistakes. The insistence on a 130mm or 140mm cannon for example is to reduce the available rounds and increase the overall weight in exchange for a redundant increase in firepower. The priority should not be moving on from the current generation of MBTs but rather to ensure that the next generation receives appropriate requirements. That is unlikely to happen so long as the concepts and doctrine for armour remain as they are. In short, concepts must shift to inform the development of optimal requirements rather than the other way about.

Beyond those systems that while perhaps poorly optimized for the future operating environment are nevertheless workable, there are many systems that retain their relevance unmodified. A good example here is bridging. Although there are some innovative improvements in the deployment systems for bridging, the reality is that it is the volume of bridging equipment available that gives a commander tactical options, not the marginal gains of peeling seconds off the launch and recovery times.[28] Investing in new bridging solutions likely means increasing the cost and complexity. The requirement, by contrast, for most NATO militaries is to substantially increase the volume of bridging across the force and for that it is much better to expand procurement of established systems than to invest in new designs.

---

[27] Given the controversy over the tank's future it may be surprising that more attention is not given to this topic, see Jon Hawkes, Sam Cranny-Evans and Mark Cazalet, 'The Tank Is Dead. Long Live the Tank', *The Wavell Room*, 1 October 2020: https://wavellroom.com/2020/10/01/a-critical-analysis-of-the-future-of-the-tank/, accessed 20 July 2022; Johnson, 'The Tank Is Dead: Long Live the Javelin, the Switchblade, the …?'; Frank Gardner, 'Ukraine War: Is the Tank Doomed?', *BBC*, 7 July 2022: https://www.bbc.com/news/uk-61967180, accessed 20 July 2022.

[28] Tom Winney, RUSI Waterways Conference: Obstacles and Opportunities for Manoeuvre, 27 April 2022.

Another example of continuity is support aviation. For the purposes of rapidly moving large quantities of materiel and personnel it is difficult to improve upon the CH-47. There are theatre-specific considerations that will drive different priorities. In the Indo-Pacific where speed and range are important for moving between atolls, the use of tilt-rotor aviation has merit. In Europe the additional speed and range is practically redundant for operationally relevant distances. The conclusions regarding attack aviation in this book are likely controversial. Essentially against proliferating threat systems their survivability is rapidly diminishing and there are few indications that there are technological solutions to their vulnerabilities. Given the immense cost of attack aviation it seems that they are going to become increasingly surpassed by UAVs. There is a strong argument to avoid significant investment in future generations of attack aviation. Although the current generation of attack aviation needs increasing enablement to survive, at present the flexibility, reach and firepower that AH-64E brings to bear makes it a capability with continued utility. That utility is expected to diminish over the next decade, but for the future life of existing platforms armies can make good use of this tool.[29]

It should finally be said that there are a range of innovative technologies that were not widely discussed in this book, but which have attracted the attention of armies. The most prominent is electric propulsion, already employed on operations for dirt bikes and other light vehicles, but not yet employed on major combat platforms. There are potential advantages to these technologies: they run quietly and very consistently and are potentially more environmentally friendly. There are also disadvantages: the tempo implications of charging and their tendency to combust. Whether the performance of battery technology will ever be sufficient to power major combat platforms has yet to be seen. Hybrid systems to enable a quieter and more fuel-efficient alternative to an APU may be a more likely iteration. These issues are not explored in this book because while interesting they do not fundamentally drive concepts of operation or force design. They may become a priority for militaries, but that prioritization is likely to reflect other factors than an increase in combat power for the relevance of the force. In that sense, the lack of detail on such matters here should not be taken to suggest that they are not important; merely that they are not important to how the force fights.

As this chapter has sought to outline transitioning the force from being optimized for mechanized to informatized warfare is partially about equipment, but also about structures, doctrine, training and mindset. Undiscussed above are the implications for the echelon structure. Nevertheless, the echelon structure will be changed considerably by the changes to networks, permissions and taskings outlined above. Given that cultural and structural change will take a long time, and that if they are not tackled then requirements for combat vehicles will continue to reinforce aspects of mechanized warfare that leave the force distinctly vulnerable,

---

[29] Jack Watling and Justin Bronk, 'Maximising the Utility of the British Army's Combat Aviation', *RUSI Occasional Paper,* April 2021: https://static.rusi.org/236_op_uk_aviation_capabilities_final_web_version.pdf, accessed 20 July 2022.

then it is important that militaries prioritize shifting the approach of their people as much as they seek to modernize their platforms. Combining the arms of the future is an endeavour that remains people centric, even if they are increasingly supported by robotic autonomous systems. The question is whether armies are prepared to make the jump to optimize for the conflicts of the future, rather than for the battles of the past.

13

An instrument of power

For what most humans call peace he held to be only a name; in fact, for everyone there always exists by nature an undeclared war among all cities.[1]

Plato

The military is ultimately an instrument of power, applied by the state and non-state actors to advance their interests. Military power sits alongside diplomatic, economic, cultural and informational instruments. How actors determine when to apply military force and against what to direct it is a function of both the security dynamics at play and the perceived capacity of their forces. The determination to reach for the military instrument is shaped by both the international security environment and what military forces can offer. Both factors can differ radically for different periods of history. For example, the methods and aims of military actions during the high Middle Ages in Europe were different to those in the 1800s. In the fourteenth and fifteenth centuries, legitimacy in Europe was intimately bound up in the person of a monarch, their perceived adherence to the Catholic faith and their reputation among their peers.[2] Because military service centred on persons rather than institutions the raising of armies depended upon the loyalty and client–patron networks of nobles. Command and control on the battlefield was built around a pyramid of loyalty, with companions and retainers of a noble following their orders. Meanwhile, the economic structure of feudalism limited the capacity to sustain a military force, while the limited availability of heavy artillery made fortresses major obstacles.[3] These dynamics created a security environment in which the capacity to raise an army depended upon the perceived legitimacy of the cause. Legitimate causes corresponded with claims either of ancient rights of title over land or a judgement of illegitimacy of another ruler. Meanwhile the size of forces realistically sustainable made for military campaigns in which the plausible objective centred on cities or specific castles within a campaign season, rather

---

[1] Plato, *The Laws of Plato*, Thomas Pangle (trans.) (London: University of Chicago Press, 1988), p. 4.

[2] Antony Black, *Political Thought in Europe, 1250–1450* (Cambridge: Cambridge University Press, 1992).

[3] For an overview of the interrelated military, political and economic changes that enabled a revolution in military affairs between the medieval and early modern eras see Andrew Ayton and J. L. Price (Eds.), *The Medieval Military Revolution: State, Society and Military Change in Medieval and Early Modern Europe* (London: I.B. Tauris, 1998).

than whole kingdoms. Any more ambitious endeavour meanwhile centred on coalition building.[4] Between campaigns there could be extensive skirmishing.

Conversely, in the nineteenth century nationalism had created the capacity for national mobilization.[5] The industrialization of both armaments production and agriculture and the expansion of infrastructure enabled the sustainment of hundreds of thousands of troops under arms. Military technology – both small arms and mobile artillery – had vastly increased the lethality of military forces and thereby created conditions in which decisive battlefield victories were possible while urban defence was of limited utility. The capacity to regenerate forces meanwhile centred on the national will to fight and therefore the justification for conflict – which shaped the perception of success and failure – began to revolve around national survival. Thus, conflict became for a time increasingly total.[6] Even when a state's objective was a limited territorial revision, the means of achieving it was often the defeat of another state and the capture of its capital, enabling territorial revision to be codified by treaty under duress.

In considering the future of how land forces may be applied – and what they may be asked to do – it is therefore important to consider the changes in how armies may operate outlined in this book and examine how this intersects with the security environment and conflict drivers that may cause states to reach for the military instrument. This chapter considers this dynamic, first by considering what may drive states to war in the future, second by examining what constraints on objectives may be imposed by the capacity of land forces to address the identified security concerns, and third by examining the decision points and options that this creates for governments.

Competition and Conflict

The definition of great power status is inexact. Nevertheless, the international system is becoming one in which there are multiple rival powers. Generally speaking, great powers are understood as states with global influence and reach, capable of pursuing an independent policy where they choose.[7] The United States and China clearly meet this criterion though China has yet to exercise its military potential globally. It is however laying the groundwork to do so.[8] Prior to its debacle in Ukraine Russia's great

---

[4] The Hundred Years War, for instance saw limited military gains lead to significant political recognition that underpinned England's claims over the French Crown, see Juliet Barker, *Conquest: The English Kingdom of France, 1417–1450* (Cambridge MA: Harvard University Press, 2012).
[5] Alexander Mikaberidze, *The Napoleonic Wars: A Global History* (New York: Oxford University Press, 2020).
[6] Clausewitz, whose theories emanated from his direct experience of conflict in this period, postulated how the pursuit of advantage drove both parties in conflict to a extremes, see Carl Von Clausewitz, *On War*, Michael Howard and Peter Paret (trans.) (Princeton, NJ: Princeton University Press, 1989), pp. 75–7.
[7] Paul Kennedy, *The Rise and Fall of the Great Powers: Economic Change and Military Conflict from 1500 to 2000* (New York: Random House, 1987), p. xxi.
[8] Sidharth Kaushal and Magdalena Markiewicz, 'Crossing the River by Feeling the Stones: The Trajectory of China's Maritime Transformation', *Occasional Paper* (London: RUSI, 2019).

power status was clear.[9] Even with events in Ukraine Russia remains self-sufficient in energy and food, has a large industrial base, capabilities that span the globe and can function as a spoiler in almost any international conflict, though it lacks the economic clout of its rivals. Nevertheless, after the invasion of Ukraine economic sanctions and its diminished prestige make Russia highly dependent upon China,[10] bringing into question its capacity for an independent policy in several theatres. India has the potential to be a great power but lacks the ambition to exercise global influence.[11] The European Union has the economic and military capacity of a great power but lacks a common foreign policy. Beyond the great powers, medium powers like the UK, France and Iran have significant fiscal and military capabilities but must largely function in coalitions to exert influence. Nevertheless, this diversification of actors and interests is creating a much more competitive security environment.

Underpinning interstate competition is hard interests. Perhaps the most combustible is energy security. The attempt to decarbonize developed economies is likely to see a significant increase in demand for electricity.[12] In the developing world the desire to raise living standards necessarily requires an increase in energy consumption. Population growth,[13] urbanization[14] and capabilities like desalination and climate control in the face of climate change will all generate increases in energy demands. Even if climate action sees a diminished demand for fossil fuels – and this is not a robust assumption – the requirement for batteries, rare earth metals, uranium and other critical resources will intensify. These resources are not distributed around the world evenly, while access to an assured source of supply depends upon global choke points that adversaries can deny. Furthermore, since the global supply of energy is a market, disruption in supply to one area will drive up prices globally.[15]

---

[9] And an active object of Russian policy, see Andrei P. Tsygankov, 'Vladimir Putin's Vision of Russia as a Normal Great Power', *Post-Soviet Affairs* (Vol. 21, No. 2, 2005), pp. 132–58; Cristian Nitoiu, 'Aspirations to Great Power Status: Russia's Path to Assertiveness in the International Arena under Putin', *Political Studies Review* (Vol. 15, No. 1, February 2017), pp. 39–48; Jeffrey Mankoff, *Russian Foreign Policy: The Return of Great Power Politics* (Lanham, MD: Rowman and Littlefield Publishers, 2012), p. 12.

[10] Oleksandr V. Danylyuk, 'Why Putin Is Turning Russia into a Chinese Client State, and How to Stop It', *RUSI Commentary*, 16 March 2022: https://www.rusi.org/explore-our-research/publications/commentary/why-putin-turning-russia-chinese-client-state-and-how-stop-it, accessed 20 July 2022.

[11] Shashank Joshi, *Indian Power Projection: Ambition, Arms and Influence*, RUSI Whitehall Paper 85 (London: Taylor and Francis, 2016).

[12] Shell Scenarios Team, 'The Energy Transformation Scenarios', Shell International, 2021: https://www.shell.com/energy-and-innovation/the-energy-future/scenarios/the-energy-transformation-scenarios/_jcr_content/root/main/section_524990089/simple/promo_copy/links/item0.stream/1652119830834/fba2959d9759c5ae806a03acfb187f1c33409a91/energy-transformation-scenarios.pdf, accessed 20 July 2022.

[13] United Nations, Population Facts, 2019: https://www.un.org/en/development/desa/population/publications/pdf/popfacts/PopFacts_2019-6.pdf, accessed 20 July 2022.

[14] United Nations, World Urbanisation Prospects, 2018: https://www.un.org/development/desa/pd/sites/www.un.org.development.desa.pd/files/files/documents/2020/Jan/un_2018_wup_report.pdf, accessed 20 July 2022.

[15] Corby Anderson, 'Rare Earths: Market Disruption, Innovation, and Global Supply Chains', *Annual Review of Environment and Resources* (Vol. 41, 2016), pp. 199–222.

Similar dynamics apply to foodstuffs. The economic efficiency of just in time manufacturing and low cost of shipping mean that while onshoring may be forced for a limited number of strategic industries, economies are likely to remain highly vulnerable to supply chain disruption.[16] For those states with insufficient energy, food and water security, or underdevelopment, the threat posed by climate change is severe, and in these circumstances there is a risk that they will be destabilized, or may instrumentalize instability to gain leverage and thus support from the states whose livelihoods they can threaten through supply chain disruption. These factors lead to a highly competitive international system in which great powers seek to secure influence.

Another arena of competition is the mechanisms of international trade. For much of the past two centuries over which time a global economy has developed the regulation and architecture of global trade has been increasingly consolidated in Europe and the United States. Basic functions like price discovery are still conducted primarily in London and New York.[17] The centrality of the US dollar to global finance means that countries today remain highly vulnerable to sanctions removing access to dollar markets. For decades countries were prepared to accept this risk because of the efficiency of trading on these financial systems, even though the United States had imposed sanctions on several adversaries. Nevertheless, over the War on Terror the United States significantly expanded its use of sanctions,[18] especially against Iran, and has subsequently applied similarly extensive measures targeting Russia.[19] China had long wished to establish a competing financial architecture controlled by Beijing, with price discovery in Renminbi.[20] The emergence of the need for a parallel market for investments and trade including Russia, Iran, North Korea and China has forced the creation of platforms and architectures so that the plumbing increasingly exists for countries to evade exposure to the US dollar. Many states will continue to accept efficiency at the expense of security from Western sanctions. However, it is also

[16] D. John Mangan and A. McKinnon, 'Review of Trends in Manufacturing and Global Supply Chains, and Their Impact on UK Freight', Government Office for Science and Foresight, February 2019: https://assets.publishing.service.gov.uk/government/uploads/system/uploads/attachment_data/file/777687/fom_trends_manufacturing_global_supply_chains.pdf, accessed 21 December 2021; UK Parliament, 'Ensuring Future Supply-Chain Resilience': https://publications.parliament.uk/pa/cm5801/cmselect/cmintrade/286/28609.htm, accessed 22 December 2021.

[17] Bingcheng Yan and Eric W. Zivot, 'The Dynamics of Price Discovery', *AFA 2005 Philadelphia Meetings* (February 26, 2007).

[18] Jay Solomon, *The Iran Wars: Spy Games, Bank Battles, and the Secret Deals That Reshaped the Middle East* (New York: Random House, 2016), pp. 142–67.

[19] Office of Foreign Asset Control, 'Ukraine/Russia-Related Sanctions Programme', US Department of the Treasury, 2016: https://home.treasury.gov/system/files/126/ukraine_overview_of_sanctions.pdf, accessed 20 July 2022.

[20] Summer Said and Stephen Kalin, 'Saudi Arabia Considers Accepting Yuan Instead of Dollars for Chinese Oil Sales', *The Wall Street Journal*, 15 March 2022: https://www.wsj.com/articles/saudi-arabia-considers-accepting-yuan-instead-of-dollars-for-chinese-oil-sales-11647351541, accessed 20 July 2022.

possible that states that disagree with or wish to diverge from US values and interests may embrace the alternative offer.[21]

Within these competitive dynamics there are clearly several drivers that may lead to conflict. First, with vulnerable states increasingly needing secure financing and supplies of food and energy, and larger powers needing assured flows of trade to underpin the financial and industrial largess that secures their influence, the alignment of states is liable to drive conflict. Here local instability is likely to be used by external powers as opportunities to secure influence by destabilizing an adversary's partners, or to intervene to support a vulnerable partner. Both dynamics encourage proxyism and intervention.[22] Where much of the twentieth century saw such proxy struggles rapidly turn into wars of attrition however, owing to an inability to sufficiently equip one party with complex weapons able to offer a decisive advantage, the war in Nagorno-Karabakh showcases how in a relatively short period of time complex weapons can be brought into theatre potentially producing decisive results.

In some cases there are also strong pull factors that may see external powers commit their own forces to such conflicts, beyond a covert or limited presence like Turkey and Russia's in Nagorno-Karabakh. The two most likely causes of great power intervention are either threats to core interests such as access to trade routes or energy, or the need to support a partner to convince others of the value of partnership. Examples of the former case could include Russian concerns about access to the Black Sea, leading to the annexation of Crimea, or Chinese concerns about its dependence on trade driving an ambition to dominate the first island chain. Another reason for intervention may be if instability in a state is perceived to threaten spill over, either to a power's homeland or to that of its allies. Here, energy demands, hunger and climate change, threatening political instability, could drive intervention. The most widespread reason, however is likely that alignment with a great power or medium power partner for a state makes sense if the guarantees it offers are credible. If they are not credible they will not deter aggression from adversaries.[23] It is therefore important for a medium or great power, seeking to use alliances and influence to assure its prosperity, to act to uphold the credibility of its offers to all its partners through the demonstration of support to a particular partner when the need arises. While adversaries may not wish to commit significant resources to a fight, the contribution of equipment offers the opportunity to fix an adversary, increasing the intensity of the fighting.

[21] Tom Keatinge, Oral Testimony to the Economic Affairs Committee, 26 October 2021: https://committees.parliament.uk/oralevidence/2928/pdf/, accessed 20 July 2022; note that there is a historical precedent, see Nicholas Mulder, *The Economic Weapon: The Rise of Sanctions as a Tool of Modern War* (New Haven, CT: Yale University Press, 2022).

[22] Amos Fox, 'Ukraine and Proxy War Improving Ontological Shortcomings in Military Thinking', *Land Warfare Papers*, vol. 148 (2022): https://www.ausa.org/sites/default/files/publications/LWP-148-Ukraine-and-Proxy-War-Improving-Ontological-Shortcomings-in-Military-Thinking.pdf, accessed 20 July 2022.

[23] Herman Kahn, 'The Nature and Feasibility of War and Deterrence', RAND Corporation, P-1888-RC, 1960; Thomas C. Shelling, *Arms and Influence* (New Haven, CT: Yale University Press, 1966); Edward Luttwak, *The Political Uses of Sea Power* (Baltimore, MD: Johns Hopkins University Press, 1974).

Incentives for direct clashes between medium and great powers seem less evident. The risk of nuclear escalation is a strong deterrent. However, where a power is not believed to be able to credibly defend an interest, inflicting localized defeat may prove attractive.[24] Similarly, misjudged aggression against a partner may force a rival power to enter direct confrontation. Direct confrontation may of course escalate, but it is worth noting that Chinese concepts of 'local wars under informatised conditions'[25] and Russian doctrinal development have emphasized limiting the geographic concentration of a conflict.[26] US concepts are more expansive, though as demonstrated in Ukraine, fears over nuclear escalation may lead the United States in such a scenario to accept a more limited theatre of operations. Medium powers, meanwhile, are unable to globalize a conflict given their available resources. Given these constraints it is evident that the future conflict environment is likely to see armed conflict over specific, strategically significant ground. It may be argued that Russia's tilt into an unrestrained military campaign in Ukraine challenges this hypothesis. Here, however, we must distinguish between Russian expectations of a short and sharp victorious campaign and the reality they found themselves confronted by. In the face of a long war authoritarian states can often better sustain an attritional battle than they can accept a defeat.[27] The former rarely threatens the regime. The latter often does. But this is not what Russian policy had envisaged to be the outcome. While wider conflict is possible therefore, the critical question as regards deterrence appears to remain whether a power believes it can achieve a rapid victory over a defined geographical area. As regards escalation, there is a difference between geographical escalation of a conflict and unrestricted use of state tools to achieve military objectives.[28]

The limits of power

That states may aspire to wield military force does not mean that their militaries can deliver what politicians demand. Aspirations must be correlated with capacity. It is therefore worth asking what inherent limits on military power are suggested by the changes in the character of fighting outlined in previous chapters.

---

[24] A pertinent example would be China's seizure of Indian territory in 2020, see 'A Border Dispute between India and China Is Getting More Serious', *The Economist*, 28 May 2020: https://www.economist.com/asia/2020/05/28/a-border-dispute-between-india-and-china-is-getting-more-serious, accessed 10 December 2022.

[25] M. Taylor Fravel, *Active Defence: China's Military Strategy Since 1949* (Princeton, NJ: Princeton University Press, 2019).

[26] Michael Kofman, Anya Fink and Jeffrey Edmonds, 'Russian Strategy for Escalation Management: Evolution of Key Concepts', *CNA* (April 2020): https://www.cna.org/archive/CNA_Files/pdf/drm-2019-u-022455-1rev.pdf, accessed 20 July 2022.

[27] Sidharth Kaushal, 'Can Russia Continue to Fight a Long War?', *RUSI Commentary*, 23 August 2022: https://rusi.org/explore-our-research/publications/commentary/can-russia-continue-fight-long-war, accessed 20 July 2022.

[28] Quiao Lang and Wang Qiangsui, *Unrestricted Warfare: China's Master Plan to Destroy America* (New York: Filament Books, 2004). The subtitle is not reflective of the original Chinese.

The first important point argued throughout this book has been that armies with sufficient sensors and fires can destroy those who lack them. The cliché that mass has a quality all of its own is in many respects deeply and increasingly misleading. There is of course a basic requirement for sufficient mass to field a fully capable force with enough magazine depth to counter the enemy. However, in a fight between a force capable of seeing first, striking further, and with ample area effect munitions, pushing more units into the struggle is simply to take heavier casualties. It does not follow that these troops will eventually wear down the defence. That Russia out massed Ukraine's artillery was of little account once Russia could not stockpile ammunition behind its guns without their being struck by long-range precision fires. More guns, or more ammunition, would not have changed this problem for the Russians. Another way in which a mass of older capabilities is not a substitute for modern capabilities is the significance of the urban assault. During the Second World War, the allies used mass to offset the lower quality of their troops in urban operations. Pushing more and more people into a battlefield geometry that is unfavourable, or against a well-prepared enemy able to outcompete the force in the close fight, is a recipe to take massive losses and to demoralize the attacking force.[29] Reinforcing a demoralized force is a recipe for collapse rather than the resurrection of an army. Once an army expends its offensive combat power they may be able to compel a defender to withdraw using massed fires or through exhaustion, but will likely destroy and render unusable the objective in the process. This reinforces why armies need to change to ensure that they have appropriate equipment and training to be competitive.

In the vignettes in the second part of this book the engagements were between the force proposed in this book against a traditional mechanized opponent. But a combat between two reformed forces would look different and it is in this context that we should consider the constraints upon military power. The new force relies upon several critical military specialisms. The most pronounced are light reconnaissance troops and assault troops. The force also needs an adequate supply of munitions and UAVs. Reconnaissance forces are hard to force generate because they must be skilled soldiers, with good fieldcraft, a technical understanding of their systems, be independently minded and comfortable working without significant support.[30] Not only are there a limited number of soldiers suitable for this task, but the time it takes to train reconnaissance troops means that once they are attrited, they are hard to replace. UAVs and screening infantry can take up some of the role but will be far less effective. Assault troops are also difficult to generate. First, there is the experience and technical expertise to have breachers and engineers and vehicle crews who know how to work in close proximity with infantry. Secondly, and in some ways more challenging is that assault operations rely on very close, rapid teamwork, trust and an aggressive *esprit de corps*. This is generated by having a close-knit community of people who know

[29] David Rowland, *The Stress of Battle: Quantifying Human Performance in Battle for Historical Analysis and Wargaming* (Bristol: The History of Wargaming Project, 2019), pp. 91–104.

[30] Requirements narrower though not dissimilar to SOF operators, see Roger A. Beaumont, *Military Elites: Special Fighting Units in the Modern World* (London: Bobbs- Merrill, 1975); Alexander Stillwell, *Military Reconnaissance: The Eyes and Ears of the Army* (London: Casemate, 2021).

each other, have trained together, and have been collectively conditioned to adopt the appropriate mindset. Such units can rarely maintain that ethos if they are heavily attrited. New units must be raised. This takes time. Units like the Iraqi CTS took ten years to build.[31] The Germans – in the context of a fully mobilized national struggle – built their storm battalions over several months, but this hollowed out experienced personnel from the rest of the force.[32] Several months, moreover, is a long time in a war. The point is that the destruction of the reconnaissance force risks leaving a unit uncompetitive in the sensing battle. The destruction or heavy attrition of the assault force meanwhile will hamper the capacity of an army to turn tactical gains into operational success.

Another way in which the force may degrade is through its munitions stocks. Precision munitions are becoming cheaper and their economy of effect on the battlefield makes them much more economical than unguided munitions. However, they are slow to make, and are unlikely to become drastically quicker to produce. With regard to precision weapons armies in contact tend to expend them faster than they can be produced. This is not necessarily the case with dumb munitions, enabling a consistent tempo. The result is that a force must judge whether to expend a high volume of precision weapons early to achieve advantage or whether by holding them in reserve they can build a favourable position after the enemy is forced to husband their remaining stocks. The depletion of stocks does not completely end the dynamics described in this book because unguided munitions enabled by precise reconnaissance and sensors can still be quite precise, but over a significantly reduced range. Nevertheless, the conclusion is that all armies will have a limited period for which they can sustain the type of fighting described in this book. Since the attack is almost always more ammunition intensive than the defence the question becomes whether a force can achieve their objective while retaining sufficient stocks to prevent counterattack.

Given that there are practical limits as to the proportion of a force that will meet the standards to form assault and reconnaissance units, while precision munitions are not easily replaced at the rate of consumption, it seems reasonable to assess that most armies will struggle to pursue more than two objectives simultaneously and that even then one is likely to be heavily weighted as the main effort. This is exacerbated by the need for dispersal for survivability and therefore the expanded frontages of units until sensor and fires dominance is achieved, reducing the number of axes that can be maintained. It is also worth exploring the implications of failure given the limited scale at which forces of this nature are likely fieldable. If steady attrition of a force's reconnaissance forces through skirmishing or assault forces through successive attacks take place then the efficiency of the force's fires system will degrade while the volume of fire necessary to enable assaults will increase. The result is that as the forces is attrited the fighting is likely to become slower, more protracted, and the rate of casualties

---

[31] Michael Knights and Alex Mello, 'The Best Thing America Built In Iraq: Iraq's Counter-Terrorism Service and the Long War against Militancy', *The War on the Rocks*, 19 July 2017: https://warontherocks.com/2017/07/the-best-thing-america-built-in-iraq-iraqs-counter-terrorism-service-and-the-long-war-against-militancy/, accessed 20 July 2022.
[32] Beaumont, *Military Elites*.

increase as the force reverts to a more traditional mechanized way of fighting, albeit one in which sensor density remains high and the survivability of stand-off sensors likely continues to make operational surprise exceedingly difficult to achieve. If one force is disproportionately attrited then it risks becoming uncompetitive.

The constraints outlined above suggest that forces that are competitive at the beginning of a future conflict are liable to have limited endurance and reach. If all goes well and the enemy's reconnaissance force is defeated, enabling assault and the taking of critical terrain, then the enemy will likely find itself struggling to regenerate capability while the attacker may be able to replenish munitions before moving on a subsequent objective. Over time the attacker may gain cumulative advantage in successive engagements as the enemy suffers disproportionate attrition and is therefore fielding lower and lower quality troops, especially in the reconnaissance function. Alternatively, it is plausible that attrition among the attacker's assault troops could cause a need to regenerate in this capability while the enemy must rebuild its reconnaissance force. If the enemy cannot defeat the reconnaissance screen and thereby enable concentration of its assault forces, then this may not be sufficient to enable them to retake lost ground. Nevertheless, a dynamic where one force cannot counterattack because it cannot concentrate and the other cannot attack further because it has insufficient troops to concentrate is likely to see an attack culminate. Most of the scenarios one can envisage for future forces therefore offer viable pathways to victory in limited conflicts over bounded geographic areas, but are not optimized for protracted fighting. The logic therefore returns to one of campaign seasons in which a force achieves or fails in its objectives before both sides are likely to seek a pause in operational tempo to replenish and reset. If, however, the conflict is over a specific piece of ground and the objective seized by the attacker enables longer-range systems to threaten theatre access, then it becomes plausible that gains are locked-in and favourable war termination becomes possible.

A final question that shapes the employment of military forces is the offence–defence balance. In both industrial and mechanized warfare the defence retained the advantage because in the defence it is not essential to move until contacted and is therefore easier to remain concealed, retain the initiative and to benefit from hard cover. Faith in the offence prior to the First World War was instrumental in poor tactical decision-making by military commanders and in the strategic expectations of what the military could deliver among policymakers. The same can be said for the Second World War, where confidence in static defences led French commanders to undervalue manoeuvre,[33] leading to their forces being dislocated and defeated.[34] In the era of informatized warfare, described in this book, advantage is retained by the defence at the sub-tactical level but the offence–defence balance is now much more contextual above sub-tactical engagements. In short, the side that has sensor dominance is likely to see first, strike first, and their strikes are likely capable of obviating the advantages

[33] Julian Jackson, *A Certain Idea of France: The Life of Charles de Gaulle* (London: Allen lane, 2018), pp. 28–46; 97–124.
[34] Julian Jackson, *The Fall of France: The Nazi Invasion of 1940* (Oxford: Oxford University Press, 2003), pp. 215–25.

of cover. A force that has lost the reconnaissance battle, therefore, is not afforded survivability by remaining in place. In many respects movement becomes critical to survival. It is this dynamic, explored in the vignette at the end of Chapter 8, that allows shaping by fire. The importance of this point is that policymakers must appreciate the constraints imposed on their forces by the loss of the reconnaissance battle and take this into careful consideration when evaluating the likely rate of attrition and the balance of combat power between forces. The ability to sense and strike precisely at reach means that units can be defeated in detail without first being isolated or severed from other echelons.

To cast the die

Taking into consideration the drivers of conflict described earlier in this chapter and the limitations in the capacity of the military instrument in the context of informatized warfare it is worth unpacking what this means in terms of how policymakers wield force and the decision points they face.

The first point of convergence between demand and capacity is that war aims are likely to be geographically limited. Successive campaigns may lead to the steady erosion of a state, but both the causes of conflict and the military capacity of states are likely to produce sequential campaigns against key geographic objectives. Furthermore, all parties are liable to seek to contain fighting rather than geographically expand a conflict. This is important because it shapes the deterrence calculations that policymakers face. If campaigns are liable to target specific objectives then the question of when to establish a deterrence posture does not hinge upon national mobilization but rather upon the prepositioning of capabilities for a more limited use of force. In most contexts therefore the relevant deterrence question is less whether State A believes it can eventually prevail against State B, but rather whether the local as opposed to the aggregate correlation of forces enables operational success.

The war in Ukraine, and the prospects of a Chinese invasion of Taiwan, may be suggested to point to the opposite: that states are prepared to pursue maximalist objectives. Here, however, it is important to consider how these conflicts are viewed by the parties concerned. For Vladimir Putin – prior to the invasion of 24 February – Ukraine was understood to be a recalcitrant Russian province. He believed there was a widespread sympathy for Russia in the country. He also believed that a fait accompli seizing a limited number of key objectives in a matter of days would bring about the collapse of wider resistance, and the unwillingness of the West to intervene or oppose the seizure.[35] The Russians intervened without mobilizing and assessed – incorrectly – that the localized correlation of forces was favourable. In short, Russia did not conduct the operation based on an assessment of Ukraine's aggregate combat power augmented with Western support, but rather based on its belief that it

---

[35] Jack Watling and Nick Reynolds, *The Plot to Destroy Ukraine* (London: RUSI, 2022): https://static.rusi.org/special-report-202202-ukraine-web.pdf, accessed 20 July 2022.

could achieve a rapid and localized victory.[36] China similarly views Taiwan as a province of China and its military activities, from the setting up of bastions in the South China Sea on reclaimed atolls to its long-range strike capabilities, are clearly intended to enable the isolation of Taiwan to achieve a rapid limited seizure. It anticipates a 'local war under informatised conditions' using long-range precision strike and nuclear threats to deter broader escalation. The deterrence question therefore is not aggregate power but power in theatre in response to the specific operational objectives of the aggressor.

A critical decision for policymakers will be when and where to deploy forces for deterrence purposes. On the one hand, given the complexity of the systems that must be deployed to be competitive this requires prioritization if it is to be credible. At the same time the force structure described in this book arguably circumvents one of the major challenges of deterrent deployments: namely adversary uncertainty as to intent. Mechanized forces deploy differently but comprise similar capabilities whether they are intended for defensive or offensive operations. Surging forces into a theatre therefore risk signalling aggressive intent even if they are there to deter aggression.[37] The advent of satellite imagery and thus the ability to interrogate logistics build ups have to some degree offered insight into whether a force is actually ready for major combat operations. Nevertheless, the separation of assault forces into a distinct function clarifies intent, since without these forces offensive combat operations are unlikely to be viable, while defensive operations remain possible with reconnaissance and fires. Thus, a credible defence can be emplaced without suggesting an intent to attack, or an intent to attack can be deliberately signalled. Clarity in messaging should be a stabilizing influence in the security environment.

For those wishing to use force therefore there is a binary choice as to whether to fight fast or slow. If the enemy has yet to fully commit a force postured to meet an attack, then an attacker may wish to strike early, aiming at the rapid capture of ground even if it does not mean the immediate defeat of the enemy's forces.[38] The risk is that speed relies on a heavy expenditure of ammunition and if the enemy's defence is more tenacious than anticipated may cause significant casualties, rendering the force vulnerable while consolidating initial gains. The alternative approach is to fight slow, to secure advantage in the reconnaissance battle and thereby deliberately attrit and wear down the opposing force, clearing a path for an assault. The probability of a sudden setback is reduced through such an approach but it offers the enemy the opportunity for mobilization and creates a political environment in which the enemy has time to adapt. Such an approach does not induce shock. What it does achieve is

---

[36] Michael Kofman and Rob Lee, 'Not Built for Purpose: The Russian Military's Ill-Fated Force Design', *War on the Rocks*, 2 June 2022: https://warontherocks.com/2022/06/not-built-for-purpose-the-russian-militarys-ill-fated-force-design/, accessed 20 July 2022.

[37] Jutta Heckhausen and Heinz Heckhausen (Eds.), *Motivation and Action* (Cambridge: Cambridge University Press, 2008). For its application to defence, see Dominic D. P. Johnson and Dominic Tierney, 'The Rubicon Theory of War: How the Path to Conflict Reaches the Point of No Return', *International Security* (Vol. 36, No. 1, Summer 2011), pp. 7–40.

[38] Daniel Kahneman and Amos Tversky, 'Prospect Theory: An Analysis of Decision under Risk', *Econometrica* (Vol. 47, No. 2, March 1979), pp. 263–91.

the preservation of the force and control over the rate of expenditure of key resources. The principal advantage in fighting to preserve the force in this way is that historically, powers unengaged in conflict have tended to be the beneficiaries of war. In a bipolar world order conflict between powers is to some extent a zero-sum game, but in a multi-polar world, where the objectives in warfare are limited, committing fully against an adversary is likely to accept risk or cede leverage to other powers.[39] To this end, a methodical rather than sudden approach offers the opportunity to retain options and balance risk in other theatres. In committing force to a geography a critical question for policymakers is whether doing so creates an opportunity for other opponents to apply pressure or pursue their own gains elsewhere. Russia risks suffering this fate in Nagorno-Karabakh as its combat power has become fixed in Ukraine, diminishing its deterrent posture towards Azerbaijan.

States may achieve the best of both worlds if they are first able to isolate their target from wider intervention and engagement. Here, the distinction between defensive and offensive capabilities is rather less clear. If a state is able to control the access points to a target and use long-range systems to prevent other states intervening then the risk of a high-tempo operation is significantly reduced. Here, China's strategic build-up of missile bases in the South China Sea is an example of how isolation can be achieved prior to a conflict.[40] The point here is that there is the capacity to positionally build up advantage in competition if the objectives for future operations can be anticipated. This gradual approach to locking in advantage is something that states with a long-term objective for territorial revision can work towards. For status quo powers this can be harder because their actions are likely to be reactive. Defensive states, therefore, need to not only look at deterrence in terms of the correlation of forces in an attack on an identified objective but also in terms of theatre access for supporting powers, and to plan proactively how the placement of forces in peacetime can lock in advantage in conflict. In the United States this is being framed as competition.[41] In the UK it is being framed as continuous operations.[42] Russia frames this activity as political warfare.[43] China conceptualizes the progressive build-up of advantage as 'crossing the water by feeling the stones', preparing for the seizure of limited objectives once the operation has been satisfactorily de-risked and the objective isolated. The critical question for policymakers, therefore, is how early and how precise they can be in prioritizing their

[39] John Mearsheimer, *The Tragedy of Great Power Politics* (New York: W. W. Norton, 2014).

[40] Kaushal and Markiewicz, 'Crossing the River by Feeling the Stones'.

[41] 'Summary of the 2018 National Defence Strategy of the United States of America': https://dod.defense.gov/Portals/1/Documents/pubs/2018-National-Defense-Strategy-Summary.pdf, accessed 20 July 2022.

[42] DCDC 'Integrated Operating Concept' (London: Ministry of Defence, 2021): https://assets.publishing.service.gov.uk/government/uploads/system/uploads/attachment_data/file/1014659/Integrated_Operating_Concept_2025.pdf, accessed 20 July 2022.

[43] Alexandr Naumov, 'Miagkaia sila' i 'tsvetnye revoliutsii' i tekhnologii smeny politicheskikh rezhimov v nachale XXI veka ['Soft Power' and 'Colour Revolutions', Technologies of Regime Change at the Beginning of the 21st Century] (Moscow: Agramak-Media, 2017); Alexandr Bartosh, *Konflikty XXI veka: gibridnaia voina i tsvetnaia revoliutsiia [21st Century Conflict: Hybrid War and Colour Revolutions]* (Moscow: Goriachaia liniia – Telekom, 2018).

efforts before a conflict. The clearer that decision, the greater the capacity for the military to prepare so that if a conflict develops, the force can achieve its objectives while preserving combat power.

A final consideration in the strategies pursued by states is the impact of informatized warfare on coalitions and alliances. Alliances, being long-term commitments by states to defend one another, require a degree of interoperability. Across NATO, few states bring the full gamut of military capability to the field and there is a long track record of composite multinational formations. The question is how this can be sustained in an era when data and technical integration must underpin interoperability. The simplest answer is to consider this by system. Within any given formation the communications, command, training and logistics support for the manoeuvre, fires and assault systems are distinct. It therefore appears sensible that within composite multinational formations a particular country takes ownership for at least one system. For the support system by contrast the critical requirement is for the command and control architecture to be standardized across the alliance, enabling multiple countries to contribute to the generation of works groups. This approach may work for NATO, but it is less achievable in international coalitions with partners outside of a formal alliance structure, or with militaries with significantly lower capabilities. Here, governments face the question of how they force generate and allocate effort to non-peer conflicts.

The War, or A War?

This book has been almost exclusively focused on what is usually described as peer-on-peer conflict, namely fighting between states able to field sophisticated military capabilities. For force planners, however, there has been a persistent challenge in retaining readiness for such conflicts while being able to conduct persistent operations against non-state or less capable adversaries. As outlined earlier in this chapter, the international security environment is likely to see food and energy instability – along with identity-based violence – continue to produce instability and conflict in several regions. Peacekeeping, non-combatant evacuation operations, intervention against violent extremist organizations and the support of key partners in competition will all likely produce demands on the military where there is not an adversary able to fight in a manner comparable to what has been outlined in this book. This was a problem Western militaries faced in the Cold War when preparations for mechanized and nuclear war on the European plain had few overlaps with persistent deployments in Africa, the Middle East and Central and South East Asia. The question arises as to how forces configured along the lines described in this book can balance these requirements.

It is firstly worth considering what has, and has not, been successful in recent low-intensity campaigns. The defeat of the Taliban in 2001,[44] the defeat of Gadhafi

---

[44] Steve Coll, *Directorate S: The C.I.A. and America's Secret Wars in Afghanistan and Pakistan* (London: Allen Lane, 2018), pp. 11–114.

in 2011[45] and the defeat of Islamic State in 2017 were not achieved through the large-scale deployment of foreign ground forces. Instead, foreign states provided intelligence, surveillance and reconnaissance support and firepower delivered by naval and air power to enable local forces. The empowerment of local forces is both resource efficient for the intervening power and does not remove the responsibility for political leadership from the partner on the ground. The aftermath of light footprint campaigns – often producing empowered militias and an unstable subsequent political environment – may lead some to question the validity of this approach. There is no evidence, however, that full-scale intervention produces a better outcome. Moreover, it is unsurprising that there are periods of instability following revolutions or successful rebellions and this process is likely unavoidable unless the local forces on the ground are themselves determined to avert it. In any case, given that commitment to major ground operations in a secondary theatre risk disproportionately weakening or fixing an external power in the context of a wider competition, it seems likely that states will continue to pursue this light footprint approach.[46]

If we accept that demand for such operations will continue and the preferred approach will continue to be based around a light footprint with partnered local forces, then it becomes possible to assess where such operations will put pressure on the force. Partnered operations rely heavily on special forces and reconnaissance troops, communications personnel, engineers and logisticians. Firepower can often be delivered by increasingly cheap medium-altitude long-endurance UAVs given the protracted period they can be on station, the precision of their effects and the distances they can cover. In addition, the force requires precision munitions, often with reduced or limited lethality payloads. At the same time, however, sub-peer adversaries are increasingly fielding long-range weapons, including ballistic missiles and their own loitering munitions. Given the lower casualty tolerance that characterizes these conflicts, defences against these threats – especially around airfields and other critical theatre access points – are a key enabler of such operations. Counter-UAS capabilities meanwhile remain necessary at all echelons, as in high-intensity conflict.

The challenge presented by the requirements outlined above is that the reconnaissance forces for such missions are precisely those that are critical in warfighting. Fortunately, these lighter forces are easier to redeploy. In addition, such out of area deployments are useful in training and building the experience of reconnaissance troops. Nevertheless, the manoeuvre system is likely to be severely stretched, especially among medium powers. The second category of defensive equipment for countering UAS and missiles are similarly vital in warfighting. The challenge with these items is that they are some of the most expensive, scarce and in demand systems at any echelon and thus, even if there is not the training and selection pipeline problem in generating crews, armies have a scarcity of this equipment. This will be a major planning constraint on out of area operations.

---

[45] Peter Cole and Brian McQuinn (Eds.), *The Libyan Revolution and Its Aftermath* (Oxford: Oxford University Press, 2015).

[46] Jack Watling and Nick Reynolds, *War by Others' Means: Delivering Effective Partner Force Capacity Building* (London: RUSI, 2021).

Relying on MALE UAVs for fires and the demand for low-lethality munitions presents a different problem; namely that these systems have very little utility in a major conflict. There is thus no economy of scale or efficiency to be gained in having stockpiles of these munitions alongside area effect and anti-armour munitions needed for warfare. MALE UAVs are likely to be provided by Air Forces in many countries, but as they are not useful for warfighting given their large radar cross section and vulnerability to electronic attack, there will be a trade-off decision to be made about whether to divert money from combat air systems. At present, the availability of multi-role fighters limits the choice imposed on air forces, but as UCAVs and other systems become more specialized this will become a pinch point for medium powers.

Another question is how transformative capabilities can support less capable partners and where the integration occurs. The short answer is that the sensor arrays described in this book are equally valuable in these kinds of conflicts, as are the fusing functions of a fire control headquarters. The information, cyber and intelligence functions of the support system will also be vital to such operations, though their outputs will need to be shared with rather than integrated into the partner force. Rather than integrating fires systems, this information is likely to be turned into briefs and shared with the partner to enable strikes, since it is unlikely that partner systems can be integrated into fire control software for both practical and security reasons. There are therefore limits to the extent of transformation at a formation level that can be technologically enabled in partnered operations. Nevertheless, the transformative technologies described in this book can be fielded where they are isolated to single platforms, or to groups of platforms constituting a sovereign expeditionary capability. The challenge for states in force generating for these operations therefore is where they can spare the capacity and how they can maintain a sufficient mass of these systems to be able to divert effort from primary theatres. As already indicated, there is value in having lower threat environments where those skills that are only to be gained through experience can be built up and matured. Furthermore, as has been persistently the case during the War on Terror – demonstrated by many of the technologies described in this book – lower intensity conflicts often enable the innovation that drives transformation of high-intensity warfighting.[47] Although there is a resource tension between the two, therefore, fighting lower intensity campaigns can see competition achieve objectives obviating the need for larger scale fighting, as well as stimulating the sustained development of the force's capabilities, tactics and expertise. If resources are well managed it is a way of keeping the military instrument appropriately sharp. If poorly managed it risks dulling the instrument and diverting resource into unproductive lines of effort. The trick, therefore, is for policymakers and the strategic echelon to fight the war before them, but never to let it dictate requirements contrary to preparedness for a war that may come.

---

[47] Sharon Weinberger, *The Imagineers of War: The Untold Story of DARPA, the Pentagon Agency That Changed the World* (New York: Bantam Books, 2018).

Conclusion

The return of major interstate warfare to Europe on 24 February 2022 arguably marks an inflection point for land forces around the world. Fears over an expanding Chinese military had already driven US defence spending to record levels.[1] Nevertheless, European military spending had been widely falling in real terms with the progressive hollowing out of forces. While armies theorized about autonomy and a revolution in military affairs, the collapse of logistical capabilities, infrastructure and ageing fleets of equipment saw diverging trends between theories and practice.[2] The invasion has prompted increases in defence spending in Germany,[3] Poland,[4] France[5] and possibly in the UK.[6] Similarly, the Russian military's poor performance is likely to spark significant introspection in Russia, Iran, China and further afield, prompting the re-evaluation of assumptions and the adjustment of acquisition and training plans. The next decade, therefore, is set to see serious bets being made about which future capabilities are most relevant and how new technologies are to be fielded. With tensions between the United States and China becoming acute, the consequences of making errors in the priorities for military modernization could be catastrophic.

There are two perils in the arguments surrounding military modernization: that nothing has fundamentally changed, and that everything has. In the former camp, legitimate concerns about a lack of combat mass, vulnerable logistics, a weak industrial

---

[1]   'World Military Expenditure Passes $2 Trillion for First Time', *SIPRI*, 25 April 2022: https://www. sipri.org/media/press-release/2022/world-military-expenditure-passes-2-trillion-first-time, accessed 20 July 2022.

[2]   Ben Wallace, RUSI Land Warfare Conference, London, 28 June 2022.

[3]   Maria Sheahan and Sarah Marsh, 'Germany to Increase Defence Spending in Response to "Putin's War" – Scholz', *Reuters*, 27 February 2022: https://www.reuters.com/business/aerospace-defense/ germany-hike-defense-spending-scholz-says-further-policy-shift-2022-02-27/, accessed 20 July 2022.

[4]   Ana-Roxana Popescu, 'Poland to Increase Defence Spending to 3% of GDP from 2023', *Jane's*, 4 March 2022: https://www.janes.com/defence-news/news-detail/poland-to-increase-defence-spending-to-3-of-gdp-from-2023, accessed 20 July 2022.

[5]   'Macron Calls for French Budget Defence Boost in "War Economy"', *France24*, 13 June 2022: https:// www.france24.com/en/france/20220613-macron-calls-for-french-budget-defence-boost-in-war-economy, accessed 20 July 2022.

[6]   'UK Defence Minister Wallace Endorses Truss for PM', *Reuters*, 29 July 2022: https://www.reuters. com/world/uk/uk-defence-minister-wallace-endorses-truss-pm-2022-07-29/, accessed 20 July 2022.

The Arms of the Future

base and the rich evidence set supporting precisely how a force should operate at high intensity and high tempo all drive towards advocacy for the renewal of Cold War formations. On the other side, there are those who argue that artificial intelligence, cyber warfare and drones are so far reaching in their implications that traditional land formations are rendered obsolete. Among this group, the speed of warfare is often framed as becoming so rapid that the notion of humans directing operations or crewing vehicles will soon become uncompetitive and therefore obsolete. The greatest danger is that military bureaucracies, steeped in concepts of operation refined over seven decades, yet captivated by the allure of technology, pursue the worst of each of these schools of thought, buying vast fleets of new platforms while fundamentally adhering to traditional concepts of operation.

The consequences of technological modernization in the absence of conceptual development are perhaps best illustrated by the First World War and the cult of the offensive.[7] Prior to that conflagration, armies around the world had poured money into technologies like the machine gun and modernized artillery while retaining an absolute faith in the power of motivated infantry to seize ground at tempo. That faith was eviscerated by barbed wire, shrapnel and automatic fire on the western front. Having failed to appreciate and anticipate the changed character of warfare new technologies and concepts had to be developed – taking years – and leaving commanders to attempt tactical innovation to try and overcome operational challenges for which they lacked appropriate tools. The casualty figures speak for themselves. Today there is a risk that the cult of manoeuvre similarly distorts military thinking. Although the manoeuverist principle that targeting enemy weaknesses and avoiding strengths is eminently sensible, the faith that there is always an exposed flank to be exploited and that subterfuge can always make up for a lack of combat power is dangerous. Against most real-world problem sets, room for manoeuvre can become significantly constrained. This is not to argue that manoeuvre is dead – just as offensive action remained possible during the First World War – but it required appropriate shaping and the right balance of capabilities to achieve the necessary tempo, concentration and surprise to make offensive action meaningful. In the future, it is necessary that manoeuvre is similarly enabled through the appropriate shaping and conducted with tools relevant to the environment.

This book has sought to traverse the ridge between the errors of believing that either everything or nothing has changed. Fundamentally it has tried to argue that the impact of new technologies on the battlefield – some quite mundane – poses fundamental problems to militaries seeking to achieve operational surprise, concentration and tempo, and that to take advantage of these capabilities armies must change how they approach command and control. The result is a battlefield on which success at the tactical and sub-tactical level will continue to be determined by manoeuvre forces, but which is operationally positional, and armies must approach operations with protracted shaping to create the conditions for successful offensive action.

---

[7] Lawrence Freedman, *The Future of War: A History* (New York: Public Affairs, 2017), pp. 2–10.

At the same time, this book has tried to outline the limitations on the employment of transformative technology by indicating the complexity of fielding new capabilities and sustaining them in the field. Swarms of drones do not simply materialize from thin air; nor can they overcome the cost and complexity necessary to achieve range, precision and survivability. They require people to launch and recover them, prioritize and determine their tasks, and depending on the task of the UAV and the balance of utility versus cost, to get forward and move through harm's way to bring them into effective range. Agile kill chains and stand-off sensors to enable decisively lethal fires are possible. But fielding these networks requires physical infrastructure, which must be established, maintained and protected. Finally, so long as fighting remains an activity driven by human interests and conducted amidst human populations it will be carried out by humans whose fieldcraft and skills will be essential to the conduct of operations. Mass still matters, but without the technologies outlined in this book is unlikely to remain competitive. Furthermore, the hypothetical force outlined in this book is not a blueprint. A force might have seventy-two rather than fifty-four howitzers in a division. It might have additional armoured battalions and fewer infantry than is outlined here. It may seek advantage in different areas than the force here described has prioritized. But the ratios, proportions and enablement necessary to bring each of these components to bear will likely continue to resemble what is here described. The scale of a competitive force, relative to the tasks ascribed to military formations, is likely to remain. To that end, seeing technology as a means of making war cheaper, armies leaner, or combat less visceral and tragic, is naïve and dangerous. Warfare will remain centred on large-scale human exertion and human suffering. It will also continue to be highly resource intensive. Those who pursue technology at the expense of the enablement outlined in this book are liable to field forces that are brittle and ultimately incapable of sustaining protracted fighting.

There are serious criticisms that could be made about the forces described in this book. One is that the book places considerable emphasis on specialist units designed around critical functions and battlefield problem sets. It does so at the expense of generalist units that can be applied against a wide variety of problems. I would contend that historically, generalist units have been favoured by armies in peacetime because it maximizes the readiness of the force to respond to a range of contingencies. In war, however, armies tend to specialize their formations to overcome specific problems. This has arguably manifested in specialist support elements attached to generalist units. Nevertheless, there is a valid debate to be had about the degree of specialization within a force.

Another major criticism that could be levied against this book is the limited attention paid to jointery or multi-domain integration, which dominates current military discourse. As outlined in Chapter 11, I believe that the air, maritime, space and cyber forces intersect with the land domain at different echelons and that the logic of each domain is likely to see divergence of mission and priorities in the highest intensity warfighting contexts. Against less capable adversaries the drivers of that divergence may be less felt and the levels of integration higher. It is also possible to view this temporally as forces strive to overcome the barriers to integration, with the winning side bringing the domains closer as a campaign advances. A different approach to this book could have been to design a multi-domain formation from first principles. Such an exercise could be interesting, with the results compared with those arrived at in this book. Nevertheless, if we look at the US or British military as good examples, while preaching multi-domain integration the services are continuing to pursue modernization agendas that make radically different assumptions about their primary mission and threats. One also suspects that to build a multi-domain formation from first principles would be exceedingly dependent upon circumstances given that different domains are liable to constitute a centre of gravity depending upon the geography being contested. A valid criticism of this book is that it does not clearly define an adversary. Arguably, however, the mechanics or character of warfare in a domain is quite consistent between adversaries. What changes is where a force may seek relative advantage and therefore the balance of capabilities employed.

There are also technologies that this book fails to consider at all. Most notable is quantum computing. This is simply because not enough is known about the implications of this technology in open sources to reliably make accurate assessments about its effects on tactical fighting. Quantum sensing and other techniques however, arguably accentuate some of the dynamics described in this book rather than contradict them. Such technologies could alter some of the judgements made in this book. Some quite specific technologies could similarly alter the balance of utility judgements pointed to in this book. If materials and design enable the substantial reduction in the acoustic signature, radar cross section and broader survivability of helicopters for example, then assault aviation may become more valuable.

Ultimately, there are many questions that this book leaves unanswered. I am confident that the problems facing land forces outlined in the first five chapters of this book are accurate. How they are overcome is debateable. If this book can encourage agreement as to the problem and stimulate a discussion about the solutions to these challenges then I believe it will have served its purpose. Given how long it takes to design, build, train to use and field military capabilities it is important that armies reach firm conclusions about how they intend to address these challenges as soon as possible. Failing to have answers to how these challenges are to be overcome risks forces lacking credibility, making conflict more likely and increasing the risks that any such conflict would be protracted and highly costly. Having a firm conception of how to combine the arms of the future is important if we are to reduce the strategic uncertainty and therefore instability that makes conflict more probable. As outlined in Chapter 13, there are plenty of drivers of conflict that will persist in the twenty-first century. To deter falling victim to conflict states must show that they are prepared for it.

Bibliography

Books

Adamy, D., *EW 101: A First Course in Electronic Warfare* (Norwood, MA: Artech House, 2001).

Adamy, D., *Introduction to Electronic Warfare Modelling and Simulation* (London: Artech House, 2003).

Alberts, D. S., Garstka, J. J. and Stein, F. P., *Network Centric Warfare: Developing and Leveraging Information Superiority*, 2nd edition (Washington, DC: DoD C4ISR Cooperative Research Program, 2000).

Aldrich, R., *GCHQ: The Uncensored Story of Britain's Most Secret Intelligence Agency* (London: HarperCollins, 2011).

Arrianus, L. F., *The Campaigns of Alexander*, de Selincourt, A. (trans.) (London: Penguin, 1971).

Ayton, A. and Price, J. L. (Eds.), *The Medieval Military Revolution: State, Society and Military Change in Medieval and Early Modern Europe* (London: I.B. Tauris, 1998).

Barker, J., *Conquest: The English Kingdom of France, 1417–1450* (Cambridge, MA: Harvard University Press, 2012).

Barry, B., *Blood, Metal and Dust: How Victory Turned into Defeat in Afghanistan and Iraq* (Oxford: Osprey, 2020).

Bartosh, A., *Konflikty XXI veka: gibridnaia voina i tsvetnaia revoliutsiia [21st Century Conflict: Hybrid War and Colour Revolutions]* (Moscow: Goriachaia liniia – Telekom, 2018).

Beaumont, R. A., *Military Elites: Special Fighting Units in the Modern World* (London: Bobbs- Merrill, 1975).

Beevor, A., *Arnhem: The Battle for the Bridges, 1944* (London: Penguin, 2019).

Beevor, A., *Stalingrad* (London: BCA, 2005).

Bergman, R., *Rise and Kill First: The Secret History of Israel's Targeted Assassinations* (New York: Random House, 2018).

Black, A., *Political Thought in Europe, 1250–1450* (Cambridge: Cambridge University Press, 1992).

Black, J., *Tank Warfare* (Bloomington: Indiana University Press, 2020).

Bowden, M., *Black Hawk Down* (London: Penguin, 1999).

Bradbeer, T. G. (Ed.), *Lethal and Non-Lethal Fires: Historical Case Studies of Converging Cross-Domain Fires in Large-Scale Combat Operations* (Fort Leavenworth, KS: Army University Press, 2018).

Bradbury, J., *The Medieval Siege* (Woodbridge: The Boydell Press, 1998).

Bronk, J., *The Future of NATO Airpower: How Are Future Capability Plans within the Alliance Diverging and How Can Interoperability Be Maintained?* (London: RUSI, 2019).

Brown, A., *Active Electronically Scanned Arrays: Fundamentals and Applications* (Hoboken: John Wiley and Sons, 2022).

Brown, L., *Technical and Military Imperatives: A Radar History of World War 2* (London: Taylor and Francis, 1999).

Brungess, J. R., *Setting the Context: Suppression of Enemy Air Defences and Joint War Fighting in an Uncertain World* (Maxwell Air Force Base, Alabama: Air University Press, 1994).

Card, O. S., *Ender's Game* (New York: Tor Books, 1985).

Carlin, J. P. with Graff, G. M., *Dawn of the Code War: America's Battle against Russia, China, and the Rising Global Cyber Threat* (New York: Public Affairs, 2018).

Cole, P. and McQuinn, B. (Eds.), *The Libyan Revolution and Its Aftermath* (Oxford: Oxford University Press, 2015).

Coll, S., *Directorate S: The C.I.A. and America's Secret Wars in Afghanistan and Pakistan* (London: Allen Lane, 2018).

Collins, L. and Spencer, J. (Eds.), *Understanding Urban Warfare* (Havant: Howgate Publishing, 2022).

Corbett, J. S., *Some Principles of Maritime Strategy* (London: Longmans, Green and Co., 1911).

Curlander, J. and McDonough, R., *Synthetic Aperture Radar: Systems and Signal Processing* (New York: Wiley, 1991).

David, S., *SBS: Silent Warriors* (London: William Collins 2021).

de Bretton-gordon, H., *Chemical Warrior: Syria, Salisbury and Saving Lives at War* (London: Headline, 2020).

de Gaulle, C., *La France et son Armée* (Paris: Tempus Perrin, 2016).

Delves, C., *Across an Angry Sea: The SAS in the Falklands War* (London: Hurst, 2018).

Fenoulhet, J., Quist G. and Tiedau, U. (Eds.), *Discord and Consensus in the Low Countries, 1700–2000* (London: UCL Press, 2016).

Ford, M. and Hoskins, A., *Radical War: Data, Attention and Control in the 21st Century* (London: Hurst, 2022).

Fravel, M. T., *Active Defence: China's Military Strategy since 1949* (Princeton, NJ: Princeton University Press, 2019).

Freedman, L., *The Future of War: A History* (London: Penguin, 2018).

Fuller, J. F. C., *On Future Warfare* (London: Sifton, Praed & Company, 1928).

Gabriel, R., *Operation Peace for Galilee: The Israeli-PLO War in Lebanon* (London: Hill & Wang, 1984).

Gormley, D. M., Erickson, A. S. and Yuan, J., *A Low-Visibility Force Multiplier: Assessing China's Cruise Missile Ambitions* (Washington, DC: Institute for National Security Studies, 2014).

Grau, L. and Glantz, D., *The Bear Went over the Mountain: Soviet Combat Tactics in Afghanistan* (Washington, DC: National Defence University Press, 1996).

Guardia, M., *The Fires of Babylon: Eagle Troop and the Battle of 73 Easting* (New York: Casemate, 2015).

Guderian, H., *Achtung Panzer!: The Development of Tank Warfare*, Duffy, C. (trans.) (London: Weidenfeld & Nicolson, 1999).

Hastings, M., *The Korean War* (New York: Simon and Schuster, 1988).

Hastings, M. and Jenkins, S., *The Battle for the Falklands* (London: Pan Books, 1997).

Heck T. and Friedman, B. A. (Eds.), *On Contested Shores: The Evolving Role of Amphibious Operations in the History of Warfare* (Quantico: Marine Corps University Press, 2020).

Heckhausen, J. and Heckhausen, H. (Eds.), *Motivation and Action* (Cambridge: Cambridge University Press, 2008).

Hooton, E. R., *Luftwaffe at War: Blitzkrieg in the West 1939–1940* (London: Midland Publishing, 2007).

Hubin, G., *Perspectives Tactiques* (Paris: Economica, 2009).

Jackson, J., *A Certain Idea of France: The Life of Charles de Gaulle* (London: Allen lane, 2018).

Jackson, J., *The Fall of France: The Nazi Invasion of 1940* (Oxford: Oxford University Press, 2003).

Jones, B., *To Rule the Waves: How Control of the World's Oceans Shapes the Fate of the Superpowers* (New York: Simon and Schuster, 2021).

Joshi, S., *Indian Power Projection: Ambition, Arms and Influence*, RUSI Whitehall Paper 85 (London: Taylor and Francis, 2016).

Kaszeta, D., *Toxic: A History of Nerve Agents, from Nazi Germany to Putin's Russia* (London: Hurst, 2020).

Kaushal, S., Byrne, J., Byrne, J., Pilli, G. and Somerville, G., *The Balance of Power between Russia and NATO in the Arctic and High North* (London: RUSI, 2022).

Keegan, J., *The Face of Battle: A Study of Agincourt, Waterloo, and the Somme* (London: Pimlico, 1976).

Kennedy, P., *Engineers of Victory: The Problem Solvers Who Turned the Tide in the Second World War* (London: Allen Lane, 2013).

Kennedy, P., *The Rise and Fall of the Great Powers: Economic Change and Military Conflict from 1500 to 2000* (New York: Random House, 1987).

Kilcullen, D., *Out of the Mountains: The Coming Age of the Urban Guerrilla* (London: Hurst, 2013).

King, A., *Command: The Twenty-First-century General* (Cambridge: Cambridge University Press, 2019).

King, A., *Urban Warfare in the Twenty-First Century* (London: Polity, 2021).

Lang, Q. and Qiangsui, W., *Unrestricted Warfare: China's Master Plan to Destroy America* (New York: Filament Books, 2004).

Lawrence, C., *War by Numbers: Understanding Conventional Combat* (Lincoln NH: Potomac Books, 2017).

Leonhard, R., *The Art of Maneuver: Maneuver Warfare Theory and Airland Battle* (New York: Random House, 2009).

Leonhard, R., *The Principles of War for the Information Age* (New York: Ballantine, 1998).

Levine, A. J., *The War against Rommel's Supply Lines, 1942–43* (New York: Praeger, 1999).

Lieven, A., *Chechnya: Tombstone of Russian Power* (New Haven, CT: Yale University Press, 1998).

Livy, T., *The War with Hannibal: The History of Rome from Its Foundation Books 21-30*, Selincourt, A. (trans.) (London: Penguin, 2004).

Luttwak, E., *The Political Uses of Sea Power* (Baltimore, MD: Johns Hopkins University Press, 1974).

Machiavelli, N., *The Prince: On the Art of Power* (London: Duncan Baird Publishers, 2007).

Mankoff, J., *Russian Foreign Policy: The Return of Great Power Politics* (Lanham, MD: Rowman and Littlefield Publishers, 2012).

McGrath, J. J., *The Other End of the Spear: The Tooth-to-Tail Ratio (T3R) in Modern Military Operations* (Fort Leavenworth, KS: Combat Studies Institute Press, 2007).

McRaven, W. H., *Spec Ops: Case Studies in Special Operations Warfare Theory and Practice* (Toronto: Random House Canada, 1995).

Mearsheimer, J., *The Tragedy of Great Power Politics* (New York: W. W. Norton, 2001).

Mikaberidze, A., *The Napoleonic Wars: A Global History* (New York: Oxford University Press, 2020).

Ministry of Defence of the Russian Federation, 'Очаговая Оборона' [Fragmented Defence], *Military Encyclopaedia* [Военная Энциклопедия], vol. 6 (Moscow: Voyenizdat, 2002).

Mulder, N., *The Economic Weapon: The Rise of Sanctions as a Tool of Modern War* (New Haven, CT: Yale University Press, 2022).

Naumov, A., 'Miagkaia sila' i 'tsvetnye revoliutsii' i tekhnologii smeny politicheskikh rezhimov v nachale XXI veka ['Soft Power' and 'Colour Revolutions', *Technologies of Regime Change at the Beginning of the 21st Century]* (Moscow: Agramak-Media, 2017).

Nordeen, L. O., *Air Warfare in the Missile Age*, 2nd edition (Washington, DC: Smithsonian Books, 2010).

Oren, M. B., *Six Day of War: June 1967 and the Making of the Modern Middle East* (Oxford: Oxford University Press, 2002).

Patrikarakos, D., *War in 140 Characters: How Social Media Is Reshaping Conflict in the Twenty-First Century* (London: Basic Books, 2017).

Payne, K., *I, Warbot: The Dawn of Artificially Intelligent Conflict* (London: Hurst, 2021).

Plato, *The Laws of Plato*, Pangle, T. (trans.) (London: University of Chicago Press, 1988).

Politkovskaya, A., *A Dirty War: A Russian Reporter in Chechnya* (London: Harvill Press, 2001).

Price, A., *Instruments of Darkness: The History of Electronic Warfare, 1939–1945* (London: William Kimber and Company, 1967).

Privratsky, K., *Logistics in the Falklands War* (Barnsley: Pen & Sword, 2014).

Rowland, D., *The Stress of Battle: Quantifying Human Performance in Battle for Historical Analysis and Wargaming* (Bristol: The History of Wargaming Project, 2019).

Ryan, M., *War Transformed: The Future of Twenty-First Century Great Power Competition and Conflict* (Annapolis: Naval Institute Press, 2022).

Sanger, D., *Confront and Conceal: Obama's Secret Wars and Surprising Use of American Power* (New York: Random House, 2013).

Scharre, P., *Army of None: Autonomous Weapons and the Future of War* (New York: W. W. Norton, 2018).

Shelling, T. C., *Arms and Influence* (New Haven, CT: Yale University Press, 1966).

Shock, J., *The US Army Barrage Balloon Programme* (Merriam Press: Vermont, 2006).

Singer, P., *Corporate Warriors: The Rise of the Privatised Military Industry* (Ithaca: Cornell University Press, 2007).

Singer, P. and Cole, A., *Ghost Fleet: A Novel of the Next World War* (New York: Houghton Mifflin Harcourt, 2015).

Slim, W., *Defeat into Victory* (London: Macmillan, 2009).

Solomon, J., *The Iran Wars: Spy Games, Bank Battles, and the Secret Deals that Reshaped the Middle East* (New York: Random House, 2016).

Stanton, N. A. et al., *Digitising Command and Control: A Human Factors and Ergonomics Analysis of Mission Planning and Battlespace Management* (Farnham: Ashgate, 2009).

Stillwell, A., *Military Reconnaissance: The Eyes and Ears of the Army* (London: Casemate, 2021).

Storr, J., *Battelgroup!: The Lessons of the Unfought Battles of the Cold War* (London: Helion, 2021).

Strachan, H., *From Waterloo to Balaclava: Tactics, Technology, and the British Army, 1815–1854* (Cambridge: Cambridge University Press, 1985).

Tacitus, G. C., *The Histories*, Wellesley, K. (trans.) (London: Penguin, 2009).

Terry, T. W., *Fighting Vehicles* (London: Brassey's, 1991).

Tomasini, E. P. and Castellini, P. (Eds.), *Laser Doppler Vibrometry: A Multimedia Guide to Its Features and Usage* (Berlin: Springer, 2020).

von Clausewitz, C., *On War*, Howard, M. and Paret, P. (trans.) (Princeton NJ: Princeton University Press, 1989).

Wahlman, A., *Storming the City: U.S. Military Performance in Urban Warfare from World War II to Vietnam* (Denton, TX: University of North Texas Press, 2015).

Walker Howe, D., *What Hath God Wrought: The Transformation of America, 1815–1848* (Oxford: Oxford University Press, 2007).

Watling, J. (Ed.), *Decision Points: Rationalising the Armed Forces of European Medium Powers* (RUSI, London, 2020).

Watling, J. and Bronk, J. (Eds.), *Necessary Heresies: Challenging the Narratives Distorting Contemporary UK Defence* (London: RUSI, 2021).

Watling, J. and Reynolds, N., *War by Others' Means: Delivering Effective Partner Force Capacity Building* (London: RUSI, 2021).

Weinberger, S., *The Imagineers of War: The Untold Story of DARPA, the Pentagon Agency that Changed the World* (New York: Bantam Books, 2018).

Whalen, R., *Bitter Wounds: German Victims of the Great War, 1914–1939* (New York: Ithaca, 1984).

Wheatcroft, A., *The Enemy at the Gates: Habsburgs, Ottomans and the Battle for Europe* (Oxford: The Bodley Head, 2008).

Wirth, W. D., *Radar Techniques Using Array Antennas* (London: Institution of Engineering and Technology, 2001).

Yeide, H., *The Tank Killers: A History of America's World War II Tank Destroyer Force* (Newbury: Casemate, 2010).

Yousheng, L., *Lianhe zhanyi xuejiaocheng [Lectures on the Science of Joint Campaigns]* (Beijing: Military Science Press, 2012).

Zenko, M., *Red Team: How to Succeed by Thinking Like the Enemy* (New York: Basic Books, 2015).

Journal Articles and Peer Reviewed Papers

'Above Us Only Stars: Exposing GPS Spoofing in Russia and Syria', *C4ADS*, 2019: https://static1.squarespace.com/static/566ef8b4d8af107232d5358a/t/5c99488beb39314c45e782da/1553549492554/Above+Us+Only+Stars.pdf, accessed 20 July 2022.

Alberts, D. S., Garstka, J. J. and Stein, F. P., *Network Centric Warfare: Developing and Leveraging Information Superiority*, 2nd edition (Washington, DC: DoD C4ISR Cooperative Research Program, 2000).

Allen, J. and Hussain, A., 'On Hyperwar', *Proceedings Magazine* (Vol. 143, No. 7, 2017), p. 1373.

Anderson, C., 'Rare Earths: Market Disruption, Innovation, and Global Supply Chains', *Annual Review of Environment and Resources* (Vol. 41, 2016), pp. 199–222.

Applegate, S. D., 'The Principle of Maneuver in Cyber Operations', 4th International Conference on Cyber Conflict, 2012, pp. 1–13.

Balis, C. and O'Neill, P., 'Trust in AI: Rethinking Future Command', *RUSI Occasional Paper* (June 2022): https://static.rusi.org/332_OP_Trust_in_AI_Final_Web.pdf, accessed 20 July 2022.

Boyd, J. R., 'Destruction and Creation', US Army Command and General Staff College, 3 September 1976, p. 1.

Bronk, J., 'Modern Russian and Chinese Integrated Air Defence Systems: The Nature of the Threat, Growth Trajectory and Western Options', RUSI Occasional Papers (January 2020).

Bronk, J. and Watling, J., 'Maximising the Utility of the British Army's Combat Aviation', *RUSI Occasional Paper* (London: RUSI, 2021).

Bronk, J. with Reynolds, N. and Watling, J., *The Russian Air War and Ukrainian Requirements for Air Defence* (London: RUSI, 2022): https://static.rusi.org/SR-Russian-Air-War-Ukraine-web-final.pdf, accessed 3 December 2022.

Chalmers, M. and Unterseher, L., 'Is There a Tank Gap?: Comparing NATO and Warsaw Pact Tank Fleets', *International Security* (Vol. 13, No. 1, 1988), pp. 5–49.

Chilton, K. and Autenried, L., 'The Backbone of JADC2: Satellite Communications for Information Age Warfare' (Washington, DC: The Mitchell Institute, 2021): https://mitchellaerospacepower.org/wp-content/uploads/2021/12/The_Backbone_of_JADC2_Policy_Paper_32-ver2.pdf, accessed 20 July 2022.

Clark, B., McNamara, W. and Walton, T., *Winning the Invisible War: Gaining an Enduring U.S. Advantage in the Electromagnetic Spectrum* (Washington DC: CSBA, 2019).

Clint, A., 'Whither Armor?', *Military Operations* (Vol. 1, No. 2, 2012), pp. 4–8.

de la Billière, P., 'The Gulf Conflict: Planning and Execution', *RUSI Journal* (Vol. 136, No. 4, 1991), pp. 7–12.

Engstrom, J., *Systems Confrontation and System Destruction Warfare: How the Chinese People's Liberation Army Seeks to Wage Modern Warfare*, (Santa Monica, CA: RAND Corporation, 2018).

Fox, A., '"Cyborgs at Little Stalingrad": A Brief History of the Battles of the Donetsk Airport, 26 May 2014 to 21 January 201', *Association of the United States Army*, May 2019: https://www.ausa.org/sites/default/files/publications/LWP-125-Cyborgs-at-Little-Stalingrad-A-Brief-History-of-the-Battle-of-the-Donetsk-Airport.pdf, accessed 20 July 2022.

Fox, A., 'A Solution Looking for a Problem: Illuminating Misconceptions in Manoeuver Warfare Doctrine': https://www.benning.army.mil/armor/earmor/content/issues/2017/Fall/4Fox17.pdf, accessed 20 July 2022.

Fox, A., 'Manoeuvre Is Dead?', *The RUSI Journal* (Vol. 166, No. 6, 2021), pp. 10–18.

Fox, A., 'On Sieges', *The RUSI Journal* (Vol. 166, No. 2, 2021), pp. 18–28.

Fox, A., 'Ukraine and Proxy War Improving Ontological Shortcomings in Military Thinking', *Land Warfare Papers* (Vol. 148, 2022): https://www.ausa.org/sites/default/files/publications/LWP-148-Ukraine-and-Proxy-War-Improving-Ontological-Shortcomings-in-Military-Thinking.pdf, accessed 20 July 2022.

Grau, L., 'Changing Russian Urban Tactics: The Aftermath of the Battle for Grozny', *INSS Strategic Forum* (Vol. 38, 1995): file:///Users/user/Downloads/1995-07-01%20Changing%20Russian%20Urban%20Tactics%20-%20The%20Aftermath%20of%20the%20Battle%20(Grau)-1.pdf, accessed 20 December 2022.

Grau, L. and Bartles, C., 'Russian Future Combat on a Fragmented Battlefield': https://www.benning.army.mil/infantry/magazine/issues/2021/Fall/pdf/5_Grau_txt.pdf, accessed 3 December 2022.

Greenwald, A. G. and Banaji, M. R., 'Implicit Social Cognition: Attitudes, Self-Esteem, and Stereotypes', *Psychological Review* (Vol. 102, No. 1, 1995), pp. 4–27.

Hägerdal, Nils., 'Starvation as Siege Tactics: Urban Warfare in Syria', *Studies in Conflict & Terrorism*, (2020), DOI: 10.1080/1057610X.2020.1816682.

Hillson, F., 'When the Balloon Goes Up: Barrage Balloons for Low Level Air Defence', Air Command and Staff College, 1988: https://apps.dtic.mil/sti/pdfs/ADA192618.pdf, accessed 20 July 2022.

Hoebeke, J. et al., 'An Overview of Mobile Ad Hoc Networks: Applications and Challenges', *Journal-Communications Network* (Vol. 3, No. 3, 2004), pp. 60–6.

Ishida, T. et al., 'Digital City Kyoto: Towards a Social Information Infrastructure', Klusch, M., Shehory, O. M., Weiss, G. (Eds.), *Cooperative Information Agents III. CIA, Lecture Notes in Computer Science*, vol. 1652 (1999), pp. 34–46.

Johns Hopkins Applied Physics Laboratory, 'The Cooperative Engagement Capability', *Technical Digest* (Vol. 16, No. 4, 1995), pp. 377–96.

Johnson, D. D. P. and Tierney, D., 'The Rubicon Theory of War: How the Path to Conflict Reaches the Point of No Return', *International Security* (Vol. 36, No. 1, Summer 2011), pp. 7–40.

Kahn, H., 'The Nature and Feasibility of War and Deterrence', RAND Corporation, P-1888-RC, 1960.

Kahneman, D. and Tversky, A., 'Prospect Theory: An Analysis of Decision under Risk', *Econometrica* (Vol. 47, No. 2, 1979), pp. 263–92.

Karako, T., *Distributed Defense: New Operational Concepts for Integrated Air and Missile Defence* (Washington, DC: Center for Strategic and International Studies, 2018).

Kaushal, S. and Markiewicz, M., 'Crossing the River by Feeling the Stones: The Trajectory of China's Maritime Transformation', *Occasional Paper* (London: RUSI, 2019).

Kessler, D. and Cour-Palais, B., 'Collision Frequency of Artificial Satellites: The Creation of a Debris Belt', *Journal of Geophysical Research* (Vol. 83, No. A6, 1978), pp. 2637–46.

Kirubarajan, T. and Bar-Shalom, Y., 'Tracking Evasive Move-Stop-Move Targets with a GMTI Radar using a VS-IMM Estimator', *IEEE Transactions on Aerospace and Electronic Systems* (Vol. 39, No. 3, 2003), pp. 1098–103.

Kofman, M., Fink, A. and Edmonds, J., 'Russian Strategy for Escalation Management: Evolution of Key Concepts', CNA (April 2020): https://www.cna.org/archive/CNA_Files/pdf/drm-2019-u-022455-1rev.pdf, accessed 20 July 2022.

Konaev, M., 'The Future of Urban Warfare in the Age of Megacities', *Focus Stratégique*, No. 88 (Paris: IFRI, 2019), pp. 34–46.

Krulak, C., 'The Strategic Corporal: Leadership in the Three Block War', *Marines Magazine* (1999).

Lambeth, B., *NATO's Air War for Kosovo: A Strategic and Operational Assessment* (Santa Monica CA: RAND, 2001: https://www.rand.org/content/dam/rand/pubs/monograph_reports/MR1365/RAND_MR1365.pdf, accessed 20 July 2022.

Lisbona, D. and Snee, T., 'A Review of Hazards Associated with Primary Lithium and Lithium-Ion Batteries', *Process Safety and Environmental Protection* (Vol. 89, No. 6, 2011), pp. 434–42.

Madhu, V. and Balakrishna Bhat, T., 'Armour Protection and Affordable Protection for Futuristic Combat Vehicles', *Defence Science Journal* (Vol. 61, No. 4, 2011), pp. 394–402.

Matsumura, J. et al., *Lightning over Water: Sharpening America's Light Forces for Rapid Reaction Missions* (Santa Monica, CA: RAND Corporation, 2000).

Matsumura, J. et al., *Rapid Force Protection Technologies: Assessing the Performance of Advanced Ground Sensors* (Santa Monica, CA: RAND, 2005).

Mead, J., 'Winning the Firefight on the Road to Warfighter', *British Army Review* (Vol. 175, Summer, 2019), pp. 64–73.

Muthanna, M. S. A., Muthanna, M. M. A., Khakimov, A. and Muthanna, A., 'Development of Intelligent Street Lighting Services Model Based on LoRa Technology', *2018 IEEE Conference of Russian Young Researchers in Electrical and Electronic Engineering (EIConRus)*, (2018), pp. 90–3.

Nitoiu, C., 'Aspirations to Great Power Status: Russia's Path to Assertiveness in the International Arena Under Putin', *Political Studies Review* (Vol. 15, No. 1, February 2017), pp. 39–48.

O'Donoghue, N., McBirney, S. and Persons, B., Distributed Kill Chains: Drawing Insights for Mosaic Warfare from the Immune System and from the Navy (RAND Corporation, 2021).

Patch, J., 'Fortress at Sea? The Carrier Invulnerability Myth', US Naval Institute Proceedings (January 2010).

Petersen, S., 'The Small Aerostat System: Field Tested, Highly Mobile and Adaptable', *AIAA 5th Aviation, Technology, Integration, and Operations Conference*, 26–28 September 2005, Arlington, Virginia.

Reading, A., 'Mobile Witnessing: Ethics and the Camera Phone in the 'War on Terror', *Globalizations* (Vol. 6, No. 1, 2009), pp. 61–76.

Reynolds, N., 'The British Army and Mass in Urban Warfare', *The RUSI Journal* (Vol. 166, No. 4, 2021), pp. 1–14.

Reynolds, N., 'Getting Tactical Communications for Land Forces Right', *The RUSI Journal* (Vol. 166, No. 5, 2021), pp. 64–75.

Reynolds, N., 'Learning Tactical and Operational Combat Lessons for High-End Warfighting from Counterinsurgency', *The RUSI Journal* (Vol. 164, No. 7, 2019), pp. 42–53.

Reynolds, N., 'Performing Information Manoeuvre through Persistent Engagement', Occasional Paper (London: RUSI, 2020).

Sampaio, A., 'Before and after Urban Warfare: Conflict Prevention and Transitions in Cities', *International Review of the Red Cross* (Vol. 98, No. 901, 2016), pp. 71–95.

Sanghvi, H. P. and Dahiya, M. S., 'Cyber Reconnaissance: An Alarm before Cyber Attack', *International Journal of Computer Applications* (Vol. 63, No. 6, 2013), pp. 36–8.

Starry, D., 'Extending the Battlefield', *Military Review* (March, 1981), pp. 31–50.

Stevens, M., 'Resistance and Information Warfare in Mosul and Raqqa', *The RUSI Journal* (Vol. 165, No. 5, 2020), pp. 10–21.

Thompson, H. and Watling, J., 'Assessing Dynamics of Control through Iranian Technology Transfer to Yemen's Houthis', *The RUSI Journal* (2022), DOI: 10.1080/03071847.2022.2148557.

Tsygankov, A. P., 'Vladimir Putin's Vision of Russia as a Normal Great Power', *Post-Soviet Affairs* (Vol. 21, No. 2, 2005), pp. 132–58.

van der Klaauw, C., 'Joint Effects: Integration and Synchronisation of Lethal and Non-Lethal Activities', *Three Swords Magazine* (Vol. 36, 2020), pp. 74–8: https://jwc.nato.int/application/files/8216/0523/5268/issue36_15lr.pdf#:~:text=Joint%20Effects%20is%20the%20integration,strategic%2C%20operational%2C%20and%20tactical., accessed 20 July 2022.

Verma, S. K., 'Security and Privacy Issues in Wireless Ad Hoc, Mesh, and Sensor Networks', *Advance in Electronic and Electric Engineering* (Vol. 4, No. 4, 2014), pp. 381–8.

Watling, J., 'Preparing Military Intelligence for Great Power Competition', *The RUSI Journal* (Vol. 166, No. 1, 2021), pp. 68–80.

Watling, J. and Bronk, J., 'Maximising the Utility of the British Army's Combat Aviation', *RUSI Occasional Paper* (April 2021): https://static.rusi.org/236_op_uk_aviation_capabilities_final_web_version.pdf, accessed 20 July 2022.

Watling, J. and Reynolds, N., *Operation Z: Death Throes of an Imperial Delusion* (London: RUSI, 2022), pp. 2–7: https://static.rusi.org/special-report-202204-operation-z-web.pdf, accessed 20 July 2022.

Watling, J. and Reynolds, N., *The Plot to Destroy Ukraine* (London: RUSI, 2022): https://static.rusi.org/special-report-202202-ukraine-web.pdf, accessed 20 July 2022.

Watling, J. and Waters, N., 'Achieving Lethal Effects by Small Unmanned Aerial Vehicles', *The RUSI Journal* (Vol. 164, No. 1, 2019), pp. 40–51.

Watling, J., Bronk, J. and Kaushal, S., 'A UK Joint Methodology for Assuring Theatre Access', *RUSI Whitehall Report* (London: RUSI, 2022).

Weeden, B. and Samson, V. (Eds.), 'Global Counterspace Capabilities: An Open Source Assessment', Secure World Foundation, April 2020: https://swfound.org/media/206970/swf_counterspace2020_electronic_final.pdf, accessed 20 July 2022.

Weizman, E., 'Walking through Walls: Soldiers as Architects in the Israeli–Palestinian Conflict', *Radical Philosophy* (Vol. 136, 2006), pp. 8–22.

Wheatley, B., 'Surviving Prokhorovka: German Armoured Longevity on the Eastern Front in 1943–1944', *Journal of Intelligence History* (2020), pp. 1–87.

Williams, I. and Shaikh, S., *The Missile War in Yemen* (Washington, DC: CSIS, 2020): https://csis-website-prod.s3.amazonaws.com/s3fs-public/publication/Williams_MissileWarYemen_WEB_FINAL_v2.pdf, accessed 20 July 2022.

Yan, B. and Zivot, E. W., 'The Dynamics of Price Discovery', *AFA 2005 Philadelphia Meetings* (26 February 2007).

Websites

'B-21 Raider', *Northrop Grumman*: https://www.northropgrumman.com/what-we-do/air/b-21-raider/, accessed 20 July 2022.

'FIRE WEAVER ™ – A Networked Combat System (Urban Scenario)', *Rafael*, 4 April 2019: https://www.youtube.com/watch?v=gJHjcukNbpw, accessed 20 July 2022.

'Houthi Attacks Reporting Monitor, Volume 1', *Embassy of the Republic of Yemen to the United States*: https://www.yemenembassy.org/wp-content/uploads/2022/03/Harm.pdf, accessed 20 July 2022.

'Lt. Gen. Sean MacFarland: Building Better Arab Armed Forces', American Enterprise Institute, 18 March 2019: https://www.youtube.com/watch?v=EWHffWl0DUY, accessed 20 July 2022.

'TROPHY® Active Protection System for AFVs', Rafael: https://www.rafael.co.il/worlds/land/trophy-aps/, accessed 20 July 2022.

Army Futures Command, NET CFT: https://armyfuturescommand.com/net/, accessed 20 July 2022.

Carleton-Smith, M., RUSI Land Warfare Conference 2021, 'Land Warfare 2021: Welcoming Remarks and Opening Keynote', London, 2 June 2021: https://www.youtube.com/watch?v=JhcGUoNo6Hk, 15:00, accessed 20 July 2022.

Carter, N., RUSI Land Warfare Conference 2016', 28 June 2016: https://www.youtube.com/watch?v=K_MRagWu8p4 06.15-06.40, accessed 7 September 2021.

Elysee, 'Notre avenir énergétique et écologique passe par le nucléaire. Déplacement du Président Emmanuel Macron sur le site industriel de Framatome', 8 December 2020: https://www.elysee.fr/emmanuel-macron/2020/12/08/deplacement-du-president-emmanuel-macron-sur-le-site-industriel-de-framatome, accessed 20 July 2022.

Hawkes, J., 'Primer: Statistical Armour', *The Institute of Tankology*, 5 March 2022: https://www.tanknology.co.uk/post/statistical-armour, accessed 20 July 2022.

Hodges, B., House of Commons Defence Committee, 6 July 2021: https://committees.parliament.uk/oralevidence/2496/html/, accessed 20 July 2022.

John Hawkes, 'Primer: Composite Rubber Track (CRT)', The Institute of Tankology, 17 January 2022: https://www.tanknology.co.uk/post/__crt, accessed 20 July 2022.

PBS Newshour, 'In Damascus, Syrians Still Seek Sense of Normal Life', 20 December 2012: https://www.youtube.com/watch?v=-FDG9kBcWII, accessed 20 July 2022.

'Танки у Росиисько-Украинськи Воино': https://www.youtube.com/watch?v=ktJNrw6d xwo&list=LL&index=2, accessed 20 July 2022.

https://www.youtube.com/watch?v=ZJgvhsgTzCc, accessed 20 July 2022.

Keatinge, T., Oral Testimony to the Economic Affairs Committee, 26 October 2021: https://committees.parliament.uk/oralevidence/2928/pdf/, accessed 20 July 2022.

MacFarland, S., 'TRADOC Mad Scientist 2017 Georgetown: Welcome to Day 2 w/ LTG Sean MacFarland', 9 August 2017: https://www.youtube.com/watch?v=Cp3NqSzSnTg, accessed 20 July 2022.

McGurk, B., 'Press Conference by Special Presidential Envoy McGurk in Erbil, Iraq', *US Department of State*, 4 September 2017: https://2017-2021.state.gov/press-conference-by-special-presidential-envoy-mcgurk-in-erbil-iraq/index.html, accessed 20 July 2022.

MoD, 'Joint Statement on Carrier Strike Group 2021 Joint Declaration Signing', 19 January 2021: https://www.gov.uk/government/news/joint-statement-on-carrier-strike-group-2021-joint-declaration-signing–2, accessed 20 July 2022.

Office of the Secretary of Defence, 'Justification for FY 2018 Overseas Contingency Operations: Counter Islamic-State of Iraq and Syria Train and Equip Fund', *Department of Defence*, May 2018: https://comptroller.defense.gov/Portals/45/Documents/defbudget/fy2018/fy2018_CTEF_J-Book_Final_Embargoed.pdf, accessed 20 July 2022.

Oryx, 'The Fight for Nagorno-Karabakh: Documenting Losses on the Sides of Armenia and Azerbaijan': https://www.oryxspioenkop.com/2020/09/the-fight-for-nagorno-karabakh.html, accessed 20 July 2022.

Perrett, B., 'Guiding Light: How Lasers Can Inform Military Operations', *Qinetiq*, 19 November 2020: https://www.qinetiq.com/en/blogs/how-lasers-can-inform-military-operations, accessed 20 July 2022.

Price, N., 'The Houthis Must Cease the Assault on Marib', *US Department of State*, 16 February 2021: https://www.state.gov/the-houthis-must-cease-the-assault-on-marib/, accessed 20 July 2022.

Raytheon Missiles and Defence, 'SM-6 Missile': https://www.raytheonmissilesanddefense.com/what-we-do/missile-defense/interceptors/sm-6-missile, accessed 20 July 2022.

Stravridis, J., 'Review', Cost Fleet Book: https://www.ghostfleetbook.com/reviews/, accessed 20 July 2022.

Sutyagin, I., 'RUSI Land Warfare Conference 2017 – Session 7', 19 July 2017, 21:54–48:00: https://www.youtube.com/watch?v=_EcrrD1dBhg, accessed 20 July 2022.

THeMIS being an example of such a platform: 'Milrem Robotics' THeMIS Combat Unmanned Ground Vehicle on Display at DIMDEX', *Milrem Robotics*,

20 March 2022: https://milremrobotics.com/milrem-robotics-themis-combat-unmanned-ground-vehicle-on-display-at-dimdex/, accessed 20 July 2022.

US Army Training and Doctrine Command (TRADOC), 'FM 100-5 Operations 1982', 1982.

Walker, S., 'Into the Grey Zone Podcast: Episode Five – Cyber Power (Part II)', *Sky News*, 3 June 2021, 06:00: https://news.sky.com/story/into-the-grey-zone-podcast-episode-five-cyber-power-part-ii-12212228, accessed 20 July 2022.

Wesley, E. J., 'AUSA Global Force Symposium: Day 3 – Opening Remarks and Keynote Speaker', 28 March 2019: https://www.dvidshub.net/video/668339/ausa-global-force-symposium-day-3-opening-remarks-and-keynote-speaker, accessed 20 July 2022.

Articles and Documents

'A Border Dispute between India and China Is Getting More Serious', *The Economist*, 28 May 2020: https://www.economist.com/asia/2020/05/28/a-border-dispute-between-india-and-china-is-getting-more-serious, accessed 10 December 2022.

'As It Happened: Ukraine Facing "Crucial" Period as Russia Focuses on East', *BBC*, 4 April 2022: https://www.bbc.com/news/live/world-europe-61032786, accessed 20 July 2022.

'Convention on Cluster Munitions', United Nations, 2008: https://treaties.un.org/doc/Publication/CTC/26-6.pdf, accessed 20 July 2022.

'Editorial: Bringing Space to Bear in Afghanistan', *SpaceNews*, 25 May 2010: https://spacenews.com/editorial-bringing-space-bear-afghanistan/, accessed 20 July 2022.

'Macron Calls for French Budget Defence Boost in "War Economy"', *France24*, 13 June 2022: https://www.france24.com/en/france/20220613-macron-calls-for-french-budget-defence-boost-in-war-economy, accessed 20 July 2022.

'Strike Me Please: Armenia's SAM Decoys', *Oryx*, 28 April 2021: https://www.oryxspioenkop.com/2021/04/strike-me-please-armenias-sam-decoys.html, accessed 20 July 2022.

'Summary of the 2018 National Defence Strategy of the United States of America': https://dod.defense.gov/Portals/1/Documents/pubs/2018-National-Defense-Strategy-Summary.pdf, accessed 20 July 2022.

'Syria: Footage Shows Islamic State Drone Blowing Up Stadium Ammo Dump', *ABC News*, 25 October 2017.

'The Conqueror of Karabakh: The Bayraktar TB2', *Oryx*, 27 September 2021: https://www.oryxspioenkop.com/2021/09/the-conqueror-of-karabakh-bayraktar-tb2.html, accessed 20 July 2022.

'UK Defence Minister Wallace Endorses Truss for PM', *Reuters*, 29 July 2022: https://www.reuters.com/world/uk/uk-defence-minister-wallace-endorses-truss-pm-2022-07-29/, accessed 20 July 2022.

'What Is Security Analysis?': https://www.doc.ic.ac.uk/~ajs300/security/CIA.htm, accessed 21 October 2021.

'Why a Huge Russian Convoy Remains Stalled North of Kyiv', *The Economist*, 4 March 2022: https://www.economist.com/europe/2022/03/04/why-a-huge-russian-convoy-remains-stalled-north-of-kyiv, accessed 20 July 2022.

'World Military Expenditure Passes $2 Trillion for First Time', *SIPRI*, 25 April 2022: https://www.sipri.org/media/press-release/2022/world-military-expenditure-passes-2-trillion-first-time, accessed 20 July 2022.

'Большая часть техники на Параде Победы прошла боевые испытания в Сирии', RIA Novosti, 6 May 2018: https://ria.ru/20180506/1519978275.html, accessed 20 July 2022.

1 German Netherlands Corps, *Corps Operating Concept*, Muenster, January 2022.

Abhdul-Ahad, G., 'After the Liberation of Mosul, an Orgy of Killing', *The Guardian*, 21 November 2017: https://www.theguardian.com/world/2017/nov/21/after-the-liberation-of-mosul-an-orgy-of-killing, accessed 20 July 2022.

Ahronheim, A., 'Israel's Operation against Hamas Was the World's First AI War', *The Jerusalem Post*, 27 May 2021: https://www.jpost.com/arab-israeli-conflict/gaza-news/guardian-of-the-walls-the-first-ai-war-669371, accessed 20 July 2022.

al-Rawhani, A., 'Marib: Local Changes and the Impact on the Future of Yemeni Politics', *LSE Middle East Centre*, 29 March 2017: https://blogs.lse.ac.uk/mec/2017/06/23/marib-local-changes-and-the-impact-on-the-future-of-yemeni-politics/, accessed 20 July 2022.

Altman, H., 'Debacle on the Donets: How Russian Forces Got Obliterated Trying to Cross a River', *The Drive*, 12 May 2022: https://www.thedrive.com/the-war-zone/debacle-on-the-donets-russian-forces-got-obliterated-trying-to-cross-a-river, accessed 20 July 2022.

Assistant Secretary of the Navy for Research, Development and Acquisition and Vice Chief of Naval Operations, 'Updated Responsibilities for Management of Naval Integrated Fire Control – Counter Air (NIFC-CA)', joint memorandum, 11 October 2002.

Australian Government Department of Defence, *Naval Shipbuilding Plan* (Canberra, 2017): file:///Users/user/Downloads/NavalShipbuildingPlan_1.pdf, accessed 20 July 2022.

Berger, D., Commandant's Planning Guidance: 38th Commandant of the Marine Corps (2019): https://www.hqmc.marines.mil/Portals/142/Docs/%2038th%20Commandant%27s%20Planning%20Guidance_2019.pdf?ver=2019-07-16-200152-700, accessed 20 July 2022.

Bronk, J., in oral testimony to the House of Commons Defence Select Committee, 'Modernising Defence Programme', HC 818, Response to Question 131, 17 April 2018.

Chang, F. K., 'Taking Flight: China, Japan and South Korea Get Aircraft Carriers', Foreign Policy Research Institute, 14 January 2021: https://www.fpri.org/article/2021/01/taking-flight-china-japan-and-south-korea-get-aircraft-carriers/, accessed 20 July 2022.

Chow, B. G. and Sokolski, H., 'U.S. Satellites Increasingly Vulnerable to China's Ground-Based Lasers', *SpaceNews*, 10 July 2020: https://spacenews.com/op-ed-u-s-satellites-increasingly-vulnerable-to-chinas-ground-based-lasers/, accessed 20 July 2022.

Congressional Research Service, 'Joint All-Domain Command and Control (JADC2)', 21 January 2022: https://sgp.fas.org/crs/natsec/IF11493.pdf, accessed 20 July 2022.

Congressional Research Service, 'Navy Ford (CVN-78) Class Aircraft Carrier Program: Background and Issues for Congress', 29 September 2021: https://fas.org/sgp/crs/weapons/RS20643.pdf, accessed 20 July 2022.

Council of the European Union, 'Directive (EU) 2015/719 of the European Parliament and of the Council of 29 April 2015 Amending Council Directive 96/53/EC Laying down for Certain Road Vehicles Circulating within the Community the Maximum Authorised Dimensions in National and International Traffic and the Maximum Authorised Weights in International Traffic', *Official Journal of the European Union* (L115/1, 6 May 2015).

Cranny-Evans, S., 'Introducing the Russian Radio-Electronic Fire Strike Concept', *RUSI Defence Systems*, 5 January 2022: https://rusi.org/explore-our-research/publications/rusi-defence-systems/introducing-russian-radio-electronic-fire-strike-concept, accessed 20 July 2022.

Cranny-Evans, S. and Kaushal, S., 'The Iskander-M and Iskander-K: A Technical Profile', *RUSI Commentary*, 8 August 2022: https://rusi.org/explore-our-research/publications/commentary/iskander-m-and-iskander-k-technical-profile, accessed 20 August 2022.

Cranny-Evans, S. and Withington, T., 'Russian Comms in Ukraine: A World of Hertz', *RUSI Commentary*, 9 March 2022: https://rusi.org/explore-our-research/publications/commentary/russian-comms-ukraine-world-hertz, accessed 20 July 2022.

Danylyuk, O. V., 'Why Putin Is Turning Russia into a Chinese Client State, and How to Stop It', *RUSI Commentary*, 16 March 2022: https://www.rusi.org/explore-our-research/publications/commentary/why-putin-turning-russia-chinese-client-state-and-how-stop-it, accessed 20 July 2022.

DCDC 'Integrated Operating Concept' (London: Ministry of Defence, 2021): https://assets.publishing.service.gov.uk/government/uploads/system/uploads/attachment_data/file/1014659/Integrated_Operating_Concept_2025.pdf, accessed 20 July 2022.

Defence Concepts and Doctrine Centre, Joint Concept Note 1/20: Multi-Domain Integration (Shrivenham: Ministry of Defence, 2020): https://assets.publishing.service.gov.uk/government/uploads/system/uploads/attachment_data/file/950789/20201112-JCN_1_20_MDI.PDF, accessed 23 November 2022.

Erwin, S., 'Report: Industry Has to Face Reality that Commercial Satellites Will Be Targets in War', *SpaceNews*, 23 August 2022: https://spacenews.com/report-industry-has-to-face-reality-that-commercial-satellites-will-be-targets-in-war/, accessed 20 July 2022.

Evans, M., 'US Army Supergun Breaks Record with Direct Hit on Target 70 km Away', *The Times*, 24 December 2020: https://www.thetimes.co.uk/article/us-army-supergun-breaks-record-with-direct-hit-on-target-70km-away-80vwdd586, accessed 20 July 2022.

Faint, C. and Harris, M., 'F3EAD: Ops/Intel Fusion "Feeds" the SOF Targeting Process', *Small Wars Journal*, 31 January 2012.

Farrer, M., 'Two Russians and One Ukrainian Arrested after Suspected Spying Raid on Albanian Arms Factory', *The Guardian*, 21 August 2022: https://www.theguardian.com/world/2022/aug/21/two-russians-and-one-ukrainian-arrested-after-suspected-spying-raid-on-albanian-arms-factory, accessed 23 August 2022.

Fisher, L., 'Soldiers and Machines Join an Army of 'Boots and Bots', *The Times*, 30 September 2020: https://www.thetimes.co.uk/article/soldiers-and-machines-join-an-army-of-boots-and-bots-mkwz9l2dt, accessed 20 July 2022.

GAO, 'Operation Desert Storm: Evaluation of the Air War', July 1996: https://www.govinfo.gov/content/pkg/GAOREPORTS-PEMD-96-10/pdf/GAOREPORTS-PEMD-96-10.pdf, accessed 20 July 2022.

Gardner, F., 'Ukraine War: Is the Tank Doomed?', *BBC*, 7 July 2022: https://www.bbc.com/news/uk-61967180, accessed 20 July 2022.

George, S., Abdul-Zahra, Q., Michael M. and Hinnant, L., 'Mosul Is a Graveyard: Final IS Battle Kills 9,000 Civilians', *Associated Press*, 21 December 2017: https://apnews.com/article/middle-east-only-on-ap-islamic-state-group-bbea7094fb954838a2fdc11278d65460, accessed 20 July 2022.

Gibbs, S., 'Your Phone Number Is All a Hacker Needs to Read Texts, Listen to Calls and Track You', *The Guardian*, 18 April 2016: https://www.theguardian.com/technology/2016/apr/18/phone-number-hacker-read-texts-listen-calls-track-you, accessed 20 July 2022.

Goble, P., 'Moscow's Plans for New Kind of Aircraft Carrier Unlikely to Be Realized', The Jamestown Foundation, 11 March 2021: https://jamestown.org/program/moscows-plans-for-new-kind-of-aircraft-carrier-unlikely-to-be-realized/, accessed 20 July 2022.

Harwell, D., 'Instead of Consumer Software, Ukraine's Tech Workers Build Apps of War', *The Washington Post*, 24 March 2022: https://www.washingtonpost.com/technology/2022/03/24/ukraine-war-apps-russian-invasion/, accessed 20 July 2022.

Hastings, M., 'Giant Carriers Are Symbols of Our National Delusions', *The Times*, 14 December 2019.

Hawkes, J., Cranny-Evans, S. and Cazalet, M., 'The Tank Is Dead. Long Live the Tank', *The Wavell Room*, 1 October 2020: https://wavellroom.com/2020/10/01/a-critical-analysis-of-the-future-of-the-tank/, accessed 20 July 2022.

Higgins, A. and de Goeij, H., 'Czechs Blame 2014 Blasts at Ammunition Depots on Elite Russian Spy Unit', *The New York Times*, 17 April 2021: https://www.nytimes.com/2021/04/17/world/europe/czech-republic-skirpal-russia-gru.html, accessed 20 July 2022.

Hoehn, J. R., *Advanced Battle Management System (ABMS)*, Congressional Research Service, February 2022: http://www.mod.gov.cn/regulatory/2019-07/24/content_4846424.htm, accessed 20 July 2022.

DCDC, 'Joint Concept Note 1/20: Multi-Domain Integration', November 2020: https://assets.publishing.service.gov.uk/government/uploads/system/uploads/attachment_data/file/950789/20201112-JCN_1_20_MDI.PDF, accessed 20 July 2022.

DCDC, 'Joint Doctrine Publication, 0-30: UK Air and Space Power', December 2017: https://assets.publishing.service.gov.uk/government/uploads/system/uploads/attachment_data/file/668710/doctrine_uk_air_space_power_jdp_0_30.pdf, accessed 20 July 2022.

US Air Force, 'The Air Force', 10 March 2021: https://www.doctrine.af.mil/Portals/61/documents/AFDP_1/AFDP-1.pdf, accessed 20 July 2022.

Hubbard, B., Karasz, P. and Reed, S., 'Two Major Saudi Oil Installations Hit by Drone Strike, and U.S. Blames Iran', *The New York Times*, 14 September 2019: https://www.nytimes.com/2019/09/14/world/middleeast/saudi-arabia-refineries-drone-attack.html, accessed 20 July 2022.

Hunder, M., 'Ukrainian Military Strikes with Western Arms Disrupt Russian Supply Lines – General', *Reuters*, 14 July 2022: https://www.reuters.com/world/europe/ukrainian-military-strikes-with-western-arms-disrupt-russian-supply-lines-2022-07-14/, accessed 20 July 2022.

ICRC, 'New Research Shows Urban Warfare 8 Times More Deadly for Civilians in Syria and Iraq', news release, 1 October 2018: https://www.icrc.org/en/document/new-research-shows-urban-warfare-eight-times-more-deadly-civilians-syria-iraq, accessed 2 January 2021.

Janovsky, J., 'Seven Years of War – Documenting Syrian Rebel Use of Anti-Tank Guided Missiles', *Bellingcat*, 4 May 2018: https://www.bellingcat.com/news/mena/2018/05/04/seven-years-war-documenting-syrian-rebel-use-anti-tank-guided-missiles/, accessed 20 July 2022.

Johnson, D., 'The Tank Is Dead: Long Live the Javelin, the Switchblade, the …?', *War on the Rocks*, 18 April 2022: https://warontherocks.com/2022/04/the-tank-is-dead-long-live-the-javelin-the-switchblade-the/, accessed 20 July 2022.

Judson, J., 'Congress Nails Runaway Blimp's Coffin Shut', *Defence News*, 27 May 2016: https://www.defensenews.com/land/2016/05/27/congress-nails-runaway-blimp-s-coffin-shut/, accessed 20 July 2022.

Karber, P., 'Lessons Learned from The Russo–Ukrainian War', Potomac Foundation, 8 July 2015.

Kaushal, S., 'Can Russia Continue to Fight a Long War?', *RUSI Commentary,* 23 August 2022: https://rusi.org/explore-our-research/publications/commentary/can-russia-continue-fight-long-war, accessed 20 July 2022.

Knights, M. and Mello, A., 'The Best Thing America Built in Iraq: Iraq's Counter-Terrorism Service and the Long War against Militancy', *War on the Rocks,* 19 July 2017: https://warontherocks.com/2017/07/the-best-thing-america-built-in-iraq-iraqs-counter-terrorism-service-and-the-long-war-against-militancy/, accessed 20 July 2022.

Kofman, M. and Lee, R., 'Not Built for Purpose: The Russian Military's Ill-Fated Force Design', *War on the Rocks,* 2 June 2022: https://warontherocks.com/2022/06/not-built-for-purpose-the-russian-militarys-ill-fated-force-design/, accessed 20 July 2022.

Kollars, N. and Moore, E., 'Every Marine a Blue-Haired Quasi-Rifleperson?', *War on the Rocks,* 21 August 2019: https://warontherocks.com/2019/08/every-marine-a-blue-haired-quasi-rifleperson/, accessed 20 July 2022.

Labs, E., 'The 2021 Outlook for Navy Shipbuilding: Prospects and Challenges in Building a Larger Fleet', *CBO,* 6 January 2021: https://www.cbo.gov/system/files/2021-01/56947-Shipbuilding.pdf, accessed 20 July 2022.

Lamothe, D., 'As Ukraine Pounds Russian Targets, U.S. Sends More Artillery', *The Washington Post,* 22 July 2022: https://www.washingtonpost.com/national-security/2022/07/22/ukraine-artillery-russia/, accessed 20 August 2022.

Mangan, D. J. and McKinnon, A., 'Review of Trends in Manufacturing and Global Supply Chains, and Their Impact on UK Freight', Government Office for Science and Foresight, February 2019: https://assets.publishing.service.gov.uk/government/uploads/system/uploads/attachment_data/file/777687/fom_trends_manufacturing_global_supply_chains.pdf, accessed 21 December 2021.

Miller, C., Scott, M. and Bender, B., 'UkraineX: How Elon Musk's Space Satellites Changed The War on the Ground', *Politico,* 8 June 2022: https://www.politico.eu/article/elon-musk-ukraine-starlink/, accessed 20 July 2022.

Mizokami, K., 'Another Ukrainian Ammo Dump Goes up in Massive Explosion', *Popular Mechanics,* 27 September 2017.

Mosul Study Group, 'What the Battle for Mosul Teaches the Force' September 2017: https://www.armyupress.army.mil/Portals/7/Primer-on-Urban-Operation/Documents/Mosul-Public-Release1.pdf, accessed 20 July 2022.

National Shipbuilding Office, *National Shipbuilding Strategy* (London: National Stationary Office, 2022): https://assets.publishing.service.gov.uk/government/uploads/system/uploads/attachment_data/file/1061201/_CP_605____National_Shipbuilding_Strategy_Refresh.pdf, accessed 20 July 2022.

Office of Foreign Asset Control, 'Ukraine/Russia-Related Sanctions Programme', US Department of the Treasury, 2016: https://home.treasury.gov/system/files/126/ukraine_overview_of_sanctions.pdf, accessed 20 July 2022.

Olejnik, L., 'Smartphones Blur the Line between Civilian and Combatant', *Wired,* 6 June 2022: https://www.wired.com/story/smartphones-ukraine-civilian-combatant/, accessed 20 July 2022.

Olson, S., 'The Danger of Space Junk', *The Atlantic,* July 1998: https://www.theatlantic.com/magazine/archive/1998/07/the-danger-of-space-junk/306691/, accessed 20 July 2022.

Osborne, C., 'Sensor Fuzed Weapons Aid Combat in Iraq', *CNN*, 19 August 2003: http://edition.cnn.com/2003/US/08/19/hln.terror.sensor.fuzed/, accessed 20 July 2022.

Paterson, S., 'Sex, Lies and Videotape', *Edelman*, 13 November 2019: https://www.edelman.co.uk/insights/sex-lies-and-videotape, accessed 20 July 2021.

Philp, C., 'Severodonetsk's Last Stand: Brilliant Manoeuvre or Reckless Waste of Life?', *The Times*, 1 July 2022: https://www.thetimes.co.uk/article/severodonetsks-last-stand-brilliant-manoeuvre-or-reckless-waste-of-life-6hzp733hc, accessed 20 July 2022.

Popescu, A., 'Poland to Increase Defence Spending to 3% Of GDP from 2023', *Jane's*, 4 March 2022: https://www.janes.com/defence-news/news-detail/poland-to-increase-defence-spending-to-3-of-gdp-from-2023, accessed 20 July 2022.

Raczynski, J., 'Kill Chain: The 7 Stages of a Cyberattack', *Reuters*, 12 October 2018.

Report of the Bloody Sunday Inquiry (London: HM Stationary Office, 2010): https://assets.publishing.service.gov.uk/government/uploads/system/uploads/attachment_data/file/279133/0029_i.pdf, accessed 20 July 2022.

Reynolds, N. and Watling, J., 'Ukraine through Russia's Eyes', *RUSI Commentary*, 25 February 2022: https://rusi.org/explore-our-research/publications/commentary/ukraine-through-russias-eyes, accessed 20 July 2022.

Riedel, B., 'In the Face of Hodeidah Assault, Yemen Is on the Brink', *Brookings*, 13 June 2018: https://www.brookings.edu/blog/order-from-chaos/2018/06/13/in-the-face-of-hodeidah-assault-yemen-is-on-the-brink/, accessed 20 July 2022.

Roberts, P. and Hewitt, D., 'Episode 29: Electronic Warfare and Cumulative Risk', Western Way of War, RUSI podcast, 17 December 2020: https://rusi.org/podcasts/western-way-of-war/episode-29-electronic-warfare-and-cumulative-risk, accessed 3 November 2021.

Rogoway, T., 'Ukraine Strikes Back: Barrage Leaves Russian-Occupied Kherson Airbase in Flames (Updated)', *The Drive*, 16 March 2022: https://www.thedrive.com/the-war-zone/44780/ukraine-strikes-back-barrage-leaves-russian-occupied-kherson-airbase-in-flames, accessed 20 July 2022.

Sabbagh, D., 'Russian Airbase on Western Coast of Crimea Damaged in Explosions', *The Guardian*, 10 August 2022: https://www.theguardian.com/world/2022/aug/09/russian-airbase-on-western-coast-of-crimea-damaged-in-explosions, accessed 25 November 2022.

Said, S. and Kalin, S., 'Saudi Arabia Considers Accepting Yuan Instead of Dollars for Chinese Oil Sales', *The Wall Street Journal*, 15 March 2022: https://www.wsj.com/articles/saudi-arabia-considers-accepting-yuan-instead-of-dollars-for-chinese-oil-sales-11647351541, accessed 20 July 2022.

Sakzewski, E., 'These Satellite Images Show Russia Has Ukraine Surrounded', *ABC News*, 23 February 2022: https://www.abc.net.au/news/2022-02-23/satellite-images-russian-troops-surround-ukraine/100827810, accessed 20 July 2022.

Shaheen, K., 'Russia's Long History of Bombing Hospitals', *New Lines Magazine*, 11 March 2022: https://newlinesmag.com/newsletter/russias-long-history-of-bombing-hospitals/, accessed 20 July 2022.

Sheahan, M. and Marsh, S., 'Germany to Increase Defence Spending in Response to "Putin's War" – Scholz', *Reuters*, 27 February 2022: https://www.reuters.com/business/aerospace-defense/germany-hike-defense-spending-scholz-says-further-policy-shift-2022-02-27/, accessed 20 July 2022.

Shell Scenarios Team, 'The Energy Transformation Scenarios', Shell International, 2021: https://www.shell.com/energy-and-innovation/the-energy-future/scenarios/the-energy-transformation-scenarios/_jcr_content/root/main/section_524990089/simple/promo_copy/links/item0.stream/1652119830834/fba2959d9759c5ae806a03acfb187f1c33409a91/energy-transformation-scenarios.pdf, accessed 20 July 2022.

Singer, N., '"Weaponized Ad Technology": Facebook's Moneymaker Gets a Critical Eye', *New York Times*, 16 August 2018.

Smithsonian Channel, 'Actual Footage of Desert Storm's First Apache Strikes', 22 May 2015, accessed 20 July 2022.

Spencer, J., 'The City Is Not Neutral: Why Urban Warfare Is So Hard', *Modern War Institute*, 4 March 2020.

Spencer, J., 'A Firsthand Account of the Battle of Mariupol', *Modern War Institute*, 25 November 2022: https://mwi.usma.edu/a-firsthand-account-of-the-battle-of-mariupol/, accessed 7 December 2022.

Spencer, J., 'Stealing the Enemy's Urban Advantage: The Battle of Sadr City', *Modern War Institute*, 31 January 2019: https://mwi.usma.edu/stealing-enemys-urban-advantage-battle-sadr-city/, accessed 20 July 2022.

Spencer, J., 'Underground Warfare in Israel and Gaza', *Modern War Institute*, 28 May 2021: https://mwi.usma.edu/underground-warfare-in-israel-and-gaza/, accessed 20 July 2022.

Spencer, J. and Geroux, J., 'Case Study #2: Mosul', *Modern War Institute*, 15 September 2021: https://mwi.usma.edu/urban-warfare-project-case-study-2-battle-of-mosul/, accessed 20 July 2022.

Spencer, J. and Ghoorhoo, H., 'The Battle of Shusha City and the Missed Lessons of the 2020 Nagorno-Karabakh War' *Modern War Institute*, 14 July 2021: https://mwi.usma.edu/the-battle-of-shusha-city-and-the-missed-lessons-of-the-2020-nagorno-karabakh-war/, accessed 20 July 2022.

Spencer, R., Charter, D., Light, F. and Mann, S., '90% of Buildings in Mariupol 'Damaged or Destroyed', *The Times*, 17 March 2022: https://www.thetimes.co.uk/article/us-to-send-800-million-in-military-hardware-to-ukraine-885r9f68q, accessed 20 July 2022.

Suess, J., 'Jamming and Cyber Attacks: How Space Is Being Targeted in Ukraine', *RUSI Commentary*, 5 April 2022: https://rusi.org/explore-our-research/publications/commentary/jamming-and-cyber-attacks-how-space-being-targeted-ukraine, accessed 20 July 2022.

Sutton, H. I., 'Chinese Navy Growth: Massive Expansion Of Important Shipyard', *Naval News*, 15 March 2022: https://www.navalnews.com/naval-news/2022/03/chinese-navy-growth-massive-expansion-of-important-shipyard/, accessed 20 July 2022.

Syal, R., 'Abandoned NHS IT System Has Cost £10bn So Far', *The Guardian*, 18 September 2013: https://www.theguardian.com/society/2013/sep/18/nhs-records-system-10bn, accessed 20 July 2022.

Trevithick, J., 'Next Generation Air Dominance "Fighter" Is Still Being Competed', *The Drive*, 28 June 2022: https://www.thedrive.com/the-war-zone/next-gen-air-dominance-fighter-still-being-competed-drones-farther-out, accessed 20 July 2022.

Trevithick, J. and Rogoway, T., 'Ukraine Strikes Back: Barrage Leaves Russian-Occupied Kherson Airbase in Flames (Updated)', *The Drive*, 16 March 2022: https://www.thedrive.com/the-war-zone/44780/ukraine-strikes-back-barrage-leaves-russian-occupied-kherson-airbase-in-flames, accessed 20 July 2022.

UK Ministry of Defence, 'Digital Strategy for Defence', April 2021: https://assets.
publishing.service.gov.uk/government/uploads/system/uploads/attachment_data/
file/990114/20210421_-_MOD_Digital_Strategy_-_Update_-_Final.pdf, accessed
20 July 2022.

UK Parliament, 'Ensuring Future Supply-Chain Resilience', https://publications.
parliament.uk/pa/cm5801/cmselect/cmintrade/286/28609.htm, accessed 22 December
2021.

United Nations, Population Facts, 2019: https://www.un.org/en/development/desa/
population/publications/pdf/popfacts/PopFacts_2019-6.pdf, accessed 20 July 2022.

United Nations, World Urbanisation Prospects, 2018: https://www.un.org/development/
desa/pd/sites/www.un.org.development.desa.pd/files/files/documents/2020/Jan/
un_2018_wup_report.pdf, accessed 20 July 2022.

US Army, 'The US Army in Multi-Domain Operations 2028', TRADOC Pamphlet
525-3-1, 6 December 2018.

US Government Accountability Office (GAO), 'Report to Congressional Committees:
Securing, Stabilizing, and Rebuilding Iraq: Iraqi Government Has Not Met Most
Legislative, Security, and Economic Benchmarks', GAO-07-1195, September 2007.

US Marine Corps, 'Expeditionary Advanced Base Operations', https://www.candp.
marines.mil/Concepts/Subordinate-Operating-Concepts/Expeditionary-Advanced-
Base-Operations/, accessed 8 September 2019.

Vershinin, A., 'The Return of Industrial Warfare', *RUSI Commentary,* 17 June 2022:
https://rusi.org/explore-our-research/publications/commentary/return-industrial-
warfare, accessed 20 July 2022.

Vremennyy Polevoy Ustav RKKA 1936 [Provisional Field Regulations for the Red Army
1936] (Moscow: People's Commissar for Defence of the USSR, 1936).

Waters, N., 'The Poor Man's Air Force? Rebel Drones Attack Russia's Airbase in Syria',
Bellingcat, 12 January 2018.

Watling, J., 'Building the Boat While Afloat: UK Commando Forces on Exercise Cold
Response 2022', *RUSI Defence Systems*, 5 April 2022: https://www.rusi.org/explore-
our-research/publications/rusi-defence-systems/building-boat-while-afloat-uk-
commando-forces-exercise-cold-response-2022, accessed 20 July 2022.

Watling, J., 'From Multirole to Modularity', *RUSI Defence Systems*, 10 December 2020:
https://rusi.org/explore-our-research/publications/rusi-defence-systems/multirole-
modularity, accessed 20 July 2022.

Watling, J. and Kaushal, S., 'The Democratisation of Precision Strike in the Nagorno-
Karabakh Conflict', RUSI Commentary, 20 October 2020: https://rusi.org/explore-
our-research/publications/commentary/democratisation-precision-strike-nagorno-
karabakh-conflict, accessed 20 July 2022.

Weeden, B., '2007 Chinese Anti-Satellite Test Fact Sheet', Secure World Foundation,
updated 23 November 2010: https://swfound.org/media/9550/chinese_asat_fact_
sheet_updated_2012.pdf, accessed 20 July 2022.

Weeden, B. and Samson, V., 'India's ASAT Test Is a Wake-Up Call for Norms of Behavior
in Space', *SpaceNews*, 8 April 2019: https://spacenews.com/op-ed-indias-asat-test-is-
wake-up-call-for-norms-of-behavior-in-space/, accessed 20 July 2022.

Weinberger, S., 'How Israel Spoofed Syria's Air Defense System', *Wired*, 4 October 2007.

Yasuyuki, S., 'The PLA's Pursuit of Enhanced Joint Operations Capabilities, NIDS China Security Report 2022: http://www.nids.mod.go.jp/publication/chinareport/pdf/china_report_EN_web_2022_A01.pdf, accessed 20 July 2022.

Zinets, N., 'Ukraine Says It Has Destroyed 50 Russian Ammunition Depots Using HIMARS', *Reuters*, 25 July 2022: https://www.reuters.com/world/europe/ukraine-says-it-has-destroyed-50-ammunition-depots-using-himars-war-with-russia-2022-07-25/, accessed 12 December 2022.

Hansard

Churchill, W., *Hansard*, House of Commons, Debate 6 June 1944, vol. 400, cols. 1207–1211.

Index